ETHICS IN THE BRITISH CIVIL SERVICE

ETHICS IN THE BRITISH CIVIL SERVICE

RICHARD A. CHAPMAN

ROUTLEDGE

First published in 1988 by
Routledge
a division of Routledge, Chapman and Hall
11 New Fetter Lane, London EC4P 4EE

Printed and bound in Great Britain by Mackays of Chatham Ltd, Kent

British Library Cataloguing in Publication Data

Chapman, Richard A.
    Ethics in the British civil service.
    1. Civil service — Great Britain — Moral
    and ethical aspects
    I. Title
    174′.93527 JN450.M8

    ISBN 0-415-00334-2

Contents

Contents

Acknowledgments

I wish to record my thanks to the following institutions and individuals for help received in various ways. The Social Science Research Council, now the Economic and Social Research Council, awarded me a small project grant, mainly for travel purposes between Durham and the Public Record Office, Kew; and the University of Durham granted me sabbatical leave for a term in 1985 to enable me to make progress with reading files in the PRO. I was very fortunate in being awarded a Hallsworth Research Fellowship in the University of Manchester for the academic year 1986/87: this enabled me to complete my research in the PRO. However, most of my time as a Hallsworth Research Fellow was devoted to writing the book. Within the University of Manchester, the Department of Administrative Studies, now the Institute for Development Policy and Management, welcomed me with understanding and friendship and provided office accommodation and facilities. Most of the book, however, was written in Broomcroft Hall in Manchester - an ideal setting for writing which also provided intellectual stimulation and exemplary cuisine. Crown-copyright material in the Public Record Office is reproduced by permission of the Controller of Her Majesty's Stationery Office. Mr D.M. Nooney, then Chief Registrar, HM Treasury, granted me access to a Treasury file on Lord Bridges. Miss Angela Raspin, Chief Archivist of the British Library of Political and Economic Science, granted access to the Diary of Professor James E. Meade and to the British Oral Archive of Political and Administrative History. Mr I.D. Shelley granted me access to the archives of the Royal Institute of Public Administration. Lord Bridges, his brother and sisters, permitted me to see family papers from Goodmans Furze, which were made available in the Guildford Muniment Room.

Many people have helped with recollections of Bridges or have answered questions on specific points of doubt or difficulty. The following were particularly generous in granting me interviews and/or with more extensive assistance: Lady Albemarle, Dr W.E.K. Anderson, Lady (Elizabeth) Arthur, Lord (Tom) Bridges, Mr Robert Bridges, Mr E.A.W. Bullock, Mr R.H.W. Bullock, Mr A.R. Bunker, Lord Cobbold, Mrs S. Corke, Sir Kenneth Couzens, Mr John C. Fernau, Sir Bruce Fraser, Mr B.T. Gilmore, Dr M.A. Halls,

Acknowledgments

Professor Sir Keith Hancock, Miss I. Hogarth, Sir John Hogg, Mr D.F. Hubback, Sir Ian and Lady Jacob, Professor R.D. Keynes, Mr I. Leadley, Sir Derek Mitchell, Mr E. Max Nicholson, Professor M.J. Oakeshott, Sir Walter Oakeshott, Dr Eunan O'Halpin, Sir Thomas Padmore, Mr Neil Rollings, Dr V. Rothwell, Brigadier J.S. Ryder, Mr J.S.G. Simmons, Mr C.H. Sisson, Professor Robert Skidelsky, Lord and Lady Trend and Sir John Winnifrith.

My special thanks must be expressed to the following who read parts or the whole of the manuscript in draft and made helpful comments: Lord (Tom) Bridges, Mr E.A.W. Bullock (Chapters 4 and 8), Mr R.H.W. Bullock (Chapters 4 and 8), Dr Duncan Bythell, Dr J.R. Greenaway, Mr Barry J. O'Toole, Mr I.D. Shelley (Chapter 6) and Sir John Winnifrith. The responsibility for the final manuscript is, of course, mine alone.

List of Characters

The following held senior positions in the British civil service when Bridges was most influential. Readers may find it useful to be able to refer to these brief details which have been extracted from *Who's Who*.

Sir Edward BRIDGES (later Lord Bridges)
born 1892. Educated : Eton; Magdalen College, Oxford. European War, 1914-18, Captain and sometime Adjutant 4th Bn Oxford and Bucks Light Infantry. HM Treasury, 1919-38; Secretary to the Cabinet 1938-46; Permanent Secretary HM Treasury, 1945-56. Retired 1956. Died 1969.

Sir Norman BROOK (later Lord Normanbrook)
born 1902. Educated: Wolverhampton School; Wadham College, Oxford. Entered Home Office, 1925; Principal 1933; Assistant Secretary 1938; Principal Private Secretary to Sir John Anderson when Lord Privy Seal 1938-9 and when Home Secretary 1939-40; Principal Assistant Secretary 1940; Personal Assistant to Sir John Anderson when Lord President of the Council 1940-2; Deputy Secretary (Civil) to the War Cabinet 1942; Permanent Secretary, Office of Minister of Reconstruction 1943-5; Additional Secretary to the Cabinet 1945-6; Secretary to the Cabinet 1947-62; Joint Secretary HM Treasury and Head of Home Civil Service 1956-62. Retired 1962. Died 1967.

Sir Christopher BULLOCK
born 1891. Educated: Rugby; Trinity College, Cambridge. European War 1915-19. Appointed to the Indian Civil Service 1915. Principal, Air Ministry, 1920; Principal Private Secretary to Churchill as Secretary of State for Air, 1919; served in same capacity 1923-30 with successive Secretaries of State; Assistant Secretary, 1929-30; Permanent Secretary, 1931-6. Dismissed 1936. Died 1972.

Sir Warren FISHER
born 1879. Educated: Winchester; Hertford College, Oxford. Entered Inland Revenue 1903; seconded for service with National Health Insurance Commission 1912-13; Deputy Chairman, Board of Inland Revenue, 1914-18; Chairman 1918-19; Permanent Secretary HM Treasury and Official Head of HM Civil Service 1919-39. Retired 1939. Regional Commissioner for Civil Defence,

North-West Region 1939-40; a Special Commissioner for London Region 1940-2. Died 1949.

Sir Oliver FRANKS (later Lord Franks)
born 1905. Educated: Bristol Grammar School; Queen's College, Oxford. Fellow and Praelector in Philosophy, Queen's College, Oxford, 1927-37. Professor of Moral Philosophy, University of Glasgow 1937-45. Temporary civil servant, Ministry of Supply, 1939-46; Permanent Secretary, Ministry of Supply, 1945-6. Provost of Queen's College, Oxford, 1946-8. British Ambassador to Washington 1948-52.

Sir Maurice HANKEY (later Lord Hankey)
born 1877. Educated: Rugby. Joined Royal Marine Artillary 1895; Colonel retired, 1929. Assistant Secretary, Committee of Imperial Defence 1908; Secretary, Committee of Imperial Defence 1912-38; Secretary, War Cabinet 1916-18; Secretary, Cabinet 1919-38; Clerk of the Privy Council 1923-38. Minister without Portfolio in War Cabinet 1939-40; Chancellor of the Duchy of Lancaster 1940-1; Paymaster General 1941-2. Died 1963.

Sir Laurence HELSBY (later Lord Helsby)
born 1908. Educated : Sedburgh; Keble College, Oxford. Lecturer in Economics, University of Durham 1931-45. Assistant Secretary HM Treasury 1946; Principal Private Secretary to the Prime Minister 1947-50; Deputy Secretary, Ministry of Food, 1950-4; First Civil Service Commissioner 1954-9; Permanent Secretary, Ministry of Labour, 1959-62; Joint Permanent Secretary HM Treasury and Head of Home Civil Service 1963-8. Retired 1968. Died 1978.

Sir Richard HOPKINS
born 1880. Educated: King Edward's School, Birmingham; Emmanuel College, Cambridge. Member of the Board of Inland Revenue 1916; Chairman of Board 1922; Controller of Finance and Supply Services, HM Treasury 1927-32; Second Secretary HM Treasury 1932-42; Permanent Secretary to HM Treasury 1942-5. Retired 1945. Died 1955.

Sir Godfrey INCE
born 1891. Educated: Reigate Grammar School; University College, London. European War 1915-19. Entered Ministry of Labour as Assistant Principal 1919; Private Secretary to Chief Labour Adviser 1920-3; Principal Private Secretary to Ministers of Labour, 1930-3; Assistant Secretary, Ministry of Labour, 1933; Chief Insurance Officer under Unemployment Insurance Acts 1944-7; Principal Assistant Secretary, Ministry of Labour, 1938;

Under Secretary, Ministry of Labour and National Service, 1940; seconded to Offices of War Cabinet, 1941; Director-General of Manpower, Ministry of Labour and National Service, 1941-4; Deputy Secretary 1942; Permanent Secretary, Ministry of Labour and National Service, 1944-56. Retired 1956. Died 1960.

Sir Roger MAKINS (later Lord Sherfield)
born 1904. Educated: Winchester; Christ Church, Oxford. Fellow of All Souls College, Oxford, 1925-39 and 1957-. Entered Foreign Office, 1928. Minister at British Embassy, Washington, 1945-7. Assistant Under Secretary of State, Foreign Office, 1947-8; Deputy Under Secretary of State, Foreign Office, 1948-52; British Ambassador to the United States, 1953-6. Joint Permanent Secretary to the Treasury, 1956-9. Chairman, United Kingdom Atomic Energy Authority, 1960-4.

Sir Thomas PADMORE
born 1909. Educated: Central School, Sheffield; Queen's College, Cambridge. Secretaries' Office, Board of Inland Revenue, 1931-4; transferred to Treasury 1934; Principal Private Secretary to Chancellor of the Exchequer, 1943-5; Second Secretary, 1952-62; Permanent Secretary, Ministry of Transport, 1962-8. Retired 1968.

Sir Edwin PLOWDEN (later Lord Plowden)
born 1907. Educated : Switzerland; Pembroke College, Cambridge. Temporary civil servant, Ministry of Economic Warfare, 1939-40; Ministry of Aircraft Production, 1940-6; Vice-Chairman Temporary Council Committee of NATO, 1951-2; Cabinet Office, 1947; Chief Planning Officer and Chairman of Economic Planning Board, Treasury, 1947-53. Adviser on Atomic Energy Organisation, 1953-4. Chairman, Atomic Energy Authority, 1954-9.

Sir Paul SINKER
born 1905. Educated: Haileybury; Jesus College, Cambridge; University of Vienna. University Lecturer, Cambridge, 1929-40. Civil servant at Admiralty 1940-5; HM Treasury 1945-50; First Civil Service Commissioner, 1951-4; Director-General, British Council 1954-68. Died 1977.

Sir Burke TREND (later Lord Trend)
born 1914. Educated: Whitgift; Merton College, Oxford. Entered Ministry of Education, 1936; transferred to HM Treasury, 1937; Assistant Private Secretary to Chancellor of Exchequer, 1939-41; Principal Private Secretary to Chancellor of Exchequer 1945-9; Under Secretary, HM Treasury, 1949-55; Office of Lord Privy Seal,

1955-6; Deputy Secretary to the Cabinet, 1956-9; Third Secretary, HM Treasury, 1959-60; Second Secretary, 1960-2; Secretary to the Cabinet 1963-73. Rector, Lincoln College, Oxford, 1973-83. Died 1987.

Sir Percival WATERFIELD
born 1888. Educated: Westminster; Christ Church, Oxford. Entered HM Treasury, 1911; Treasury Remembrancer in Ireland, 1920-2; Principal Assistant Secretary, 1934-9; Deputy Secretary, Ministry of Information, 1939-40; First Civil Service Commissioner, 1939-51. Retired 1951. Died 1965.

Sir Horace WILSON
born 1882. Educated: Kumella School, Bournemouth; London School of Economics. Entered Home Civil Service 1900; Principal Private Secretary, Ministry of Labour, 1919-21; Permanent Secretary, Ministry of Labour, 1921-30; Chief Industrial Adviser to HM Government, 1930-9; Permanent Secretary, HM Treasury and Head of Civil Service, 1939-42. Died 1972.

Sir Henry WILSON SMITH
born 1904. Educated: Royal Grammar School, Newcastle upon Tyne; Peterhouse, Cambridge. Entered Home Civil Service 1927; Secretary's Office, General Post Office, 1927-9; HM Treasury, 1930; Assistant Private Secretary to the Chancellor of the Exchequer, 1932; Principal Private Secretary, 1940-2; Under Secretary, HM Treasury 1942-6; Permanent Secretary, Ministry of Defence, 1947-8. Additional Second Secretary, HM Treasury, 1948-51.

Sir John WINNIFRITH
born 1908. Educated: Westminster; Christ Church, Oxford. Entered Home Civil Service 1932; Board of Trade, 1932-4; HM Treasury, 1934-59; Permanent Secretary, Ministry of Agriculture, Fisheries and Food, 1959-67.

Introduction

This book is a sequel to *Leadership in the British Civil Service: A Study of Sir Percival Waterfield and the Creation of the Civil Service Selection Board*. Like the earlier volume, it has its origins in the recognition by members of the Fulton Committee and others in the 1960s that one of the serious gaps in the public administration academic literature was the absence of research studies on eminent civil servants. In 1980 I began a research project intended as a contribution towards remedying this defect. Originally I planned to write a single volume presenting comparative studies of three leading civil servants who had made their mark on the British civil service in earlier years of the twentieth century. I chose Sir Warren Fisher, Sir Edward (later Lord) Bridges and Sir Percival Waterfield, and began with Waterfield because I thought that he and his work would be the most straightforward part of the project: Waterfield's main contribution as a career civil servant was focused on one fairly well documented achievement, the creation of the Civil Service Selection Board (CSSB). The Social Science Research Council supported my research with a grant of £2,950 for the whole project embracing the three civil servants and the comparative analysis. In the event, two books have been published and discussion and analysis has been included in each.

As the research progressed I realised that I had more material than I anticipated. There was more than enough on Waterfield and CSSB to justify a separate monograph. During that work I expanded my knowledge of files in the Public Record Office and also developed expertise in using them. These skills were particularly valuable in this larger project on Bridges. However, I doubt whether I shall write my intended study of Fisher, for three reasons. First, my original grant has run out and it is now very difficult to obtain even modest funds towards my expenses in reading files in the Public Record Office (which is some 300 miles from Durham). Secondly, my study of Bridges was greatly helped by the award of a Hallsworth Fellowship, and good fortune in obtaining a second such Fellowship seems as unlikely as lightening striking twice in the same place. Thirdly, someone else is already preparing a book on Fisher and even if his approach is quite different from mine it seems unlikely that there is a market for two studies on Fisher. For the time being, therefore, after writing this book on Bridges, I shall turn my attention to a different area of research.

This study of Bridges, and of his work as Head of the Civil Service, has been a difficult task for a variety of reasons. First, there is relatively little useful material to work on . Bridges himself was unsympathetic to officials keeping diaries or private papers relating to their work because in his view officials are quite different from politicians or other public persons. Officials tend to work in the shadows and that is consistent with the conventions and traditions of the British civil service. If officials were to keep diaries they might be tempted to publish them and that might damage the convention of ministerial responsibility (at least, that is how the argument appears to have been presented by Bridges). It is therefore not surprising that Bridges, whose influence in the civil service was primarily through the example he set, not only kept no official diary, but also kept hardly any papers, even of a personal and non-official sort, relating to his official duties. The papers from his home have hardly any bearing on his time as Secretary to the Cabinet or as Head of the Civil Service. Instead they are an assortment of bits and pieces about such interests as Box Hill, All Souls College, the Calouste Gulbenkian Foundation and the Royal Institute of Public Administration. Hardly any documentary material therefore exists for a conventional biography.

Secondly, some of the material that does exist and might be relevant for such a study is not yet available. For example, one imagines that there might be relevant material in the over 2,000 boxes of Churchill's papers deposited in Churchill College, Cambridge. Unfortunately, however, the entire collection of Churchill papers is completely closed to all scholars until ten years after the completion of the series of biographical volumes on Churchill which Martin Gilbert is still writing. A second example concerns files that remain closed in the Public Record Office for periods longer than thirty years - this happens for reasons which cannot, it seems, be officially disclosed, except in terms of the conditions specified in the Public Records Acts, though it is obvious that some sort of continuing sensitivity is involved. Thus the evidence from the Treasury to the Committee of Inquiry on Intermediaries, which might contain important material about ethics and standards of conduct in public life, is closed until 1999. Another example concerns the file relating to the appointment of the Chairman of the 1953-55 (Priestley) Royal Commission on the Civil Service, which is closed until 2029. This file might reveal details of any contribution Bridges made in the selection of the Chairman. Such closures increase the difficulties of this sort of research, especially when available material is already very thin. It is not surprising that there have been so few biographies published on leading civil servants.

Sometimes material is not available because it has simply not been released to the Public Record Office by a government department, even after thirty years since the last entry on the file. If there is no information in the PRO Search Room, then researchers cannot know about a file's existence and for all practical research purposes it simply does not exist. This happened with the 'Bridges Collection' of files which consists of files that were in his Private Office when he retired. In many cases these files contained no entries since the 1940s, though some had material going up to 1956. My detailed searches of Treasury lists in the PRO, supplemented with extensive enquiries over three or four years, did not lead me to them, and it was only my persistence in relation to a peculiar reference to a pseudonymous article by Bridges in the *Cambridge Journal* that eventually revealed their existence. In fact the 'Bridges Collection' of over 400 files turned out to be of crucial importance to understanding how Bridges worked and what attitudes he held on many topics; they fundamentally changed the direction of my research.

Thirdly, much of Bridges' work was in discussion with individuals privately or at meetings. Sometimes minutes record what he said but rarely are they full enough to convey much personal detail. It seems he only wrote detailed 'Notes for record' when something looked potentially sensitive or was particularly important. Again, much of his time seems to have been spent reading and amending drafts prepared for him by others. This is consistent with the general pattern of work in the civil service, but in such circumstances it is not always easy to work out Bridges' personal impact or contribution. The exceptions are sensitive issues, like cases in personnel management, but there are dangers in using them without caution because it is easy to misinterpret as typical something that was, in fact, far from typical.

The focus for this book is Bridges' career as Head of the Civil Service. Some of his colleagues have reflected that his most important work may have been earlier in his career, when he was involved in the rearmament policies in the 1930s and while he was Secretary to the Cabinet during the Second World War. Sadly, however, the existing material on these, and the evidence of Bridges' personal contributions to them, are less than his reputation suggests his contributions actually were. One reason for this is that the preparation of papers for the War Cabinet was not conducted according to the requirements of a normal filing system and little of the working papers remain (compared, for example, to the record of decisions and copies of the papers that were formally presented to the Cabinet). From the existing material it is not now possible to work out the personal contributions Bridges made. Therefore, concentrating on the period from 1945 to 1956, when Bridges was Head of the Civil Service, enables the maximum use to be made of the available material. In fact, this seems to be all there is.

Consequently this book is based primarily on the gleanings from many hundreds of files (nearly 2,000 of them), most of which contain very little material on or by Bridges. The work has been like a jigsaw puzzle in which the pieces have been put together not according to a picture or following the guidelines of a detailed research methodology carefully worked out in advance, but instead according to what can be made of the pieces that are available. It was simply not possible to produce, in advance, a detailed research methodology or to adopt an acknowleged and already tried typology, as is nowadays often expected in research in the social sciences.

Fortunately, supplementary resources of a peculiarly valuable sort still exist. By making as much sense as possible of available documentary evidence, lessons have emerged about how government actually worked in the 1940s and 1950s, and especially about the personal contributions of such an eminent individual as Edward Bridges. An important facet of my methodology has therefore been to see whether the chapters and sections I have written seem to ring true to individuals who worked with Bridges. Happily, a number of them are still alive and this procedure made valuable use of their willing co-operation. Not much more can come from them, however. Partly, this is because the events to which this book relates are now long ago and memories of them are unreliable. Partly, it is also because memories of Bridges himself and the valuable contributions he made are now enveloped in a rosy glow of high regard and goodwill towards an ex-colleague who clearly had many attractive qualities. Critics of Bridges are scarce and difficult to find. There must have been critics thirty or forty years ago, of course, and without consulting them it is difficult to give a balanced assessment of Bridges and the contributions he made.

The book concentrates on Bridges' work in the context of Whitehall while he was Head of the Civil Service. This may at first seem a surprising, perhaps even a disappointing constraint, but it is not unfair to Bridges. As Head of the Civil Service, Whitehall was his area of operations and although he was very active in the politics of Whitehall his political activities were limited to that sphere. Furthermore, the civil service in the 1940s and 1950s was not the subject of intense political debate and ideological conflict in the way that it attracted such attention in other periods, especially the 1960s. Bridges was probably personally responsible to a large extent for the low profile of the civil service while he was its Head, though the attitudes of political leaders and the consensual nature of Westminster politics were also relevant factors. An important point to remember is therefore that in some respects the worlds of Westminster and Whitehall were separate and though it might be interesting to know more about the thoughts and attitudes of politicians on some of the issues covered in this book, their opinions are hard to come by. One reason is that politicians may have themselves known little; another is that what they may have known does not feature in their memoirs because political memoirs are largely written for reasons quite different from academic research studies.

The chapters in this book focus on selected areas of activity, and in some respects on particular incidents or developments, for three reasons. First, they all constitute interesting issues where research material exists. However important Bridges' contribution may have been to winning the Second World War through the key role he played as Secretary to the Cabinet, it is impossible now to make an authoritative study of the relevant events or to analyse properly the detailed work he did: the research material does not exist. The topics chosen for the various chapters in this book have therefore been selected because material *does* exist on them. Secondly, enquiries of his ex-colleagues and others who knew Bridges and his work have confirmed that these are not misleading topics to study in depth, and no-one has said that the accounts that emerge give a misleading picture of Bridges in the context of his work as Head of the Civil Service. In other words, it is reasonable to use them as a tool in this particular biographical exercise. Thirdly, though scholars may debate at length which areas or topics they might ideally prefer to study, and the preferred order in which they should appear, within a book on key areas of public administration in Britain during the period after the Second World War, these topics are very likely to appear on most lists somewhere in the order of priorities. For example, personnel management, the political attitudes and political behaviour of civil servants, the machinery of government, open government, generalist administration, the role of civil servants in relation to the constitution, and the education and training of civil servants are all topics not only worth investigation but also worth relating to each other in the context of one of Britain's most eminent public servants.

Another point which it is necessary to make clear at the outset is that Bridges appears today as typical of his generation and of his social class. Critics, particularly critics of generalist administration, may point to his education at Eton and Oxford, to his war service, to his club memberships, and to the social circles in which he moved. They may also comment that there is not much evidence that he had any acquaintance with, or understanding of, people from different backgrounds or different age groups. Indeed, in some respects Bridges typifies and epitomises the concept of a narrow, self-confident, self-contained elite to which terms like 'Mandarins' and 'the Establishment' are conventionally applied. Questions may be asked not only about his conception of 'the national interest' but also about the real ends (conscious or unconscious) for many of his activities. Furthermore, critics may argue that, in effect, he helped perpetuate the concentration of real power in the hands of an elite by controlling, or at least strongly influencing, recruitment to key positions in the public services, and by surrounding 'the administration' in an aura of mystery and secrecy which no outsider could penetrate. Sometimes the evidence suggests that whilst his political and ideological values were soundly based in his background, they were also somewhat ordinary. Readers of this book may gain the impression that he believed that the British system of government was as nearly perfect as could actually be achieved, that the civil service had a key role to play in maintaining the high standards of the system of government, and that the most effective civil service was one run in the way he said it should be. There are indications in this book to substantiate such comments. But it should also be said that Bridges was typical of his generation of civil servants as well as typical of his background and education, and although he may have been self-confident, he was also a very private person.

Had Bridges been alive today it seems unlikely - at least to the writer of this book - that he would have chosen 'ethics' as a key word in the title for this study. However, Bridges clearly had unambiguous standards for himself and he expected (or assumed) them to exist in others. It therefore seems not unreasonable to use the work 'ethics' in the title for this book although the book is neither a philosophical treatise nor a handbook to guide civil servants into how they should behave. Whilst he undoubtedly contributed much to the ethos and traditions of the civil service, it is the impression he made on those who worked with him and his lasting contribution to the administrative culture, especially through indicating what was or was not proper behaviour, that made so deep an impression on this particular researcher who has for many years been concerned in one way or another with Bridges' contribution to both the practice and the study of public administration.

In the end what I am saying is that I have done my best with the available material and tried to produce a study which allows the facts to speak for themselves. Nobody had more material at an earlier date because the files were not then available. Nobody seems likely to have much more material at a later date because the current survival rate for Bridges' contemporaries is not high. What emerges is, I hope, a double contribution to the literature. First, this book is to a large extent, though with limitations, a biography. Readers should be able to feel that they have been introduced to a great civil servant - possibly the greatest British civil servant of this century - and it is hoped that by reading to the end of the last chapter they will have a reasonable appreciation of what motivated him, what his standards were, and how he went about his work. Consequently the book contains insights into *why* Bridges was such a successful civil servant. Secondly, this book offers an original contribution to the public administration academic literature. It reveals much about the profession of government, encompassing both civil servants and politicians, in the twentieth century. It draws attention to topics that were sensitive in the middle decades and in some cases are still sensitive today. More than this, it raises questions about the methods of work and standards expected of civil servants that are of major importance at the present time.

Richard A. Chapman
University of Durham

1

Edward Bridges 1892-1969

Edward Bridges was 'the man with a million secrets'.[1] Once he was likened to 'a very nice maiden aunt - but the most formidable one in history'.[2] Lord Helsby doubted 'whether anybody in recent years contributed so much to our national life over so wide a span'.[3] Lord Franks found him to be 'a completely exceptional man, combining the highest intellectual distinction with a shining integrity, and all with a great zest for the enjoyment of life'.[4] Sir Paul Sinker regarded him as 'a mighty oak', but added that 'in his work he was so unassuming, friendly and boyish'.[5] Sir John Winnifrith said that he was 'one of the greatest civil servants this country ever had'.[6]

Bridges occupied some of the highest offices in the land; he was at the centre of government during war and peace; numerous honours were conferred on him. He could be a stern master but he was also known for his unswerving loyalty to his colleagues and for his great kindness and willingness to take trouble to help others in need. He inspired admiration and affection. Above all, he was a man of integrity, devoted to the public service, an example to others because he embodied all the qualities widely thought to be required in an ideal civil servant. His was the most significant influence on the British civil service in the mid-twentieth century; more than anyone else he set a particular stamp on its character and moulded its ethos and traditions.

Edward Bridges: biography

Edward Ettingdene Bridges was born on 4 August 1892 at Yattendon Manor in Berkshire.[7] He was the third of three children and the only son of Robert Seymour Bridges, later Poet Laureate, and his wife (Mary) Monica, daughter of the eminent architect Alfred Waterhouse. Both Bridges' maternal grandparents were from long established Quaker families. Robert Bridges' father died when he was only nine years of age, and as a result of the sale of most of the family property he inherited enough money to devote himself to writing and literature. After leaving Oxford, where he graduated in Greats, and an interval of travel, he qualified in medicine at St Bartholomew's and for a time practised it. He was selected to be Poet Laureate by Asquith and served from 1913 to 1930. Another distinguished member of the family was Edward Bridges' cousin, Lieutenant-General Sir Tom Bridges, who became well known to the public for his enterprise in rallying two battalions of the British Expeditionary Force at St Quentin in the retreat of 1914 during the First World War. He later took part in the evacuation of General Denekin's White Russian Army and the withdrawal of the Greek Army from Asia Minor. In 1922 he became Governor of South Australia: he died in 1939.[8]

Edward Bridges' life was greatly influenced by his family background and by his early years at Yattendon Manor. His father, thanks to his private income, was spending all his time on literature, and was writing poetry and prose essays and compiling the Yattendon Hymnal. Consequently it is not surprising that libraries always meant a lot to Edward Bridges. The family homes at Yattendon and, later, at Boars Hill near Oxford, were full of books. In Bridges' own home most of the bedrooms had books up to the ceiling. To Bridges a house without books seemed a very dead and soulless affair.[9] Although the children rarely left Yattendon village except for an occasional journey to Newbury by pony cart, there was a constant stream of literary and musical visitors. In bringing up his children Robert Bridges followed his own tenet in the introduction to *The Spirit of Man*: 'The reader is invited to bathe rather than to fish in these waters'. On that principle the family was given a good soaking in music and literature. It was not only a question of listening to music. The whole family were competent to make it and played Purcell, Handel and Mozart among themselves and with neighbours. Bridges himself played the clarinet well when young.[10]

From his early years at Yattendon Bridges took an intense interest in the surrounding countryside. He knew it intimately and made his own collection of large-scale ordnance maps. Later, in 1923, he sought and was granted permission from the Treasury to take out a patent for a method of folding maps which he invented and in which the Director of the Ordnance Survey was not interested.[11] He invented this during an Easter walking tour and the invention enabled a map to be held open on the particular section where a walk is taking place; it is still in use.[12] His love of the country remained with Bridges all his life and he was happy, with only the slightest encouragement, 'to declare his delight, his joy and faith in the English village'. When, for example, he addressed the National Conference of Parish Councils in 1952 he outlined his deep rooted 'conviction in the virtues of life in the country', adding: 'I have found ... that as you come to a better knowledge of the past, and to a fuller understanding of how the village of to-day has grown out of the village of the past, so your affection for the village will grow, and with it your fellow feelings for all who live in it, and your determination to serve it to your utmost'.[13]

He also acquired an interest in architecture and collected the ground plans of all the English and many of the Continental cathedrals. He was passionately interested in Gothic buildings. He was also a good draughtsman, as his sketchbooks full of pencil drawings testify.[14] He had toyed with the idea of becoming an architect when young. After his retirement from the civil service he was able to develop this interest further, especially in his work for the Oxford Historic Buildings Fund.

Bridges' early education was far from happy. In 1902, at the age of ten, he went to Horris Hill, near Newbury, and stayed there for four years, but he disliked the school and did not do particularly well; he left for Eton in 1906 without getting a scholarship. He was much happier at Eton, where he received a grounding in the classics; but here also he was not particularly successful academically. However, it was at Eton that he decided to become a history specialist, largely because he was so influenced by his history tutor, Mr C.H.K. Marten, who later became Provost of Eton. Bridges recorded that from Marten he learnt a great deal 'about how to get inside a subject, how to order his thoughts and how to set them out in an orderly convincing way'.[15] He learned far more from him than from any other teacher at Eton or Oxford and, largely because of Marten's teaching, Bridges won a History Demyship at Magdalen College, Oxford, to which he went in 1911. Here he started to read Greats with the object of taking his degree in two and a half years, going on to read Modern History in the next eighteen months, and then trying for a Prize Fellowship. He was awarded a First in Greats in July 1914, but, owing to the war, he never read History. After the war Bridges took the All Souls Prize Fellowship examination in 1919 and 1920.[16] This led to the award of an All Souls Fellowship in 1920 - a non-stipendiary Prize Fellowship with no prescribed duties except attending College Meetings. His proposed course of study, approved by the College on 29 October 1921, was 'The Development of English Administration, 1855-1906'. He held this Fellowship simultaneously with his post in the Treasury until 1927 (and became a Fellow of All Souls again from 1954). He always felt that he had a historical bent of mind[17] and he developed this interest, in reading and writing, whenever he had the time and opportunity, even though his interest could not be developed as seriously as he would have preferred.

In September 1914 Bridges had joined the 4th Battalion Oxfordshire and Buckinghamshire Light Infantry and was on active service in France with the 145th Brigade from March 1915 to March 1917. The Battalion War Diary records that on 21 August 1915 Second Lieutenant Bridges joined the Battalion in the trenches at Hebuterne: the conditions were appalling and in the winter of 1915-16 there was 2-4 feet of water in the trenches. He became Lieutenant in May 1916 and later was promoted to Captain and Adjutant. He was awarded the Military Cross in January 1917. At 7.00 a.m. on 2 March 1917, when Bridges was serving in the Front Line opposite La Maisonette, Herbecourt, he was severely wounded by a bullet which shattered both bones in his right arm; he carried a fragment of the bullet in his arm for the rest of his life.[18] He returned to England, then later, on 24 November 1917 a Medical Board decided that he was sufficiently fit to be assigned to clerical work for a period of not less than six months. According to Winnifrith, the Treasury heard (because its officials had many links with Oxford) 'that Bridges, who had established his reputation at Oxford as a man with a first-class brain and a highly ordered way of thinking and expressing his thoughts, was available and persuaded the War Office to let him come to the Department'.[19] Clerical duties in the Treasury were thought to be just the job for an adjutant and Bridges consequently became a temporary administrative assistant from 11 December 1917. He soon made his mark and when the Medical Board on 26 March 1918 pronounced him fit for home service the Chancellor of the Exchequer, as well as Treasury officials, pleaded to be allowed to keep him until he was fit for overseas service. On 29 October 1918 he was passed fit for active service again, though there is some doubt whether he actually reached his Battalion, then serving at the Front Line in Italy,[20] before hostilities ceased.

After the war Bridges competed in the reconstruction competition for what were then called Class I Clerkships in the civil service; but before the results were known the Treasury reemployed him as a temporary administrative assistant from 6 November 1919 to 11 January 1920. His first significant assignment was to serve as secretary to the Committee on the Remuneration of Scientific and Technical Officers. Sir Malcolm Ramsay, then Controller of Establishments, decided that if Bridges was successful in the competition he would be assigned to the Establishments Department, and on 6 November he wrote that because of the special aptitude and promise he had shown during his temporary appointment '... My Lords have no hesitation in recommending that if successful under the Selection Scheme he should be permanently assigned to the Treasury as an Assistant Principal'.[21] His established appointment, as a result of his success in the competition, dated from 12 January 1919 and he was paid a salary of £300 (£100 above the minimum of the scale, in view of his previous experience). After only eighteen months as an assistant principal Bridges was promoted to principal in June 1920. This was indeed rapid promotion.

The next fourteen years were, as Winnifrith put it in his Biographical Memoir, 'of the utmost value and significance in his later career'.[22] It covered four main fields. For almost the whole of this period he was assigned to establishment work, involving the scrutiny and control of the numbers, grading and conditions of service in government departments. Secondly, for almost a year, from May 1933 to April 1934, he served in a division responsible not only for the establishments but also for the functional expenditure of the common service departments: the Post Office, Stationery Office, Office of Works, etc. Thirdly, he served as secretary to a number of important committees, including three Royal Commissions. Fourthly, Bridges was attached to the Estimates Committee of the House of Commons, which gave him valuable experience of House of Commons committees. Then, for about four years before his appointment in 1938 as Secretary to the Cabinet, he was primarily concerned with rearmament.

During this period Bridges therefore gained wide experience of all aspects of establishment work. He began in the Establishment Officer's division concerned with establishments in the Treasury itself and in its ancillary group of departments. Later, from 1927 to 1934, he served as Deputy Establishment Officer of the Treasury. During this period he acquired considerable understanding and insight into the conditions of service in government departments generally, including pay. In addition, he served from November 1926 as the Official Side Secretary to the National Whitley Council - an opportunity to gain experience which was subsequently of enormous value to him because dealing with the Civil Service Staff Associations was an important part of his work as Secretary to the Treasury and Head of the Civil Service.

Secondly, Bridges served as secretary to a number of very important departmental committees and Royal Commissions. The influence of his father's high standard in the use of language was a considerable asset in this work, as was his own natural talent, and Bridges acquired a reputation for his skill in drafting memoranda and reports. His first departmental committee, as already mentioned, investigated the pay of scientific and technical officers. Then, in 1921, he became secretary to the Middle Eastern Committee under the chairmanship of Mr J.E. Masterton Smith.[23] In 1922 he was secretary to the Sub-Committee (for the Foreign, Home and Colonial Services) of the Committee on the Reduction of National Expenditure. In July 1924 he served as secretary to the Foreign Office enquiry held by Lord Blanesburgh and Sir Maurice de Bunsen.[24]

In a debate in the House of Lords in 1968 Bridges said he believed he was the only living person to have served as secretary to three Royal Commissions.[25] He still holds that record: it is unlikely to be broken. From September 1928 to April 1929 he was secretary to the Royal Commission on Police Powers and Procedure. The chairman, Lord Lee of Fareham, set a terrific pace in order to complete the report in seven months and Bridges and Geoffrey Kirwan of the Home Office (they were joint-secretaries) corrected the verbatim reports during the night following each session so that they were available for the Commission the next day. A few months after the Royal Commission reported, Bridges was appointed secretary to the (Tomlin) Royal Commission on the Civil Service, which sat from October 1929 to September 1931. This gave him even more insight into the problems and personalities of the civil service. Bridges' last Royal Commission was on Lotteries and Betting, which sat from June 1932 to May 1933. Bridges was secretary to this Commission and Mr (now Sir) Alexander Johnston of the Home Office was assistant secretary. The chairman was Sir Sydney Rowlatt who had recently retired from being Mr Justice Rowlatt. Bridges' tact and other qualities were at first tested by the chairman's conviction that it was his job to draft the report, and that to allow anyone else to produce a draft would have been as unsuitable as having called in someone to draft his own judgments. Bridges weaned him of this idea by redrafting or presenting fresh drafts of earlier chapters and in the end the report was in fact drafted by Bridges, with Johnston's help.

Each of these commissions provided experience and resulted in reports which enhanced Bridges' stature in the civil service. In 1922 Lord Crawford, the chairman of the Sub-Committee on the Reduction of National Expenditure, reported on Bridges in the most glowing terms: '... His judgment is good, his temper imperturbable and there is a shrewdness withal ...'.[26] Lord Lee of Fareham wrote to Sir Warren Fisher on 23 March 1929 expressing his complete satisfaction with Bridges as secretary to the Royal Commission on Police Powers and Procedure.[27] And in July 1931 Lord Tomlin, writing of the imminent issue of the Report of the Royal Commission on the Civil Service, said of Bridges and Mr (later Sir) Harold Parker (the assistant secretary): '... Apart from the fact that they ... are both delightful people to work with, they have proved themselves in functioning for us something almost more perfect than anyone is entitled to expect in this imperfect world ...'.[28]

Bridges was promoted to assistant secretary on 1 April 1934 and was put in charge of the division responsible for the pay and conditions of service of the three armed Services. In October 1934 he also took charge, during the illness of its head, of the division dealing with the other expenditure i.e. the Supply expenditure on armaments and works, of the three Service departments. In 1935 he was relieved of the double burden of being also Deputy Establishment Officer; but he remained in charge of what was later called the Defence Matériel Division until June 1938. During this period of intense activity, when the fighting Services were being prepared for dealing with the increasing threats from Hitler, there was a great deal of committee work and inter-departmental co-ordination by the Treasury.[29] Many briefs were prepared for the Chancellor when defence expenditure was being discussed in Cabinet and Cabinet committees. In these circumstances heavy demands were made of Bridges. His capacity for hard work and drafting abilities were widely recognised and he acquired, according to Winnifrith, 'a great and completely deserved reputation for the skill with which he was able to assimilate the sense of any proposition and to single out the points which the Chancellor should take'.[30]

Towards the end of his life Bridges himself gave a brief account of this period of his career when he wrote some notes for S.W. Roskill who was then writing his biography of Lord Hankey. Bridges wrote:

> ... In the years up to 1938 - that is 1935-38 - when I was Head of the Division of the Treasury which dealt with Defence, my contact with the Military was not with the top level, namely the Chiefs of Staff. My contact was at the level of the Directors of Plans or their representatives. Thus I used to sit as Treasury representative on Committee of Imperial Defence committees dealing with defence policy and expenditure, i.e. the Home Defence Committee and the Overseas Defence Committee on which the representatives of the Service departments would be the directors of plans or their representatives. At that level disagreements would be expressed between the representatives of the three Services, differences really based on differing views as to what part would be played in a future war by Air or by artillery - guns sea-based or land-based ...[31]

Bridges was promoted principal assistant secretary in January 1937 and when Sir Maurice Hankey retired in the summer of 1938, Fisher recommended him for appointment as Secretary of the Cabinet. Neville Chamberlain approved and he began his new duties on 1 August 1938. His formal title was Secretary of the Cabinet and Permanent Secretary of the combined offices of the Cabinet, Committee of Imperial Defence, Economic Advisory Council and Minister for the Co-ordination of Defence. He was assisted by two deputies: Sir Rupert Howarth, who was Clerk to the Privy Council and Deputy Secretary to the Cabinet, and Colonel H.L. (later Lord) Ismay, Secretary to the Committee of Imperial Defence, who was promoted to the rank of Major-General in 1939.

Of his appointment Bridges later wrote: 'nobody was ever more surprised than I was when I was appointed Secretary to the Cabinet. I never had the faintest idea that I could be considered for the post ...'.[32] It was a critical time: Munich may have provided a brief breathing space but war seemed inevitable and the machinery for government in time of war, already in draft, had to be scrutinised and brought up to date. Bridges received many letters of congratulation on his appointment which was recognised by some of his correspondents as the most important post in the kingdom (or even, as Professor George Catlin suggested, in the empire). One member of Bridges' family made a comment in her letter that showed particular insight into his personality and standards as well as into the nature of the position: '... the mere fact of your presence in the room will make it harder for ignoble decisions to be taken'.[33]

The Cabinet office in 1938 was still a small organisation. Hankey had been its only head since it evolved during the First World War, many of the staff had been recruited by him and, as Winnifrith has explained, 'there was considerable antipathy to the idea of change either in procedure or organisation'.[34] The introduction of a new head from outside the existing office staff could have resulted in disaster had the person appointed lacked sensitivity for dealing with the personalities and difficult situations which developed. Fortunately, however, a remarkable partnership arrangement emerged. Although Bridges was responsible for the efficient working of the general office machine, he gave Ismay entire responsibility for the activities of the military side and for co-ordinating the plans and intelligence of the service and supply Ministries under the Chiefs of Staff. Bridges focussed his personal attention on the civil and political side. Bridges and Ismay had little in common - their tastes, interests and general attitudes were different; but they respected each other and each admired the other's effectiveness. On the outbreak of war the War Cabinet Office moved from Richmond Terrace to new offices in Great George Street and the fortifications and rooms used for sleeping and working there may still be seen, preserved as they were during the Second World War, in the recently opened museum.[35] Under Bridges as Secretary, the Offices of the War Cabinet became the nerve centre of the war effort, manned day and night. It was a remarkably successful combination of civil and military personnel and much of the team spirit that emerged was directly inspired by Bridges personally.

As Secretary, Bridges was responsible for recording the deliberations of the War Cabinet and its committees. In this he introduced a style different from Hankey's - Hankey had never taken a single note, relying on his memory entirely, a practice Bridges did not follow.[36] Instead of recording the statements of individuals during discussions Bridges simply marshalled the arguments, usually without attributing them. Bridges also briefed the Prime Minister on the handling of the business. Although he had no executive responsibilities outside his own office he undoubtedly had an immensely important position in the government machine. Bridges was always being consulted by those making or contributing to decisions; he and Ismay oiled the wheels of the machine and ensured that it was always ready to respond to the Prime Minister. He regarded it as one of his main functions to see that decisions were taken when needed - and put into immediate effect - and to ensure that, before any decisions were taken, all the relevant facts had been assembled and the right people consulted. A large part of his working day was spent in consultations to ensure that his departmental colleagues took the initiative in putting forward their problems for decision and that they provided all the facts, figures and arguments needed for informed decisions. By 1943, strategic and civil policies were being co-ordinated by the Lord President's Committee which enabled the Prime Minister and War Cabinet to concentrate on war policy: support for the Lord President's Committee became a separate organisation within the Cabinet offices, concentrating on home affairs. This facilitated the development of detailed plans for the reconstruction period after the war, developments which became more formal when the Ministry of Reconstruction was set up under Lord Woolton. Bridges played an important part in designing this organisation and in ensuring that it was staffed by experienced officials who had been trained in his own methods (at first Norman Brook and then William Gorell Barnes).[37]

There were four ways in which Bridges' personal qualities enabled him to become an outstanding leader of the Cabinet Office. First, there was his own selfless energy and infectious enthusiasm. He maintained a dedication to his work which was an inspiration and encouragement to others and became an essential contribution to keeping up morale in the office. Secondly, he appointed or influenced the appointment of staff to key positions. For example, Bridges had a great deal to do with the success of the Ministry of Production which operated as a small high powered secretariat and advisory staff - it worked alongside the Cabinet Office and Bridges ensured that it was manned with properly trained staff. In this matter of staffing Bridges made use of his earlier experience on establishment work in the Treasury (his experience in this aspect of the work of the Cabinet offices also proved of value in his subsequent work as Head of the Civil Service). Thirdly, Bridges brought together a wide variety of people - serving officers, scientists, politicians and civil servants - and encouraged them to work together: but whenever they ran into deadlock they would come, individually or collectively, to Bridges to help them find a way out. Bridges could usually achieve this because of his unrivalled knowledge of the government machine, his openness and honesty in the presentation of argument, his skill in the formulation of questions for discussion, and his capacity for giving himself wholeheartedly to the problems of the moment. Fourthly, Bridges was always being called on to deal with new problems such as the submarine menace, the growing information on the new German weapons (the V1s and V2s), and, later, the post-war administration of German-occupied territory. His advice was also sought on numerous international matters, though the Foreign Service was for most practical purposes separate from the home civil service: significant examples are Bridges' attendance at both the Yalta and Potsdam conferences. Indeed, while Bridges was at its head, the Cabinet Office itself acquired something of an international reputation and its practices and procedures became models for new organisations such as the OECD, NATO and the United Nations.

It must not be thought that, because Bridges had a unique combination of relevant qualities for this work, the work was either easy or without difficulties. As Winnifrith says, and as everyone who worked with Bridges during the war agrees, the strain on Bridges was terrific.[38] The main cause of stress was Churchill's own methods of work. This meant that meetings were often called well into the night. It also meant that submissions to the Prime Minister were expected to be expressed on one page of typescript. Consequently Bridges often had to rewrite drafts prepared by his staff so that they met more precisely the Prime Minister's requirements, and this called for a great deal of intellectual effort within rigid time constraints.

Bridges often slept in the office to meet these demands. He tried to keep for himself the twenty-four hours from 6 p.m. on Saturday to 6 p.m. on Sunday when he went home to Headley Heath, though even these respites had to be cancelled in emergency and his leave was often interrupted by the telephone. His home on the edge of the country became an important means of replenishing his energies. In 1922 Bridges had married Katherine, second daughter of the second Lord Farrer, himself the son of T.H. Farrer who had been Permanent Secretary to the Board of Trade, and who was raised to the peerage in 1893. Kitty Bridges was known to be a great support and comfort to Bridges in these strenuous days. Even when the pressures eased Bridges did not use the time for a more complete break or for catching up on sleep. Instead he kept available what he called his 'cold table', a collection of papers on topics of lower priority put aside for such moments. During his period as Secretary of the Cabinet one of these topics was the War Histories. Bridges was aware that the histories of the First World War had still not been completed and he was determined that a similar fate should not befall the histories of the 1939 war: they also attracted his personal attention because of his interest in history. Although at the end of the war Bridges was almost certainly unconscious of the importance of the part he had played, those who worked with him or saw him at work had no doubt about the contribution he made to history. Churchill, in particular, appreciated Bridges' abilities and in *Their Finest Hour* he wrote:

> ... That no ... friction occurred between the military staff and the War Cabinet was due primarily to the personality of Sir Edward Bridges, Secretary to the War Cabinet. Not only was this son of a former Poet Laureate an extremely competent and tireless worker, but he was also a man of exceptional force, ability and personal charm, without a trace of jealousy in his nature. All that mattered to him was that the War Cabinet Secretariat as a whole should serve the Prime Minister and War Cabinet to the very best of their ability. No thought of his own personal position ever entered his mind, and never a cross word passed between the civil and military officers of the Secretariat.[39]

When Sir Richard Hopkins retired at the end of February 1945 from his post as Permanent Secretary to the Treasury and Head of the Civil Service, Churchill was in some difficulty about his successor. Bridges was the obvious person for the appointment but Churchill did not want to lose his services as Secretary to the Cabinet. He was always unhappy about changes in his personal staff and he was very concerned not to appoint a successor to Bridges, to whom Ismay would be subordinate. Therefore it was arranged that 'as a temporary measure, to meet the special circumstances of the war and the period of the peace settlement, Sir Edward Bridges was to continue as Secretary to the War Cabinet, with Mr Norman Brook to help him in a new post of Additional Secretary to the War Cabinet'. Simultaneously, Bridges was to be Permanent Secretary to the Treasury and Head of the Civil Service. After the General Election in July 1945, when Mr Attlee had succeeded Churchill as Prime Minister, it was agreed that Bridges should concentrate on his Treasury position and the Headship of the Civil Service. It is this period in his career, his last eleven years of service, that is the main focus for the later chapters of this book.

Bridges was not a financial or economic expert and did not claim to have professional experience in these areas. Nevertheless he made a major contribution to these aspects of government through his interest in the machinery of government. This interest, and his sense of responsibility and duty towards all aspects of work in the Treasury, encouraged him after his retirement to give a number of important lectures on such topics as 'Treasury control' and 'The elements of any British Budget'. These receive special attention in chapters 5 and 7. In addition, Bridges was also occasionally drawn into economic negotiations which had sensitive political and administrative dimensions: an important example was the part he played at the end of the negotiations for the American loan in 1945. However, Bridges' most significant contributions were not to the detailed technical aspects of resolving financial problems but to the political judgements and advice being offered to ministers. His machinery of government work illustrates the way Bridges enhanced the professional standing of administrators. On a big problem Bridges would summon 'a meeting of the Greybeards' as he called his senior colleagues, and together the permanent secretaries would develop and agree a view on the problem before it was propounded to ministers.

The second main feature of Bridges' headship of the civil service was the way he co-ordinated, enthused and directed his colleagues; operating by example rather than precept to ensure that his view on the role of the Treasury prevailed throughout the department and his view on the civil service was known generally throughout the civil service. Occasionally his views would be expressed in a significant letter circulated from the Treasury; more frequently they became known through constant meetings with groups of colleagues or in separate discussions with individuals involved in a particularly difficult problem. His leadership was never assertive; nearly always it was the outcome of time-consuming behind-the-scenes activities; frequently it was achieved through intermediaries. Numerous examples could be quoted to illustrate this approach, but there are none better than the ways Bridges engineered the defence of the civil service when it was being attacked. His method was not to speak or write authoritatively as Head of the Civil Service, denouncing criticism with, perhaps, the self-righteous overtones of an injured party. Instead he preferred to get the civil service defended by others, usually ministers. Attacks on the civil service were rarely left without reply or defence from someone in authority and often the substance of replies was personally planned and prepared and/or provoked by Bridges. Two examples, typical of many that could be quoted, illustrate this. In 1950 a pamphlet was published entitled *Keeping Left* which contained what Bridges regarded as 'a beastly reference to officials in the Treasury and the Bank of England'. Bridges ensured that it was drawn to the attention of the Chancellor of the Exchequer who wrote a sharp letter on 21 January 1950 to Sir Richard Acland, one of the authors, saying that the attack on 'certain officials' was wholly unjustified and made out of ignorance, and asking him to withdraw the wholly unjustified accusation.[40] Another example concerned the publication in 1953 of *Diplomatic Twilight* by the ex-diplomat Sir Walford Selby. This was a bad book (all reviewers agreed) written, as Bridges wrote to Lord Vansittart, 'by a very stupid man'. The book contained numerous errors and also an attack on Sir Warren Fisher. Bridges discussed the matter with his Treasury colleagues and also with Sir William (later Lord) Strang (Permanent Under Secretary of State, Foreign Office, 1949-53) who, Bridges noted, 'obviously thought Selby an extremely poor public servant - one who ought never to have attained such a high post'. Vansittart clearly thought Bridges should have publicly corrected the record and personally defended those who had been unjustly criticised. In a letter to Bridges dated 5 May 1953 he wrote: 'I really do think it time that you took your part in preventing history from being falsified like this'. But this was not the way Bridges operated. He did not think it right that civil servants should engage in public controversy. Instead, after the book had been slated by reviewers, a Question was raised in the House of Lords by Viscount Elibank which enabled the Marquess of Reading to respond, on 8 July, with an authoritative reply: this ended public discussion on the matter.[41] Bridges' apparently confident and masterly control of difficult situations inspired great loyalty from his colleagues. Sir Ian Jacob, who served under Ismay in the War Cabinet Secretariat, wrote: 'we would all have done anything he asked of us'; and Mr (later Sir) Walter Adams, Director of the London School of Economics wrote: '... My admiration and affection for him were akin to worship'.[42]

Bridges' style of leadership depended more on influence than public statements which might focus attention on himself. It could be justified constitutionally because in the British system of government ministers have a duty to defend their officials. It could be justified tactically because there are certain advantages in being defended by a disinterested but well-informed third party when an unjust or ill-informed criticism is publicised. More important, this means of responding was consistent with Bridges' approach to doing good works discreetly - it may have had a scriptural basis; it was certainly consistent with the Quaker influence from his maternal family background. Some further examples of this aspect of Bridges' leadership are considered in chapters 3 and 7.

One of Bridges' most time-consuming activities as Head of the Civil Service concerned personnel work, or establishment work as it is generally called in the civil service. His views on education and training, in particular his work towards implementing the recommendations of the Assheton Committee[43] and his relationship to the Royal Institute of Public Administration reveal a lot about Bridges' attitudes and beliefs. These matters are considered further in chapters 2 and 6. However, it is in his dealings with those cases that were referred for his personal attention that one sees examples of his extraordinary strict morality. This morality guided his own behaviour and, although it was not written down, it influenced the behaviour of others who had contact with Bridges. As Winnifrith put it: 'There were no directions, very few written instructions, but the word passed - all the quicker because it was not written - and all concerned knew what they had to do and what was expected of them'.[44] Winnifrith also remembers a relatively minor incident that made a great impression on him. Bridges had invited him to Goodmans Furze (the family home at Headley Heath) and Winnifrith was playing a game of cards with the children who were not doing at all well. It was a simple game and lent itself to 'manipulation' and he thought it would be a kindness to the children to throw away some of his chances to win. After the children had left Bridges expressed his disapproval to Winnifrith: that was not the right way to behave and it was certainly not the way to bring up children. This impressed Winnifrith and he never forgot the incident: as time went on he saw more and more manifestations of this high standard in Bridges' determination for facts to be recorded accurately and for arguments to be presented fairly.[45] This was almost certainly the attitude referred to by Sir William Armstrong, in his obituary, as Bridges' 'very fundamental honesty'.[46] In some circumstances, however, especially when someone had behaved badly, Bridges' high moral code could appear like a form of ruthless righteousness.

In fact, such incidents were outward manifestations of Bridges' beliefs. He explained what he believed in an interview in 1953, recorded in Britain but broadcast on the Columbia Broadcasting System Network in the United States. In the following extract the fourth paragraph is from the penultimate draft but it was subsequently softened to remove the implication of a kind of ruthless self-righteousness. Although it may seem rather unfair to include a paragraph that Bridges later changed by re-drafting, it gives such a clear insight into this aspect of Bridges' philosophy of life that it seems too valuable to lose it (the final version of the fourth paragraph is, in fairness to Bridges, printed in the footnote):

... To me there is nothing more deep-rooted than that we are under an obligation as to how we should live our lives. You can express this by saying that certain actions are right and others wrong. Or you can call it a belief in a spiritual order of things, which gives a value and meaning to our actions that they would not otherwise possess.

It was from the example of those among whom one was brought up that, as a child, one first learned to see spiritual things expressed in terms of human conduct and human endeavour, and that as a young man one first formed a picture of the kind of person one wished to be.

No doubt the qualities which one most respects change as one becomes older. Today I put highest courage, patience and tolerance; the desire and capacity to understand one's fellows to the utmost and to serve them; a pretty ruthless determination to stick to the best; and last, relentless pursuit of the truth. Much of my working life is spent in trying to find out why certain things happen, in testing arguments and in assessing what is likely to come to pass if a certain course is decided upon. And I have come to feel that no-one can hope for even a fair measure of success in such work unless he sets about it with an almost crusading zeal to find the truth, and a most scrupulous regard for it when found.

There is then, as I see it, a clear obligation on all of us to set before ourselves some such model as this and to do one's best to get as near to it as one can, and my belief that this is so does not need the support of any argument based on the consequences of one's actions ....[47]

This broadcast was particularly interesting because Bridges, an essentially private person, could be easily persuaded to broadcast on overseas services. Perhaps broadcasting did not seem like an intrusion into his privacy because he was speaking to a microphone in a small room without a visible audience. Nevertheless it seems remarkable that he was prepared to do this, not just willingly but almost enthusiastically, especially when the 'This I believe' series claimed, in 1953 and 1954, to be 'the most listened to programme in the United States', was 'broadcast around the world daily in six languages' and also had a 9,500,000 newspaper syndicated circulation each week.[48]

Bridges did not depend only on others when the civil service needed defending. On a number of important occasions he defended the civil service through his own writing and lectures. Some examples are considered in chapters 6 and 7 but a rather unusual approach was provoked in 1950 by a pseudonymous article 'The Civil Service in 1950', published in the *Cambridge Journal*. Bridges' Private Secretary, Mr T.J. Bligh, had been sent a copy by Mr (later Sir) Edward Hale, who worked in the University Grants Committee, and Bligh passed it to Mr (later Sir) Thomas Padmore, Sir James Crombie, and Bridges. Bridges wrote to Michael Oakeshott, the editor of the *Cambridge Journal*, saying how maddening the article was, because 'while some of the statements it makes are shrewd and near the mark, others are pretty badly off the mark, and a number contain a percentage of truth but stop short of stating the full facts'. This approach to being economical with the truth,[49] by using incomplete evidence, was unacceptable to Bridges. He asked Oakeshott to consider publishing a reply and Oakeshott agreed that it could be signed pseudonymously. In fact the article in reply was drafted by Bridges himself, shown to Mr A.P. (later Sir Paul) Sinker, Mr John Maud (later Lord Redcliffe-Maud), Padmore, and Mr S.C. Leslie; then, after he had made a few minor amendments (the article remained substantially as originally drafted) Bridges sent it to Oakeshott with a covering letter that did not reveal that the article was his own work at all: '... The author or authors of it ask me to say the following to you ....[50]

Bridges retired from the civil service at the end of 1956. It was rumoured that he would go earlier. Indeed, there was press speculation in May 1951 that the most likely man to be offered the Wardenship of All Souls College was Sir Edward Bridges, '... But he may feel that he must finish his full term at Whitehall'.[51] There had, in fact, already been contingency planning involving Brook moving from the Cabinet Office to become Permanent Secretary to the Treasury and Padmore moving to the Cabinet Office. In the event, after the 1951 General Election, when Churchill became

Prime Minister again, he insisted on keeping Brook as Secretary to the Cabinet and he wanted Bridges to remain in office.[52]

Bridges had a very active and enjoyable retirement. He gave many lectures and broadcasts, wrote quite a lot (much more than is generally known) and was enthusiastic about everything with which he was associated. He was particularly active in public work of various sorts, as the following examples indicate.

Activities which combined Bridges' interest in nature and the countryside with his self-imposed duty to public service benefited greatly from his retirement. For example, for over 30 years he was deeply involved with the local committees responsible for National Trust properties near his home at Headley Heath and on Box Hill. For a long time he was Vice-Chairman and later Chairman of the Box Hill Management Committee. Over the years he gave a variety of talks about Box Hill to local groups. In 1952 he wrote a Preface to *The Book of Box Hill*, a pamphlet by G.E. Hutchings, published by the Friends of Box Hill, which provided an interesting account of the history, the trees, flowers and grasses that grew there; and about the birds and beasts in the woods. When the print of 5,000 copies ran out in 12 or 13 years Bridges and J.H.P. Sankey, Warden of Juniper Hall Field Centre, revised it and the second edition was available from mid-1969, just before Bridges died.[53] Bridges could also be fairly easily persuaded, especially after his retirement, to take an interest in schemes to preserve the natural environment. One example occurred in the late 1960s in connection with an enquiry instituted by Mr Anthony Crosland, the Minister of Housing and Local Government, about the proposed Sports Centre at Appleby in Westmorland. The scheme would have been a threat to agriculture and to rare flowers which grew there (pyrola minor and Bird's nest orchid). Bridges wrote various letters expressing his concern, including one to Lord Kennet, the Joint Parliamentary Secretary, Ministry of Housing and Local Government. After the enquiry the minister refused planning permission for the Sports Centre.

Churchill's high regard for Bridges was reciprocated and when Churchill died Bridges was one of the pall-bearers at his funeral. He broadcast a tribute to Churchill on the BBC 'Today' programme, 25 January 1965, which was subsequently published in *The Listener* and in a book of *Tributes to WSC*.[54] Then, in 1966, Bridges and others were shocked by the publication of details from the diary of Lord Moran, Churchill's doctor, portraying Churchill in an unfavourable light.[55] Together with Lord Normanbrook, Mr (now

Sir) John Colville, Sir John Martin, Sir Ian Jacob and Sir Leslie Rowan, Bridges contributed to a reply, edited by Sir John Wheeler-Bennett and published by Macmillan in 1968.[56] At his own expense Bridges sent numerous copies of the book to influential ex-colleagues and friends. Characteristically, the authors agreed that they would not receive any royalties from the book but instead royalties went towards the cost of copying the Churchill Archives in Churchill College, Cambridge, so that the original documents might be properly preserved.[57] Churchill, as Chancellor of Bristol University, conferred the honorary degree of Doctor of Laws on Bridges in 1946.

After he was raised to the peerage in 1957 Bridges became a fairly active participant in the House of Lords where he sat as a Cross-Bench Peer. His contributions were characterised by meticulous preparation, in relation to both facts and individuals. For example, in 1963 he contributed to the debate on the Robbins Report on Higher Education (he was asked to do so by Sir Robert Aitken, on behalf of the Committee of Vice-Chancellors and Principals). He also made contributions to less important matters which attracted his interest: for example, in 1967 he was a significant agitator at the lack of prior notice or consultation by British Railways when the exit from the Down platform at Oxford station was closed.[58]

From 1954 Bridges was again a Fellow of All Souls College, Oxford, under the statute that provided for the election of Distinguished Persons. This took a lot of his time and energy during the mid-1960s when reforms were being considered. At that time there was a proposal that All Souls should become the British equivalent of the Institute for Advanced Study at Princeton. In the College Bridges belonged to a group (he regarded himself as a sort of 'unofficial self-appointed Opposition Chief Whip') that felt that the College should remain an active and vital part of the University of Oxford and that this should involve direct responsibilities in teaching as well as research.

On 11 February 1965 Bridges was one of five representatives of All Souls to give evidence before the Franks Commission of enquiry into the University of Oxford. At that time All Souls, the College without any students, was being widely criticised: it was criticised for not fully living up to its income, for voting itself a lot of free living, and for having an administrative budget that was high in relation to its expenditure on academic purposes. It had considerable surpluses, and had been giving so generously to a variety of causes that it appeared, to some critics, more like a charitable foundation than a college. Bridges was an enthusiastic advocate within the College of the proposal that the College should assume responsibilities for a number of graduate students and should provide accommodation for them: this proposal was approved by the College early in 1965. However, on 6 November 1965, after Bridges and others had given their evidence to the Franks Commission, the College rescinded its decision to admit students. Bridges felt very miserable about this. In a letter to the President of Trinity College, Oxford, he said 'I feel it is shameful'. He also drafted a letter of resignation, but after taking advice from friends did not send it. The whole episode was another example of Bridges' high moral standards. He made it clear to the Warden, John Sparrow, that if the College reversed its decision he would not play any further part in the government of the College. In a letter to Lord Sherfield on 3 November 1965, three days before All Souls changed its mind, he wrote: '... I want to argue strongly, and I hope persuasively, the case against reversing the College's decision. But I think it would weaken the force of what I have to say, if I accompanied it by the threat of possible resignation if the point of view I argued was not accepted ...'.[59]

In 1952 Bridges was given the rare honour (for a non-scientist) of election to a Fellowship of the Royal Society ('... nothing has ever given me so much pleasure').[60] Numerous other honours were also conferred upon him: he was knighted in 1939, appointed GCB in 1944, GCVO in 1946, made a Privy Councillor in 1953, raised to the peerage in 1957, and appointed Knight of the Garter in 1965. He received honorary degrees from the universities of Oxford, Cambridge, London, Bristol, Leicester, Liverpool, Reading and Hong Kong.

On 24 February 1945 the Provost and Fellows of Eton College unanimously elected Bridges as a Fellow (i.e., a member of the Governing Body of the College). In the late 1940s he was very active in planning the College Appeal which was launched in November 1950 and led to extensive schemes of reconstruction and renovation. As a result of the appeal the College raised £490,000 by 1958. He continued as an active Fellow of Eton until 1968.[61] He was elected an honorary Fellow of Magdalen College, Oxford in 1946; of University College, Cambridge[62] in 1965; of the London School of Economics (where he was Chairman of the Court from 1957 to 1968); and of the Royal Institution of British Architects. From 1960 to 1962 he was Chairman of the Committee to study the relationship between Cambridge University and its colleges. In 1963 he was appointed chairman of the committee to consider training in public administration for overseas countries.[63]

In 1957 both Prime Ministers Anthony Eden and Harold Macmillan wrote to Bridges to persuade him to accept the chairmanship of the Royal Fine Art Commission and he agreed to do this, succeeding Lord Crawford (with whose father he had worked in the 1920s on the Sub-Committee on the Reduction of National Expenditure), and continuing as Chairman until March 1968.[64] His other chairmanships included the British Council from 1959 to 1967, the Pilgrim Trust from 1965 to 1968, and the Oxford Historic Buildings Fund in 1957. Bridges retained a devoted memory of his father and spent much of his spare time ordering his letters and papers.

One facet of Bridges' character is important to record but difficult to express because of an apparent contradiction in the evidence. Although many people have said Bridges was fun to work with, mainly because he so thoroughly enjoyed his work, his sense of humour was of an impish intellectual sort so that, for example, he took a delight, without malice or rancour, in deflating the more pompous members of the official community. It was a sense of humour that was sophisticated and sensitive but not frivolous - as Lord Trend put it: 'it reflected an impatience with anything that was superficial or irrelevant to the task in hand'.[65] Consequently some people, Sir Robert Birley for example, thought the secret to understanding Bridges lay somewhere in his sense of humour,[66] while others thought he had no real sense of humour at all. In spite of his self-effacing modesty it was not unusual for people to be ill at ease in his presence and to find him 'not at all easy to talk to'. He was a rather austere man who went his own way. He was not gregarious and had few close friends: often he would have what passed for his lunch brought to his room or he would take lunch on his own, in earlier years at the United University Club, or in later years at the Athenaeum. Bridges had a remarkable combination of personal qualities which greatly impressed people who worked with him. There are numerous references to 'his wonderful gift of eternal youth', to his 'wisdom and goodness', to the 'sense of fun which he brought to everything he touched'. *The Times* said in 1950 that 'No man of comparable authority in the Commonwealth is so little known to his contemporaries ... Sir Edward Bridges possesses most notably that combination of personal modesty and intellectual power which makes the born civil servant'.[67]

When William Armstrong was preparing his obituary on Bridges he asked colleagues for assistance (as is quite normal in the civil service). One particularly valuable reply came from Sir William Murrie who wrote:

... I have a very vivid memory of that old leather sofa in Edward's room. Some of the stuffing was leaking from it and the hole out of which it came was covered by a rug. But always by the end of any talk during which you had been sitting beside him on the sofa the rug was ruffled - as ruffled as Edward's hair - such was his restlessness. The darting mind - and how his mind did that! - was matched by a bouncing, swift turning body, his feet often lifted from the floor and his hand now and then running through his hair in a very characteristic gesture. There was a gusto and an absence of pompousness or solemnity that made him like a schoolboy.

I feel that his handwriting was very revealing. I supose that basically it must have come from his parents who were, I think, interested in calligraphy. The strokes reminded me of the flowing brushwork of a painter: but on top of that was all the dash, the impetuosity, the panache of his temperament. I always found it a pleasure to look at anything he had written - even his most hurried scribbles - because one felt the artist in every line.

... Edward's generosity in giving everyone a chance to do his best in his own way. He tried, I think, to make our very different talents flower, without imposing too much conformity - indeed without imposing *any* conformity in a conscious way, though he could not help making us into a team by his example and personality. I felt too, very strongly, that he was never jealous of someone else's doing well or being afraid of being outdone or supplanted. I remember Lawrence Burgis contrasting him with Hankey in this respect. One felt that all this sprang from his feeling that the only thing that mattered was to get the work done as well as it could be by the instruments at his disposal and that no feeling of lack of sympathy with the personality or methods of work of any of the staff must stand in the way of achieving this ...

... But I think he was, with all his qualities, rather a shy person and that beneath the schoolboy-like informality and rather boisterous fun there was a difficulty in making human contacts and perhaps a slight lack of warmth. He wasn't very good at breaking bad news. But then how few are![68]

Edward Bridges died on the heights of Winterford Heath on 27 August 1969: only his wife was with him at the time - they had gone to enjoy the view over the North Downs which he loved so much. [69]

The Head of the Civil Service

The main purpose of this book is to provide an account and analysis of selected aspects of Bridges' career as Head of the Civil Service. There are two reasons for concentrating on the period from 1945 to 1956, the last eleven years of his civil service career. First, Bridges' contribution to the practice and study of public administration are so significant that they warrant a study in as much depth as possible using the meagre resources available, including the official files now released for the first time (thirty years after 1956) and whilst the memories of officials who served with him are also available. Secondly, though his career as Secretary to the Cabinet may indeed have been of crucial importance to the history of the United Kingdom, there is even less documentary evidence relating to that part of Bridges' career. He did not keep an official diary and he went out of his way to discourage his colleagues from recording their work experiences. Hankey, his predecessor as Cabinet Secretary, had kept a diary, which he used in writing his memoirs. When the time came for Hankey to seek permission before publication it was Bridges who ultimately had to decide. It took Bridges five months from receiving the request from Hankey before they met to discuss it. Bridges was very concerned about the effect the memoirs would have on the confidential relationship between ministers and their officials. Numerous revisions were made but Bridges was still not satisfied. As Bridges put it:

> Your book exposes, often in great detail, the working of this relationship [between ministers and official advisers], and the extent and degree to which Ministers were dependent on particular occasions on the help given by their officials. I fear that publication of all this material would have a very unfortunate effect on the relationship to Ministers, not only of your successors as Secretary to the Cabinet, but also of the Permanent Heads of the great Departments, and also of the

Civil Servants who, in other capacities, stand in a specially trusted relationship to Ministers.

...if your book were published it would make me personally self-conscious in my dealings with the Cabinet, and it would make Ministers generally much more chary of speaking freely to members of the Cabinet Secretariat, unless and until, as might well be the case, it was decided to promulgate some general rule against the keeping of diaries by members of this Office.[70]

On some occasions Bridges simply told colleagues they should not keep diaries, on other occasions his views percolated through opinions expressed in files dealing primarily with other matters. An example of this concerned the request, considered by Bridges in 1953, to permit the publication of the papers of W.J. Braithwaite (who had been a Special Commissioner for Income Tax and had died in 1938). Bridges commented that he had the nasty thought that besides having kept official documents he might also 'have written one of these diaries describing in familiar terms exactly how the Ministers he had worked for had and had not behaved'.[71] Furthermore, it seems that Bridges' working papers from the offices of the War Cabinet no longer exist. While Secretary to the Cabinet his work was not geared to the sort of filing system normally found in administrative departments; instead he preferred the Hankey system of 'skins' - envelopes in which were thrust the drafts and any other relevant documents leading up to a Cabinet paper. The records of Cabinet decisions and relevant final versions of official papers have survived, of course, but it is difficult if not impossible to work out from them the personal contribution of Bridges. As Churchill remarked on one occasion, the Cabinet records, as written by Bridges, were 'incredibly discreet'.[72] If Bridges had intentionally set out to prevent anyone writing a biographical study of his career he could hardly have been more successful or made the task more difficult. Therefore there can never be a complete record and evaluation of his official career: all that can be offered is a study of the remaining evidence. More evidence has been preserved from the period when Bridges was Head of the Civil Service. There is no doubt about the importance of this period, not only in terms of major developments but also in terms of what is revealed about the more routine work of the Head of the Civil Service.

The Headship of the British Civil Service is a position of both potential power and enormous influence. It is also an office about which remarkably little has been written. Therefore it is necessary to give a brief explanation of the history and duties attached to the office before proceeding to consider some aspects of Bridges' own occupancy of the position.

In the British system of government executive authority is vested solely in HM Government: officials, however high in rank, in theory, and in the last resort in law, exercise no executive authority of their own. The supreme Head of the civil service is the Sovereign and the ministerial Head is the Prime Minister (with, in recent years, a junior minister who has responsibility for day to day matters affecting the civil service). This arrangement, along with the growth of the civil service as a unified service, has a remarkably short history. The King's Civil List was finally relieved of civil service expenditure as recently as 1832. Before 1855 there was hardly the beginnings of a service-wide organisation because recruitment and promotions were almost entirely dependent on patronage and there was no standard system for pay or personnel classification. A service only emerged in the third quarter of the nineteenth century when recruitment for all classes of posts was placed on a regular basis. The Treasury emerged as the central department of management because of its fund-raising role and in particular its responsibility to present to Parliament the Estimates for expenditure from the various departments of state. Treasury sanction then became required to decide on the numbers, pay and classification of the civil establishments, and the most senior permanent official in the Treasury came to be recognised as the principal position in the civil service.[73]

According to a Treasury account of the matter, the title of Permanent Secretary to the Treasury was introduced with the Treasury reorganisation in 1867. It is possible, but not certain because the files were declared lost many years ago, that the official Headship of the Civil Service also originates from 1867.[74] Maurice Wright, however, casts doubt on the significance attached to 1867, believing that it did not confer on anyone the title Official Head of the Civil Service.[75] In 1872 Robert Lowe, Chancellor of the Exchequer, referred in the House of Commons to the Secretary of the Treasury as head of the civil service,[76] though this reference could be interpreted as no more than a reference to the fact that he stood first in his profession, because he was head of the most important department. According to Fisher, by 1878 it had become 'a well established fact' that the Permanent Secretary to the

Treasury was Head of the Civil Service.[77] Following the recommendations of the MacDonnell Royal Commission on the Civil Service (1912-14)[78] and the Select Committee on National Expenditure which reported in 1917,[79] Treasury control over the organisation of the civil service was strengthened. In 1918 the Haldane Committee on the Machinery of Government recommended that there should be a separate branch in the Treasury specialising in establishment work and studying all questions of staff recruitment, classification and routine business generally.[80] In 1919 the Treasury was reorganised. Instead of having three permanent secretaries, with the retirement of Sir Robert Chalmers and the departure of the other two permanent secretaries (Sir Thomas Heath and Sir John Bradbury) at the end of the year to take up new appointments, it was decided to revert to the arrangement of having only one. Fisher was appointed to the post of Permanent Secretary and in addition there were to be three Controllers of Departments, who were to rank, under the directions of the permanent secretary, as Secretaries of the Board and to have the status in the civil service of heads of departments. A Treasury minute dated 4 September 1919 left no doubt about the duties attached to the top post. It said: 'The functions of the Permanent Secretary would include responsibility for the organisation of the Treasury, for the general supervision and co-ordination of the work of the Treasury as a whole, and for advising the Board. He would act as Permanent Head of the Civil Service and advise the First Lord in regard to Civil Service appointments and decorations'.[81] Sir Horace Hamilton has said that there is no evidence that Fisher was in any way responsible for the scheme. Fisher's version of the proceedings was that he was not sent for by ministers until after they had reached decisions about the future organisation of the Treasury.[82] In any case, ministers were themselves keen on the new arrangement; Austen Chamberlain, Chancellor of the Exchequer, wrote to Fisher on 24 August 1919: '... I attach special importance ... to the recognition of the position of the Permanent Secretary ås Head of the Civil Service'.[83] Later, Fisher explained the position of the Permanent Secretary to the Treasury as being 'deliciously vague, floating, somewhere rather Olympian'.[84]

When Fisher was appointed Whitehall was still in practice a collection of departments. Fisher was determined to alter this and to make the civil service a coherent whole. According to Bridges it was a deliberate part of this policy that he created, or revived for himself, the title of Head of the Civil Service and he deliberately publicised it or even over-publicised it not, in Bridges' opinion, for self-aggrandisement, but to make the civil service conscious of itself; indeed, Bridges thought that it was for the same motives that he encouraged civil service cricket and rugger teams. In 1949 Bridges reflected on this:

> ... Looking backwards, I am myself disposed to think that he made two errors of judgment in what he did in this way. The first is that I think the title "Head of the Civil Service" (the word "official" was only added later) was probably a mistake although I have not been able to think of any easy and satisfactory alternative ...
>
> The second error, which was also a matter of form and not of substance, was that he officially and formally attached the title "Head of the Civil Service" to the post of Permanent Secretary to the Treasury and used it in all the books of reference ....[85]

This caused political controversy in Westminster from time to time. It also attracted antagonism from the Foreign Office. For example, some politicians thought they saw in the increasing cohesion of the civil service a threat to ministerial responsibility - though it is fair to add that others strongly disagreed. On 1 April 1926 Sir Austen Chamberlain again gave his strong support to the arrangement. He wrote: 'I regard the 1919 decisions as vital to the efficiency of the Civil Service'.[86] On two occasions in 1926 the Prime Minister, Mr Stanley Baldwin, answered Parliamentary Questions about the post, with replies drafted by Fisher. He made it absolutely clear that although the official Head of the Civil Service had the duty of advising, with the best advice in his power, the Prime Minister in regard to all the more important appointments throughout the civil service, the responsibility remained with the Prime Minister and his ministerial colleagues.[87] Bridges thought that Fisher antagonised a group in the Foreign Office mainly because he opposed what would have been an unworthy appointment to be Under Secretary of State. This antagonism also became associated at a later date with a Foreign Office vendetta against the Treasury arising from their dislike of the part played by Sir Horace Wilson, Fisher's successor, in foreign affairs. This was at least in part because Wilson, before he became Permanent Secretary to the Treasury, had been Mr Neville Chamberlain's personal assistant and had accompanied him to Berchtesgarten and elsewhere when neither the Foreign

Secretary nor any Foreign Office experts were present.[88]

Bridges, being at the centre of Treasury establishments work for in this summary.[89] Consequently he felt he had to avoid anything which would lead to the continuance of the old controversy over the title. Indeed, he not only abstained from ever himself using the title of Official Head of the Civil Service, he struck it out of all the reference books. He also said that if it could be proved that the title was still a real cause of offence he would not object to it being altered, but he added: 'having considered the matter very carefully, I am strongly against any alteration in the present position. Any steps to alter the position would, in fact, bring the whole controversy into prominence again'.[90]

Bridges' own appointment to the position in 1945 was not without an interesting pre-history. When Wilson retired from the post in 1942 he suggested that he should be succeeded by Sir Arthur Street, then Permanent Secretary to the Air Ministry. It seems that at that time Churchill may have been considering Bridges for the dual appointment of Secretary of the Cabinet and Secretary of the Treasury. Wilson discounted the practicality of the suggestion on the grounds that the burden of work in the Treasury was heavy and likely to remain so, and he argued that it would be quite impossible for the Treasury duties to be carried out efficiently if the holder of the post was also obliged to attend Cabinet meetings and meetings of Cabinet committees. It seems that Bridges, as Secretary to the War Cabinet, was also asked for comments on this suggestion. Bridges wrote that criticism would link up with the contention that an altogether undue load would be put on the shoulders of the holder of the combined post. He suggested that the only way to meet this criticism would be to have two joint secretaries of the Treasury so that the senior one would be responsible for questions of civil organisation generally while the other could be responsible for the Treasury business generally and for the efficiency of the department. Churchill responded: 'Surely the Secretary to the Cabinet should be the "Official Head of the Civil Service" and the Secretary to the Treasury deal with Treasury matters only. Try thinking along these lines'.[91] In the event, Bridges remained at the Cabinet Office and Sir Richard Hopkins (with whom Churchill had worked as Chancellor in 1924) became Secretary to the Treasury.

The question arose again when Hopkins retired in 1945. This time Churchill took a firmer line and told Bridges to prepare proposals for devolution within both the Treasury and the War Cabinet Office. Other officials were also involved in these proposals. Bridges discussed the matter with the Chancellor of the Exchequer and with Hopkins and they agreed that Norman Brook was the best person to serve as Deputy Secretary in the Cabinet Office – he had already worked there for 20 months up to December 1943, when he became the chief official assisting Lord Woolton as Minister of Reconstruction. Mr J.A.C. Robertson assisted the discussion by writing a paper outlining the duties of the Permanent Secretary to the Treasury as official Head of the Civil Service. On 20 January 1945 the Prime Minister sent a minute to the Chancellor of the Exchequer saying it had been decided that at least as long as the war lasted and during the period of the peace negotiations Bridges should continue in general charge of the War Cabinet Office, retaining the title of Secretary of the War Cabinet, but he would also become Permanent Secretary to the Treasury. Bridges' duties as Head of the Civil Service were as outlined in Robertson's paper: '... responsibility for the organisation of the Treasury, for the general supervision and co-ordination of the Treasury as a whole and for advising the Board. He will act as permanent Head of the Civil Service and advise the First Lord in regard to Civil Service appointments and decorations'.[92] The paper also made it absolutely clear that the consent of the Prime Minister was required for the appointment (or removal) of Permanent Heads of Departments, their Deputies, Principal Finance Officers and Principal Establishment Officers.

Bridges gave careful consideration to how he would carry out his responsibilities. In a letter to Sir Ernest Barker in 1948 he said he had thought a lot about the official title of headship of the civil service and added: 'it is one of the few things which I believe I really understand'.[93] It was a post that had from time to time been the centre of political controversy, it was also a post which Churchill had become particularly worked up about in the 1920s when he was Chancellor of the Exchequer and Fisher was in the Treasury. On 16 November 1925 Churchill was so exasperated that he drafted a letter to Fisher which in fact he never sent. This letter is quite revealing about the position of Permanent Secretary to the Treasury at that time and about the relationship of its then incumbent to Churchill as Chancellor. Churchill wrote:

> ... During the year I have been at the Treasury I have received scarcely any assistance from you in the very difficult task I have been endeavouring to discharge. I only recall three Minutes which dealt with Treasury business. The first a rather

facetious rejection by you of some suggestion on the improving and regularising of the form of office papers in accordance with the practice of other Departments; the second a Minute proposing to spend a considerable sum of money on the purchase in this over-burdened year on recreation grounds for Civil Servants; the third showing the impossibility of any reduction in the emoluments or number of the Civil Service. Sometimes as much as three months have passed without my seeing you or receiving any official paper from you, and on any of the occasions when we met, it has only been because I have directly summoned you.

I am aware that you do not regard yourself in any way responsible for assisting the Chancellor of the Exchequer and that you reserve your functions entirely for the First Lord of the Treasury. You have been careful to impress this upon me and I have not challenged your interpretation of your duties. I must say however that it is an interpretation very different from that which after nearly twenty years experience in Ministerial Office I had supposed was the practice, and I cannot conceive that any of your distinguished predecessors have not been accustomed to give more constant and effective assistance to the Chancellor of the day, whether in regard to the controlling of expenditure or the framing of finance. Such knowledge as I possessed led me to suppose that the Secretary to the Treasury was the right-hand man and fellow-worker of the Chancellor of the Exchequer and the leading official figure in the whole business of the Treasury ...'.[94]

The next year, when Churchill was more balanced about the situation he contented himself with sending a short note to Fisher making similar points but more briefly: '... I am of course always ready to see you, though I have not been so fortunate in this respect during the 18 months I have been at the Treasury ...'.[95]

It seems that by this time the work of Head of the Civil Service had assumed priority for Fisher. In fairness to Fisher, he left the three Controllers to get on with their work without interference and even Churchill in his most critical mood in 1925 (in the letter he did not send to Fisher) acknowledged that he had been ably served by the very accomplished heads of the branches of the Treasury 'for whose selection you are I believe entitled to much credit'.[96] The work of Head of the Treasury did not diminish, instead it increased - as illustrated in subsequent chapters of this book. Moreover, it was an office associated not only with political controversy. It was also a position of managerial sensitivity when Bridges was appointed. Lord Roberthall has recalled that Bridges came in to the Treasury as Permanent Secretary over the heads of two very senior Treasury officials, Sir Wilfrid Eady and Sir Bernard Gilbert. Although these officials were, in 1945 (according to Roberthall) rather extinct volcanoes, Bridges' sensitivity to persons meant that he was rather 'nervous about them and too deferential to them about their views'.[97]

In several respects Bridges was the disciple of Fisher. On economic matters he relied on advice from his specialist colleagues and on drafts prepared for him by them. However, he occasionally played an important personal role. A good example was during the 1945/46 discussions on economic aid: Bridges was apparently the only official present during crucial discussions in London.[98] Then Attlee and his principal colleagues found it so difficult to believe the American condition about convertibility within a year that Bridges was despatched to Washington to check on Keynes' judgment.[99]

Wilson in 1942 had summarised what he saw as the duties of the Head of the Civil Service. It was quite clear to him that the status of the position conferred no right of interference in matters of policy in other departments. The special responsibility of the post related to the Government's servants rather than to the Government's policy. In a paper which he wrote on 5 May 1942 he listed the main duties as:

1) When a vacancy arises in posts of Permanent Heads of Departments, their Deputies, Principal Finance Officers or Principal Establishment Officers, it is his duty to submit advice for the consideration of the Prime Minister and of the Minister of the Department in which the vacancy occurs.
2) He deals with Civil Service Honours.
3) Closely connected with (1) is his duty of exercising a general oversight over the organisation and well-being of the Civil Service. He should be the man to whom the Permanent Heads of other Departments would naturally turn for counsel and advice in their difficulties.[100]

It is important to understand how Bridges saw the Headship of the Civil Service when he was appointed. He wrote that he was very aware that one or two of his predecessors in the previous thirty years 'had gained the reputation of seeking to exercise more influence or power (I'm not sure which is the right word) than was right for a Civil Servant. It would be bad for the Civil Service if that came to be said about me'.[101] He was also aware that the criticisms of the job all attached themselves to particular individuals.[102] The duties were all important; the title mattered little.[103]

According to Bridges the reality of the position was that the Permanent Secretary to the Treasury exercised certain functions in relation to the whole civil service and the chief of these was acting as adviser to the Prime Minister in regard to civil service appointments.[104] However, he recognised the changes that had taken place in the central organisation of the government machine since 1938 (when he was promoted from the Treasury to become Secretary to the Cabinet). He said that after the war no-one would think of describing this central organisation without describing the role played by the Cabinet Office. The Treasury, too, had changed and was beginning to look more like a Central Economic Department. He continued:

> When I was appointed to the Treasury I made up my mind that, whatever else I did, I would try to foster the development of a better central government machine in which both the Treasury and the Cabinet Office would play their due part, and the relation of the two would be more clearly understood throughout Whitehall. I think that this relation has improved a lot and is better understood. But I have not made nearly as much progress in this direction as I had hoped. This is partly on account of the sheer pressure of events. But it is not only that. My instinct is that it would be unwise to force the pace; and that a good deal must develop by evolution and practical experience before we attempt any formal re-definition of this part of the government machine.[105]

It is an indication of Bridges' genuine modesty that he seemed not to appreciate his own role in this. It could be argued that his two greatest achievements were in this field of the machinery of government. First, he converted the central machinery to achieve its war purpose. Secondly, he adapted the central machinery to the requirements of the period of post-war reconstruction and to meet the demands of the 1945-51 Labour Government. His main achievements were, however, inseparable from other responsiblities he exercised as Head of the Civil Service. They were also inseparable from and cannot be understood without some appreciation of his personal and philosophical approach to the tasks of administration and the profession to which he had devoted himself, in particular his profound belief in generalist administration.

Generalist Administration

Although in the House of Lords Debate on the Fulton Report Bridges referred to the generalist as 'this mythical creature,'[106] Bridges himself excelled in what others have called the generalist approach to administration in the British civil service. Anthony Seldon, in his monumental study *Churchill's Indian Summer*, uses the word 'excelled' in this context [107] because it was quite evident from Seldon's extensive researches in oral history that this was the way Bridges was seen by many of his contemporaries. Lord Redcliffe-Maud, in an interview with Seldon, remarked that Bridges 'was always number one until he retired' and Seldon concluded that Bridges was 'the outstanding civil servant in Whitehall since his appointment as Secretary to the Cabinet in 1938'.[108] Nevertheless, it was the approach to management exemplified and expounded by Bridges that was the focus for critics because it was thought to be not sufficiently professional and inadequate in terms of training and expertise in economics.

The term 'generalist' in this context achieved prominence from the criticisms associated with it in the Fulton Report where, in the highly controversial first chapter, the Report said that 'The Home Civil Service today is still fundamentally the product of the nineteenth-century philosophy of the Northcote-Trevelyan Report' and referred to the tradition that had developed of 'the "all-rounder" as he has been called by his champions or "amateur" as he has been called by his critics'.[109] The Report stated that 'the Service is still essentially based on the philosophy of the amateur (or "generalist" or "all-rounder")'[110] and indicated how it worked:

.. all-round administrators were ... supported by non-graduates to do executive and clerical work and by specialists (e.g. Inspectors of Schools) in those departments where they were needed. A man had to enter the Service on completing his education; once in, he was in for life. The outcome was a career service, immune from nepotism and political jobbery and, by the same token, attractive for its total security as well as for the intellectual achievement and social status that success in the entry competition implied.[111]

The Fulton Committee argued that the civil service in the twentieth century faced new tasks. It explained:

> The ideal administrator is still too often seen as the gifted layman who, moving frequently from job to job within the Service, can take a practical view of any problem, irrespective of its subject matter, in the light of his knowledge and experience of the government machine ... (The) cult of the generalist ... is obsolete at all levels and in all parts of the Service.[112]

The reason why the Fulton Committee was so critical of the generalist administrator was that, as the Report said, many adminstrators

> do not develop adequate knowledge in any aspect of the department's work ... Often they are required to give advice on subjects they do not sufficiently understand or take decisions whose significance they do not fully grasp. This has serious consequences. It can lead to bad policy making; it prevents a fundamental evaluation of the policies being administered; it often leads to the adoption of inefficient methods of implementing these policies ... and it obstructs the establishment of fruitful contacts with sources of expert advice ....[113]

Professor Lord Simey, in a powerful reservation to Chapter 1 of the Report argued that the chapter was unfair to the civil service, mainly because it failed to recognise the many achievements and qualities of the British civil service and gave a misleading impression of its future potentials. He argued not for something approaching revolutionary changes, but for 'encouraging the evolution of what is basically the present situation, given the necessary amendments in direction and emphasis'. He did not agree that '"the service is essentially based on the philosophy of the amateur (or 'generalist' or 'all- rounder')"' and asserted that 'It is true that modern economic and political organisation needs high specialism, but it also needs more general qualities of judgement and decisiveness, and the ability to understand how the reshaping of values may be embodied in and implemented by public policy'. He stressed 'the importance of the fundamental qualities of judgement which are vital to the successful prosecution of government business' and added 'I have little sympathy with the argument that the Civil Service today must be fundamentally changed because the Administrative Class which dominates it is typified by the "gifted amateur" ... I do not ... accept that there is a "cult of the generalist" in the Service today or that the "generalist" is obsolete at all levels'.[114] Bridges came out firmly in support of Simey during the House Lords debate, saying that if he had been a member of Lord Fulton's Committee he would certainly have joined Simey in signing his minority report.[115]

It is critics of the generalist rather than supporters who have given some of the clearest statements of his main characteristics. Three examples illustrate this. Professor Harvey Walker, writing in the 1930s, detected a 'lack of knowledge and appreciation, on the part of the administrators, of the affairs of the outside world, except in so far as they pertain to their work'; a 'lack of knowledge of the activities and policies of the departments of government, other than those in which they serve'; and 'a failure to consider public administration as a science with a body of fundamental principles, and the insistence on treating it as an art or mystery revealed only to those who have followed the initiatory rite through which they have passed, or alternatively as a faculty inborn, which is denied to all who are not blessed with it at birth'.[116]

Thomas (later Lord) Balogh, writing in the 1950s about the Establishment of Mandarins, referred to 'that special mysterious art, Administrative Capacity' which was said to depend on 'an attitude of effortless superiority, combined with cultured scepticism'. He added: 'Positive knowledge and imagination, assertion of the social against the private interest, were obviously not looked for. The negative qualities were thought to be best attained by a judicious mixture of breeding, "character building" and a purposefully useless, somewhat dilletante, erudition which would keep "dangerous thoughts" well away ... Anything smacking of vocational training and technical knowledge was severely discountenanced'.[117]

Lord Crowther-Hunt, writing in the 1970s, gave details of the clear picture, built up by the Fulton Committee's Management Group, of the ideal administrator as seen by the civil service:

He is a man (or woman) of good education and high intelligence who can take an overall view of any problem, irrespective of the subject matter, in the light of his knowledge and experience of the government machine. The "generalist" is an expert in the processes of government - a craft to be picked up mostly by experience on the job. The role of the administrator is that of the intelligent layman whose unique and vital contribution is an intimate knowledge of the government machine. This background enables him to synthesise the views of specialists both within and without the government machine and to evaluate them in terms of what is feasible.[118]

Critics of generalist administration have therefore made a very significant impact through their writings and in public debate. This debate, however, has been largely one-sided. The quantity and quality of replies and exposition in favour of generalist administration has been overwhelmed by the critics who have enjoyed the advantage of the mid-twentieth century fashion to criticise British institutions. Generalist administrators have, in contrast, been handicapped because most practitioners in the civil service have not been free to write and speak in public about their work. It is true the First Division Association produced a valuable paper about it in their evidence to the Fulton Committee,[119] but there has been little else to help balance the discussion except for Bridges himself. It would be difficult to imagine a better example of generalist administration: Bridges excelled at it. His career embodied both the variety of experience and the personal qualities sought by those who approved of generalist administration. Moreover, Bridges was in many respects an authoritative exponent and leading advocate. He explained it on numerous occasions in official contexts and in his published writings and lectures. There are therefore two reasons why it is necessary to present an outline of his views in this introductory chapter. First, his exposition is important for understanding how generalist administration was seen from an outstanding practitioner of it. Secondly, an understanding of it is necessary for appreciating the subjects discussed in subsequent chapters of this book.

Bridges' conception of the work of an administrator must be seen in the context of his views of modern democratic government in general and the development of the British approach to public administration in particular. 'All governments', he said, 'are overburdened'[120] - and that, according to Bridges, was why some of the practices of administrators developed in the ways they have. However, in the British context there was an additional important feature that should be seen from its origins in the political history of the eighteenth century: 'the civil service is non-political, and free from party bias or allegiances'.[121] As Bridges explained: 'The action taken by Parliament in that century to prevent the corruption of Parliament itself by patronage resulted in a series of Acts which limited, and clearly defined, the number of Ministerial offices which could be held by Members of Parliament. These Acts brought into being a sharp distinction between political and non-political offices; and prevented anything in the nature of a spoils system in this country'.[122] In the nineteenth and twentieth centuries he distinguished three main causes which brought about something which could be described as 'a "service" in the place of a series of departmental staffs, separated off from each other, distant and jealous'.[123] These were first, the introduction of a common system of recruitment for all departments. Secondly, the transfer of staff between departments. Thirdly, after 1920, when it was formally laid down that the assent of the Prime Minister was required to appointments to the top posts in all departments, the way the whole civil service was taken by the Prime Minister and his advisers as their field of selection for appointments to the top posts. The process of breaking down the isolation of departments went further during and immediately after the Second World War, partly because of the effect of total war on the service which led to so many transfers between departments but also because of the growing inter-dependence of departments and the importance of economic factors which affected all aspects of government.[124] Bridges, who might have been an academic historian[125] had he not become a civil servant, emphasised in this way the importance of Britain's history for understanding the British civil service.

Nevertheless, he thought there were important comparisons to be made between the academic life and work in the civil service. In evidence before the 1953-5 (Priestley) Royal Commission on the Civil Service he acknowledged that one of the factors which helped in civil service recruitment was that the job was interesting, though he also argued that the demands and challenge of the work meant that it resulted in 'a more strenuous life than that of many people outside'.[126] He always stressed that the chief need of the civil service was 'to be able to recruit the ablest people'[127] and he was pleased that the service had attracted such good candidates. Of those who joined the civil service he thought it fair to say that they nearly all had in common: 'a disposition to find public affairs of interest; no desire or intention to take part in political life; and a readiness to work as a member of a team, rather than to seek personal glory'.[128] However, the great achievement of introducing competitive examinations was that departments were 'successful in recruiting first class material from the universities' - 'men who brought to their work the happy blend of scholarship and ebullience that one finds in a university'.[129] On another occasion he wrote 'I have no doubt that ... "university entry" to the Civil Service has been an outstanding success: and that it has provided the Civil Service with a succession of first rate administrators'. He then argued, again, that there was a fairly close affinity between the qualities developed in the universities and those needed in the civil service:

> In both you have to cultivate the capacity to analyse complicated situations, and to set out the results clearly and accurately. You cannot do that unless you have an inner determination to find out the right answer at all costs: unless you are always on your guard not to allow yourself to be swayed by the preconceptions or prejudices which we all have about any subject, before we have really studied it. Above all, you must not allow your sympathies to get entangled with what looks like an ingenious and satisfactory solution to your problem, before you have finished your collation and analysis. You must be ready to accept an awkward fact which shows that you have been on the wrong lines, and to start all over again.
>
> As I see it, both in academic life and in the Civil Service you need this combination of intellectual integrity (horrid phrase), with the ardour of the chase. Moreover this combination of qualities has been of value to the Civil Service in another way. It is the pride of the Civil Service that it is non-political, and that it can serve Governments of all parties with equal loyalty and obtain their confidence. And this confidence is, perhaps, the more easily obtained by a Civil Service whose general attitude is slightly detached and withdrawn.[130]

Although Bridges recognised that the civil servant's task was changing in character and becoming, perhaps, rather more difficult than before, and that therefore even greater care was needed over recruitment and training, he did not think the changes caused him to alter his views about 'the fundamental soundness of the principles on which the report of 1854 rests'.[131] In particular, he added, after the publication of the Fulton Report, 'it would be a mistake to have this preference for relevance'.[132] Previously, in the public debates preceeding the setting up of the Fulton Committee, Bridges had tried to set the record straight concerning the number of administrative civil servants who had, in fact, relevant professional training. He recalled that when he first joined the Treasury there were only one or two people on the staff with a professional training in economics, but by 1964, in the two branches of the Treasury dealing with economic co-ordination, ten out of twelve of the staff had professional economic training. Furthermore, if, in 1964, you took the four top grades in the administrative class (assistant secretary to permanent secretary) thirteen per cent had degrees in science and mathematics.[133]

On the suggestion that there should be more short term secondments into and out of the civil service, Bridges was sympathetic, though he believed that the academic world was 'the best place with which to arrange exchanges'. He made it quite clear that he did not think secondments of civil servants to business was the right approach. He argued that the civil servant, at a fairly early age found himself engaged on work which combined management functions with considerations of policy. 'It is rare in business for any except the more senior officers to be engaged on this combination of duties. A civil servant transplanted temporarily into business could not, without a considerable apprenticeship, take on the businessman's job: and the same is true the other way round'.[134] In evidence to the Fulton Committee he wrote:

I have felt for some years that we could with advantage go some way towards the practice in, say, the USA where persons of particular experience and knowledge are brought in from business or universities for a period of years to do particular duties.

I am sure there is a lot to be gained from this. But it is important that this should not be done in a way which carries with it the implication (a) that the persons brought in are the personal nominees of particular Ministers and (b) that they are given positions which allow them a more direct access to Ministers than their colleagues in the permanent Civil Service.[135]

The civil servant in modern times has to adapt to his developing environment. Although Bridges believed some academic qualities were necessary in an administrator, other qualities were also necessary. The emphasis of the duties of the civil servant now extends beyond the writing of minutes and memoranda in the safe seclusion of his office. On behalf of the minister he is now called upon, more than ever before, to meet members of the public, either in their individual capacities or as representatives of industries or groups. Consequently, 'While never forgetting that he is the servant of the Minister, and is acting throughout with delegated authority from the Minister, he must show himself alert, knowledgeable of his business, and able to give a good account of it. He must also show understanding of the troubles of the public'.[136]

The political environment, especially the relationship between officials and ministers, is a distinctive feature in the work of a generalist administrator. In commenting on the suggestion (later proposed to the Fulton Committee) that a minister should have 'his own little *cabinet* in the French sense - a sort of central office through which he runs the whole department', Bridges said:

> It is significant that one wants to use the French pronounciation here. It is an idea foreign to us, with political overtones.
>
> I dislike this idea a good deal. It implies that a department is unable or unwilling to serve all ministers loyally and effectively, irrespective of party. I can see no need for a *cabinet* in a department unless one believes that only with the help of such an office is it possible for a minister to get his schemes carried through his department. And this just is not true ....[137]

Another respect in which this relationship became evident was in discussions about conditions of service, especially pay. For example, Bridges always felt very strongly that the position of senior civil servants as advisers to ministers, and with very close relations to ministers, made the procedure of compulsory arbitration less appropriate than in other fields. Civil servants had never been paid commercial rates, nor did they expect to be so paid. However, just because the work they did was interesting, it did not seem fair to say to them: 'Well, I know you work very hard, but it is a very interesting job and we will not pay you the full rate'.[138] A procedure therefore had to be developed which would recognise the peculiar position of civil servants in matters like pay-bargaining.

Bridges stressed on various public occasions that top administrators had 'the professionalism of the layman' because although they had real skills and qualifications, their skill was not the same as the professionalism of a doctor, or a lawyer, a chemist or an engineer. A civil servant had also to be well aware of the political content of his work:

> He will not be a trustworthy adviser unless he has studied the general national outlook, as illustrated particularly in Parliament ... and accepts this as the general background against which he works. At the same time, he is perhaps the least political of all animals, since the departmental experience of which he is the exponent ... is part of the stock of things which are common to all political parties. It is something which stands apart from the creed of any political party and thus makes a Civil Servant avert himself, almost instinctively, from party politics ... he is a student of public opinion, but no party politician.[139]

According to Bridges the administrator needed what might be described 'either as a general understanding of the main principles of organisation or as a kind of rarified common sense'[140] - by which he meant not the sort of common sense that can be divined by abstract reason, but common sense based on experience and the exercise of judgement. 'The really wise administrator shows a fine distinction about the points he can concede and the points on which he must stand firm. He may seem to be giving a lot away, but at the end of the day you will find that he has conceded nothing of importance'.[141] Whilst he will make use of the advice of specialists, including those who have instinctively studied and acquired skills in resolving problems of organisation, these are not qualifications or skills which he will personally seek to acquire. Instead he will rely on the power of rapid analysis, the capacity to recognise the essential points in a situation, a sense of timing, and a capacity to predict implications and perceive future problems and conditions.

Bridges thought it important that administrators, like all men and women whose work depends on using their brains, should have an intense curiosity and burning enthusiasm - a desire to master their subject. But their enthusiasm should be tempered by both an absolute intellectual honesty, so that judgement was held in suspense until a particular problem was mastered ('He will not venture an opinion until he has mastered the facts, and these he will set out accurately and clearly')[142]; and a good conscience, so that mistakes can be admitted promptly, then forgotten. It did not involve 'leadership' in the everyday sense of that word because for Bridges 'leadership' carried overtones of conscious bossiness and moral rectitude, which he found 'pretty repulsive'.[143] Nevertheless, he recognised the need for such personal qualities as imagination and perseverance, by which he meant the capacity to understand people, and 'to be the conductor of the orchestra'.[144] Consequently, Bridges saw the permanent head of a government department as 'general manager responsible for seeing that the Department as a whole is properly organised and running smoothly and is able to provide, either directly himself, or through one of his senior colleagues, advice at short notice on any part of the field'.[145] Essentially, Bridges saw the work of an administrator in the British civil service as an art - an art which can only be learnt on the job:

> ... I suppose that if I was going to learn to row, I might start by reading a book with diagrams which would show mathematically the precise angle behind the rigger at which the oar should be applied to the water in order to give the greatest leverage. I doubt if good oarsmen are made that way. Others think that these raucous noises which the coach shouts through the megaphone have more than psychological value. One gets much nearer the mark when one sees the coach get down into the boat and use his own arms and legs to show the young oarsman what he is doing wrong. But for my part I believe that many of the best oarsmen learned a great deal from the mere fact of rowing in a good crew behind a really good oarsman, for the good style and good rhythm proved as catching as the measles.[146]

The Report of the Fulton Committee made damning criticisms of the generalist administrator and all its recommendations were designed to move the British civil service away from what it described as the cult of the generalist. Critics of generalist administration have been eloquent and persuasive in their criticisms of it. In recent years no-one has done this more effectively than Lord Crowther-Hunt, who served as a member of the Fulton Committee, was later a minister in the Labour Government of 1974-79, and was a university teacher and Rector of Exeter College, Oxford.[147] However, observers from other countries have often regarded the British civil service as having good features worth copying, and in some cases[148] there have been calls for more attention to be paid, in particular, to the development of generalist administrators. Difficulties then arise because there has been so little firm evidence available about what is involved and how a generalist administrator works in practice. This book should help to provide some relevant information about this British experience. By concentrating on key elements in the work of Bridges as Head of the Civil Service, the role of one particular generalist adminstrator is described and analysed, thus shedding light on what Bridges himself, on one occasion, called 'one of the least understood of professions'.[149]

Notes

1. *The Daily Telegraph*, Obituary, 29 August 1969.

2. *Ibid.*

3. Laurence Helsby to Lady Bridges, 30 August 1969, Goodmans Furze Papers, Box 9.

4. Oliver Franks to Lady Bridges, 1 September 1969, Goodmans Furze Papers, Box 9.

5. Paul Sinker to Lady Bridges, 31 August 1969, Goodmans Furze Papers, Box 9.

6. Sir John Winnifrith, at Lord Bridges' Memorial Service, 15 October 1969, Treasury file: T118.

7. Much of the material in this biography section is derived from John Winnifrith, 'Edward Ettingdean Bridges - Baron Bridges, 1892-1969', *Biographical Memoirs of Fellows of the Royal Society*, Vol 16, 1970 (The Royal Society, London, 1970), pp. 37-56; E.T. Williams and C.S. Nicholls (Editors), *Dictionary of National Biography, 1961-1970*, (Oxford University Press, Oxford, 1981), pp.132-6; and *The Times*, Obituary, 29 August 1969.

8. See General Sir Tom Bridges, *Alarms and Excursions*, (Longmans, London, 1938).

9. Lord Bridges, when opening Reading University Library, 15 May 1964, Goodmans Furze Papers, Box 9.

10. Information from the present Lord Bridges. The Precentor (Director of Music) at Eton, Dr Henry Ley, told him in about 1941 that Edward Bridges had been a good clarinettist at Oxford before the First World War.

11. Treasury file: T118.

12. John Winnifrith, 'Edward Ettingdean Bridges - Baron Bridges, 1892-1969'.

13. Sir Edward Bridges, 'The Village in History', *Parish Councils Review*, New Series, Vol 1, 1950, pp. 1-12.

14. Information from the present Lord Bridges.

15. Quoted by John Winnifrith, 'Edward Ettingdean Bridges - Baron Bridges, 1892-1969'.

16. Information from the present Lord Bridges.

17. Lord Bridges to HM The Queen, 27 April 1965, Goodmans Furze Papers, Box 7.

18. PRO/WO95/2764 and information from the present Lord Bridges.

19. John Winnifrith, 'Edward Ettingdean Bridges - Baron Bridges, 1892-1969'.

20. PRO/WO95/4251

21. Treasury file: T118.

22. John Winnifrith, 'Edward Ettingdean Bridges - Baron Bridges, 1892-1969'.

23. PRO/WO32/5891.

24. Treasury file: T118.

25. 295 H.L. Deb., 5s., cols. 1173-6 (24 July 1968).

26. Treasury file: T118.

27. *Ibid.*

28. *Ibid.*

29. See G.C. Peden, *British Rearmament and the Treasury 1932-1939*, (Scottish Academic Press, Edinburgh, 1979).

30. John Winnifrith, 'Edward Ettingdean Bridges - Baron Bridges, 1892-1969'.

31. Bridges to Roskill, 3 December 1968, Goodmans Furze Papers, Box 9.

32. *Ibid.*

33. Letter from Margery Fry (Bridges' cousin), Goodmans Furze Papers, Box 9.

34. John Winnifrith, 'Edward Ettingdean Bridges - Baron Bridges, 1892-1969'.

35. Cabinet War Rooms (Imperial War Museum), Clive Steps, King Charles Street, London SW1A 2AQ.

36. Information from the present Lord Bridges.

37. John Winnifrith, 'Edward Ettingdean Bridges - Baron Bridges, 1892-1969'.

38. *Ibid.*

39. Winston S. Churchill, *The Second World War, Vol. II: Their Finest Hour*, (Cassell, London, 1949), pp.17-18.

40. PRO/T273/335.

41. PRO/T199/474.

42. Lt Gen Sir Ian Jacob to Lady Bridges, 29 August 1969; Walter Adams to Lady Bridges, 29 August 1969, Goodmans Furze Papers, Box 9.

43. *Report of the Committee on the Training of Civil Servants*, [Cmd. 6525], (HMSO, London, 1944).

44. John Winnifrith, 'Edward Ettingdean Bridges - Baron Bridges, 1892-1969'.

45. Sir John Winnifrith, interview in 1985.

46. Sir William Armstrong, 'Edward Bridges 1892-1969', *Public Administration*, Vol. 48, 1970, pp. 1-2.

47. PRO/T273/222. In the broadcast version the last paragraph quoted read: 'There is then, as I see it, a clear obligation on us all to set before ourselves a pattern of life which reflects, as far as each of us may, something of the spiritual and other-worldly. That those who live their lives in this spirit give much comfort to their fellows is clear enough, but the obligation surely goes deeper than that'.

48. *Ibid.*

49. The phrase received wide publicity when quoted from Sir Robert Armstrong's evidence in the New South Wales Supreme Court in connection with the application by the British Government for an injunction against Mr Peter Wright and the Heinemann Publishing Company in Australia. See *The Times*, 19 and 20 November 1986.

50. PRO/T273/234.

51. *The Daily Telegraph*, 15 May 1951.

52. John Winnifrith, 'Edward Ettingdean Bridges - Baron Bridges, 1892-1969'.

53. Goodmans Furze Papers, Box 4.

54. Maurice Ashley (Ed.), *Tributes to WSC*, (BBC Publications, London, 1965).

55. Lord Moran, *Winston Churchill: The Struggle for Survival, 1940-1965*, (Constable, London, 1966).

56. Sir John Wheeler-Bennett (Ed.), *Action This Day: Working with Churchill*, (Macmillan, London, 1968).

57. Goodmans Furze Papers, Box 3.

58. Goodmans Furze Papers, Box 5.

59. Goodmans Furze Papers, Box 9.

60. Sir Edward Bridges to Lord Adrian, 7 April 1952, Goodmans Furze Papers, Box 9.

61. Goodmans Furze Papers, Box 5.

62. University College, Cambridge, became Wolfson College on 1 January 1973.

63. Department of Technical Co-operation, *Report of the Committee on Training in Public Administration for Overseas Countries*, (HMSO, London, 1963).

64. Goodmans Furze Papers, Box 5.

65. E.T. Williams and C.S. Nicholls (Editors), *Dictionary of National Biography, 1961-1970*.

66. Sir Robert Birley to Lady Bridges, 29 August 1969, Goodmans Furze Papers, Box 9.

67. *The Times*, 22 May 1950.

68. Treasury file: T118.

69. Goodmans Furze Papers, Box 9.

70. Bridges to Hankey, 30 November 1944. Quoted by John F. Naylor, *A Man and An Institution: Sir Maurice Hankey, the Cabinet and the custody of Cabinet Secrecy*, (Cambridge University Press, Cambridge, 1984), p. 271.

71. PRO/T273/223, Bridges to Padmore, 27 April 1953.

72. PRO/T273/228, Churchill to Bridges, 27 June 1947.
73. Richard A. Chapman, 'The Rise and Fall of the CSD', *Policy and Politics*, Vol. 11, 1983, pp. 41-61.
74. PRO/T199/351.
75. Maurice Wright, *Treasury Control of the Civil Service 1854-1874*, (Clarendon Press, Oxford, 1969). See also The Rt Hon Lord Bridges, *The Treasury*, (George Allen and Unwin, London, 1964), Ch. 17 and Appendix 7.
76. 210 H.C. Deb., 3s., cols. 847-8 (5 April 1872).
77. PRO/T199/351.
78. *Fourth Report of the Royal Commission on the Civil Service*, [Cd. 7338], (HMSO, London, 1912), paras. 92-102.
79. *Second Report from the Select Committee on National Expenditure, together with the Proceedings of the Committee*, H.C. 151, (HMSO, London, 1917).
80. *Report of the Machinery of Government Committee*, [Cd. 9230], (HMSO, London, 1918). paras. 19-21.
81. PRO/T199/351.
82. Sir H.P. Hamilton, 'Sir Warren Fisher and the Public Service', *Public Administration*, Vol. 29, 1951, pp. 3-38.
83. PRO/T199/351.
84. Public Accounts Committee, 30 April 1936, Q. 4443, Quoted by Sir H.P. Hamilton, 'Sir Warren Fisher and the Public Service'.
85. PRO/T199/352, Bridges to Helsby, 16 October 1949.
86. PRO/T199/351, Chamberlain to Fisher, 1 April 1926.
87. 191 H.C. Deb., 5s., cols. 2093-5 (18 February 1926) and 192 H.C. Deb., 5s., cols. 518-20 (24 February 1926).
88. PRO/T273/381. See also 459 H.C. Deb., 5s., cols. 713-23 and 725-7 (10 December 1948).
89. Lord Bridges, *The Treasury*, Ch. 17.
90. PRO/T199/352.
91. PRO/T199/352.
92. PRO/T199/352, J.A.C. Robertson 'Permanent Secretary to the Treasury as official head of the Civil Service', 8 February 1945.
93. PRO/T199/352, Bridges to Barker, 31 March 1948.
94. PRO/T199/415.
95. PRO/T199/415, Churchill to Fisher, 29 April 1926.
96. PRO/T199/415, Churchill to Fisher, 16 November 1925.
97. Lord Roberthall, Transcript of Interview, British Oral Archive of Political and Administrative History, British Library of Political and Economic Science. See also the Chancellor of the Exchequer's uneasiness about the quality of staff in the Treasury and the heavy burden on some of them in 1947: PRO/T273/241.
98. PRO/T273/242.
99. Francis Williams, *A Prime Minister Remembers: The War and Post-War Memoirs of the Rt Hon Lord Attlee*, (Heinemann, London, 1961), p. 133. See also Sir Alec Cairncross, *Years of Recovery: British Economic Policy 1945-51*, (Methuen, London, 1985), pp. 108 and 114.
100. PRO/T199/351.
101. PRO/T273/74, Bridges to Attlee, 5 November 1946.

102. PRO/T199/352, Bridges to Padmore, 21 September 1949.

103. Lord Bridges, *The Treasury*, p. 173.

104. PRO/T199/352, Bridges to Padmore, 21 September 1949.

105. PRO/T273/74.

106. 295 H.L. Deb., 5s., cols. 1173-6 (24 July 1968).

107. Anthony Seldon, *Churchill's Indian Summer: the Conservative Government 1951-1955*, (Hodder and Stoughton, London, 1981), p. 545, fn. 6.

108. *Ibid.*, p. 107.

109. *The Civil Service, Vol. 1 Report of the Committee 1966-68*, [Cmnd. 3638], (HMSO, London, 1968), paras. 1 and 3.

110. *Ibid.*, para 15.

111. *Ibid.*, para 4.

112. *Ibid.*, para 15.

113. *Ibid.*, para 40.

114. Lord Simey, 'Reservation to Chapter 1', in *The Civil Service*, Vol. 1, pp. 101-3.

115. 295 H.L. Deb., 5s., cols. 1173-6 (24 July 1968).

116. Harvey Walker, *Training Public Employees in Great Britain*, (McGraw-Hill, New York, 1935), p. 13.

117. Thomas Balogh, 'The Apotheosis of the Dilettante: the Establishment of Mandarins' in Hugh Thomas (Ed.) *The Establishment*, (Anthony Blond, London, 1959).

118. Peter Kellner and Lord Crowther-Hunt, *The Civil Servants: An Inquiry into Britain's Ruling Class*, (Macdonald and Jane's, London, 1980), p. 33.

119. Memorandum No. 15 submitted by the Association of First Division Civil Servants, *The Civil Service, Vol. 5(1), Proposals and Opinions: Evidence submitted to the Committee under the Chairmanship of Lord Fulton, 1966-68*, (HMSO, London, 1968).

120. The Rt Hon Lord Bridges, *The State and the Arts*, Romanes Lecture, 1958, (Oxford University Press, London, 1958), p. 4.

121. Sir Edward Bridges, *Portrait of a Profession: the Civil Service Tradition*, (Cambridge University Press, Cambridge, 1950), p. 6.

122. *Ibid.*, p. 6.

123. *Ibid.*, p. 8.

124. *Ibid.*, pp. 11-12.

125. Lord Bridges, 'The Treasury as the most political of departments', The Pollak Lecture, delivered at the Graduate School of Public Administration, Harvard University, December 1961.

126. *Evidence taken before the Royal Commission on the Civil Service, 1953-5*, Q. 97, 96.

127. 295 H.L. Deb., 5s., cols. 1173-6 (24 July 1968).

128. Lord Bridges, 'The Relationship between Ministers and the Permanent Departmental Head', *The W. Clifford Clark Memorial Lectures, 1964*, (Institute of Public Administration of Canada, Toronto, 1964), p. 9.

129. Sir Edward Bridges, *Portrait of a Profession*, (Cambridge University Press, Cambridge, 1950), p. 15.

130. Sir Edward Bridges, 'The Reforms of 1854 in Retrospect', *The Political Quarterly*, Vol. 25, 1954, p. 321.

131. *Ibid.*, p. 323.
132. 295 H.L. Deb., 5s., cols 1173-6 (24 July 1968).
133. *Whitehall and Beyond, Jo Grimond, Enoch Powell, Harold Wilson, three conversations with Norman Hunt, with a comment by Lord Bridges*, (BBC Publications, London, 1964), p. 64.
134. *Ibid.*, p. 65.
135. Bridges' paper for the Fulton Committee, 23 August 1967, Goodmans Furze Papers, Box 9.
136. Sir Edward Bridges, 'The Reforms of 1854 in Retrospect', p. 323.
137. *Whitehall and Beyond*, p. 69.
138. *Royal Commission on the Civil Service, 1953-55, Evidence*, (HMSO, London, 1954), Q. 95, 96, 172.
139. Sir Edward Bridges, *Portrait of a Profession*, pp. 27-8.
140. Sir Edward Bridges, 'Administration: What is it? And how can it be learnt?' in A. Dunsire (Ed.) *The Making of an Administrator*, (Manchester University Press, Manchester, 1956), p. 6.
141. *Ibid.*, p. 14.
142. Lord Bridges, 'The Relationship between Ministers and the Permanent Departmental Head', p. 9.
143. The Rt Hon Lord Bridges, *Commemoration Day Address 23 October 1958*, (Imperial College of Science and Technology, London, 1958).
144. Sir Edward Bridges, 'Administration: What is it? And how can it be learnt?' p. 14.
145. Lord Bridges, 'The Relationship between Ministers and the Permanent Departmental Head', p. 10.
146. Sir Edward Bridges, 'Administration: What is it? And how can it be learnt?' p. 23.
147. Peter Kellner and Lord Crowther-Hunt, *The Civil Servants: An Inquiry into Britain's Ruling Class*; Rt Hon Lord Crowther-Hunt 'The Failure to Reform the Civil Service' in Arthur Shenfield *et al, Managing the Bureaucracy* (The Adam Smith Institute, London, 1986).
148. For example, J.J. Deutsch, 'Some thoughts on the Public Service', an informal address to the annual meeting of the Ottawa Chapter of the Canadian Political Science Association, later published in the *Canadian Journal of Economics and Political Science*, Vol. 23, 1957, pp. 183-91, and reprinted in J.E. Hodgetts and D.C. Corbett, *Canadian Public Administration*, (Macmillan, Toronto, 1960), pp. 297-304.
149. Sir Edward Bridges, *Portrait of a Profession*, p. 33.

2

Personnel Management

Personnel management in its widest sense is the process of appointing the best possible staff, then looking after them so that they will want to stay and give of their best to their jobs.[1] It is not an activity reserved only for specialists: anyone who manages people must from time to time practise personnel management. In addition to this general use of the term it has become a specialist type of management. In this sense personnel management aims to achieve efficiency and justice in an organisation through fair terms and conditions of employment and by helping to ensure that employees achieve satisfaction from their work.[2] Personnel management techniques and methods of analysis have been developed with beneficial results since the nineteenth century, though the most significant advances occurred during and soon after the First World War. These have included developments in such aspects as recruitment, training, labour relations, pay structures and negotiations and staff welfare. In Britain, as in other advanced countries, personnel management has its own Institute with its own professional qualifications. Its origins can be traced to the Welfare Workers Association, founded in 1913, which, after changes in its name, became the Institute of Personnel Management in 1946.

Although personnel management must exist in all fields of employment and, indeed, is widely practised as a profession in British industry and commerce, in the British civil service it has not been a type of work generally held in high regard. Until comparatively recently personnel management was not recognised as a distinctive activity. It was not something for which people were thought to need training; it was simply an aspect of day to day work which generalist officials did by the application of commonsense to particular management problems involving staff.

Nevertheless, for many years, in all departments of the civil service, there has been a relatively small number of staff engaged in establishments work. However, establishments work is not the same as personnel management. It has different values and goals arising to a large extent from the system of accountability and control originating from the relationship between Parliament and the administration: it has never been primarily concerned with the needs of individuals to achieve satisfaction from their work. Establishments work may be traced back to the nineteenth century when Treasury approval became necessary for all schemes for recruitment of staff, and Treasury sanction was specifically required in respect of numbers, pay and classification of all civil establishments. A separate branch specialising in establishments was created within the Treasury after the Haldane Committee on the Machinery of Government recommended in its report in 1918 that

> In the Treasury there should be a separate branch specialising in ... 'establishment' work, and studying all questions of staff, recruitment, classification, etc., and routine business generally. Such a branch would be in close touch and constant communication with the officers in other Departments charged with the duty of supervising the 'establishment' work. It would also keep itself acquainted with what was being done in business circles outside, and perhaps in foreign countries. Probably special arrangements would be required for recruiting the staff of this branch so as to provide for the necessary expert knowledge.[3]

As already mentioned, the reorganisation of the Treasury in 1919 implemented some of the Haldane Committee's recommendations. There were to be three departments within the Treasury: Finance, Supplies Services and Establishments. The Controller of the Establishments Department, like the other two Controllers, was given the status of head of a government department (under the Permanent Secretary who had ultimate responsibility for its general control and who was also Head of the Civil Service). The work of establishments at that time encompassed the organisation of civil establishments, questions of personnel and remuneration, conditions of service and superannuation. On all these matters the Treasury had acquired the responsibilities to advise Treasury ministers and through them the Cabinet, and to give effect to Cabinet decisions, according to the principles and practice of accountability within the British system of government. This general oversight derived, historically, from the power of the purse and in particular from the Treasury's responsibility for the presentation to Parliament of the Departmental Estimates. Establishments was important, but it was regarded as ordinary Treasury work, not requiring special training or expertise.

In the civil service more generally an ethos developed that staff were often posted to establishments work if they were not really up to the intellectual demands of administrative work. Some Establishment staff in departments of government therefore tended to be rather unexciting officials, sometimes those who were a bit worn out by previous work, sometimes those promoted from the executive class, and generally people not expected to rise higher in the civil service. Establishments was, essentially, a type of work aptly referred to in civil service terminology as a form of management as distinct from administration[4] because it tended to be at arms length from the political environment and the development of policy, for both of which the really outstandingly able staff were always in short supply. This ethos was typical of what the Fulton Committee criticised.

A striking contrast to this general picture is the experience and practice of establishments work by Bridges. From early in his official career his assignments were typical of work in the Treasury Establishment Officer's department; but in two ways Bridges went further than the typical official engaged in this sort of work. First, he found it interesting and genuinely accepted the challenge involved in the problems he tackled. Secondly, although he used the terminology associated with civil service establishments work he in fact practised personnel management in both the widest and the specialist sense in which the term is used. He was always concerned with personnel policy-making as well as with implementation; he was frequently concerned with issues that were politically sensitive; he was keen to develop personnel management techniques including staff forecasts, staff ceilings, staff inspectors, O and M and periodic reviews;[5] and he personally spent a lot of time on promotions and in resolving difficulties in individual cases. It might, of course, be argued that establishments work in the Treasury involved more intellectual demands than establishments work elsewhere, and there are certainly examples of Treasury establishments officials who later became permanent secretaries in other departments. Nevertheless, the point is worth stressing that this was work for which Bridges was peculiarly well suited and which provided a satisfying link from the beginning of his career to the end.

It has already been explained that, during Bridges' time as Head of the Civil Service, he had important personnel responsibilities in making recommendations for most of the senior appointments in the civil service. Therefore the first section of this chapter will explain the procedure for top appointments at the time when Bridges was responsible for them, illustrated with examples from the cases with which he was concerned. The second section will deal with the human consideration and sensitivity which characterised his treatment of selected personnel cases. A synopsis of a few individual cases will illustrate more completely how Bridges worked and the personal standards he applied in this type of work. The third section will be mainly an appreciation of Bridges' approach to personnel management and the influence he exercised as a result of this aspect of his work. Later chapters are devoted to the political attitudes of civil servants and the education and training of civil servants.

It is clear that personnel management was one of the more time-consuming aspects of Bridges' work as Head of the Civil Service. It is also beyond doubt that he was outstandingly good at it, though he may not have used the terms now preferred by specialists in this type of management.

Procedure for senior appointments

Although Treasury approval was required for the numbers, grading, remuneration and conditions of service of all staff in government departments, most of these duties were carried out by the subordinate officials specifically concerned with establishments matters in the Treasury. This left three important personnel duties for the personal attention of the Permanent Secretary as Head of the Civil Service. They were: advising the Prime Minister and the Minister of the Department concerned on appointments to posts of Permanent Secretary, Deputy Secretary, Principal Finance Officers and Principal Establishment Officers; dealing with Civil Service Honours; and exercising a general oversight of the organisation and well-being of the civil service - by being the man to whom permanent heads of other departments could turn for counsel and advice when difficulties arose.

Fisher, as part of his determined effort to make the civil service into a coherent whole, gave high priority to the selection of men for the most senior positions. Indeed, in a letter of advice to his successor in 1939 he placed this in 'a category of importance by itself'.[6] His successors, Wilson, Hopkins and Bridges, continued carrying out these duties as Fisher had done[7] and also gave this responsibility the highest priority. Bridges in particular believed, though because he was personally concerned he recognised that he was not in a position to say so, that the arrangement worked well and to the general satisfaction of Whitehall.[8]

It is important to understand the processes leading up to recommendations for appointments to the most senior positions in the civil service. Bridges was convinced that it was not a task that could best be performed by a Board. Instead, it was a matter that called for much personal consultation and thought. He reached this conclusion for three reasons. First, in filling any important post it was necessary to consult five or six persons before a formal recommendation could be made, but it was not the same five or six people who were best able to give advice on each case. Even when the civil service was much smaller than it is now, using a Board with fixed membership did not appear as good as less formal consultations with those most intimately concerned with the work. In addition, it was helpful to have consultations with selected individuals, both in the department and in other departments with which comparisons might be made. Secondly, when requiring the frankest and most searching judgement of the potential candidates, Bridges found that more confidence and freedom could be achieved at a meeting of two people than at a meeting of a formally constituted Board. Thirdly, he felt the job of giving advice to the Prime Minister in these cases was more complicated than 'forming an order of merit of the candidates for a particular post'. He put it like this: 'It is much more like that of placing the members of a cricket eleven in the field in the way which will give the strongest result for the team as a whole. It is no good settling that a particular man is the best slip fielder in the eleven if you find that you have got to ask him to keep wicket'.[9]

He went on to argue that the advice given to the Prime Minister by the Permanent Secretary to the Treasury in these matters therefore did not rest simply on the personal judgement of any one man: 'It represents an objective judgement, given after the best guidance and help available from many quarters'.[10] What he did not make clear in any known statements was that if a senior appointments system was to operate successfully in this way in the public service it required considerable confidence in the integrity and competence of those making the judgements. Of course mistakes would occur from time to time because it is impossible to be scientific or infallible when so much depends on human factors, but in general the results must surely have been acceptable for the system to continue in the way Bridges ran it. It was much later, when William Armstrong had become Head of the Civil Service, that the system became more formal with the appointment, as now, of the Senior Appointments Selection Committee to advise the Head of the Civil Service, who in turn advises the Prime Minister.[11]

It is probably also true to say that the largely informal system of consultation practised by Bridges and his immediate predecessor and successors could be more specific and uninhibited about particular individuals. The civil service before the Second World War was, of course, considerably smaller than it is now ar.d it was therefore easier for its Head to know personally a large proportion of the officials in the upper echelons. Those who were Bridges' contemporaries, or just slightly younger than him and more junior in the civil service, included many who were to rise to senior positions in the civil service as it expanded during and after the war. Because of their common social and educational background many people in this fairly small group knew each other, or of each other, in other contexts. Bridges put this well when he said in 1954: 'Today there are many strong bonds between the Universities and the Civil Service: the bonds of personal friendships: the sympathy which comes from a similar outlook and upbringing: and contacts in many matters of common interest'.[12] Furthermore, the speed and complexity of government work is now quite different from the pace in the 1940s and 1950s. Even though at the time many of the officials may have felt they were fully stretched, time was found for maintaining a complex pattern of informal consultation processes about promotions at the top of the civil service. In practice a lot depended on good informal networks at various levels in the service, but especially among those occupying the more senior posts. It is hardly surprising, however, that the process was regarded as mysterious and seemed to some of its critics to have some of the characteristics of a Renaissance court.[13]

This informal network developed in various ways in addition to contacts through the social and educational backgrounds of particular officials. One way was through service on departmental and interdepartmental committees. There have always been many of these and their unintended consequences have never been fully examined: examples may be seen in Chapter 5 on the Machinery of Government, and in the section on the departmental view in Chapter 7. Another way was to make full use of less structured formal and informal networks that existed for other purposes. For example, Bridges occasionally used the weekly meetings of second secretaries in the Treasury (originally formalised to co-ordinate economic policy)[14] to discuss establishment business. He also received special support from the second secretary in charge of establishments work who was active in going round Whitehall and seeing people in departments to discuss these matters in a general way.[15] A further way was to institute new informal systems.

Bridges, in his personnel management activities, did not hesitate to use all these opportunities when they seemed appropriate and advantageous. Numerous examples of informal networks available to Bridges for personnel management and other purposes could be quoted in illustration but two will suffice.

The first example arose in 1944 when there was a problem about senior departmental ministers leaving the country without obtaining the King's permission. This was a misdemeanour of potential importance because departments needed to know that when their senior minister was not available another Cabinet minister was prepared to deal on their behalf at Cabinet level with matters of general importance affecting their interests. A notice was accordingly prepared and circulated by the Prime Minister to all ministers of Cabinet rank reminding them of this requirement but it had little effect because it was addressed only to ministers and was not necessarily seen by their officials. Bridges, as Cabinet Secretary, decided that a much better way to ensure compliance was to get the Prime Minister's Principal Private Secretary to write to his fellow private secretaries indicating what was expected of them as watchdogs of their masters. This seems a minor but good illustration of Bridges' skill in using an informal communications network to achieve compliance for what he believed to be the public interest.[16]

The second example concerned the development by Bridges of a new institution: the Permanent Secretaries' Dining Club. The idea originated in the autumn of 1946 and involved a monthly gathering of 10 or 12 officials dining together. Each paid his own bill. The number attending was kept small so that conversation could remain general instead of developing in small groups. The attendance was different each month and it seemed to work well because there are later references to these dinners. Bridges used them as an opportunity to inform himself, but they also enabled permanent secretaries to get to know each other and exchange news. In addition the dinners must have helped to develop confidence between colleagues and to facilitate further bilateral contacts at the highest levels in the civil service.[17]

These were the sorts of contacts which enabled the process of informal consultations for senior appointments to work well when Bridges was Head of the Civil Service. It should, however, be emphasised that the process applied not only to appointments to senior posts inside the civil service but to certain jobs outside it as well - and in the period immediately after the Second World War this became no mean task. The nationalisation programme meant that numerous government appointments had to be made to boards. This became such a demanding task that it was decided that the Treasury would have to maintain a list of suitably qualified persons who might be invited to serve on the boards of newly nationalised industries. This need coincided with the recognition in the Treasury, early in 1945, that a more formal system should in any case be created for maintaining a record of potential persons to serve on government committees and commissions. The result was the beginning of what is now popularly known as the 'great and the good' - a record of individuals who might be acceptable and willing to serve in public positions.

From its beginning, the 'great and the good' was intended by Treasury officials to be a general utility list in the sense that although specialists were not included 'it was always the intention to select for inclusion in the list those who would take a broad commonsense view on subjects unconnected, as well as on subjects connected with their field of special knowledge'.[18] The essence of the approach was that the list should consist of all-rounders, that it should be selective, and that it should be available at the centre of government as a general list to which departments could make reference by applying to the Treasury.

When it first began Bridges proposed a panel (which he thought could be drawn mainly from the Forces and the business world, together with Treasury officials) to draw up the list. The panel was to have no formal terms of reference but each member would be asked to prepare, 'either from his direct personal knowledge or from reliable sources known to him, a list of further names'; the panel would then meet to compile a new and improved list. Bridges added: 'We doubt whether it would be appropriate to use such a panel for interviewing. To call likely people (who would usually be very busy men) for interview and to have to explain that there was nothing immediately in view except inclusion in a Government list would make the existence of a Government list publicly known and would give it a degree of formality which would be rather embarrassing'.[19]

The Chancellor of the Exchequer, Dr Hugh (later Lord) Dalton agreed with Bridges' proposal but it does not seem that a panel as envisaged was formally set up. Instead, names were collected on an informal basis whenever suggestions were made and the record was maintained in the Treasury by a senior official. At this time there was an unprecedented need for names of people willing to serve in various capacities and Bridges was prepared to accept - and, indeed, to solicit - suggestions in confidence from all sources thought to be reliable. Two examples illustrate how the list grew. At dinner on 17 December 1946 Bridges met Mr G.E.B. Abell, the Private Secretary to the Viceroy of India. Abell suggested that Lord Linlithgow was well worth bearing in mind for the chairmanship of a really important public board or corporation. Bridges immediately wrote to J.A.C. Robertson, the assistant secretary in charge of the list: 'You might see that his name is noted on our lists. It is, I think, true that his politics are rather to the Right. But I am not sure that he has displayed this very prominently, and he might well be acceptable'.[20] On 18 March 1947 Bridges wrote to Sir Alan Barlow: 'Another very promising name which has been mentioned to me, which might serve for the London Transport Board, is General Sir William Slim, who will be free at the end of this year. He is a man of absolutely first class ability and would be very good with staff'.[21]

It was a great advantage to Bridges, when placing individuals in positions of responsibility, to be at the centre of a communications network that served other purposes as well as personnel management. The development of this network was facilitated because people in established positions in all walks of life called on Bridges in his office. His discretion could be relied upon; but more importantly, he was inevitably an influential and powerful man. Individuals called for brief interviews at their own request or because Bridges asked them to, to give or to receive advice, or simply to convey information. For example, Lord Moran called on Bridges on 29 March 1950, at his own request, to let Bridges know what he thought about the costs of the National Health Service and the state of the medical profession.[22] Such visits helped Bridges to acquire an overall appreciation of numerous governmental interests which might not otherwise have come to his attention. They also enabled him to accumulate information and insights into the personalities involved.

A regular weekly visitor - once or twice a week, according to Lord Cobbold in his evidence in 1960 to the Radcliffe Committee on the Working of the Monetary System[23] - was the Governor of the Bank of England. Sometimes his visits must have been just routine, but on occasion they could be particularly significant. In 1955, for example, the Governor had heard in advance that the Fleck Report[24] was to contain criticisms of the organisation of the National Coal Board, though it would not deal with personalities. The Governor wanted Bridges to know that in his opinion there should be a new Chairman of the NCB (to replace Sir Hubert Houldsworth). This coincided with discussions Bridges was already having on the subject with Sir John Maud (later Lord Redcliffe-Maud), Permanent Secretary at the Ministry of Fuel and Power, and also with the Chancellor of the Exchequer and others. Eventually it was agreed that Houldsworth should continue as Chairman but only for a limited period, when he would be succeeded by Mr (later Sir) James Bowman.[25] Such discussions must have been very time-consuming, but they often contributed to agreed solutions to problems - agreement that was achieved mainly through Bridges' patient persuasion and his sensitivity to others.

Bridges tended to look for the same sorts of generalist qualities and strong support from persons whose judgement he trusted, irrespective of the field for the top appointments. For example, in 1948 he wrote that the qualities to be sought in appointing a new Deputy Master of the Royal Mint were: 'plenty of shrewd commonsense; power to get on with people; and the capacity to make the staff of the Mint, which is largely industrial, feel that their interests are looked after with consideration and that the family atmosphere of this organisation is maintained'.[26] Another example is in a letter Bridges wrote to Sir Thomas Lloyd of the Colonial Office. In it he referred to Eric Speed: '... of whose ability as an administrator I have the highest respect. I think he gets down to the point very quickly, even if he has no particular previous experience of the subject matter'.[27]

A further example concerned appointments to the Anglo-Iranian Oil Company.[28] In 1950 Bridges became heavily involved in appointments to the Board of this Company, one of the largest and most important companies in the country and one in which the Government had a controlling interest, and he exercised his influence accordingly. When Sir William Fraser (later Lord Strathalmond), the Chairman of the Company, felt he was not being invited to as many functions as his position in his view warranted, Bridges wrote to H.G. Vincent, Secretary to the Government Hospitality Fund, suggesting that, when opportunity offered, Fraser should now and again be invited to a certain number of gatherings. He added : 'If you feel able to fall in with this, it would be very helpful indeed to me'.[29] In 1951 the Persian Government 'nationalised' the oil industry in South Persia and the situation became delicate for a number of reasons. Part of the background was the Persian Government's desire to give greater recognition to Persian national dignity at a time when oil profits were prodigiously high and the AIOC was exporting these profits abroad as well as keeping great reserves in the bank. There were indications that the British Government was mishandling the situation politically. In addition, the Company had become the centre of tension locally (mainly because it was employing local contractors who under-paid their employees, rather than employing workers direct; and the slum conditions of the housing for its employees was a cause for serious concern).[30] Bridges became heavily involved for three reasons. First, he had been responsible for recommending the appointment of the Chairman and Government directors. Secondly, he was involved because the Treasury was concerned about the revenue implications and its Overseas Finance interests. Thirdly, Bridges had frequent contact on the subject with the Bank of England, the Foreign Office, and the Ministry of Fuel and Power.[31] Even before the actions of the Persian Government Bridges was making comments about the suitability of the senior management of the AIOC. In mid-1950 he noted that he regarded Sir William Fraser as a 'complete totalitarian' who did 'very little in the way of consultation with his colleagues'. The Vice-Chairman, Mr Heath Eves, he regarded as 'a little ineffective'.[32] He also thought that too many of the other members of the Board were departmental specialists and that what the Board lacked was men of general all-round ability, who could see the Board's affairs against the wider background.[33]

These reservations were made more clear because of the actions of the Persian Government in 1951. On 7 July Bridges chaired an important meeting in the Treasury with representatives of the Company and government departments concerned. He said that the morale of the Company was at a low ebb and a new Chairman was clearly needed. Sir William Fraser was lacking in the wider political qualities that were necessary for the difficult period ahead. He continued by saying that 'It was not necessary in choosing a new name to look for someone with commercial experience, but rather for a broad outlook and statesmanlike qualities, and a name, moreover, to impress outsiders'.[34]

Sometimes when Bridges was being asked for suggestions of names for posts that stretched his competence he was inclined to seek advice from persons he trusted whether or not their experience was really relevant for the advice sought. This happened, for example, when names were being considered for posts at the United Nations Organisation.[35] The files show that Bridges particularly valued the opinions of Sir Godfrey Ince, Sir Frank Lee and Sir Norman Brook. Another feature of the appointments files, a feature which is related to certain aspects of the administrative culture, is that certain phrases became standard without their meaning being questioned in the context of particular positions. For example, Mr Frank Roberts wrote to Bridges in 1954 about the post of Chief of Personnel and Establishment at the United Nations: 'We think it most important that whoever is selected should be quite first class'.[36] Similarly Lord Swinton, when suggesting Sir Alexander Clutterbuck as a suitable man for the post of Chairman and Director-General of the British Council wrote: 'He is of course an absolutely first class man, and quite fit to be Head of a Government Department'.[37]

One surprising feature of appointing officials to senior positions was that the potential appointees for top appointments did not themselves always participate in the selection procedure. They did not necessarily apply for the posts nor did they always even know they were being considered.[38] A not infrequent tactic was for individuals to be 'sounded out' concerning their willingness to undertake a particular assignment without any firm offer being made; sometimes this led to confusion about the conditions or even about whether the post was being offered.[39] On one occasion information was leaked (though not through the civil service) that a candidate - in this case Professor Lionel (later Lord) Robbins - was being deleted from the shortlist for the post of Chief of the Research Division at the International Bank of Reconstruction and Development when he did not even know he was being considered for it.[40] It was rather embarrassing when Robbins discovered from a press journalist that he was supposed to have rejected the offer.

Another example of similar confusion concerned the offer of the position of Chairman and Director-General of the British Council to Sir Robert Fraser. After it was agreed that Fraser should be offered the post Winnifrith wrote:

> When I told Fraser the glad news I found that he was not just waiting for news about a post which he had hypothetically agreed to accept. He said that the interviews he had had with Padmore and Bridges had not given him the impression that he was being asked to say whether, if invited, he would be willing to give a firm acceptance ... he says he would wish to examine the conditions of appointment before he finally commits himself ...[41]

Later Fraser turned down the offer of the post and Mr A.P. (later Sir Paul) Sinker was appointed.

The evidence quite clearly indicates how important the informal network was, not only for collecting information about possible appointees, but also for 'sounding them out'. However, it would be a mistake to assume that a more formal style of interviewing was never used. In many cases interviews were held, especially towards the end of Bridges' time as Head of the Civil Service. For example, in 1955 when a new permanent head (at deputy secretary level) was to be appointed to serve the Commissioners for Crown Lands, five candidates were interviewed by Bridges for about 20 minutes each.[42] The same sort of interview procedure was customarily used for recommending the appointment of private secretaries to the Prime Minister.[43] One of the reasons for this increasing formality was that Bridges was very unhappy about recommending for appointment people he did not personally know. As the civil service had expanded and Bridges had become established at the top, his own informal network no longer reached all the potential candidates. In 1945, when Mr E. Barnard was being recommended to Bridges for promotion to the second in command post at the Department of Scientific and Industrial Research, Bridges wrote:

> I am not prepared to put this man forward for Deputy Secretary without knowing something more about him. He seems to have entered the Civil Service in 1919 and to have been promoted to PAS in 1943. In other words he was an Assistant Secretary until 2 years ago. He may be the 'cat's whiskers' but if so it seems very odd that nobody ever seems

to have heard of him in the last 25 years ...[44]

During further detailed enquiries, Bridges commented, on 14 June 1945: 'I hate appointing chaps I do not know'; but later he recommended this particular appointment to the Prime Minister and Attlee approved on 23 October 1945.

In considering names for top appointments a great deal depended not only on oral discussion to collect information and assess possible appointees, but also on getting the agreement of all the interested parties. Detailed records were not always made of these discussions but they frequently involved Bridges personally in addition to the Head of the Establishment side of the Treasury. Often Bridges would consult other officials when he met them at meetings or at the Athenaeum when he went to lunch there.[45] He would also sometimes consult ministers at lunch or dinner engagements. All these discussions and 'soundings out' were conducted with great courtesy and tact. In all aspects of this side of his work Bridges took particular care to be sympathetic to the human elements and personal circumstances of individuals. Sometimes, however, he was rather limited in his knowledge on the wider front and the impression gained from the files is that certain important appointments were made in a rather amateur in-house fashion.

Part of the reason for this apparent amateurishness was that there was only a limited field of candidates for consideration. When the post of Civilian Instructor at the Imperial Defence College was vacant General Sir William Slim, the Commandant, was very concerned that nobody should be appointed who was not a 'tip top' man; but some of the staff at the IDC thought that the Foreign Service was the only possible source for obtaining a really first class man as Civilian Instructor.[46] This may have been true in the sense that senior officials in home departments often felt and said that they could not spare their most able staff for secondment to such duties. Other sources of candidates for such positions were simply not considered. It may be wondered, for example, why in the late 1940s there was apparently no consideration of persons who had served in government during the war on a temporary basis, and who therefore had relevant knowledge and experience, but had since returned to other occupations. Some of them, if they had known about such opportunities, might have been keen to be considered.

One of the other constraints on the appointments system was that only a small number of officials were involved in this selection work. They in turn did not have unlimited contacts, especially since confidences had to be respected; much depended on informal enquiries; and mutual trust was essential among those involved in the discussions. It is not, therefore, very surprising that certain names were proposed over and over again. Moreover, it should be noted that there were certain advantages of control over persons already in the civil service, or in the ranks of retired civil servants; and there would be less control, or opportunities for easy influence, if complete outsiders were appointed. Occasionally an unenthusiastic 'candidate' who had been selected for an important post was referred to Bridges for him to explain how important the job was and, if all else failed, to put it to the 'candidate' that 'it was his public duty to accept'.[47] Indeed, it seems to have been normal to assume in conversations with Bridges that people always had uppermost in their minds a genuine anxiety to do what was right or what was best in the public interest.[48]

This conception of the national interest is crucial for understanding how Bridges operated as Head of the Civil Service. It is well illustrated in the procedure for making appointments to senior positions. Clearly, Bridges enjoyed this part of his work. Though he sometimes may have assumed a proprietorial air it was a proprietorial air without any personal interest except his own job satisfaction in doing his best: he became the channel for expressing the national interest. In the British system of government it is sometimes thought that the national interest can only be defined by the Government in power. Indeed, this was the line of argument by Mr Justice McCowan in the 1985 trial of Clive Ponting.[49] It may also be argued that constitutionally the Government must make the final determination of what the national interest is, because the Government is assumed to have the confidence of the people as a result of being elected. Furthermore, in some instances the Government alone knows all the details of any current controversy: for reasons of complexity and security full details cannot always be made known publicly.

In practice, however, the national interest in many matters has to be conceptualised and expressed daily by civil servants simply because such expressions are required more often than it is possible for ministers to consider it. This involves an attitude of mind reflecting the traditional approach of the non-partisan, personally disinterested bureaucrat within the British system of government. Bridges spoke of this from time to time and his approach is well illustrated from the comments he made in one of his broadcast talks on the BBC Overseas Service. He said: 'A good civil servant has to be more anonymous and unselfish in his work than those in other walks of life ... the traditional outlook of the modern Civil Service is one that recognises that the interests and welfare of the whole country come first, and that the closer and more intimate loyalty to the Department, although it is nearer at hand and more vivid, must take second place'.[50] On another occasion he added that civil servants should be influenced 'by no thoughts of private advantage or advancement'; they should have 'no end in view but that the work may be carried out faithfully and well'.[51]

Civil servants sometimes use the national interest or the public interest in their day to day work as a yardstick in controversies and as a guide in their own work. If the government does not make clear what the national interest is, the civil service in practice fills the gap. Civil servants' understanding of this concept, like their appreciation of integrity and similar values, is acquired through processes of education, training and socialisation. Questions about some of these matters are discussed further in subsequent chapters. Difficulties may arise or become intensified when individual civil servants are known publicly to be actively associated with particular expressions of the national interest - a case in point concerned William Armstrong when he became personally identified with the policies of the Heath Government and in some circles was referred to, with irony, as the 'Deputy Prime Minister'.

The importance of civil service conceptions of the national interest, illustrated so well in the procedure for making senior appointments, must not be underestimated in the British system of government. The civil service position can be criticised for having elitest overtones, for originating from the social class to which senior civil servants belong, and because conceptions of the national interest are disseminated by socialisation and do not easily fit into programmes of education and training. It may also be criticised because it has the potential to endanger the government's own position in the political system, especially when the government does not make its position clear or is not united in its interpretation of the national interest. On the other hand, there is a sense in which civil servants have (or were thought to have) their service to the state in common. As Bridges himself put it on one occasion: 'What unites us is the bond that we are all servants of the State, whether we are Permanent Secretaries or postmen, whether we are architects who design Government buildings or lawyers who draft Parliamentary bills'.[52]

Even though it may be a concept that is difficult to define and explain, the national interest has practical relevance in terms of British public administration (as it did, especially, when Fisher and Bridges were Head of the Civil Service). It is a crucial element in differentiating establishments work in government departments from the work of personnel management in other contexts. Furthermore, it introduces into management processes a political dimension that is not generally found in industry and commerce. However, interpretations of the national interest as illustrated here can only have practical significance if there is mutual trust and respect among those operating the system. Much therefore depends on the personal qualities to be found in the most senior officials.

Examples of sensitive management and difficult cases

One of Bridges' most outstanding qualities was his capacity to listen to other people talking about their difficulties, then to respond sensitively. He explained his approach by saying that handling people was 'mainly a question of sympathy and understanding, but trained and disciplined to an unusual degree'. When conducting a difficult interview his advice was to 'practice the art of thinking of the man you are talking to ... You must learn to see him as he thinks of himself; you must get to know something of the hopes and feelings which he is probably trying to hide from you'.[53]

One of the facets of Bridges' sensitivity in this area was his ability to give wise advice. However, in relation to personal cases it seems that often the much appreciated wisdom he appeared to offer was little more than the crucial opportunity for someone to work out his or her own solution to a difficult problem by exploring with Bridges the implications of various possibilities. However, when he felt it necessary Bridges could be very decisive. This was not unusual where he felt sympathy towards a colleague experiencing misfortune: then he might do something to help, sometimes without revealing what he had done. He would also appear decisive when a colleague had behaved in an unworthy manner: then he was likely to apply his scrupulous moral standards with results that could be predicted.

These qualities were greatly appreciated by his colleagues. Soon after Bridges had become Head of the Civil Service Mr (later Sir)

Frank Lee wrote to Bridges after he had been appointed to the post of Deputy Secretary at the Ministry of Supply: 'I went away from our talk on Friday cheered and fortified ... and I should like you to know how grateful I am for the constant inspiration and kindness which you have given me. It is a great and abiding honour to be a member of a Service which has you at its head'.[54] When Bridges retired from the civil service Dame Evelyn (later Baroness) Sharp wrote to him: 'Your encouragement and your invariable readiness to listen to one's troubles and to give advice have been a real source of strength and confidence to me in my short period as Permanent Secretary; and I know that my colleagues feel the same'.[55] After Bridges died others also recalled this quality. Sir Arthur fforde wrote: 'He seemed always to have time for all and sundry'.[56] Lord Helsby wrote: '... what I chiefly remember now, as many others will do, is his great kindness and willingness to take infinite trouble to help in case of need ...'[57] Sir Robert Birley wrote: 'He could be very decisive when necessary, but he was always ready to listen to the other side and in the end one came to recognise a kind of inner humility'.[58]

Although he was always busy Bridges generally found time to see people. After officials were appointed to senior positions Bridges would invite them to call on him for a chat, so that he could get to know those he did not feel he already knew, and so that he could personally make it clear to them that should they ever wish to see him in the future they were always welcome to call. It was his practice to have periodic talks with each permanent secretary about the form and promise of his deputy secretaries and under secretaries, often asking at the end the question who he would himself suggest as his successor if he were to be struck down by a bus. Bridges kept notes of all these talks and these notes were used as a running conspectus of the position of higher posts throughout the civil service.[59] He would also sometimes ask less senior officials to call on him to explain what they were doing if their work was of particular interest to him. In this way Mr N. Baliol Scott, a temporary under secretary unknown to Bridges, who, in 1949, was conducting an inquiry into the organisation of the Ministry of Supply, was invited to Bridges' office for half an hour's informal chat, to find out how his inquiry was progressing.[60] When senior officials retired Bridges generally wrote them personal handwritten notes of thanks and good wishes for the future.[61]

These indications of Bridges' interest were encouraging to officials and through them his general attitude towards others became widely known within the civil service. If they felt their own position was fully justifiable and that of others was not, they could feel confident of his support, and his experience was always valuable and available to them. But if they had done wrong they similarly knew what to expect: justice might be tempered with mercy, it would be fair according to the rules, and it would be given by someone widely respected and trusted - but penalties might also follow and if Bridges disapproved they would be left in no doubt of his feelings.

These qualities became particularly evident when ministers wanted a change in their senior officials: a procedure known to Bridges and others within the civil service as 'a change of bowling'. Col N. (later Sir Norman) Scorgie was moved for this reason from the Ministry of Information in 1941 (where he was temporarily serving, during the war, on transfer from H.M. Stationery Office). Even though it was widely recognised that Scorgie's minister, Mr Brendan (later Lord) Bracken, had been at the Ministry for such a short time that they hardly knew each other, and therefore there could have been little scope for the development of personal friction, the move was a great worry to Scorgie. Bridges probably knew about it at the time but he was reminded of it later. Scorgie was worried simply because the move was likely to be interpreted in the civil service as an indication that he had blotted his copybook in some way.[62] In 1952, Mr Duncan Sandys (now Lord Duncan-Sandys), then Minister of Supply, twice told his permanent secretary, Sir Archibald Rowlands, that he wanted to get rid of one of his deputy secretaries and have him replaced by another official of his own choice. Rowlands saw Bridges about this and it was agreed that Bridges should seek an opportunity to say to the Minister 'that I very much disliked the suggestion of Ministers asking that their permanent civil servants should be moved because they did not like the shape of their noses or the colour of their eyes'.[63]

In 1946 Sir Percival Robinson was moved from the Ministry of Works because the Prime Minister and the Minister of Works wanted 'a change of bowling'. In this case, however, Attlee apparently thought a change might contribute to speeding up the implementation of the Government's post-war housing programme. Bridges had already, in February 1946, talked to Robinson because the Treasury had not received a copy of the Report by Sir Ernest Holloway on reorganisation within the ministry, and Robinson had had to explain that the oversight had been due to carelessness on his own part. Bridges told him he was glad to hear the explanation and added that the episode could be regarded as closed (the record of the meeting, however, makes the gentle reprimand fairly clear). It was less than two months later that the Prime Minister said he wanted Robinson moved. Bridges defended Robinson strongly in a very firm minute to the Prime Minister in which he stressed Robinson's good qualities and achievements and argued that allegations about his capacities in running the department had not been clearly formulated, nor had any opportunity been given for him to rebut them. Bridges explained that the Minister of Works had seen Robinson but had not told him that he was dissatisfied with his work. Bridges had also seen Robinson who had said he would not wish to continue in the Ministry of Works if ministers wanted him moved, provided that he was not asked to leave under a cloud of vague and undefined charges. Bridges argued:

> If a change is to be made in the post of Permanent Secretary soon after the recent debate on shortages of housing components, the two events are only too likely to be associated. I am afraid of comment to the effect that in this case a novel constitutional practice has been adopted, namely, that when a Department comes under strong criticism, the right course is to remove the Permanent Secretary. I am sure that this criticism would be made very forcibly if Sir Percival Robinson were to be transferred to some post of considerably lesser importance. In other words, while this bowler may be taken off, he must be given a useful and important place in some other part of the field. Anything less would be not only unjust to the individual concerned, but would run the risk of impairing the confidence and morale of the Civil Service.[64]

Bridges therefore proposed that Robinson should be appointed as a Government director in the Anglo-Iranian Oil Company.

Occasionally, a high-level transfer had a very serious effect on the individual involved. This occurred, for example, in the case of Sir Frank Tribe who was on the verge of a nervous breakdown as a result. In 1946 Tribe, Permanent Secretary at the Ministry of Food, was transferred to the post of Comptroller and Auditor-General. Tribe had previously been Permanent Secretary at the Ministry of Fuel and Power (1942-5), Permanent Secretary at the Ministry of Aircraft Production (1945) and had been appointed to the Ministry of Food in 1945. His last move, to Comptroller and Auditor-General, was arranged simply because his minister, Mr John Strachey, who had been appointed Minister of Food in 1946, disliked him. Tribe was deeply affected by the experience, especially by the manner in which it came about. He had little doubt that the move would be interpreted as an indication that he had been a failure in his post.

The story as it emerges from the file[65] was as follows. Tribe was called to see Bridges on Wednesday evening, 10 July 1946, and learned that he was to be moved from the Ministry of Food because his minister had so decided. Tribe expected to hear details from his minister the next day but was not called to see Strachey until Friday morning 12 July. Strachey then said that no doubt Tribe had learned from Bridges of his decision. Tribe said that he had, but that he felt that he was entitled to know the reasons for the move. He added that he felt Strachey had no reason to doubt his loyalty, nor had Strachey indicated dissatisfaction with the way he was running the office: Strachey agreed. Strachey said he had no specific complaint to make but he would summarise the matter by saying that he had reached a decision that it would be in the public interest to 'have a change of bowling'. Beyond that he was not prepared to say anything. Strachey told him that his successor, Sir Percivale Liesching, would arrive to take up duty at the ministry the next Tuesday, and he thought it better if Tribe terminated his service in the ministry on that day, Friday, though Strachey added that he would not object to Tribe coming into the office on Monday to clear up matters. Tribe spent an agonising weekend trying to recall incidents which might have led to Strachey's decision; the only disagreements he could recall were very insubstantial.

Bridges saw Tribe again the next week and was very kind and understanding. He also wrote him a particularly warm and sympathetic handwritten letter on Thursday 18 July in which he said: 'You know, I hope, how unhappy this has made me'. This was greatly appreciated and the next day Tribe replied saying that he would keep Bridges' letter among his treasured possessions. He added, 'I am so sorry that I should have caused you all this worry; yours is certainly not an enviable job, but, as far as I know, you have the whole Civil Service behind you to a man, and we would all do anything we could to help you at any time'. This story adds to the details given in Hugh Thomas' biography of Strachey. It seems surprising that Thomas should conclude that Strachey was successful with his officials and knew how to use them to their best advantage.[66] After getting Tribe moved, Strachey did not see eye-to-eye with Liesching, his successor; but Liesching was in a strong position since, as Thomas comments, 'no minister could expect to dismiss two permanent secretaries - though Strachey tried'.[67]

Another case combining Bridges' concern for an individual with his punctilious regard for propriety arose from the retirement of Sir James Helmore, Permanent Secretary at the Ministry of Supply.[68] Helmore had, in 1953, been having a difficult time with his minister, Duncan Sandys, and on 2 December he called on Bridges to let off steam. In doing so he asked whether Bridges had taken seriously his threat to resign. Bridges said he had, and knew Helmore felt unsettled; but he attached great importance to Helmore remaining in the civil service as he had a valuable contribution to make and could not easily be replaced.

Helmore expanded on the irksome features of the civil service. He found dealing with ministers trying and reminded Bridges that he had never wanted to be a permanent secretary. Secondly, he disliked the underpayment, including lack of amenities, in the civil service. Thirdly, he disliked the continuous over-work and never having time to see anybody except his colleagues and the people he did business with. All this led him to the view that he would like to go when he was 50. Bridges afterwards wrote a note saying that he thanked Providence that this was still two and a half years ahead, and therefore it was a headache that someone else would have to tackle.

As Helmore left, he told Bridges that he had been asked whether he was willing that his name should be sent in for a KCB. He asked whether he could be sure that Bridges, or whoever sat in his shoes in two and a half years' time, would not say it was a cad's trick to take a KCB and then resign in three years. Bridges said that the argument about staying or leaving the service did not seem to him to depend on acceptance of a KCB now that Helmore had been Head of the Department for eighteen months. Bridges guaranteed that he, at any rate, would not use that particular argument, although he would use every other argument which occurred to him insofar as he might be concerned in the matter.

Helmore called again on 13 January 1956 for a discussion about staffing in his department. The question then arose as to whether he or Bridges should see the minister. Helmore said that the minister regarded Bridges as rather formidable and Bridges replied: how ridiculous. Helmore said that that was what he had always said!

Bridges then said that he would offer to go to see the Minister of Supply but if he did it would create a buzz in the ministry. Would Helmore therefore ask the Minister to look in on Bridges one day soon on his way to the House of Commons?

Four days later Bridges was told that the Secretary of State for Air had told Sir Maurice Dean (his Permanent Secretary), who had passed on to the Treasury a rumour that Helmore was leaving the civil service to join the Hawker Group. Bridges quickly contacted Helmore and told him of the rumour that the Secretary of State had heard. Helmore said the rumour was untrue, though Hawkers might have been thinking of making him an offer. The firm he was thinking of joining when he left the civil service - as the Bank of England already knew - was S.G. Warburg and Co. Bridges then sent for Dean and told him the facts without mentioning Warburgs.

It was later agreed that Helmore was to leave the civil service on 1 July. He discussed with Bridges the details of his resignation and the statement that would be made about his joining Warburgs. Helmore also raised another point, as recorded by Bridges:

> Helmore told me that S.G. Warburg and Co were going to make him a tax-free payment in respect of the superannuation privileges which he is foregoing by his retirement, i.e. presumably the extra pension which he would have earned if he had stayed in the Service until he is 60. He also intends that this payment should be made to him before he actually started.
>
> I said I was not quite sure about this. It seemed to me that there were possible objections to a Civil Servant receiving a payment from a firm and thereby putting himself under a firm obligation to them before he actually retired. Sir James at this looked very naughty and said that, although he was telling me about this, he had not asked me to say that I approved it or did not approve it: but in any case he was going to do it whatever I said. I said that notwithstanding the attitude he had adopted, having been informed of the position, I must make up my mind whether it was or was not proper: and I should proceed therefore to think the matter over and let him know how I felt ...

Bridges next sought the advice of colleagues. Winnifrith informed him that there were no precedents on this particular experience but added:

If we look at the matter as one of principle, I cannot see any escape from the conclusion that it is grossly improper for a civil servant to be under obligation to a commercial firm by having received from them a large sum of money before he leaves the public service.

On the other hand, Sir J. Helmore is perfectly entitled to say that before he finally burns his boats and retires from the Civil Service, he must provide for his future, but I cannot see that it is at all essential that he should actually have his assurance in the form now suggested. If the compensation is to have the form of a lump sum, surely it could be held by a third party as stakeholders until he actually retires. I think he ought to be pressed strongly to have sufficient feelings for the Service he is leaving to do this.

On 29 March Bridges wrote to Helmore about the arrangements for the announcement of his retirement. He then went on:

I am afraid I feel much more difficulty about the suggestion that the firm which you are going to join should make a payment to you while you are still in Government service in respect of superannuation privileges which you are foregoing by your retirement. I don't know that a ruling on this precise point has ever been given but it does seem to me to be inherently unsuitable that a civil servant should receive such a payment from a private firm while still in the service of the State. I hope that you can arrange without difficulty that the payment should be deferred until you have actually retired. I should add that I mentioned this last point to the Financial Secretary who felt very strongly that it would be wrong for such a payment to be received by a civil servant before he had actually retired.

Helmore then sent a draft of his resignation letter for Bridges to see before he actually wrote the final version. In it he outlined the arrangement for the compensation sum he was to receive. Bridges personally redrafted this and a new draft of the final paragraph was typed and sent by Mr D.J. (now Sir Derek) Mitchell to Helmore. Helmore used this new draft for inclusion in the resignation letter he sent on 5 April 1956:

Dear Bridges,

As you have known for a long time, it has been my intention to retire from the public service at the age of 50 (which I reach on 1st July next) and I now think I ought to put on record with you that I have been offered, and have accepted, a directorship with S.G. Warburg and Co Ltd to take effect as soon as I am free. You told me informally some time ago that the provisions of Cmd. 5517 would not apply to this, but I ought to put in writing to you that so far as I know, the Ministry of Supply have no relationship of any kind with this firm and that my only official dealings with them were on one occasion as long ago as 1948 or 1949 when, as Second Secretary in the Board of Trade, I presided over some meetings between some Americans, the British Travel and Holidays Association and Warburgs, to see if it were possible for an American hotel firm to set up a hotel in London. Nothing came of this and Warburgs dropped out, though the Americans have continued their enquiries through other channels (still with no result as far as I know).

As part of the discussions between Warburgs and myself about the terms on which I shall join them, it has been agreed that I am to have a capital payment as compensation for the less good superannuation arrangements which they can make as compared with those which I would have had if I had stayed in the Civil Service. I told you that they had sent me a cheque as soon the agreement had been made: but you said that you would regard it as unsuitable that the sum in question should be at my disposal while I am still a serving Civil Servant. I have therefore asked the firm to keep the money for me until after the date of my retirement.

Yours sincerely,

James Helmore.

Helmore also enclosed a personal letter:

Dear Edward,

My conscience would not be clear if in sending you this letter I failed to apologise for all the fuss and bother I have caused over the subject matter of paragraph 2.

Yours ever,

James.

The last example, intended to give special insight into the personnel facets of Bridges' work, concerns the Privy Council Office.[69] In February 1951 Sir Eric Leadbitter, Clerk to the Privy Council, indicated that he wished to retire from the public service when he reached the age of 60 in June. The Lord President, Mr Herbert (later Lord) Morrison, proposed that Mr F.J. Fernau, Leadbitter's Deputy, be appointed to replace him. Padmore, who at that time was Head of the Establishment side of the Treasury, saw Leadbitter and acquired details of Fernau's career. Fernau, a graduate of Oxford University, who had been called to the Bar in 1925, was 48 years of age in 1951 and had been a civil servant since 1925. Leadbitter said he was entirely happy about recommending the appointment. Fernau had the ability and personality to do the job well. He was liked at the Palace and by the other people with whom he came into contact. Leadbitter argued in favour of Fernau's appointment and Padmore recommended it to Bridges. Bridges then spoke to Sir Alan Lascelles at the Palace who said he found Fernau lively, sensible and obliging and saw no reason against the appointment. Bridges also spoke to Sir William Blatch, the Inland Revenue Solicitor (under whom Fernau had previously worked). Blatch said he had kept in touch with Fernau: he had found him an excellent mixer and an energetic worker with a good mind. Blatch had been sorry to lose him when he transferred from the Inland Revenue to the Privy Council Office, and he thought Fernau deserved advancement. On 15 February 1951 Bridges therefore recommended the appointment to the Prime Minister, telling the Prime Minister that the Lord President was proposing to submit Fernau's name to the King, because this particular appointment was made by the King in Council. Bridges added: 'I am satisfied that Mr Fernau is altogether suitable for this appointment'. Next day, Attlee gave his approval. Fernau's appointment as Clerk to the Privy Council was from 30 June 1951.

Just over a year later, on 29 July 1952, Lascelles had a talk with Bridges. He said that since Leadbitter had left they (at the Palace) no longer felt that they had the rock of stability in the Privy Council which they were accustomed to. They did not feel that Fernau was reliable: he was mercurial, temperamental and not always clear about his facts. Speaking in great confidence, Lascelles said he had the impression that Fernau 'lifted his elbow' and was suffering from the reactions of over-stimulus or that he was suffering from some nervous complaint. He added, without provocation, that it would not break their hearts at the Palace if there was a change. Bridges and Padmore saw Lord Salisbury, who had by then succeeded Morrison as Lord President, and said that, because there was some suspicion of serious disease, such as T.B., the position should be properly investigated and that Fernau should be sent to see Dr W.E. Chiesman, the Treasury Medical Adviser. The Lord President saw Fernau who confirmed that he had sometimes felt too ill to attend the office, indicated that he was generally worried about it, and leapt at the idea of seeing Chiesman.

Chiesman found no evidence of serious disease but sent Fernau to St Thomas's Hospital for a general check-up. Chiesman reported back to Padmore that Fernau's wife had died a couple of years earlier and he was living in rather unsatisfactory circumstances in a flat with his sister: there was also some suggestion (not made by Fernau) that he might be finding some consolation in drink.

In or about August 1952 Fernau went into St Thomas's Hospital where no serious illness was found apart from unsatisfactory teeth and arrangements were made to deal with this problem. Chiesman again reported to Padmore, saying that Fernau was a nervous and somewhat eccentric character and any failure to discharge his duties satisfactorily should in future be treated as a matter of discipline rather than as a medical matter. This was reported to the Lord President who again saw Fernau. Fernau was told that if he felt unwell he must get proper medical advice.

In February 1953 Padmore heard that Fernau had been out of the office for most of the previous three weeks, no-one knew where he was, it was thought that he might be drinking to excess, and he had so far forgotten himself as to appear at a recent Privy Council without any teeth. Padmore checked on some of these details with Mr W.G. (later Sir Godfrey) Agnew, Fernau's deputy. Padmore then sent for Fernau, who came to see him on 5 February. Padmore asked him what was going on, and whether if he was on sick leave the sick leave was properly certificated. Fernau explained that he had had such serious troubles with his teeth that he had been to a Harley Street specialist as a private patient. He had informed Lascelles of his difficulties and said that the Queen with great kindness had him to lunch in his toothless state and provided him with a meal that he was capable of eating. However, his toothlessness had upset his digestion and he had been back to St Thomas's for treatment which remedied the digestive troubles but left him feeling feeble. He had also had influenza and had been on sick leave for a few weeks. He expected to be back at work soon.

Padmore discussed the whole situation with him and emphasised the need for proper medical care and certification when Fernau was sick. Padmore did not charge him with drinking because he felt he had no evidence for doing so, but he told Fernau to see Chiesman again. He also told Chiesman to check on Fernau's statements and to ask him bluntly whether he was drinking and, if so, to stop it.

On 8 February 1953 Salisbury wrote to Bridges for an urgent meeting to discuss information he had learned from Agnew about Fernau. Meanwhile he said that Fernau should be sent on leave and suspended from all duties immediately. Apparently Salisbury saw Bridges the same day and discussed the latest aspects of the problem. Bridges saw Fernau the next morning and told him he was suspended from duties on Salisbury's authority. Fernau agreed that there were irregularities in his accounts and said that he knew he would have to go, but that he hoped it would be done without loss of prestige and dignity to the Privy Council Office and the public service. Meanwhile, Padmore found out from Agnew details of Fernau's absences; he also learned that there were in the office empty gin bottles numbering hundreds and that Fernau was drinking gin by the tumblerful. The financial irregularities were that Fernau had been borrowing from the petty cash in exchange for I.O.U.s and that these borrowings had amounted to £208 and 12 shillings. This was regarded as a particularly serious matter because Fernau was the Accounting Officer for the department and by signing the appropriation account had by implication stated that the balances were correct - which was not true to the extent of the I.O.U.s. Padmore saw Fernau on 10 February and told him the extent of the irregularities that he had found out from Agnew. Fernau said he hoped to refund the money he had borrowed and gave some details of his personal circumstances which had led to his difficulties: his second wife, with whom he had been happily married, had been ill with depression for some time and had committed suicide in October 1950.

Considerable further discussion then occurred between the Lord President, Bridges, Padmore, the Treasury Solicitor, the Comptroller and Auditor-General, the Director of Public Prosecutions and others. Salisbury said he and Lascelles hoped it would be possible to award a pension (i.e. for 27 years' service), but Bridges and Padmore explained that pensions were dependent on good and faithful service and in view of the financial aspects there could be no question of a pension. Even this was not quite as it first appeared because Agnew, unknown to Fernau, had been so concerned to avoid scandal in connection with the Privy Council Office that he had quixotically repaid the debt to the petty cash in exchange for the I.O.U.s; there had therefore been no actual loss to the Exchequer. Bridges saw Fernau again on 23 February and told him, in effect, that he would be dismissed if he did not resign (which Bridges, when asked, advised him to do). It was not made clear to Fernau whether or not there would also be legal proceedings. Fernau asked for time to think about his position and repeated his intention to repay the loan. On 24 February Fernau called on Padmore and told him that he intended to 'accept the offer of acceptance of his resignation'. Later that day he submitted his resignation in writing. Some of the money was recovered by witholding Fernau's balance of salary (i.e. for the period up to the date when he was suspended) and this was passed to Agnew. Agnew was reimbursed for the rest when his promotion to succeed Fernau was backdated.

It soon became known in the Treasury that Fernau was indebted to moneylenders and within a few months Fernau was declared bankrupt at the Bankruptcy Court in Carey Street, London. He told the Court the whole story, including that he had been drinking a bottle and a half of gin a day. Publicity was minimal: as the proceedings developed Padmore reported to both Bridges and the Lord President, the Lord President was informing Lascelles at the Palace, and the Prime Minister was also being informed by the Lord President. All this was possible because, as Padmore put it in a note dated 10 June 1953: 'The Official Receiver is of course a civil servant and we can legitimately expect his co-operation'. Fernau became a solicitor's clerk later in 1953, with pay of about £6 a week (when he was Clerk to the Privy Council his salary was £2,250 p.a.);[70] he reformed from drinking but after a long illness died in 1968, aged 65 years.[71]

This story has various facets as far as Bridges and personnel management in the civil service are concerned. First, to an observer some thirty years later it seems rather harsh that Fernau had to leave the civil service without a pension. The possibility of this sort of penalty is, however, one of the disadvantages of a non-contributory pension. Had Fernau been a stronger character and physically in better shape in 1953, or had he sought advice from a union or staff association (it seems he did not belong to the First Division Association) the situation may have been different. His behaviour may have been foolish and his disregard for office rules may have justified dismissal, but his state of mind was not that of a criminal - even though Padmore's note of 18 May 1953 makes the Treasury attitude quite clear: 'The fact is that Mr Fernau stole this money from the Exchequer'. The denial of a pension after nearly 28 years of apparently loyal service now seems severe. Secondly, the story reveals a lack of proper control over the Privy Council Office which Bridges immediately took steps to remedy by suggesting that it might be linked with another organ of central government such as the Cabinet Office. As Bridges put it to the Lord President in a letter of 13 March 1953: 'there was not really a full-time job for the Clerk to do and the office had become something of a Civil Service backwater which no-one at the official level could keep an eye on'. However, this was not the only significant case of underemployment that came to Bridges' attention[72] and one wonders why more effective measures were not taken at the time to deal with it. One also wonders why no questions were asked about the appointments procedures which led to Fernau's promotion to headship of a subordinate department only shortly before the events which led to his virtual dismissal from the civil service. Thirdly, the case reveals an attitude of ruthless righteousness among Treasury officials in punctiliously applying rules to a situation that, in retrospect, may have justified a review of personnel welfare arrangements. Where a civil servant of previous good conduct suffers family misfortune including the suicide of his wife and as a consequence drinks so heavily that his immediate colleagues confirm that he is openly drinking tumblerfuls of gin and had hundreds of gin bottles in his office, then the lack of sophistication in civil service personnel management - especially accountability and welfare - may indeed justify some of the harshest criticisms of the Fulton Committee. The main emphasis at the time, however, was to minimise any publicity and to avoid embarrassment to the civil service and, in particular, the Privy Council Office. It seems to have been more in pursuit of this concern, than in consideration for Fernau or good management practice, that so much time and effort was spent on the case by so many highly paid senior officials and ministers.

Bridges was always concerned to avoid embarrassment to the civil service (and also to ministers), but he was also sympathetic to individual civil servants who found themselves in difficulties not of their own making. His personal qualities were very important on such occasions and his standards were widely known. He was respected even though, because he was such a private individual, few people really felt they knew him. He was also outstandingly hard-working: he spent a great deal of time considering and planning possible staff moves to cover key positions and he did this with sensitivity towards the individuals involved.[73] He did not shirk difficult interviews with colleagues, as when he had to tell someone that his chances of promotion were poor[74] or that it was thought someone had reached his ceiling as far as future prospects were concerned.[75] He also did not shirk telling ministers when he thought they were behaving badly: as will be illustrated later. Although he could usually only offer colleagues sympathy, encouragement and advice this was often all that was required, especially from such a powerful figure. Occasionally Bridges had to deal with friction between government departments or between individual civil servants. He generally did this by getting the disputants together in his office and, where necessary, acting as a sort of referee.[76] In relation to the most senior posts Bridges only had a constitutional responsibility to make recommendations to the Prime Minister. In practice, however, he had almost complete power because no-one had a better command of all the relevant details and his recommendations were therefore usually, though not invariably,[77] accepted. Consequently, in many cases the only role left for ministers during their short careers in particular departments was the possibility of a veto.

Bridges' personnel management experience in context

It would be unfair to Bridges and his colleagues, and misleading as an insight into personnel management processes in the British civil service, to leave the examples of cases quoted in this chapter without providing more information about their context. The strong moral constraints of Bridges' character fitted easily into some of the puritan constraints of the public sector environment. The general approach is well illustrated by part of the advice Sir Gregory Hardlines, the fictional character in Trollope's *The Three Clerks*, gave to some of the first civil service candidates to be selected by competitive examination. Bridges quoted this in some of his own lectures. Hardlines told the candidates:

> ... that they should look on none of their energies as applicable to private purposes, regard none of their hours as their own. They were devoted in a peculiar way to the Civil Service, and they should feel that such was their lot in life. They should know that their intellects were a sacred pledge entrusted to them for the good of that service, and should use

them accordingly. This should be their highest ambition.[78]

This may have been the advice of a fictional character but in fact it was not very different from the official advice given to civil servants. For example, Mr B.D. (later Sir Bruce) Fraser in 1941[79] quoted, as if it were a code of conduct, the 1928 Report of the Board of Enquiry appointed by the Prime Minister to investigate certain statements affecting civil servants. The report said that 'The first duty of a Civil Servant is to give his undivided allegiance to the State at all times and on all occasions when the State has a claim upon his services ...'[80]

The consequences of this approach are well illustrated from earlier this century in connection with industrial action. One disciplinary tactic was to use the non-contributory pension entitlement to discourage strikes by reducing by 10% the pension eligibility of individuals who took industrial action. Winston Churchill explained the rationale when he wrote in 1922 to the Governor General of Gibraltar:

> ... the principle upon which Parliament has proceeded in giving legal sanction to the award of pensions to Civil Servants is that they should have rendered faithful and satisfactory service; and this primary condition could not be held to have been satisfied in the case of servants of the State who by striking have endangered or prevented the carrying on of the public service, for which His Majesty's Government is responsible to Parliament and the community.[81]

It was, in fact, this principle which was used to punish Fernau for borrowing from the petty cash.

Other examples to illustrate the Treasury attitude to staff problems may be quoted from the 1920s, when Bridges was working in the Treasury Establishment Officer's department. In 1926 Mr A.W. Barron, an officer in the Rochdale office of the National Insurance Audit Department, was discovered to be augmenting his salary by professional work in his spare time and the case was referred to Bridges who, on 23 October 1926 wrote: 'It seems to me that it is unbecoming for a Civil Servant to be the auditor of a public Company'.[82] Bridges' advice was that Barron should be told to stop his spare time work because attendance elsewhere during working hours, even on a day of leave, was contrary to clause 17 of an Order in Council of 10 January 1910. He also advised that if Barron continued his outside work and if his work appeared to be less satisfactory than it should be, then he might be transferred to a post a considerable distance from Rochdale. On another minor case, in 1929, also referred to the Treasury for advice, Bridges wrote: '... Saturday afternoon being a half holiday "when the state of public business permits", it is clear that there is an implied obligation on Civil Servants to attend for duty on Saturday afternoons when required to do so'[83] - the implication being that no civil servant should engage in a commitment on a Saturday afternoon that might prevent him from being always ready for such service.

In these and other matters Bridges had no personal interest to pursue. His application of the rules may now appear somewhat inflexible but, as a Treasury civil servant, he also was bound by the rules. These rules, it must be emphasised, originated in Parliament and reflected the attitudes and standards of society when they were introduced. As not only a good civil servant, but an outstanding Treasury official, Bridges was a master of the rules. He worked on establishment matters for most of his service up to the Second World War. As already explained, establishments work was different from personnel management because it was a hard-line approach to staffing problems - a hard-line approach originating from financial accountability to Parliament. This approach was quite different from the softer approach of those personnel management enthusiasts who emphasised the need to enable staff to give of their best and favoured welfare services for staff. Not only were there no resources specifically allocated by Parliament for such purposes, it was far from clear that such approaches to personnel management were academically respectable or effective in practice. It must be emphasised that few officials could have known the rules as well as Bridges did. He worked hard, receiving considerable satisfaction from his work and he acquired a solid grounding in practical experience in the Treasury. This experience included service as secretary to the Official Side of the National Whitley Council and Secretary to the Tomlin Royal Commission on the Civil Service.

When he became Head of the Civil Service Bridges made full use of the network of contacts he already had, in order to continue the emphasis that Fisher had established on selecting the best people for senior appointments. This was by no means a burden. Bridges admired what Fisher had achieved for the civil service and continued the procedure for staff appointments along the same

lines. It is important to remember, too, that whilst he found being
Permanent Secretary to the Treasury a strenuous job, it was also one
that brought many satisfactions.[84] There is plenty of evidence to
suggest this, but two typical examples illustrate it well. After it was
announced in 1968 that Sir William (later Lord) Armstrong was to
be the new Head of the Civil Service, Bridges wrote to him: 'I am
more delighted than I can say that you have been appointed to
succeed Laurence as Head of the Civil Service ... Whatever else
people may say about me, it was owing to me that you came into
the Treasury'.[85] Bridges was also far from unaware of the
importance of his work and the power he had in the conscientious
exercise of his responsibilities: in this respect, too, his participation
in the activity of administrative politics was an important source of
satisfaction. With perhaps more than a hint of regret, he wrote to
Padmore on 13 September 1956: 'The time is fast approaching
when I should cease to make plots about filling the two top levels
in Civil Service ...'.[86]

Constitutionally, of course, Bridges could only make
recommendations. The doctrine of ministerial responsibility was
the main reason behind his determination to observe confidentiality
until after an appointment was announced. It was important to find
out whether a potential candidate would be prepared to accept an
appointment before a formal offer was made, otherwise
embarrassment could follow. Just as it would be quite improper to
reject an invitation from the Queen, so the same sort of attitude
applied also to invitations from lesser mortals like Prime Ministers
and Ministers. The principle was the same, even if the form
was less pure. Normally, but not always, ministers accepted
recommendations from their well-informed and well-prepared
officials. Occasionally they had ideas of their own about particular
appointments. These could easily be accommodated within official
programmes - not so much because ministers' ideas were secondary
but more because the programmes were drawn up with built-in
flexibility and after an appreciation of the way the government and
ministers' minds were working.

Bridges' attitudes were detached in many respects; and in the
best traditions of a Weberian bureaucrat, Bridges saw himslf, as
others also saw him, as a sort of super office secretary - though this
did not mean that Bridges was completely lacking in emotions. A
splendid example of one of his emotional reactions arose from a
turnover article in *The Times* in 1966. Mr A.W. Wyatt of the
Treasury sent Bridges a photocopy because he knew Bridges,

though retired, would be interested. When a second article appeared a few weeks later Bridges was 'perfectly furious'.[87] He drafted a letter to *The Times* and sent a copy to Helsby because, Bridges said, it might console Helsby to know how angry he was and also it might amuse him to read Bridges' first reaction. The letter was never sent to *The Times*. Instead, Bridges talked to Lord Strang about the possibility of organising a debate in the House of Lords. Strang suggested it might be better if Bridges wrote a paper for the Fulton Committee and after trying out a draft on Helsby, Bridges wrote to Fulton on 14 January 1967.

The articles in *The Times*, by 'A Correspondent', were about patronage, especially in relation to appointments to senior posts in the civil service and to appointments outside government departments. The first article[88] drew attention to the promotion system for senior appointments and argued that there were inadequate safeguards against patronage. The system was, it said, 'defended by many respectable persons who hold the courtier-like doctrine that the man promoted to under-secretary should not necessarily be the best man, but the man whom the permanent secretary gets on with best'. It drew attention to the role of the Treasury in selecting for itself an elite from other departments, then letting these officials influence appointments elsewhere: 'As early as 1936, it was noted that in the years since the 1914-18 War, out of 48 headships of departments, 10 had gone to men previously at the Treasury'. It emphasised that, even after the then recent publication of Bridges' book on *The Treasury*,[89] the central direction of senior appointments was surrounded in secrecy: it argued that it should be better known and less formal. It also argued that the managerial centre of the civil service would command more confidence if it were divorced from the Treasury.

The second article[90] drew attention to such developments as over 500 advisory councils and 2,000 tribunals, together with details of numerous bodies that today are known as quangos.[91] It argued that 'For former civil servants, the plums are on the boards of corporations, and the bread and butter is in the departmental entourage and in the galaxy of ephemeral committee and similar assignments'. It argued that this amounted to 'a largely undiluted and old-fashioned patronage system'. It drew attention to the scope for civil servants to find jobs for themselves with the facility (as enjoyed by Helmore - see above) 'by which a civil servant can freeze his pension before retiring and receive it in a modified form when he attained that age in other employment'. The author also argued that although there were good reasons for retaining a ministerial patronage system there were equally good reasons for the reform of its civil service counterpart.

In his draft letter to Fulton, enclosing his notes on the article in *The Times* on 15 November 1966, Bridges dealt with all the points that annoyed him most, repeating and elaborating what he had written in his book. His points were eminently reasonable - but, to a reader twenty years later (even if not to a senior Treasury official in the mid-1960s) the two articles in *The Times* may also appear reasonable examples of fair comment. One example illustrates Bridges' approach. On the statement that 'The selection of teams, however, seems to dispense with the basic principle of promotion by merit', Bridges wrote:

> This appears to be a misunderstanding of a remark in Chapter XVII that it is not a question of forming an order of merit of candidates for a particular post, because you have to consider many posts. And I used the cricket analogy that it is no use settling that X is your best slip fielder, if you have got to ask him to keep wicket. In other words the simple fact that A may on balance be the strongest candidate for post X does not mean that he should be appointed to that post. A may be far more badly needed for post Y for which he is ideally suited; whereas B and C could do X nearly as well as A.

The plain truth emerges that any system of selection for senior appointments will depend to a large extent on the quality and suitability of the selectors. This is as true today as it was when Bridges was Head of the Civil Service. The present system involves a Senior Appointments Selection Committee and originates from William Armstrong's time as Head of the Civil Service, though suggestions for instituting such a reform date from the time of the Second World War. H.E. Dale, for example, wrote in 1941 that '... if all selections for the highest offices were made and were known to be made by a committee ... it should dispel the least shade of the disheartening suspicion that in Whitehall talent and industry are not the only path to success'.[92] The proposal was also debated in Parliament in the 1950s.[93] In the 1960s, the Fulton Committee thought that the role of the Head of the Civil Service in senior appointments gave too much responsibility to a single individual and created the impression that his recommendations to the Prime Minister were within his sole discretion. It added: 'Many civil servants criticise this - we think rightly'.[94] It recommended that the Head of the Civil Service should be assisted in this task by a committee, including not more than two eminent people from outside the civil service. It was following the publication of the Fulton Report that, in 1968, a committee was first set up to assist the Head of the Civil Service, though without the participation of outsiders.

This Senior Appointments Selection Committee now normally meets monthly and is intended to satisfy critics of the previous system (as operated by Bridges and his immediate successors). The Committee is a collegial body which, on a basis of consensus, advises the Head of the Civil Service, who in turn advises the Prime Minister. It is thought to include about six permanent secretaries and a couple of senior specialists. It proceeds on a basis of the highest confidentiality so that until sometime in the late 1970s its papers were not circulated in advance, but were made available at the meetings.[95] In practice its procedures continue to be shrouded in secrecy. Outsiders still play no part in them.

There is now a growing volume of what William Plowden, in his Preface to the recently published Report of a Working Group of the Royal Institute of Public Administration, has called anecdote and speculation about alleged abuses, conflicts, undue personal influence and about the 'politicisation' of the civil service. He added: 'Such speculation is likely to be encouraged by the shortage of reliable information'.[96] The RIPA Report therefore contains information about the present arrangements for making senior appointments; it also proposes changes to make the procedures more open and subject to external (non-political) scrutiny. It suggests that the civil service should be 'opened up' with more flexible career patterns and more opportunities for recruitment from outside to the highest posts in the service.

However, a study of Bridges' experience, with all the defects of amateurishness that are so apparent to an observer reading the files forty or fifty years after the events, also has some positive features worth recalling. Bridges, in the best tradition of Fisher, tried to develop a loyalty to the civil service. He did this in various ways and his efforts were helped by the way the Treasury exercised control over the civil service. Much of this control has now been dissipated. One of the practical reasons for setting up the Senior Appointments Selection Committee was to respond to the consequences of economies in the civil service. The economies resulted in more delegation to departments with less control by the

Treasury. Now there is no longer a central agency with these controls. First the central personnel management functions were taken from the Treasury and given to the Civil Service Department. Then they were redivided and either passed back to the Treasury or passed to the Management and Personnel Office within the Cabinet Office. At the same time the Financial Management Initiative inaugurated in the 1980s has resulted in more delegation to departments and units. All these changes may be interpreted as reforms - but one of their consequences has been effectively to curtail, if not prevent, the sort of consultations practised by Bridges in relation to senior appointments.

Another feature of contemporary Britain worth comparing with Bridges' time is the interest in more open government. It could, of course, be argued that confidence in the informal system operated by Bridges was not only acceptable because of the trust and respect Bridges generally inspired, it was also acceptable because so little was known about it. The main reason for strict confidentiality was the civil service interpretation of ministerial responsibility. Now, with demands for more open government and changes in the relationships between civil servants and ministers,[97] it is possible for commentators to be more informed and more critical of Bridges' system of making senior appointments. Perhaps the defects of the system, and some of the unfortunate appointments that resulted, did indeed contribute to Britain's decline in terms of economic policy-making in the post-war period, as some critics have argued.[98]

A further change relates to the national interest, as the concept was known and interpreted by Bridges and others. Since Bridges' time as Head of the Civil Service there has been a rise in militancy by civil service unions: official strikes have demonstrated very clearly that conflicts may now exist between the sectional interests of staff and the national interest.[99] However, recent events must also not be considered in isolation. An examination of union activity in the civil service is likely to demonstrate that it is in part, if not mainly, a reaction to other changes in the system of government. An explanation of recent union activity may be more complex than at first appears.

Much of the relative harmony during the time when Bridges was Head of the Civil Service must be attributable to his personal qualities and the skills in personnel management which he demonstrated. The approach to office management which he practised is well illustrated in a letter Bridges wrote in 1955 to

Professor J.R.M. (later Sir James) Butler who was then preparing for publication the Grand Strategy volumes in the series on the History of the Second World War. Bridges was explaining that what made the Offices of the War Cabinet work so well could not be illustrated adequately by the arrows and dotted lines on an organisation diagram but by something quite different. He went on:

> The real effectiveness of the machine depended on the fact that the Secretariat of the War Cabinet and all its committees was a fairly small body who all lived together in the same building and knew one another well and made a practice, under orders from their superiors, of keeping in the closest touch with the Secretaries of the Committees which dealt with subjects which touched and probably overlapped. It was the result of this day to day contact between all members of the Secretariat that overlapping or gaps were avoided; and that subjects were steered into the Committee in which they would be most expeditiously and speedily considered, and that conflicts of jurisdiction were avoided. Then again the whole constitution and working of the Cabinet Committee system has always avoided a legalistic outlook. If it was obviously right and convenient that a paper should not follow the normal channel but should be submitted to some other Committee, or that a joint meeting of two bodies should be held, or that a paper should skip out a stage and go direct to the Defence Committee or Cabinet because of lack of time, then it was so arranged. All this was made possible by two things. First the close and harmonious working together of the members of the Secretariat, and secondly the confidence which all members of the Committees had in the Secretariat, who were thus enabled to arrange matters so that business was dealt with speedily and harmoniously.[100]

Bridges did much to inspire team spirit and had a natural talent for developing personal contacts and operating as a politician (in the strictly non-party sense) within the Whitehall administrative system. This helped not only the personnel management processes within the civil service as a whole but also other responsibilities he exercised personally. One of these was advising the Prime Minister on the award of honours to civil servants. Because of his wide understanding of work in the civil service and of the officials within it he could better than anyone else form a judgement for submission to the Prime Minister on the relative claims of various officials. In any case he had a formal responsibility in this context because as Permanent Secretary to the Treasury he was Secretary to the Order of the British Empire and his duties included making recommendations for the grant of membership of the Order in any class. Bridges was also the Chairman of the advisory a selecting body for many other honours.[101]

Although some features of personnel management as practised by Bridges still remain, no-one will ever again play such a key role in the British civil service. There are practical reasons for this, associated with recent institutional changes - including the current responsibilities of the present Head of the Civil Service (who is also Secretary to the Cabinet) and the creation of the Senior Appointments Selection Committee. There have also been management changes associated with new techniques including the Financial Management Initiative and the development of a more professional approach to personnel management. However, there have also been changes in the attitudes of politicians and in their expectations of the civil service. It is not only the civil service that has changed. The political environment within which it operates has changed. It would be quite extraordinary if there had not also been changes in the British civil service.

Notes

1. Adapted from Maurice Cuming, *The Theory and Practice of Personnel Management*, (Heinemann, London, 1968; Fourth edition, 1980).

2. Adapted from the definition published by the Institute of Personnel Management. See Maurice Cuming, *The Theory and Practice of Personnel Management*.

3. *Report of the Machinery of Government Committee*, [Cd. 9230], (HMSO, London, 1918), para. 20.

4. See Richard A. Chapman, 'Administrative Culture and Personnel Management: 'The British Civil Service in the 1980s', *Teaching Public Administration*, Vol. 4, No. 1, 1984, pp. 1-14.

5. PRO/T273/201, Bridges to Bligh, 5 January 1950.

6. PRO/T199/351, Fisher to Wilson, 15 May 1939.

7. Lord Bridges, *The Treasury*, (George Allen and Unwin, London, 1964), p. 176.

8. PRO/T199/352, Bridges to Helsby, 19 October 1949.

9. Lord Bridges, *The Treasury*, p. 177.

10. *Ibid*.

11. Richard A. Chapman, *Leadership in the British Civil Service: A Study of Sir Percival Waterfield and the creation of the Civil Service*

Selection Board, (Croom Helm, London, 1984), Ch. 5.

12. Sir Edward Bridges, 'The Civil Service Tradition', BBC (GOS) Broadcast talk, 1954. Script in PRO/T273/222.

13. C.H. Sisson, 'The Civil Service After Fulton', *The Spectator*, 20 February 1971, p. 250. Reprinted in W.J. Stankiewicz, *British Government in an Era of Reform*, (Collier Macmillan, London, 1976), pp. 252-62.

14. PRO/T273/381, Bridges to Trend, 17 June 1948.

15. Report of an RIPA Working Group, *Top Jobs in Whitehall: Appointments and Promotions in the Senior Civil Service*, (Royal Institute of Public Administration, London, 1987), p. 19.

16. PRO/T273/212. For another example see PRO/T273/324.

17. PRO/T273/219. See also PRO/T273/376.

18. PRO/T273/346, Johnson to Lord President, 16 November 1945, and Robertson to Bridges, 22 November 1945.

19. PRO/T273/346, Bridges to Chancellor of the Exchequer, 9 August 1946.

20. PRO/T273/347, Bridges to Robertson, 17 December 1946.

21. PRO/T273/347, Bridges to Barlow, 18 March 1947.

22. PRO/T273/329. For other examples see PRO/T273/64 and PRO/T273/75.

23. *Committee on the Working of the Monetary System, Minutes of Evidence*, (HMSO, London, 1960), Q.260. See also Richard A. Chapman, *Decision Making*, (Routledge and Kegan Paul, London, 1968), Ch. 5.

24. National Coal Board, *Report of the Advisory Committee on Organisation*, (Chairman: Dr A. Fleck), (National Coal Board, London, 1955).

25. PRO/T273/250.

26. PRO/T273/123.

27. PRO/T273/179, Bridges to Lloyd, 25 February 1948.

28. On the early history of the Company (it became Anglo-Iranian in 1935 and British Petroleum in 1955), see R.W. Farrier, *The History of the British Petroleum Company, Vol. 1, The Developing Years 1902-1932*, (Cambridge University Press, Cambridge, 1982). Vol. 2 has not yet been published.

29. PRO/T273/360, Bridges to Vincent, 30 October 1950.

30. PRO/T273/362.

31. PRO/T273/363.

32. PRO/T273/360, Bridges' 'Note for Record', 18 July 1950.

33. PRO/T273/360, Bridges' 'Note for Record', 27 October 1950.

34. PRO/T273/364.

35. PRO/T273/25.

36. PRO/T273/25, Roberts to Bridges, 19 July 1954.

37. PRO/T273/26, Swinton to Butler, 31 August 1953.

38. PRO/T273/40.

39. PRO/T273/27.

40. PRO/T273/38.

41. PRO/T273/26, Winnifrith to Nicholls, 5 August 1953.

42. PRO/T273/78.

43. PRO/T273/86.

44. PRO/T273/83, Bridges to Robertson, 25 April 1945.

45. PRO/T273/151.

46. PRO/T273/29.

47. PRO/T273/46.

48. For examples, see PRO/T273/61, PRO/T273/62, PRO/T273/111, PRO/T273/127 and PRO/T273/129.

49. Richard Norton-Taylor, *The Ponting Affair*, (Cecil Woolf, London, 1985), p. 103.

50. Sir Edward Bridges, 'The Civil Service Tradition', BBC (GOS) Broadcast talk, 1954. Script in PRO/T273/222.

51. Sir Edward Bridges, 'Professional Standards: The Civil Servant', BBC (GOS) Broadcast talk, 1952. Script in PRO/T273/222.

52. *Ibid.*

53. Rt Hon Lord Bridges, *Commemoration Day Address 23 October 1958*, (Imperial College of Science and Technology, London, 1958).

54. PRO/T273/126, Lee to Bridges, 17 November 1947.

55. Dame Evelyn Sharp to Bridges, 17 October 1956, Goodmans Furze Papers, Box 9.

56. Goodmans Furze Papers, Box 9.

57. Lord Helsby to Lady Bridges, 30 August 1969, Goodmans Furze Papers, Box 9.

58. Sir Robert Birley to Lady Bridges, 29 August 1969, Goodmans Furze Papers, Box 9.

59. Draft of 'How the Treasury Exercises Civil Service Patronage', a note of points on *The Times* article 15 November 1966, for possible enclosure with the letter to Lord Fulton, 14 January 1967, Goodmans Furze Papers, Box 9.

60. PRO/T273/126.

61. PRO/T273/131.

62. PRO/T273/129.

63. PRO/T273/127, Bridges' 'Note for Record', 1 April 1952.

64. PRO/T273/151, Bridges to Prime Minister, 8 April 1946.

65. PRO/T273/90.

66. Hugh Thomas on John Strachey in E.T. Williams and C.S. Nicholls (Editors), *Dictionary of National Biography, 1961-1970*, (Oxford University Press, Oxford, 1981).

67. Hugh Thomas, *John Strachey*, (Eyre Methuen, London, 1973), p. 238.

68. PRO/T273/127.

69. PRO/T273/118.

70. *British Imperial Calendar and Civil Service List, 1953*, (HMSO, London, 1953).

71. Information from Mr J.C. Fernau.

72. For another example, see PRO/T273/42.

73. For examples, see PRO/T273/76 and PRO/T273/111.

74. For example, see PRO/T273/152.

75. For example, see PRO/T273/49.

76. For examples, see PRO/T273/299 and PRO/T216/121/EM811/798/01. See also Richard A. Chapman, *Leadership in the British Civil Service*, Ch. 4.

77. For examples, see PRO/T273/2 and PRO/T273/150.

78. Anthony Trollope, *The Three Clerks*, (Oxford University Press, Oxford, 1858), 'The World's Classics Edition', 1907, p. 130. See also PRO/T273/222.

79. PRO/T162/726/E8641/021/01, Minute by B.D. Fraser, 19 September 1941.

80. *Report of the Board of Enquiry appointed by the Prime Minister to investigate certain Statements affecting Civil Servants*, [Cmd. 3037], (HMSO, London, 1928), para. 56.

81. PRO/T162/384/E9062, Churchill to Smith-Dorrien, 13 March 1922.

82. PRO/T162/625/E12810/1.

83. PRO/T162/625/E12810/3.

84. Sir Edward Bridges, 'A Day in the Life of the Permanent Secretary to the Treasury', BBC (GOS) Broadcast talk, 1952. Script in PRO/T273/222.

85. Bridges to Sir William Armstrong, 9 January 1968, Goodmans Furze Papers, Box 9.

86. PRO/T273/114.

87. Bridges to Helsby, 21 November 1966, Goodmans Furze Papers, Box 9.

88. *The Times*, 15 November 1966.

89. Lord Bridges, *The Treasury*.

90. *The Times*, 20 December 1966.

91. See Anthony Barker (Editor), *Quangos in Britain*, (Macmillan, London, 1982).

92. H.E. Dale, *The Higher Civil Service of Great Britain*, (Oxford University Press, London, 1941), p. 227.

93. 509 H.C. Deb., 5s, cols. 925-6 (12 December 1952) and 514 H.C. Deb., 5s, cols. 1685-1717 (24 April 1953). See also the leading article in *The Times*, 12 December 1952, and PRO/T215/113.

94. *The Civil Service, Vol. 1, Report of the Committee, 1966-8*, [Cmnd. 3638], (HMSO, London, 1968), para. 260.

95. Report of an RIPA Working Group, *Top Jobs in Whitehall*, Ch. 3.

96. William Plowden, 'Preface' in Report of an RIPA Working Group, *Top Jobs in Whitehall*.

97. Richard A. Chapman and Michael Hunt (eds.) *Open Government: A Study of the prospects of open government within the limitations of the British political system*, (Croom Helm, London, 1987).

98. For example, see Hugh Thomas (Ed.) *The Establishment*, (Anthony Blond, London, 1959); Max Nicholson, *The System: the misgovernment of modern Britain*, (Hodder and Stoughton, London, 1967).

99. Barry J. O'Toole, 'Morale in the Higher Civil Service: the Symbolic Importance of the FDA's decision to Join the TUC', *Public Administration Bulletin*, No. 47, April 1985, pp. 18-38.

100. PRO/T273/72, Bridges to Butler, 5 January 1955. See also John Ehrman, *History of the Second World War, United Kingdom Military Series: Grand Strategy, Vol. VI, October 1944 - August 1945*, (HMSO, London, 1956), p. 377.

101. PRO/T199/351.

3

Political Attitudes and Political Behaviour

It is not only in personnel matters that public administration differs from business management. Anyone who fails to recognise the essential differences, especially in the British context, must be myopic, or ignorant, or over-enthusiastic to change the nature of public administration. In this context it should be remembered that the British civil service works under the supreme control of a committee accountable to over six hundred elected 'shareholders', of whom up to about three hundred are likely at any one time to be opposed to current policies. Any fairly large section of this body is able to raise a set debate on any part of the organisation's business or on any transaction they may select at almost any time. The leaders of the opposition group are at liberty to propose that the committee, or at least the 'director' responsible for the mistake, shall be publicly reprimanded; and if the proposal is carried, the 'director', and perhaps the whole committee, will have to resign at once. In addition, any of the 'shareholders' is entitled at any time to ask any question he chooses about any matter of the business, from issues of broad policy down to the smallest detail, and to have a full and accurate reply within two or three days. Furthermore, the 'shareholders' with these rights and powers sit at the organisation's supreme headquarters for several hours a day, on five days a week, for about eight months of the year.[1]

Within such an environment the daily management of the organisation proceeds; but as a consequence the most important work of the most senior management officials is not in practice concerned so much with management as with politics in the most comprehensive and non-partisan sense of the word. The senior officials give precedence to matters arising from Parliament and its members, and they develop attitudes and skills appropriate to meeting the demands of this political environment. Consequently, the relationship between the permanent officials and the elected politicians has become both non-partisan and professional - in the same sense that other professions develop standards of conduct and norms of behaviour in relation to their clients.

Its non-partisan nature is one of the most characteristic features of the British civil service in modern times, and Bridges probably did more than anyone else to foster and further this non-partisan approach to public service. He was always willing to expound upon the relationship which he thought should exist between politicians and permanent officials within the British system of government. He also took steps to correct any misapprehensions drawn to his attention. When necessary he contributed either formally or informally to official discussion on this relationship to ensure that the non-partisan principles were both practised and also enshrined in appropriate documents. Above all, he personally observed with meticulous propriety the standards he thought should apply. This chapter outlines Bridges' approach to the subject and considers his contribution to the Masterman enquiry and the implementation of its recommendations.

The non-partisan civil servant

By the time Bridges became Head of the Civil Service he was already an acknowledged authority on the practice of the British constitution. Since his days at Eton and Oxford he was interested in its development as a study in history. His academic interests were supplemented by his experience of dealing with particular issues in the Treasury and as Secretary to the Cabinet. When he became Head of the Civil Service he also assumed responsibility for upholding the best features and traditions of the British civil service, including, above all, its tradition of party political neutrality.

Bridges explained this non-partisan role of the British civil service on a number of occasions. For example, in his famous essay, *Portrait of a Profession*, he suggested that the non-political character of the civil service received its main imprint in the eighteenth century. Although patronage continued until towards the end of the nineteenth century, 'a characteristic convention was established that, while Ministers could use their patronage to appoint to official posts persons who had some claim upon them, such appointments were not disturbed by subsequent administrations ... by a process of instinctive good sense, it came to be accepted that permanence carried as a corollary a certain standard of conduct and discretion - namely conduct compatible with loyal service to whatever Government is in power'.[2] On another occasion he explained:

> There is nothing in which we British Civil Servants take more pride than the fact that we can and do serve all governments with equal loyalty: and that whatever Government is in power, there is the same confidence between Ministers and their permanent advisers. We believe intensely that a non-political Civil Service such as ours makes for a more efficient system of government than one in which changes have to be made in the top posts whenever a Government of a different political complexion takes over.[3]

Bridges recognised that men and women joined the civil service for a variety of reasons, but he thought it 'fair to say that they nearly all have these points in common: a disposition to find public affairs of interest; no desire or intention to take part in political life; and a readiness to work as a member of a team, rather than to seek personal glory'.[4] He quoted with approval from Herbert Morrison's book *Government and Parliament*. In that book Morrison said that his readers could be assured that the British civil service was loyal to the government of the day. Morrison explained that:

> The relationship between the Minister and the civil servants should be - and usually is - that of colleagues working together in a team, co-operative partners seeking to advance the public interest and the efficiency of the Department. ... The partnership should be alive and virile, rival ideas and opinions should be fairly considered, and the relationship of all should be one of mutual respect - on the understanding, of course, that the Minister's decision is final and must be loyally and helpfully carried out, and that he requires efficient and energetic service.[5]

Bridges described in some detail this relationship between ministers and civil servants. He said 'the Permanent Head's supreme loyalty is to his Minister. It is his duty to serve him to the utmost of his power, and to give him all the help he needs'.[6] He also said:

> It must be for the Permanent Head ... to see that both he, himself, and the Department as a whole are working in harmony with the Minister's ideas.
>
> The working life of a Permanent Head calls, I think, for a greater measure of self discipline than almost any other occupation. But the effort required is greatly rewarded: in the friendship and mutual gratitude between the partners, and in the satisfaction of what can be achieved for the public good.[7]

This had consequences not only for policy and management, but also for the civil servant's conception of politics and political influence.

Bridges maintained that policy and management were inseparable and 'the essence of the relationship of the Permanent Head to his Minister is that there can be no clearly defined limits demarcating their spheres of action'.[8] This intermingling of policy and management was 'at the very heart of the partnership between the Minister and the Permanent Head of the Department. On the one hand policy cannot be formed, and the measures to give effect to it determined, without the knowledge and experience which the Department possesses. On the other hand the Department, in executing policy, is dependent on continuous guidance, direction and authority from above'.[9] Civil servants looked at a particular matter from the point of view of continuity of administration and were concerned that decisions contributed to the development of a well-ordered piece of administration.[10] When the details of policies were being planned or re-shaped the burden of the work fell on civil servants. However, Bridges qualified this by pointing out that civil servants:

> will be working in close touch with a Minister who will give directions from time to time as to how the work should be studied and will receive reports of what is going on. He may specify from time to time points to which he attaches special importance. He may say that on political grounds a solution on some line would be easier to put across. He may on occasion go so far as to say that some proposal is so open to political objection that he doubts if it will prove to be feasible. But I have yet to learn that any hard line can be drawn in this

long process between the objective study of facts and political considerations. Is not every important issue of Government policy likely to have political overtones? But is there any reason why a Civil Servant should refrain from giving all the help and advice that he has to offer, or why a Minister should not welcome all the help that he can get, simply because the matter in hand has a political angle? Perish the thought.[11]

This understanding of the relationship of policy and management had consequences for the civil servant's conception of politics. In essence, it was a non-partisan conception. Bridges put it like this: 'In the British Civil Service, when we speak of "political influence" we mean rather the extent to which the Cabinet, or Ministers in their submission to the Cabinet, are influenced by their view of what the House of Commons or the general public will tolerate on any particular issue'.[12] On another occasion he said that by politics he meant 'broad judgments as to what will be the reaction of the community to a particular course of action'.[13] In commenting on the suggestion that a minister should have 'his own little *cabinet* in the French sense - a sort of central office through which he runs the whole department', Bridges found it significant that 'one wants to use the French pronunciation here. It is an idea foreign to us, with political overtones'. He said:

> I dislike this idea a good deal. It implies that a department is unable or unwilling to serve all ministers loyally and effectively, irrespective of party. I can see no need for a *cabinet* in a department unless one believes that only with the help of such an office is it possible for a minister to get his schemes carried through his department. And this just is not true.[14]

In one of his broadcast talks Bridges stated the position particularly clearly. He said:

> ... the essence of the relationship between Ministers and Civil Servants is that it is a confidential one; a relationship in which each can speak to the other with perfect frankness and confidence, and with the knowledge that what he says is for the ear of the other only, and will go no further.
> ... It's our duty and privilege to serve and give advice to whatever Government is in power, with equal fidelity, with

equal devotion.

We civil servants believe intensely in this conception of a body of men and women which serves all governments alike. We believe that both the country and Ministers are better served in this way than they would be under any other system.

You'll see that the system requires that civil servants should be equally acceptable as advisers to Labour Ministers or Conservative Ministers. This can only happen if civil servants are free from all taint of party allegiance; and there's a rule that all civil servants save those in a fairly subordinate capacity, must take no open part in party politics ... The rule is of long standing and it's well observed.[15]

Whilst 'a Civil Servant is bound to be well aware of the political content of his work ... he is perhaps the least political of animals since the departmental experience of which he is the exponent ... is part of the stock of things which are common to all political parties. It is something which stands apart from the creed of any political party and thus makes a Civil Servant avert himself, almost instinctively, from party politics'.[16] Whilst a civil servant was, in Bridges' view, a student of public opinion, he was no party politician. One reason for this is that civil servants who have served ministers from both the political parties, and have experience of seeing the inner workings of the machine, come to recognise that 'if neither party is as near perfection as it claims to be, so neither is half as bad as its opponents would make it out to be. Their experience leads them to see the good and the bad points on both sides ...'.[17]

Consistent with these beliefs, Bridges' career was a model of non-partisan political activity and high sensitivity to potential political embarrassment. He defended the civil service (or ensured that it was defended) when critics suggested that officials were not neutral, and he avoided circumstances or occasions where there was any possibility that his own position might be misconstrued. Nevertheless, he never shirked giving advice or responding to questions, even on delicate matters, when he felt it was his duty to take such action. This is well illustrated by the following examples, chosen from among many in the official files.

The first example concerns a number of articles critical of the civil service, published in *Tribune* over the years 1946 to 1949. On certain occasions these articles were also critical of particular civil servants. In November 1946 an article implied that Bridges and his senior colleagues were not impartial as between the Conservative and Labour parties; and that being essentially Tories, they were incapable of giving unprejudiced service to a Labour minister other than one who was strong enough to keep them in their places. The article also cast serious doubt on the integrity of civil servants in general. Bridges was upset by this, mainly because he felt sure the propagation of such ill-founded comment was 'bad for the morale of the Civil Service and contrary to the public interest' and he sent a note about it to Mr T.L. (later Sir Leslie) Rowan, the Prime Minister's Private Secretary.[18] Rowan passed the note to the Prime Minister, who sent it to Dr Hugh Dalton, Chancellor of the Exchequer, who sent for Bridges. Dalton also sent for Mr Mallalieu, who had written the article, and after seeing the Chancellor, Mallalieu called on Bridges. They had a friendly talk, but Bridges told him: 'although I thought I knew the Permanent Secretaries throughout the Service very well, I did not know how any of them had voted in the last election; and as regards about 25 or 30 or more, I would not like to bet which way they voted'.[19]

The second example concerns Sir Donald Banks. When, in 1946, Banks had written the manuscript of his book *Flame Over Britain*,[20] it was referred to Bridges for comments. Bridges took a strong line about it because he thought '... that for a former Civil Servant to publish a book in which he criticised other Departments would tend to weaken the confidence with which matters were discussed between colleagues'. Bridges sent for Banks and when he saw him on 7 May 1946 he told him that his book should be rewritten in order to eliminate its partisan tone. Banks took this very well and went away to revise his manuscript.[21]

The third example occurred in 1952 when a series of six Panel Discussions on 'Some Administrative Problems Ahead' was sponsored by the Institute (now the Royal Institute) of Public Administration. Each of the weekly discussions had four distinguished panel speakers and the events were advertised by an attractive poster. Bridges saw the poster and noted that Sir Robert Fraser, Director-General of the Central Office of Information, was taking part in the discussion on 27 October 1952, on 'The Citizen and the Administrative Maze'. The discussion was to focus on such questions as 'How can the citizen learn of the official regulations which govern his duties and rights?' and 'Can administrative methods be simplified for his benefit?' Fraser was the only civil servant on the panel (the other speakers were Douglas Houghton MP, broadcaster in the 'Can I help you?' series; Miss K.M. Oswald,

National Secretary of the Citizens' Advice Bureau Service; and S.K. Ruck, Deputy Chief Welfare Officer, London County Council). Bridges was immediately anxious because he felt that Fraser's position was delicate by virtue of the Government's views about propaganda and Fraser's previous background (he was a Leader Writer for the *Daily Herald* from 1930 to 1939, before he joined the Ministry of Information). Bridges wrote to Padmore on 29 September 1952: 'Do you think it would be a good thing for you or I to warn him of the difficulties and dangers of the ill-judged publicity which might follow on this discussion and to suggest to him that he should mind his step rather carefully?' Later, Bridges wrote to his Private Secretary, T.J. (later Sir Timothy) Bligh, 'Please find a suitable occasion to get Sir R.F. to look in'.[22] Fraser must have taken to heart Bridges' advice because, the next year, when he was being considered for the position of Director-General of the British Council, Bridges wrote: 'He has lived up entirely to the non-political and non-partisan ideal of a Civil Servant since he took on Government service ...'.[23]

The fourth example took place when, in the autumn of 1949, Sir Edwin (now Lord) Plowden, then Chief Planning Officer, H.M. Treasury, was disturbed by statements in the press that his name was 'mud' with the Tory Party. He saw Bridges and explained how awkward it would be for him if, at the following election, a Conservative Government was returned and promptly dismissed him from office with contumely. Bridges was sympathetic and said that as he had helped to persuade him to accept the planning job in the public interest Plowden should not be exposed in this way. Bridges added that he would take informal steps to clear the position up. He first spoke privately to Mr Henry Hopkinson MP, who had once been a colleague in the Cabinet Office, then he wrote letters to Hopkinson on 21 December 1949 and 5 January 1950 He argued strongly on behalf of Plowden, and concluded:

... So you will see that there is really nothing about Plowden's present job which really has any political flavour about it. You will, I know, sympathise with my point of view as someone who has responsibilities for the manning of the higher posts in the Civil Service. Is it not unfortunate that when a man is doing an essential public job, and doing it really well, without any political bias, he should feel hampered by the fear that on a change of Government his appointment may suddenly be terminated - and terminated too in a way which might reflect adversely on the work he had been doing, and therefore damage his future.[24]

The fifth example illustrating Bridges' non-partisan approach happened in 1952 when Sir Godfrey Ince, Permanent Secretary to the Ministry of Labour and National Service, made a public statement in Nottingham that was interpreted by Sir Donald Fergusson, Permanent Secretary to the Ministry of Fuel and Power, as being contrary to Government policy. Fergusson wrote a strong letter to Bridges on 4 April saying that Ince's action 'was unprecedented and quite contrary to all recognised rules governing the conduct of Civil Servants', and he added that if Bridges did not see Ince about it he would report the matter to his minister. In due course, on 6 May, Bridges raised the matter in a jocular spirit with Ince and found that Ince thought that what he had said was in accord with the views of the Chairman of the National Coal Board. Bridges indicated that Ince's speech had given rise to a remote rumbling of thunder in certain other departments, but Bridges seemed pleased to have kept the issue a low key one. However, Ince continued making public speeches and in February 1954 there was a leading article in *The Times* referring to one of his speeches. There were also reports in *The Times*, the *Financial Times*, the *Daily Herald* and the *Manchester Guardian*. Bridges again had a word with Ince and warned him of the danger that questions might be asked about him doing the Minister's work. Bridges noted: 'I have no doubt that the moral of what I said sunk home and I don't think I hurt any feelings'.[25]

After his retirement Bridges became, on occasions, even more active in defence of his colleagues who were unable to defend themselves. A significant example occurred in 1966 when Nora Beloff wrote an article in *The Observer* in which she said: '... Sir Thomas (Padmore) has run the Ministry of Transport since Mr Marples' heyday in 1962. He does not share Mrs Castle's enthusiasm for an integrated transport system, and his removal would have breached the accepted Civil Service mythology that officials have no private views of their own ...'.[26] (It was some time later, with the publication of *The Castle Diaries*, that Mrs Castle revealed that she had tried to get Padmore moved when she became Minister of Transport in 1965).[27] Bridges was furious when he read the article in *The Observer*. He wrote to *The Times*:

... the advice given by civil servants to their ministers is confidential, as the Prime Minister has recently reaffirmed. The rumours which have been given currency cannot be based on any authentic information; and it is wholly unfair that civil servants who cannot reply, and whose professional code prohibits them from revealing what advice they have given, should be attacked in this way. Nothing does more to undermine the confidence of the Civil Service as a whole, and its capacity to get on with its work, loyally serving the Government of the day as a permanent Service must do, than this kind of baseless attack on the professional integrity of those who carry the heaviest responsibilities.

Experience over many years shows that a factor which has had great influence on recruitment in any given period is the view taken by public opinion of its leading public servants: the sort of people who hold the senior posts, the nature of the duties for which they are responsible, and the general esteem in which they are held.

A series of statements belittling and denigrating the work and standing of some of its senior members can only worsen recruitment to the Civil Service.[28]

The next week he again wrote to *The Times*:

... no Civil Servant worth his salt can ever disclose what view he has taken in advising his Minister, and recent gossip about the views of individuals has plainly been as wide of the mark as it is unfair ...

The main point of my letter of February 18 was that the proper functioning of a permanent Civil Service depends on certain conditions. Of these, one of the most important is that the advice given by senior Civil Servants to their Ministers is confidential.[29]

Bridges' determination personally to maintain these standards is characterised by three illustrations. First, after Bridges had retired Lord Kemsley wrote asking him whether, at some future occasion, *The Sunday Times* could communicate with him. Bridges also received an approach from *The Times*. In his reply to Kemsley he said he would have one qualification: '... if I contributed anything which touched on public affairs, it should be pretty objective. I would not want anyone to say that a former Secretary to the Treasury had gone out of his way to be critical of the policy or leaders of either political party ...'.[30]

The second illustration concerns part of Bridges' evidence to the Masterman Committee on the Political Activities of Civil Servants. Bridges told the Committee on 15 July 1948 that he did not subscribe to any political party, but if he wanted to do so he would be very careful not to subscribe in such a way that anybody would find out he had done so. He thought that everyone in the higher ranks of the civil service 'would feel it incumbent upon them to observe that amount of discretion'.[31]

The third illustration occurred in 1949 when Edward Muir, of the First Division Association, wrote to Bridges suggesting he might become a member of the FDA. Bridges replied:

> ... I have thought this over, and I am afraid that the short answer must be that I cannot do what you suggest. The reason is that there are certain occasions on which it would, I think, be an embarrassment to me to be a member of the Association, even if my only connection with it was to pay you 10s. a year. I am sorry, but there it is.[32]

A good example of Bridges ensuring that his own position was defended when he was the focus of controversy occurred in 1948. In early November Attlee asked Bridges to serve as one of the five representatives of H.M. Government on the Committee to be set up in Paris to consider and report on the steps to be taken towards a greater measure of European unity. When the appointment became known Churchill commented about the Head of the Civil Service becoming involved in partisan politics. He also made reference to the unfortunate results in the case of Sir Horace Wilson. Bridges was disturbed by this and wrote to Laurence Helsby, then Prime Minister's Private Secretary, about it on 19 November.[33] He stressed that since being appointed Head of the Civil Service he had tried extremely hard to avoid anything which would keep alive the controversy about the Head of the Civil Service. He added that if more needed to be said about this matter he would be glad if the following two points could be brought out. The first was that he had not been appointed as a British Government representative but because he was thought to have had a wide experience of governmental and inter-governmental affairs and it was thought that this experience would be useful to the Delegation. Secondly - because it exploded the parallel with Sir Horace Wilson - Bridges' appointment had the full concurrence of the Foreign Office (and he added that it might be an advantage if this second point could be stated by a spokesman of the Foreign Office). In the event, however, the controversy quickly passed, and in the House of Commons debate Dalton, then Chancellor of the Duchy of Lancaster, referred to Bridges and said: '... there is no man in this country ... who has a better knowledge of the details and machinery of government and how it works ... He is an expert, and as such he is, of course, adviser to me'.[34]

Bridges recognised the significance of his position as adviser and, in a wholly non-partisan sense, was a very active and successful politician. Giving the sort of advice which only he, as a professional, could give, was a source of great satisfaction. He made this clear in evidence to the Priestley Royal Commission on the Civil Service when he explained that the day he became assistant secretary was the most important day in his official life until he became a permanent secretary. Promotion to that particular level in the civil service meant going through an important door: 'You were head of a division; you were running your own show, and when the permanent secretary or the Minister wanted to know about a particular thing, it was you he sent for; you produced a memorandum and gave the advice, and in your own little way you were "it"'.[35]

There were, of course, numerous occasions when the advice Bridges gave was clearly political and he was never averse to acting politically. Sometimes this was because he was asked for his advice as an expert on how government worked, sometimes he acted politically in the interests of the civil service (i.e. a facet of his style of leadership), sometimes he was prompted to do so simply by his conception of the public good. Again, there are plenty of illustrations that could be quoted but the following are a few examples.

First, there was considerable concern in 1945 about the post-war housing situation. According to Sir Malcolm Eve, who saw Bridges on 13 June, the problem was aggravated by a lack of any clear definition of responsibility in the Ministry of Works. On 15 June Bridges spoke about it to Sir Percival Robinson, the Permanent Secretary. He told Robinson that he had learned from several sources that not much progress had been made in settling the lines of responsibility in the Ministry of Works. Robinson agreed that this was so, and said it was because the Minister, Mr Duncan Sandys, could not make up his mind about the proposals put to him. Bridges recorded:

I said that if it would be of any help to him, he could tell his Minister from me that it was common gossip in Whitehall that nobody in the Ministry of Works knew what his job was, for the reason that no proper system of responsibility had been laid down; and that he, Sir Percival Robinson as the Permanent Secretary responsible for administration, should press his Minister very strongly to put the matter right without delay ...[36]

The second example took place when Bridges was chairing a steering committee on Economic Development which was responsible for producing the 1947 White Paper on Economic Planning. The Cabinet agreed that the Prime Minister should put his name to a Foreword stressing the seriousness of the situation. This Foreword was in fact prepared by Bridges but he felt it wise not to include (as the Cabinet had suggested) reference to the difficulties inherited from earlier administrations. In his minute to the Prime Minister Bridges explained:

> With respect, it seems to me that if this direction is carried out literally, it would completely nullify the main purpose of the White Paper itself and of the foreword. I do not see how it is possible at one and the same time to call for a united effort from the whole nation to meet a grave national crisis, and to include a passage with the deliberate purpose of introducing an element of party strife.
>
> May I also add this. As I said in my minute of 12th February, a foreword by the Prime Minister to a White Paper is unusual but I believe it is fully justified by the present situation. On the other hand, I feel that you might expose yourself to the risk of criticism if the foreword were to differ from the White Paper in that it included Party political matters.
>
> I hope I have not exceeded my brief in setting out these points. I should not have felt happy if I had not brought them to your notice.[37]

A third example occurred in 1948 when the Chancellor of the Exchequer thought it would be possible to reform the law on betting and gambling without first having another Royal Commission on the subject, and he referred to this in his budget speech. Bridges sought advice from colleagues in the Treasury and on 3 May sent the Chancellor a carefully reasoned paper outlining the arguments for and against creating a new Royal Commission. The general advice from the Treasury and the Home Office was to let sleeping dogs lie. However, the most interesting aspect of Bridges' advice was really both political and practical. He argued that the last Royal Commission had taken a year and if there was to be a new Royal Commission it might report before the next General Election, which would almost certainly be embarrassing to the Government. He added: 'The legislative programme for the next two sessions of Parliament is pretty full up already. I would have thought it was quite likely that you would not get a Betting Bill until the first or second session of the new Parliament. And there will be some practical advantage in not having the Royal Commission's report until a year or so before the legislation is to be introduced'. In fact, the terms of reference and membership of the new Royal Commission were not announced until 11 February 1949. At first sight, this may appear to be a case of civil servants blocking the intentions of ministers. However, their views did not originate from ideological or partisan interests but in terms of the practicalities of the proposal. From the perspective of the civil servants the Government had to be reminded of its heavy legislative programme and they also had to be asked how much priority should be given to this issue.[38]

A fourth example concerned rearmament. In 1950 Bridges wrote to William Armstrong about Rearmament and U.S. aid for it, saying:

> ... the position on the paper about defence finance really affects our economic and financial position over the next two or three years fundamentally; and from this point of view I imagine that the Prime Minister would probably wish for a final decision to be taken at a meeting of the Cabinet. If it is not, there is always a risk of difficulties with Ministers in charge of the social services - risks which may repercuss on the Treasury.
>
> I am sure that all this is in the Chancellor's mind but I thought there would be no harm in my putting it down in a note.[39]

The fifth illustration of Bridges giving political advice happened in 1951 when Mr Harold Macmillan (later Lord Stockton) the newly appointed Minister of Housing and Local Government, persuaded

W. and T. Avery Ltd to release Sir Percy (later Lord) Mills, with whom Macmillan had worked during the war, in an honorary capacity to help with the drive to increase house building. Macmillan obtained Bridges' advice on how to do this and consequently Mills was initially appointed 'To review the arrangements for carrying out the housing programme and to advise Ministers ...' However, Bridges warned Macmillan on 26 November that he was absolutely convinced that to appoint Mills to a post of this nature without first defining its duties and relating its responsibilities to the rest of the organisation could only lead to muddle and confusion, and incidentally also to friction. Later, Macmillan proposed to give Mills a prominent position in other areas of the department's work, which had no connection with housing. This seemed to Sir Thomas Sheepshanks, the Permanent Secretary, to cut at the root of his own authority and usefulness and he pointed out to Macmillan the dangers of importing a friend into a very high post in a department to deal with matters of a general administrative character. He warned that the example might be followed by subsequent Governments. Sheepshanks informed Bridges what had happened and sought his advice.

In April, while Sheepshanks was on holiday, Bridges called on Macmillan to say that he would not have a happy department unless he took his Permanent Secretary into his confidence and let him know what he meant to do, and did not try all sorts of clever tricks behind his back. On 23 May Bridges saw Sheepshanks again about the curious antics of his Minister but they agreed it would be a mistake for Bridges to see Macmillan again, to tell him how badly he was behaving, because he was probably incorrigible - but it was also agreed that if Bridges met Macmillan for some other reason he would take advantage of the opportunity to tell Macmillan privately how difficult he was making the working of the whole office by his ridiculous behaviour.[40]

These examples illustrate Bridges' approach to the political attitudes and political beliefs of civil servants. It was an approach distilled from years of contact with civil servants and ministers, but also influenced by the example of Warren Fisher and others and by the experience of significant cases. When distilled by Bridges into succinct statements of principle in his lectures and broadcasts, what Bridges had to say quickly became revered and widely used for teaching about the British civil service. Indeed, it has become a feature of the literature on the British civil service to derive precepts of public administration from experience rather than from laying down *a priori* canons or codes of practice.

By example, too, Bridges made a significant contribution to public administration practice. Whilst he was sensitive to issues that involved partisan elements he steered clear of any known association with them - by the time he became Head of the Civil Service he may have been incapable of adopting a partisan line. However, this did not prevent him from behaving politically in the public interest or in the interest of constitutional propriety or to protect the civil service or particular individuals within it.

Bridges and the Masterman Enquiry

One of the major controversies during Bridges' career as Head of the Civil Service concerned the rights of civil servants to participate in partisan, or potentially partisan, political activities. The setting up of the Masterman Committee and the events following the publication of its report are important to this study for two reasons. First, they provide an illustration of some of the sensitive issues associated with political attitudes and political behaviour. Secondly, and more importantly, Bridges' major and extremely time-consuming role in the deliberations surrounding this enquiry clearly indicates the political nature of some aspects of his work.

The independence of the civil service from party politics is achieved in three main ways. First, by the method of appointments; secondly, by tradition; and thirdly, by civil service regulations.

How the method of recruitment is used for this purpose was explained in evidence given to the Masterman Committee on the Political Activities of Civil Servants by Sir Percival Waterfield, First Civil Service Commissioner. In his evidence on 16 November 1948 Waterfield explained:

The man we are looking for is above all things a man who is capable of taking an objective view of any problem presented to him and of advising upon it impartially and judicially. If he is subjective, biased or prejudiced from the start, he is not really suitable for the administrative class of the Civil Service; so we do take a great deal of pains to discover whether a man can view these questions in such a way, not from the angle of political partisanship, but in regard to any kind of question of whatever nature such as well-educated, intelligent young persons think about, and our questions are particularly directed to discover the answer to that question.[41]

This approach was further emphasised in other evidence to the Committee. For example, Mr S.P. (later Sir Paul) Osmond, writing about the attitude of higher civil servants in a paper dated 14 June 1948, said: '... if his approach to public affairs is a party one, he lacks at least one qualification for an administrative career ... in the public service'.[42]

The extremes to which the civil service has been known to go in preserving its party political neutrality can be illustrated by various examples, one of the most noteworthy of these being the advice from Mr B.W. (later Sir Bernard) Gilbert in connection with the 1926 case of an ex-service temporary clerk in the Scottish Board of Health who was active in local political organisations. Gilbert wrote: 'I think he should be blacklisted ... the fact that when he had to make a choice between the two (the objectionable offices and reemployment) he chose to retain the political office probably denotes not only political convictions but also an opinion that they were likely to last longer than a temporary clerkship'.[43]

As far as tradition is concerned, there can be no better illustration than the evidence to the Masterman Committee from Bridges. He explained on 15 July 1948 that the experience of the civil servant

> ... leads him to be a different kind of animal altogether from the politician. The whole training you have in the Civil Service leads you, when you tackle a problem, first of all to direct yourself to getting the facts; you are given a statement and you say, 'Is this really so, why is it so, and what evidence does it rest upon?' and you check it and counter-check it and you say 'I wonder whether this is really true, let us ask somebody who has got a different angle of approach to it' and then you look to see what the different consequences of it are and finally you are in a position to put something up to your Minister which is really pretty hard boiled as far as facts and probable consequences are concerned. That sort of training does by degrees induce an outlook and a frame of mind which is quite different from the politician's ... I think that people who have lived that sort of life for some years ... definitely have an outlook of mind which does not lead them to be either Conservative or Labour or hostile to Conservative or hostile to Labour. It is a different outlook of mind.[44]

It is, however, the third way of achieving independence from party politics, by regulations, that is the main focus of this section. As far as possible, Bridges avoided issuing regulations. He disliked having to prohibit something which was not previously prohibited, and he disliked interfering with people's private lives unless it was absolutely unavoidable.[45] However, it was necessary to have some basic rules of guidance in particular circumstances, especially where political activities were concerned.

In 1921 the Labour Party Conference had passed a resolution pressing for the removal of the ban upon Parliamentary candidature by civil servants. The demand was aired in Parliament and the press and the Prime Minister Mr Lloyd George (later Earl Lloyd George of Dwyfor) received a deputation from the Labour Party on 18 August 1921. The question did not become acute, however, until the first Labour Government came to power. The Government was then pressed by sections of the civil service to grant civil servants equality of civil rights with the Navy and Army (in particular this meant the right to stand for Parliament). On 22 March 1924 Mr Philip (later Lord) Snowden, then Chancellor of the Exchequer, received a deputation from the staff organisations affiliated to the Civil Service National Whitley Council, and promised to order an enquiry. The Committee on Parliamentary Etc Candidature of Crown Servants was therefore appointed under the chairmanship of Lord Blanesburgh to enquire into 'the existing regulations governing the candidature for Parliament and for municipal bodies of persons in the service of the Crown'. It enquired into the existing regulations (Statutes, Orders in Council and departmental rules) and also the unwritten rules on the subject, and considered whether there should be any changes. The staff associations affiliated to the National Whitley Council argued that the existing restrictions were unnecessary and alluded to the distinction drawn between civil servants and members of the armed forces. In general, the Blanesburgh Report supported the existing arrangements: in using the language of another sphere of activity, it said 'there is a middle course between forbidding Crown servants to play cricket and extending to them the necessary facilities to become full-time members of county elevens or even to undertake Australian tours'.[46] The main recommendations of the Committee were that the existing ban on the Parliamentary candidature of civil servants without prior resignation should be maintained but that industrial employees in the Service Departments should be free to stand as Parliamentary candidates without resigning.

The Committee reported in 1925, after a change of Government had occurred. During the period between the presentation of the Report and the announcement of the Government's attitude to it, the Committee's recommendations were discussed at staff association conferences and resolutions of disapproval were received at the Treasury. Meanwhile, the Report was submitted to the Cabinet by Churchill, then Chancellor of the Exchequer. Without consultation with the Staff Side, the Government announced, on 7 July 1925, that they had decided to give effect to the Committee's recommendations so far as they were unanimous. The Staff Side was apparently not consulted at any stage about the implementation of the Report's recommendations.[47]

Bridges, while engaged in establishments work in the Treasury, had much to do with the Blanesburgh enquiry and its follow-up. He prepared the Order in Council which implemented the Blanesburgh recommendations[48] and also organised meetings in the Treasury to discuss the use of words and phrases in the Blanesburgh Report and in the Order in Council.[49]

From the 1920s Bridges also had experience of dealing with civil service unions and acquired opinions and attitudes which may have influenced him for the rest of his civil service career. For example, in 1927 he wrote of the Civil Service Civil Rights Defence Committee:

...it is in actual fact in the closest possible touch with the TUC and the Labour Party. The Committee is in fact just such an example of the intimate connection between Civil Service Associations and political parties as it is desired to avoid.

For this reason I think that we should, if possible, be extremely chary of recognising this Committee...

Much might be said as to the political activities - lobbying etc - of Civil Service Associations. However much we dislike it, it is virtually impossible to stop this sort of thing.[50]

From time to time after Blanesburgh reported political activities other than Parliamentary candidature became sensitive. One example occurred in 1941 when the Executive Committee of the Civil Service Clerical Association passed various resolutions for the more effective prosecution of the Second World War. These included calling for a purging of the public services of 'Munich' elements, removing the ban on the *Daily Worker*, and the immediate establishment of a Second Front. This caused considerable debate in the Treasury. Mr B.D. (later Sir Bruce) Fraser proposed disciplinary action against the civil servants concerned and also argued for other possible actions including withdrawal of the Certificate of Approval held by the CSCA in accordance with the Regulations made under Section 5 of the Trade Disputes and Trade Unions Act 1927[51] (this would have made it illegal for any established civil servant to be a member of the Association). Mr E.H. (later Sir Edward) Ritson also argued for firm action: 'No one should be in doubt where we stand, and the limit of Civil Service freedom in political matters should be clearly established'.[52] Bridges was not officially involved in the issue but it is unlikely that he was unaware of the feelings expressed in the Treasury; he may also have been consulted. He was almost certainly aware that in May 1943 the Staff Side of the National Whitley Council asked for some relaxation of the restrictions on the political activities of civil servants.[53]

The 1927 Act, which placed considerable constraints on trade unions, was passed when political passion had been aroused by the general strike. Section 5 of the Act dealt specifically with civil service organisations and one of its main effects was to prevent established civil servants from belonging to associations which were associated with political parties, or from being affiliated to organisations containing non-civil servants. It was intended by this means to preserve the impartiality of the civil service. Over the years since 1927 blind eyes were turned to various things that were contrary to the letter or to the spirit of Section 5 and no great harm appeared to follow.[54]

There were a number of attempts to repeal the Act, including a deputation from the General Council of the TUC led by Mr E. Bevin which saw Mr Neville Chamberlain, the Prime Minister, in February 1939. There was also a TUC attempt in 1941 to get the Act repealed, and when that failed a special effort was made by the General Council of the TUC to persuade the Government to repeal Sections 5 and 6 only (i.e. the Sections of the Act which referred specifically to established civil servants and persons employed by local and public authorities). It is therefore not surprising that civil service staff associations were delighted when the Labour Government, elected in 1945, pledged itself to repeal the Act.[55]

The prospect of repealing the 1927 Act stimulated the associations to reconsider what might be done to resolve the anomalies about personal political activities by civil servants (towards which a blind eye had also been turned in some departments). Sir Alan Barlow in the Treasury had taken the line that nothing could be done about the political activities of individual civil servants until the controversy about Section 5 of the Trade Disputes and Trade Unions Act had been resolved. In the autumn of 1945 the Chairman of the Staff Side of the National Whitley Council therefore wrote to the Chancellor of the Exchequer pointing out that the repeal of the 1927 Act was now settled policy and asking for a decision on the other matter. In particular he suggested that there should be a relaxation of the restrictions on political activities of the lower grades in the civil service. Part of their complaint was that the rules were being applied unevenly in different departments. Bridges wrote a covering note for the Chancellor in which he admitted that there were differences between the practice of departments. He said that an enquiry might show that in certain respects the position could be made easier. He then added: 'But on the whole I believe that there is very little wrong with the present position. Moreover, in a matter of this kind there is a good deal to be said for a certain absence of rigidity, and I should deprecate the attempt to lay down a precise code as to what civil servants in particular grades or departments can and cannot do with propriety'.[56] He advised delay until after the Bill to repeal the 1927 Act had received its Second Reading; Dalton agreed. He also suggested an outside body to look into the matter, involving representatives of the main political parties; Dalton thought not. Bridges suggested telling the Staff Side that there was nothing seriously wrong with the present position. Dalton responded: 'Don't commit yourself to this'.

The Chancellor brought the matter to the attention of the Cabinet committee chaired by the Lord President on 16 November 1945 when it was considering the Second Reading of its Trade Disputes and Trade Unions Bill (which was to repeal the 1927 Act). The Lord President's committee thought this might be a more complex problem than at first appeared and therefore proposed that a small committee of ministers should examine the question and report back on it.[57]

The committee of ministers was quickly set up under Dalton, then Chancellor of the Exchequer. Its other members were Mr J. Chuter Ede, Home Secretary, Mr G.A. Isaacs, Minister of Labour and National Service, the Earl of Listowel, Postmaster General, and Mr A.V. Alexander, First Lord of the Admiralty: the secretaries were Mr W.S. (later Sir William) Murrie and Miss D.C.L. Hacket, both from the Treasury. At its first meeting, on 9 January 1946, the committee had a general discussion, exchanging their views on the subject. For its second meeting, on 31 January, it asked for a draft report to be prepared by officials to show the background to the problem, the existing rules, and recommendations in accordance with the views so far expressed by the committee.[58] When Bridges saw the draft he immediately called a meeting of a group of permanent secretaries on 6 February. Sir Donald Fergusson (Ministry of Fuel and Power) was unable to attend. But he felt very strongly about the matter and was extremely concerned about the draft Bridges had sent him of the report prepared for the ministerial committee. He said: 'There has been an increasing tendency in recent years for Civil Servants to be encouraged to become closely associated with the Labour Party ... Unless it is checked I forsee a situation in which Party politics will intrude into and impair the ordinary administrative work of Departments'.[59] After the meeting Bridges wrote a minute to the Chancellor drawing attention to the administrative difficulties that would follow from any relaxation of the rules along the lines being proposed. He put the position forcefully: 'I hope that I shall not be thought to be exceeding my function if I suggest ...' He then proposed that for the civil service in general, 'the existing rule against participation in politics should be retained and restated in categorical terms', but that the manipulative grades should be allowed the same political freedom as any other citizens, so long as they did not take part in political activities in uniform, in official time, or on official premises (but they should continue to be debarred from actual Parliamentary candidature).[60]

Bridges was invited to be present at the third meeting of the committee, on 5 March 1946, when his minute to the Chancellor and the draft report were discussed. He told the committee that he was very concerned that if there was to be greater freedom, departments would demand more precise definitions with more detailed guidance and if a dividing line were drawn between staff at different points in different departments it would have a serious effect on the team spirit in the civil service. The committee appreciated the administrative difficulties that might result from a relaxation of the restrictions but agreed that civil servants in the minor and manipulative grades should be permitted to become Parliamentary candidates without resigning. Because the existing rules had broken down, and many lower grade civil servants were already engaged in political activities, Bridges' proposals would in fact have limited the freedom then being enjoyed by some officials.

The Home Secretary felt that what was needed was a code of professional etiquette. The general sense of the committee was in favour of maintaining and, if possible, extending the existing degree of freedom and Bridges was therefore asked to consider whether there was any way the committee's intentions could be met without giving rise to the administrative difficulties he had outlined. Bridges again consulted a number of his senior colleagues (he wrote to them on 22 March and 17 April, then held a meeting in his room on 24 April).[61] He then wrote a further report which was circulated on 3 May 1946. This paper resolved some of the complexities by proposing a definition of 'minor and manipulative grades' for this purpose and also proposed revised rules for 'minor' political activities in the national field by non-industrial civil servants. However, Miss Hacket had no doubt that Bridges' view was 'that *any* alteration in the existing rules might have such disastrous consequences that the administrative difficulties did not really matter by comparison'.[62] It was clear that ministers would not have the time to spare to resolve all the issues themselves but it was also recognised that a committee of civil servants would be quite unsuitable for resolving the matter. The Chancellor, encouraged by Bridges, therefore began considering other ways to deal with the problem, including the possibility of an outside committee. Bridges' views were very clear on this:

> It seems to me this whole question of the political activities of civil servants is inherently one which should be dealt with on a non-party basis and obviously there is no better way of dealing with it than on the basis of the findings of an impartial Committee which would be universally accepted, and to put it bluntly, any very direct treatment of this subject might inadvertently stir up a degree of political controversy which would prevent, to some extent at any rate, that happy result of the impartial non-party treatment of this subject.[63]

Bridges took a leading part in preparing for this committee. He played an important role in drafting its terms of reference and proposing names for the committee. One of his first suggestions for chairman was Sir Oliver Franks, but this was vetoed by Dalton who wrote: 'Don't put Franks on to this second-class job. He is wanted if available for higher things'. After further extensive consultation Bridges recommended that Sir Philip Morris should be chairman. Later, after Morris declined, Mr J.C. (later Sir John) Masterman,

Provost of Worcester College, Oxford, was invited instead. Bridges was clearly very anxious about the subject and how it should be resolved. Indeed, in confirming his anxieties to Sir Donald Fergusson he added: 'If I have anything to do with it, I am determined to see to it that evidence is given not only by the Treasury but by the Permanent Heads of several other departments, particularly those who have staffs up and down the country which come into contact with the public'.[64] In fact, nineteen official witnesses from different departments were called and gave evidence to the Masterman Committee.[65]

The ministerial committee, however, did not meet again for nearly two years. During this period there was a change in the Chancellorship (Cripps succeeded Dalton) and also changes in the other membership. When it reconvened on 7 January 1948 the Postmaster General, then Mr Wilfrid Paling, emphasised that he was being pressed to alter the existing rules for Post Office staffs and he was therefore looking for early action on this matter. In addition, the Chancellor had been asked to receive a deputation from the Staff Side of the National Whitley Council, which was expected to urge much wider latitude than was ever being contemplated by the committee. After discussion, it was agreed to recommend to the Cabinet that an outside committee should be appointed.[66]

The membership of the committee was publicly announced on 14 April 1948: it had ten members, including the chairman. Bridges knew Masterman fairly well, not only from Oxford connections, the United University Club and their membership of the dining club to which they both belonged, but also through Eton College where they were both members of the governing body. Others on the committee included Mr. D.N. (later Sir Norman) Chester, Fellow of Nuffield College, Oxford, who had worked in the Cabinet Office during the war; Sir Richard Hopkins, who had been Permanent Secretary to the Treasury 1942-45, and who, effectively, became Vice-Chairman of the committee;[67] and Dame Myra Curtis, then Principal of Newnham College, Cambridge, who had been a civil servant 1915-41. As soon as Masterman was appointed he wrote on 4 April to Cripps, saying he would like a brief discussion with him. Masterman then invited Mr F.C. Newton, of the Treasury, who was to be the committee's secretary, to lunch at the United University Club. He also discussed his assignment with Bridges when they met at the United University Club before attending 'The Club' dinner on 27 April at the Charing Cross Hotel.[68] Masterman felt it right to have these informal discussions before his meeting with the Chancellor.

The terms of reference for the Masterman Committee were 'To examine the existing limitations on the political activities (both national and local) which may be undertaken by civilian Government staffs and to make recommendations as to any changes which may be desirable in the public interest'. Newton, as secretary to the committee, had an important role to play. The decisions about who to invite in certain categories of witnesses were essentially his and the committee's programme of work was largely prepared in advance of its first meeting. At the first meeting, on 18 May, Newton reported on the intentions of the Chancellor of the Exchequer in setting up the committee; the committee then agreed to invite Bridges to attend the second meeting, to give an introductory account of the existing position. Throughout the proceedings Newton kept Bridges in touch with the committee's progress; he also discussed with Bridges the contents of the note he was to send (on 27 May) to Heads of Departments, inviting them to give evidence.[69]

Bridges took a very close interest in the work of the committee as it proceeded: presumably he received copies of the minutes but he was also in frequent contact with Newton as well as seeing other members of the committee from time to time. When he gave his own evidence, early in the proceedings, it was a masterly performance. He was well primed about the sort of questions to expect and had the time and resources to prepare himself for the occasion. For example, Bridges was provided with a very detailed outline for his evidence, drafted by Newton and approved by Mrs Johnstone[70] (who, as Miss Hacket, had been one of the secretaries to the earlier ministerial committee). This draft was also circulated for comment to a number of colleagues in the Treasury. Both Newton and Johnstone were at this time working under the direction of Winnifrith who also took a close interest in their work. In addition, while Bridges' evidence was being planned and prepared he called a meeting on 23 March of twelve other permanent secretaries and three other Treasury officials to exchange views with them and so that they could have time to prepare their own evidence.[71] At the meeting, for which Newton acted as secretary, they were also provided with copies of Bridges' draft evidence (which, by then, had also been discussed and commented on by a number of Treasury officials). The draft was further amended after the meeting on 23 March. The general view at the meeting was that the introductory paragraph should be strengthened to place much greater emphasis on the need to maintain a non-political civil service which was in a position to give loyal service to the Government of the day, notwithstanding political changes. Other amendments were also proposed and Bridges agreed that the memorandum should be redrafted and copies of the revised version would be circulated to those who had been present.[72] Later, Bridges sent a copy to the Chancellor of the Exchequer with a covering note in which he said:

> I imagine that you would wish me to speak for myself and say what I believe and not to speak as the mouthpiece of Ministers. Nevertheless I would like you to know the general line I am going to take and I would like to feel that you are not unsympathetic to it.[73]

Further amendments were later made to the draft in June. When the final version was prepared Bridges sent it to a large number of heads of departments. This procedure seems to have been followed for two reasons. First, Bridges wanted his paper to be as nearly perfect as possible (and he was grateful for even the most minor suggestions for improvement). Secondly, it expressed the general concensus of the most senior civil servants - although it was, of course, presented as Bridges' personal opinions - and it was therefore likely to be used by them as an *aide memoire* when thinking about their own evidence.

Bridges' oral evidence was a masterly performance for another reason as well. He gave his evidence in a style that was both characteristically courteous but also contained fairly clear guidance towards the line on which he hoped the committee would report. At one point he put it like this:

> I feel it is rather impudent perhaps even to suggest a summary of the sort of points you might take, but if I am not going too far, I have a sketch of something which seems to me might be right. It would fall under four heads. The first would be factual and historical. The committee might draw attention to ... The third would be - and this depends on what you are going to say in the rest of you report - for my purposes I assume you might be basing yourself on something like the line of demarcation which I suggested to you but if it is a different line the argument is much the same only it would be

put with more or less emphasis ... Then we come to the last point, the really important point as to what is said about the future. The line I would humbly recommend to you is that you would say that you do not advocate any alteration of the law, that as regards nearly all the Associations catering for the grades above the line, it is very unlikely they would wish to affiliate to any political party, and that as regards civil servants above the line the Committee do not think it necessary to say more than that they thought it right to leave the matter in the main to the good sense of those concerned and relying on them if the Government accepted the Committee's recommendations to pay regard to those recommendations as a general guide as to the way in which they should govern themselves - no new rule, no change in the law, an exposé of the whole position and an injunction as to the need for rather greater discretion in a way which I hope will not cause ill-feeling or stir up any controversy.[74]

After the sixth meeting of the committee, Bridges provided a paper for circulation defining the grades which would fall above and below the line of demarcation he had proposed in an earlier memorandum.[75] Later, when the report was being drafted, the committee asked Bridges to give further evidence. Bridges immediately asked Newton for guidance on the questions he might expect - then he asked Newton to collect the information he would need for the answers. Newton was useful in other respects, too. As Bridges put it on 10 February 1949:

I do not think I dealt very successfully with the last point which the Masterman Committee put to me about permission for civil servants to talk at unofficial conferences and so forth. I think it would be useful if you could let me know a little bit of the sort of evidence they have had on the subject and if we could discuss the matter with the Third Secretary concerned ...[76]

In return, Bridges offered valuable help to Newton. For example, on 4 February Bridges prepared a note on 'Association Activities' which began: 'This is my idea of the substance - not the wording - of the line I would like the Committee to take ...' This note was later revised by Bridges, with Padmore's help, and a final version was sent to Newton on 8 February 1949. Paragraphs 75 and 76 of the published report are word for word from this draft by Bridges.[77]

The report of the Masterman Committee was published in June 1949. It said that the Committee had tried to find a balance between two conflicting principles. One was the desirability in a democratic society for all citizens to have a voice in the affairs of the State and for as many as possible to play an active part in public life. The other was that 'The public interest demands the maintenance of political impartiality in the Civil Service and of confidence in that impartiality as an essential part of the structure of Government in this country.'[78] (these words were very similar to passages in Bridges' memorandum submitted to the Committee on 2 July 1948).[79] The Committee reasserted that 'the political neutrality of the Civil Service was a fundmental feature of British democratic government and essential for its efficient operation.' However, it suggested that 'in applying the general principles a distinction could be made between those grades whose participation in political activities might imperil public confidence and the efficiency of the civil service, and those whose activities would involve no such risk. It therefore recommended that a line of demarcation be drawn below the administrative, professional, scientific, technical, executive, clerical and typing grades and, apart from certain exceptions, above the minor and manipulative and the industrial grades. Those below the line would be permitted greater liberty than those above it'.[80] It concluded that the results of its recommendations, if accepted, would be 'to maintain the existing limitations ... subject to variations in detail'.[81]

The Report was signed by the Committee on 26 April. On 31 May Cripps signed a memorandum for the Cabinet about the Report. He said: 'In my view the report is a good and sensible document. Moreover, it is unanimous (save on one very small point) and it comes from a strong and impartial Committee representing all shades of political opinion. My recommendation to my colleagues is that the report should be accepted'.[82] The Cabinet considered the matter on 21 June and decided that the Report should be published and also that the Chancellor should make a statement at the time of publication that they had decided to accept its recommendations. In a written answer to an arranged Parliamentary Question in the House of Commons the Chancellor of the Exchequer therefore announced on 28 June 1949 that copies of the Report would be available in the Vote Office after Questions, that the Government had decided to accept the Committee's recommendations, and that detailed arrangements would be promulgated as soon as possible.[83] The press comment on the Report was not unfavourable. The only editorial comment was a favourable leading article in *The Daily Telegraph*; the *Daily Herald* and *The Worker* suggested that the National Staff Side were to ask for a postponement of action until they had considered it. It is unlikely that the Chancellor took these actions without consulting Bridges, especially as Bridges has written of Cripps' practice of holding morning meetings with his senior advisers,[84] but there appears to be no record of any consultation before the Chancellor's announcement in the House of Commons. In any case, the timetable and order of events at this stage seems to have been set by the Cabinet.

The unions reacted strongly. They were upset for three main reasons. First, in their opinion more anomalies would be caused than already existed if the recommendations were implemented. The unions felt that if a line had to be drawn, it was proposed to be drawn in the wrong place. Secondly, because the existing rules were not in fact observed in relation to local government, the recommendations would restrict freedoms. Thirdly, the Government announced the adoption of the Report before consulting the Staff Side of the National Whitley Council: indeed, its acceptance of the recommendations was given in the House of Commons before the unions had an opportunity to read the Report. On 29 June Mr A.J.T. (later Sir Albert) Day, Chairman of the Staff Side of the National Whitley Council, wrote to Cripps asking him to delay putting the recommendations into effect until the Staff Side had considered the position. Before he went on leave on 30 June Day told Newton he thought that the Report was 'deplorable'.[85] Newton, writing to Padmore, said that Day was 'obviously piqued' because the Masterman Committee had rejected the Staff Side's suggestions. The CSCA issued a circular on 4 July referring to 'the hypocrisy of the report with its platitudinous references to the integrity of the civil service' and said that its recommendations would create such absurd anomalies as to make its proposals quite unworkable.[86] Stanley Mayne, on behalf of the Institution of Professional Civil Servants, also protested in a short, well-argued letter to the Financial Secretary to the Treasury.[87]

When the Staff Side of the National Whitley Council met on 7 July it asked its secretary, T.R. Jones, to write immediately to Cripps asking him to defer action on the recommendations until they had been considered by the National Whitley Council. Jones wrote to Cripps the same day. He also wrote immediately to Bridges asking him to call a meeting of the Council 'at the earliest possible moment'.[88] Mr Peter Freeman put down a Question for answer in the House of Commons on 13 July. Bridges, writing to Padmore about it, said: 'Judging by Mr Peter Freeman's Question, and the protests, the Staff Side are trying to work up an agitation that the Masterman Committee's Report puts the clock back and is an illiberal document. We must not allow this to have any success and must concert counter-measures. Please consider this'.[89] On 12 July Newton wrote a note for consideration by the Official Side of the National Whitley Council referring to the representations that had alleged the Masterman Report was an illiberal document. He stressed that it was important that the misrepresentation should not succeed.[90]

Bridges wrote to Masterman on 13 July (the letter being drafted by Newton) asking for clarification about the meaning of paragraph 87 in the Report, about participation in local government activities.[91] The Staff Side was interpreting that paragraph as preventing a civil servant above the line but who had received permission to stand as a local candidate, from sitting on the same platform as other candidates wearing party labels, joining in a combined election address with them, and canvassing on behalf of other candidates of the same party. Consequently, they were arguing that a new restriction was being recommended.

This indicated the extent to which the Staff Side was getting worked up. The real reason, however, was that as they had raised the issue in the first place, they felt they ought to have been consulted before the Government announced its acceptance of the recommendations of the Masterman Committee. The position was made worse when the matter was raised in an adjournment debate in the House of Commons and the Report was poorly defended by a junior Lord of the Treasury on his first appearance at the despatch box.[92] Furthermore, as Masterman noted, the Conservative Opposition in the House of Commons was being both opportunist and obtuse.[93]

In the Treasury it was, in fact, Newton and Padmore who received the numerous protest letters and decided what should be done about them. After formal acknowledgement they were simply added to the file. Bridges was, however, kept fully informed. He asked Newton[94] to check on the evidence to see what the Staff Side and associated bodies had said about the anomalies of the existing position, which they were now alleging: Newton replied immediately with all the references.

On 16 July Bridges wrote to his colleagues on the Official Side of the National Whitley Council. He outlined the situation to them, indicated that he thought there would be some doubt about the meaning of paragraph 87 of the Report, about participation in local government, and argued that 'As the government have accepted the Masterman Report without waiting to hear what the general public or the officials of the Staff Associations think about it, it is imperative that we should not appear in any doubt as to what the report means,' and convened a meeting of the Official Side on 19 July to discuss their position.[95]

The meeting of the Official Side on 19 July, with Bridges as Chairman and Newton as Secretary, included ten departmental representatives plus two from the Treasury. It focused its discussion on the potentially controversial aspects of participation in local government. The general opinion of the Official Side was that the report was a good one, they believed there was no evidence in departments of agitation against it, and they decided that at the meeting of the National Whitley Council on 22 July (the first to be held for eight years) their role would be to listen to the Staff Side's case without discussing the merits of their arguments: any comment was to be confined to points of fact.[96]

The meeting on 22 July was a large gathering. Apart from the Chairman and the secretaries from both the Official Side (Newton) and the Staff Side (Jones) there were forty-two others present. After the Staff Side's case was clearly and forcefully presented by Day, who argued for a compromise somewhere between the Staff Side's original proposals (i.e. freedom exercised with discretion) and the Committee's recommendations, the Official Side withdrew to discuss their reactions. It was agreed at the meeting to report the discussion to ministers and reconvene the next week; meanwhile, no action would be taken on the Masterman Report. On 26 July the Liaison Committee of the Labour Party received a delegation from Labour Members of Parliament, including some of the 'Civil Service' MPs. Two days later, on 28 July, the Cabinet agreed to suspend action on the Masterman recommendations for the time being.

After the meeting Bridges immediately sought advice from his colleagues by circulating a memorandum and soliciting comments. He was particularly anxious to discuss the line of action to be recommended to ministers. Although he stressed the strength of feeling in the Staff Side, Bridges recalled that no consultation with the Staff Side had occurred after the Blanesburgh Committee reported in 1925. However, he recognised how important were the tactics to be adopted. He added: 'I think it is open to question whether the Government would be wise even at this stage to refuse to listen in Whitley discussion to what the Staff Side have to say. We should be on more secure ground in holding to the conclusion of the Masterman Report if we had done so'.[97]

Bridges called a meeting of permanent secretaries on 29 July. They were concerned about possible weakening of the Masterman proposals and felt strongly that the question of the political activities of civil servants was a matter of high Government policy, not a Whitley matter. Nevertheless, it was thought prudent to see what sort of compromise the Staff Side was prepared to accept. This meeting was followed, the next day, by an adjournment debate in the House of Commons, which showed that pressure would be brought by the civil service unions on MPs, irrespective of party. There was a very poor attendance for the debate and criticisms were made from both sides of the House — mainly because of the Government's acceptance of the recommendations of the Masterman Committee without consultation. Newton prepared a draft brief for Capt. J.W. Snow, who replied in the debate on behalf of the Financial Secretary.[98] Soon afterwards Bridges gave an account of events to the Prime Minister, together with his comments on them, suggesting that he might be permitted to find out from the Staff Side what their suggestions might be.[99] Attlee agreed: 'The question of the political rights to be allowed to Civil Servants is a matter of high State policy. There cannot, in my view, be any question of negotiation on the general principles ...'.[100]

After initial discussion on 22 August between Padmore, Bridges and Day, Bridges wrote to Day about this on 23 August, inviting him to submit the Staff Side's recommendations within the general principles of the Report. In reply, the Staff Side submission was dated 31 August. This was discussed by Bridges and permanent officials and on 16 September some Treasury officials were sympathetic to the Staff Side reaction. The consequences of the Masterman recommendations were expected to do away with the vagueness and uncertainty of the existing rules but this would mean some tightening up and new restrictions in many departments. As Mrs D.R. Williams (who acted as secretary to the 16 September meeting) had put it to Padmore on 9 September 1949: 'The Masterman Committee was not set up because there was any suggestion that the existing rules were too lax, either on paper or in practice, but primarily in order to consider whether increased freedom could be granted ...'.[101]

The details of these developments were written up by Mrs E.M. Abbot, subsequently amended by Padmore and Bridges, then referred to Cripps and Attlee. Attlee decided that the matter should be considered again by the Cabinet. Bridges' advice to the Chancellor at this time was perfectly clear: 'My advice is ... that the original decision to accept the Report as a whole should stand.' He considered possible concessions to the Staff Side and recommended they be rejected. He went on:

> You yourself took the view that the Government should decide either to accept the report as a whole as it stands or reject it. The Government decided on acceptance and events subsequent to that decision have not shown that it was wrong ... The Staff Side are seeking concessions which are inconsistent with the main theme of the Report and which are opposed by the whole weight of my senior colleagues, and which could not be considered without the risk of undermining the traditions of the Civil Service.[102]

This paper by Bridges, when Bridges' personal advice was deleted and other passages had been redrafted by Padmore in the light of comments by Cripps, became the substance of a paper from the Chancellor of the Exchequer to the Cabinet.[103]

At about this time Day again called on Bridges because he was concerned that those officials Masterman had recommended should be freed of restrictions should indeed be freed before the General Election (which was expected to be soon). Bridges promised to examine this point and let him know the result. The consequence was that the Government decided to implement all the Masterman recommendations to free certain groups of staff from all restrictions (i.e. those below the line of demarcation suggested in the Report); for the rest, to maintain the existing practice; and to postpone further consideration of the matter until towards the end of 1950 These arrangements were announced in Parliament on 1 November 1949.[104] During the winter months the main consequence in the Treasury was that discussion on the Masterman controversy was suspended. The election took place in February.

However, in September 1949, the Trades Union Congress had passed a resolution calling for 'Civil Rights for Civil Servants' and regretting the Labour Government's announcement of acceptance of the Masterman Report without any discussion with the civil service trade unions. After the election, on 2 March 1950, Vincent Tewson, General Secretary of the TUC, acting on instructions from the executive committee, sent a copy of the TUC resolution to Cripps and asked for consultations between the Government and the unions.[105] This was reinforced when Day wrote to Bridges on 19 April, saying that as the General Election was in February and the end of the year was now only eight months ahead, the Staff Side felt discussions ought to begin.[106] As a consequence Padmore wrote to Bridges on 2 May:

> we have to decide
> a) whether to embark now or soon on Whitley talks;
> b) if so, what our representation is to be
> c) what instructions we are to propose that Ministers should give us ...

Bridges then called another meeting of permanent secretaries on 18 May 1950. The meeting agreed that there had been no significant rule-breaking during the General Election, though a few minor incidents were reported. Bridges said that the Staff Side had asked for another meeting of the National Whitley Council, and added that they had suggested that detailed discussions might be resumed by a sub-committee. Although Bridges personally thought the Staff Side's suggestions should all be refused, he recognised that this would be likely to lead to renewed agitation and that ministers were not likely 'to stand pat in face of such a campaign.' It was therefore important to consider the tactics to be followed. The general opinion was against postponing a review of experience during the General Election but against offering concessions; it was also against setting up the proposed sub-committee. Instead, it favoured using the meeting of the National Whitley Council, as requested by the Staff Side, as an opportunity to listen to what the Staff Side had to say. Bridges consulted Cripps about this proposed procedure and Cripps agreed. Bridges therefore called a meeting of the Official Side on 12 June, and this was followed by a meeting of the full National Whitley Council (again, of forty persons). As no progress was made the meeting was soon adjourned. The Staff Side said they had already offered clear proposals in writing and were prepared to discuss them in a smaller forum. The Official Side said they were unable to agree to discussions in less than a meeting of the full Council. Immediately after the adjournment Bridges reconvened the Official Side. After discussion it was agreed to ask ministers to approve the opening of discussion on the Staff Side proposals, with a view to discussing whether any compromise solution would be possible, on the understanding that the Government would not be committed to the acceptance of any conclusions that might be reached. Afterwards, Bridges wrote to the Chancellor of the Exchequer reporting what had happened and proposing a joint committee from the National Whitley Council.[107] Cripps noted that 'upon this *very political issue* the PM must first be consulted.' Later, on 11 July, Attlee wrote: 'I agree.'

Bridges and Day corresponded about the arrangements, including the timing for the joint committee and it was agreed to have the first meeting in the autumn, after the main period for summer leave had passed. Bridges called another meeting of the Official Side in his room on 3 October 1950 It was a particularly free meeting which discussed the operational experience of the rules in the various departments with special reference to canvassing at local elections and the problems of exactly where a line might be drawn to differentiate the free from the restricted staff. This was useful preparation for the first meeting, on 4 October, of the joint committee (at which there were nineteen participants). That meeting was devoted to emphasising and discussing the general position of the two sides: the discussion was led by Dame Evelyn Sharp (for the Official Side) and Day (for the Staff Side). The second meeting was on 27 October. The procedure, which Bridges encouraged, was for the Official Side to explain their point of view and give the Staff Side an opportunity to discuss it and understand it before any compromise solutions were put forward. The consequence was the gradual emergence of a 'grey class,' an in-between class neither clearly free nor clearly unfree, intermediate between the grades indubitably above the line of demarcation and those indubitably below it. Discussions continued at the next meeting, on 15 November. On 22 November Bridges summoned a meeting of the Official Side to discuss details of the proposal for a 'grey class' (or what Sir John Maud, later Lord Redcliffe-Maud, preferred to call 'No man's land'). Bridges wrote after the meeting to all members of the Official Side, with an account of what had been discussed. Meanwhile there was a great deal of correspondence between the Treasury and departments about the details of the proposal for a 'grey class.'

The joint committee met again on 6 December and discussed the exact extent of the 'grey class' and how anomalies might be accommodated. On 3 January 1951 Bridges again called a meeting of the Official Side to seek their views on details of the 'grey class' idea and it was agreed that before the next joint meeting Bridges and Padmore would see Day privately, to let him know where the Official Side intended to stand firm. This private meeting between Bridges and Day, with Padmore in attendance, was on 15 January 1951 and it was agreed that at the next joint meeting detailed proposals on the 'grey class' would be presented by the Official Side. A note of this meeting was sent by Padmore next day to all members of the Official Side.

The joint committee met again on 18 January. Bridges recapitulated on the committee's discussions so far and the idea of the 'grey class' was formally proposed in relation to national political activities. On 25 January Day saw Bridges and Padmore and said he thought the Staff Side might be prepared to accept the 'grey class' idea if they could first have a joint discussion on other matters including participation in local government. Bridges called another meeting of the Official Side on 7 February to discuss participation in local government. After the meeting Mrs Abbot produced a paper outlining the Official Side's proposals and this was circulated to all members of the Official Side and also to various departments for particular comments. Throughout the discussions Bridges was very anxious that the proposals should be kept strictly confidential. These details were reported to the next joint meeting, on 20 March, which was also provided with copies of the details of the Official Side's proposals. At the joint meeting on 6 April further details were discussed, together with counter-proposals from the Staff Side. This was followed by another meeting of the Official Side on 2 May, which reached decisions on the line to be taken by the Official Side on each of the points raised by the Staff Side. Bridges then again saw Day privately to brief him about progress by the Official Side, in preparation for the joint meeting on 17 May. In July Day told Mrs E.M. Abbot that the Staff Side were now ready for another meeting. As with all the other stages this meant that Mrs Abbot wrote detailed briefs for senior Treasury officials, outlining the outstanding issues. Before the meeting, on 20 July, Day called on Bridges, apparently at Bridges' request, to give him a private and informal preview of the Staff Side's position. As Bridges said in a note to Padmore: 'had we not better find out privatim what the oracle is going to say before the meeting. And the oracle had better be told that it will not be possible to make any top-hat submission to Ministers before the recess?'[108] The Official Side then met on 25

July to discuss a paper, prepared in the Treasury, on the present position. This was immediately followed on the same day by a joint meeting with the Staff Side. This latter meeting resolved most of the outstanding difficulties: there were only two outstanding problems (on canvassing and the position of junior executive officers and analogous grades) on which agreement was not reached.[109] The next step was for a report to be submitted to Treasury ministers giving details of what had been agreed. However, Bridges warned that even though the preparation of this submission would begin at once, it would be quite impossible for ministers to consider it before the Parliamentary recess.

The report which emerged from these detailed, time-consuming discussions was unique in that the Official Side were going on record as agreeing with certain proposals, and disagreeing with others, without having the slightest idea what would be the views of ministers. As Mrs Abbot put it in a minute of 22 November 1951:

> In the event Ministers may not accept any of the recommendations agreed or otherwise; or they may agree with them all. Thus there is a risk of disclosure of a difference of opinion between Ministers and the Official Side. Disclosure of such a situation is never a good thing, but where the question at issue is the political activities of the Civil Service (and fundamentally the politicisation of the Civil Service) disclosure would be extremely unfortunate.[110]

Winnifrith was also concerned about this and sent Mrs Abbot's minute on to Bridges with a covering note in which he explained two points. First, that it was necessary to keep the report confidential and prevent it being published by the staff. Secondly, he recalled that when the Masterman Report was published the Staff Side managed to make a lot of political capital out of what they described as the precipitate action of the Government in adopting the Masterman proposals without any form of consultation or discussion with the Staff. He said: 'We must not give them any chance of doing this again'.[111] Bridges agreed. He minuted that he thought it better if he told the new Financial Secretary (there had been another General Election in 1951 and there was now a Conservative Government) what was afoot before seeing the Staff Side: 'Otherwise, if there is a leakage, Ministers may wonder what we have been up to'.[112] A four page draft was then prepared by Mrs Abbot which Bridges sent to the Financial

Secretary on 5 December 1951. It summarised the developments, drew attention to the difficulties encountered and ended not insignificantly with the sentence: 'It will probably be desirable for the Treasury Ministers to give the Staff Side a chance to make their views known to them orally, before the matter is submitted to the Cabinet'.[113] Mr John (now Lord) Boyd-Carpenter wrote on it: 'Read with much interest. JAB-C 7.12.51.'

Meanwhile, in the Treasury, Mrs Abbot and her colleagues, with much consultation with others, proceeded to write drafts of the final report. When Bridges commented on a draft he permitted himself what he referred to as two little jokes. Where, at paragraph 21 it referred to 'thought and heart-searching on both Sides' he wrote 'I do *NOT* admit to searching my heart n'existe pas.' And at the then paragraph 24 he made an insertion. The relevant sentence read: 'It may be that the modern canvasser is usually instructed not to seek to persuade or to indulge in argument.' Bridges added: 'This is not, of course, a matter on which the Official Side are well qualified to express a view.'

The Staff Side agreed with most of the report but suggested a few minor amendments. More polishing of the draft followed. The final version of the report was agreed in April 1952.[114] On 1 May Mrs Abbot minuted: 'Mr Day told me today that the National Staff Side had approved the Committee's report. He emphasised the desirability of speedy action now - the longer the delay the more the likelihood of a leakage.' On 6 May Mr Douglas Houghton put down a Parliamentary Question for answer on 15 May: 'To ask the Secretary to the Treasury whether any agreement has yet been reached on the Civil Service National Whitley Council concerning the civil rights of civil servants and matters arising from the Masterman Report: and whether he can make a statement.' Mrs Abbot noted:

This was embarrassing and while we were considering what to do about it Mr Day telephoned me and said he assumed it was an arranged question! I disillusioned him on this, and said I was a bit annoyed that a member of the Staff Side, who had presumably attended the Staff Side meeting on 1 May, should have put us in the position of either (a) having to disclose that the Committee had finished its discussions. This was true but not a good thing to disclose, or (b) avoiding (a) by saying this was not a subject for "agreement" on the Council. This was true but its reiteration was not calculated to help matters.

Mr Day's annoyance was no less than mine and he said he would see if he could persuade Mr Houghton to withdraw the Question.

Next day, the Question was withdrawn.

The final draft was submitted to ministers on 19 May, together with a minute by Bridges. Some of the most important passages in his minute were:

6. My first point is to indicate very broadly the nature of the compromise on which we have agreed provisionally and ad referendum. What we have done is to introduce a category of Civil Servants intermediate between the two categories envisaged by the Masterman Committee - i.e. those who have complete freedom and those who are forbidden to engage in any activities associating them publicly with political parties. Civil Servants in this intermediate category would be eligible for partial, but quite considerable freedom.

7. The second comment is that throughout I have made it abundantly clear that, contrary to the normal Whitley procedure whereby officials, in negotiating, only put forward proposals which they have reason to believe are acceptable to Ministers, in these discussions we have reversed the procedure. We were attempting to produce an agreed scheme, and it would then be for Ministers to say whether, on grounds of broad general policy, the scheme was acceptable. Ministers are, therefore, in no way committed to this report.

8. My third point is that Ministers will rightly ask whether, in reaching this compromise, I and my colleagues think that we have given away anything which is essential for the preservation of the tradition of a non-political/non-partisan Civil Service.

Have we, in other words, been drawn on to go a little further than we should in the desire to reach a compromise?

9. If I am to be wholly candid, I must admit that, for my part, I have been anxious to reach a compromise; and my anxiety was sharpened by the fear that important political influences in this country might well have to yield to political clamour in this matter and make concessions far beyond those which it has been necessary to make in order to reach this compromise.

10. But while I have had this anxiety in my mind I do not, in

fact, believe that the agreed scheme gives away anything that matters.[115]

Bridges concluded by confidently recommending ministers to accept the report. On procedure, he pointed out that he had promised the Staff Side an opportunity to make their views known to ministers - especially so that they could explain their position on the two points on which agreement had not been reached (i.e. canvassing and the position of junior executive officers). In a separate note Mrs Abbot and Winnifrith both argued for the Chancellor as well as the Financial Secretary meeting the Staff Side. Bridges reinforced this. R.A. Butler (later Lord Butler) agreed in a minute which said: 'I am not likely to have much to do in the near future. RAB 30.6.52.' There was a further delay because Day went on leave, but the meeting took place on 16 July. Butler received a detailed brief from Mrs Abbot and also advice from Bridges which included such comments as: 'As the Chancellor will know, Mr Day is not one of the most succinct of speakers. Nevertheless I think it is important that the Staff Side should feel that they have a really good run for their money tomorrow and are allowed ample scope to express their views' and 'Above all I think it is imperative that the part taken by any official representatives at the meetings should be an entirely silent one'.

Later, officials (but mainly Mrs Abbot) produced a draft paper for the Chancellor to submit to the Cabinet. Because of summer leave its submission was, however, delayed until October. It proposed that the scheme embodied in the report should be accepted; on the issues of canvassing and the position of junior executive officers the Staff Side proposals were rejected. It was agreed that the issue was so important that the Government's decision should be announced in a White Paper to be laid before Parliament (no legislation was necessary to give effect to the decision) and also the Opposition would be informed of the position privately before the White Paper was laid.

Padmore wrote a brief, dated 21 October, for the Chancellor of the Exchequer because it was thought this might be helpful in clarifying the position when the civil rights of civil servants was raised on the adjournment in the House of Commons on 27 October 1952.[116]

On 28 January 1953 Day called on Bridges to protest about the long delay in getting a decision on the political activities of civil servants. Bridges noted: 'I did a certain amount to calm him down, but expect that we shall, before long, get a letter from him making some protests at the long delay'.[117] Bridges also wrote, on the same day, to Norman Brook, Secretary to the Cabinet, telling him that Day had called and made a dignified but firm protest about the long delay. He added: 'I shall have to send a reply to the Staff Side and I shall be glad to know whether I can hold out any hope that the matter will be decided shortly. If it is not, the position will soon become very difficult indeed.'

Brook replied to Bridges on 31 January saying that he had asked the Prime Minister to take this paper at one of the Cabinet's meetings the next week and the Prime Minister had agreed. In fact the Cabinet approved the recommendations on 12 February and agreed that a White Paper should be issued.[118]

Bridges wrote to Masterman on 25 February to tell him in the strictest confidence what had been agreed about his committee's recommendations and on 10 March he sent him a copy of the White Paper - this was Bridges' own idea, so that Masterman had a copy simultaneously with the appearance of the news in the press.[119]

An apparently arranged Parliamentary Question by W. Glenvil Hall on 12 March asked the Secretary to the Treasury whether he now had any statement to make on the political activities of civil servants and the Financial Secretary replied that the Government's decisions were set out in a White Paper available in the Vote Office that afternoon. He added that the conclusions provided for freedom to take part in certain political activities for substantially more civil servants than under the existing regulations without, in the view of the Government, prejudicing in any way the political impartiality of the civil service, to the maintenance of which the Government attached the greatest importance.[120]

On publication of the White Paper there was wide press coverage and the Staff Side issued a press statement regretting that on both points on which the Official and Staff Sides held opposing views the Government had decided against the Staff Side. Meanwhile, officials in the Treasury were preparing drafts of an Establishments Circular to implement the decisions[121] (this took some time, however, and the approved version was not issued until 14 August 1953).[122]

The account of the Masterman Report and its consequences is revealing in a number of respects. First, it reveals an interesting relationship between the post-war Labour Government and the civil service. The pre-history of the Masterman enquiry, going back to the early 1920s but especially the period of the General Strike, was evidently important in influencing subsequent attitudes in the unions and also in the Labour Party towards the rules against the participation by civil servants in political activities. This contributed to the Labour Party's commitments in its Election Manifesto, especially its pledge to repeal the 1927 Trade Disputes and Trade Unions Act. Furthermore, some senior civil servants (like Fergusson) were clearly apprehensive about the increasing significance of unions in the civil service and the relationship of the unions to the Labour Party. These were genuine apprehensions relating to the increasing participation in national political discussions by civil service unions - and they were genuine because senior civil servants had such an overriding concern to maintain the political impartiality, in the partisan sense, of the civil service. There is no evidence that any civil servant involved in the discussions had a clear partisan allegiance, let alone an allegiance against the Government in power. Nevertheless, they shared an understanding of what the constitutional and management consequences might be, if the civil service became politicised. They also shared a strong determination to prevent this happening. As P.J. Grigg wrote in his book *Prejudice and Judgment*, civil servants in general are the secular enemies of the House of Commons.[123] This was therefore an issue on which they could be easily united.

Furthermore, pressures to reduce the restrictions on civil servants participating in political activities have always been more evident when the Government has been other than Conservative. This can be traced to the 1920s when there were Labour Governments, again during the time of the post-war Labour Government (1945-51), and also in the 1970s under the Wilson/Callaghan Government. Whenever such governments have been succeeded by a Conservative Ministry the lack of sympathy of the government to union pressures has resulted in the issue fading from view.

Secondly, forty years after the Masterman saga, when conditions are somewhat different, it seems quite extraordinary that a Government should announce its acceptance of the Masterman proposals, when it knew how sensitive were the issues involved, in a written answer to a Parliamentary Question. The matter was then seriously aggravated when, in the adjournment debate on 30 July 1949, the Government took so little care to defend its position. This example of the effects from the political environment on the activities of the administrative system is, however, not without parallels in more recent years (e.g. the Thatcher Government's unilateral decision to dispense with the Pay Research Unit in 1981, and in 1984 its decision to ban unions at the Government Communications Headquarters). Clearly, the evidence from the late 1940s suggests that ministers did not have prior discussion with Bridges about the procedure to be followed before the announcement was made to accept the Masterman recommendations - this, however, seems out of character for Cripps and his colleagues.

Thirdly, once the embarrassing situation had erupted following the Government's acceptance of the Masterman proposals, Bridges was determined to give the problem his full attention. The way he went into action, especially to counter the pressure from the unions, was an outstanding example of a political administrator in action. His personal role is particularly revealing. He was clearly acting in a highly political manner, as Head of the Civil Service, to protect the interests and traditions of the civil service as he saw them. The episode clearly indicates the skilful way in which he set about achieving his aims. In the first instance he pressed hard for an impartial committee to investigate the issue. Part of his normal duties then required him to help suggest names to serve on the Committee, and he was thus able to influence the selection in favour of members whose views he knew and approved or whom he thought would sympathise with his approach. When it came to the presentation of evidence, not only did he present his own views in a careful and influential manner, but he was also able to influence the evidence of other witnesses, especially that of permanent secretaries. Indeed, so adroit was he at this that he was even able to contribute indirectly to writing sections of the report. It must be emphasised, however, that Bridges did this for no personal motive except the satisfaction of leading the civil service in the direction he thought it should go and upholding its traditions. Nevertheless, he was acting unbureaucratically (in Weber's ideal sense) because he was not merely carrying out without affection or enthusiasm the instructions from his political masters. As is often the case, the line between the development of policy and its implementation is more complex and sophisticated than the approaches in elementary textbooks suggest: this is well illustrated by the Masterman enquiry and the implementation of its recommendations.

Political attitudes and political behaviour

The constitutional implications of any change, intended or unintended, from an impartial civil service should not be ignored. A change towards a less impartial civil service would have radical consequences in terms of the relationship of the executive and the legislature within the British system of government. Ministers might cease to have confidence in the support of their subordinates and this in turn would probably affect the public estimation of the civil service. The consequences might affect the largely unwritten nature of the constitution as well as the relationships of its essential institutions. Any change would certainly affect the powerful position of the civil service in the system of government. Where ministers are strong there is plenty of evidence that the civil service loyally carries out their instructions. But where ministers are weak, not clear in their own minds, or are too hard pressed to give adequate attention to complex issues, then the power of the civil service tends to increase for perfectly understandable reasons. Padmore illustrated this well in the minute quoted in this chapter where he drew attention to the need to decide what instructions officials should propose that ministers should issue to them. Bridges also illustrated this when he referred to the partnership of officials and politicians for the public good: the benefits being 'friendship and mutual gratitude' of individuals who, more often than not, already had much in common. It is an essentially professional relationship: in some senses it is akin to a master/servant relationship with expectations of unquestioned loyalty; in other senses it is akin to the relationship between a professional and a client, with the professional knowing exactly how the system works and in a sometimes superior manner requesting instructions.

This also has other implications which a healthy political system may need to question from time to time. Bridges believed that the machinery of democratic government in Britain depended very largely on maintaining the political impartiality of the public service. But this may not necessarily mean that countries without such an impartial bureaucracy are necessarily undemocratic: much depends on the nature of the society, on the roles of the other elements in the system of government, how they are structured and how they work together. In Britain, however, a mystique is often associated with the system, involving its secretiveness and at the same time expecting unquestioned confidence in the civil service.

It is sometimes believed that the gentleman in Whitehall knows best; and that the gentleman who dares to question Whitehall is no gentleman.[124] Whether or not this is true, that it is expressed in this way may reveal something of the attitudes to government in British society - or, if not in the society, then in some sections of the civil service. Some of these issues will be considered further in chapter 6, on education and training, and in chapter 7, on the constitution.

There is as much evidence now as there ever was, that civil servants have a different outlook and a different frame of mind from ministers. Evidence from survey research for the Fulton Committee in the 1960s confirms much that Bridges said and wrote on the subject. Some quotations from civil servants during the research illustrate this well: 'However favourable to one party a civil servant is, he soon becomes aware of the ineptitudes of any party ... we see the merits and demerits of any particular policy;' 'If you are emotionally concerned about party politics you don't become a civil servant;' 'Civil servants tend to admire politicians who are business-like rather than amateur; this is irrespective of party'.[125] The same sort of attitude was reflected in the evidence given to the Masterman Committee by Professor W.A. Robson. He said: 'I think most civil servants regard politics with a good deal of good-natured contempt. They seem to combine immense deference for the ministerial office with a contempt for the holder of it, that is their compensation'.[126] The lesson emerges that when officials work closely with the political system, they are more likely to develop an a-party attitude to politicians.

Nevertheless there may also be cause for concern. As this chapter shows, officials sometimes have to make assessments not only of what ministers will stand for but also what ministers will stand up for. Civil servants are often in these circumstances concerned about what is practical; but again, assessing practicalities is sometimes a matter of considering what is politically possible as well as what is administratively possible: it is by no means unknown for civil servants to have to consider both perspectives. Furthermore, there are ethical implications when civil servants have to decide what advice they should give as well as ethical facets to implementing instructions. Any discussion that proceeds further in this direction, however, may soon become involved as much with how ministers should behave as with how civil servants should behave. As this chapter indicates, questions should sometimes be raised at least as often about the conduct of ministers as about the conduct of officials.

Several aspects of the discussion in this chapter about the political attitudes and political behaviour of civil servants are as important and relevant to contemporary concerns in the late 1980s as they were to topics in public discussion during the 1940s. The subject of political attitudes of civil servants is revived from time to time, and with good effect, by politicians of all major political parties as well as by unions and staff associations. The Masterman Committee and the 1953 White Paper were followed twenty-five years later by the Armitage Committee on the Political Activities of Civil Servants. The Armitage Committee was set up because in 1970 the National Staff Side asked for further relaxations for the restricted category. The Civil Service Department looked into the question but the Staff Side was not satisfied with the relaxations proposed and asked for a complete reappraisal of the question. This was set up by the Prime Minister in 1976, and the Committee reported in 1978.[127] Its recommendations included reducing the numbers of civil servants in the restricted category principally by transferring the higher executive officer and executuve officer grades to the intermediate category (the 'grey class'), rationalisation of other arrangements, and the institution of an appeal body for those who feel aggrieved by departmental decisions. Its recommendations have not been implemented, however, because the discussions on them with the Staff Side, which began in 1978[128] under the Callaghan Government and continued in 1979[129] under the Thatcher Government, seem to have run into a fallow period during which civil servants took major strike action and the Civil Service Department was abolished.

There is continuing debate about accountability and loyalty of civil servants. The current variation of the debate questions the need for a career civil service[130] and includes positive suggestions for appointing officials who are more evidently committed to the Government in power. Some of the debate has been influenced by comparative studies, looking at British experience and the experience of other countries, but this is sometimes unhelpful because of the lack of any clear and agreed understanding in the United Kingdom of the idea of the state (which, apparently, is a word that occurs in only one of our statutes, the Official Secrets Act).[131] An official in the British civil service is still expected to have an almost supreme dedication to his minister; and there will always be scope for discussion about how enthusiastic a civil servant can or should be and to what extent it is an advantage to have officials who are sympathetic towards particular policies. An

137

example of enthusiasm which was at first highly regarded but which later led to personal disaster for an outstanding civil servant is the case of Sir Christopher Bullock. This case, and Bridges' initiative in trying to resolve it, is considered in the next chapter.

Notes

1. The approach in this opening paragraph has been influenced by H. E. Dale, *The Personnel and Problems of the Higher Civil Service*, Sidney Ball Lecture, 1943, (Oxford University Press, London, 1943).

2. Sir Edward Bridges, *Portrait of a Profession: The Civil Service Tradition*, (Cambridge University Press, Cambridge, 1950).

3. Sir Edward Bridges, 'The Civil Service Tradition', BBC (GOS) Broadcast talk, 1954. Script in PRO/T273/222.

4. Lord Bridges, 'The Relationship between Ministers and the Permanent Departmental Head', *The W. Clifford Clark Memorial Lectures, 1964*, (The Institute of Public Administration of Canada, Toronto, 1964), p. 9.

5. Herbert Morrison, *Government and Parliament: A survey from the inside*, (Oxford University Press, Oxford, 1954), pp. 318-19. Quoted by Lord Bridges, 'The Relationship between Ministers and the Permanent Departmental Head', p. 15.

6. Lord Bridges, 'The Relationship between Ministers and the Permanent Departmental Head', p. 13.

7. *Ibid.*, p.16

8. *Ibid.*, p.16

9. *Ibid.*, p.8.

10. *Ibid.*, p.14.

11. Lord Bridges, 'The Treasury as the Most Political of Departments', The Pollak Lecture, Graduate School of Public Administration, Harvard University, 1961, p. 17.

12. *Ibid.*, p.16

13. Lord Bridges, 'The Relationship between Ministers and the Permanent Departmental Head', p. 14.

14. Lord Bridges in *Whitehall and Beyond, Jo Grimond, Enoch Powell, Harold Wilson, three conversations with Norman Hunt, with a comment by Lord Bridges*, (BBC Publications, London, 1964), p.69.

15. Sir Edward Bridges, 'A Day in the life of the Permanent Secretary to the Treasury', BBC (GOS) Broadcast talk, 1952. Script in PRO/T273/222.

16. Sir Edward Bridges, *Portrait of a Profession*, p. 27.

17. Sir Edward Bridges, 'The Civil Service Tradition'.

18. PRO/T273/232, Bridges to Rowan, 19 November 1946

19. PRO/T273/232.

20. Sir Donald Banks, *Flame Over Britain: A Personal Narrative of Petroleum Warfare*, (Sampson Low, Marston and Co Ltd, London, 1946).

21. PRO/T273/230.

22. PRO/T273/178.
23. PRO/T273/26
24. PRO/T273/139.
25. PRO/T273/103.
26. *The Observer*, 13 February 1966
27. Barbara Castle, *The Castle Diaries 1974-76*, (Weidenfeld and Nicolson, London, 1980), p.41.
28. *The Times*, 18 February 1966
29. *The Times*, 28 February 1966
30. Goodmans Furze Papers, Box 5.
31. PRO/T215/92.
32. PRO/T215/81, Bridges to Muir, 22 February 1949.
33. PRO/T273/381.
34. 459 H.C. Deb., 5s., cols. 725-6 (10 December 1948)
35. *Royal Commission on the Civil Service, 1953-55, Evidence*, (HMSO, London, 1954), Q. 1388.
36. PRO/T273/205.
37. PRO/T273/307, Bridges to Prime Minister, 14 February 1947.
38. PRO/T273/35.
39. PRO/T273/289, Bridges to Armstrong, 24 October 1950.
40. PRO/T215/191.
41. PRO/T215/95.
42. PRO/T273/101.
43. PRO/T162/909/E13264/2.
44. PRO/T215/92.
45. PRO/T215/92.
46. *Committee on Parliamentary Etc Candidature of Crown Servants, Report of the Committee appointed by the Lords Commissioners of His Majesty's Treasury (the Blanesburgh Report)*, [Cmd. 2408], (HMSO, London, 1925), para. 49.
47. PRO/T215/182.
48. PRO/T162/729/E12794/01/3.
49. PRO/T162/729/E12794/01/4.
50. PRO/T162/832/E8641/1, Bridges to Upcott and Scott, 16 February 1927.
51. 17 and 18 Geo V Ch. 22.
52. PRO/T162/726/E8641/024/01, Ritson to Padmore, 19 September 1941.
53. PRO/T215/101, Winnifrith to Johnstone and Newton, 1 March 1948. See also PRO/T162/909/E13264/2.
54. PRO/T162/832/E8641/3.
55. Labour Party Manifesto, 1945: 'Let us Face the Future: A Declaration of Labour Policy For the Consideration of the Nation', in F.W. S. Craig (Editor), *British General Election Manifestos 1918-1966*, (Political Reference Publications, Chichester, 1970), p.99.
56. PRO/T162/909/E13264/2.
57. PRO/CAB21/1729.
58. PRO/CAB130/8.
59. PRO/T162/909/E13264/2, Fergusson to Bridges, 5 February 1946
60. PRO/CAB21/1729, Bridges to Chancellor of the Exchequer, 21

February 1946

61. PRO/T162/909/E13264/3.

62. PRO/T215/103, Johnstone to Winnifrith, 5 March 1948. See also PRO/T162/909/E13264/2, Bridges to Hacket, 13 February 1946

63. PRO/T215/97. See also PRO/T162/909/E13264/3, Bridges to Padmore, 19 April 1947.

64. PRO/T215/90, Bridges to Fergusson, 27 January 1948.

65. *Report of the Committee on the Political Activities of Civil Servants*, [Cmd. 7718], (HMSO, London, 1949), p. 34.

66. PRO/CAB21/1729.

67. J.C. Masterman, *On the Chariot Wheel,* (Oxford University Press, Oxford, 1975), p. 267.

68. PRO/T215/90.

69. PRO/T215/101.

70. PRO/T215/99 and PRO/T215/101.

71. PRO/T215/103.

72. PRO/T215/103.

73. PRO/T215/104.

74. PRO/T215/97.

75. PRO/T215/100.

76. PRO/T215/106

77. PRO/T215/106 and *Report of the Committee on the Political Activities of Civil Servants,* [Cmd. 7718].

78. *Report on the Political Activities of Civil Servants*, para. 37.

79. PRO/T215/104.

80. *Report on the Political Activities of Civil Servants*, paras. 64-5.

81. *Ibid.*, p. 32.

82. PRO/T215/109 and PRO/T215/223.

83. 466 H.C. Deb., 5s., col. 77 (28 June 1949).

84. PRO/T273/214.

85. PRO/T215/182.

86. Civil Service Clerical Association Circular NL/GEN/5/49. See also PRO/T215/108.

87. PRO/T215/108, Mayne to Glenvil Hall, 14 July 1949.

88. PRO/T215/108.

89. PRO/T215/182, Bridges to Padmore, 7 July 1949.

90. PRO/T215/182.

91. PRO/T215/182.

92. 467 H.C. Deb., 5s., cols. 3005-24 (30 July 1949).

93. J.C. Masterman, *On the Chariot Wheel*, p. 268.

94. PRO/T215/108, Bridges to Newton, 19 July 1949.

95. PRO/T215/109, 'National Whitley Council: Masterman Report, A Note for the Official Side by the Permanent Secretary to the Treasury'.

96. PRO/T215/109.

97. PRO/T215/109, Memorandum by the Permanent Secretary to the Treasury, 26 July 1949.

98. PRO/T215/182.

99. PRO/T215/109.

100. PRO/T215/182.

101. PRO/T215/182.

102. PRO/T215/182, Bridges to Chancellor of the Exchequer, 28 September 1949.

103. PRO/T215/182, 'The Masterman Report on Political Activity by Civil Servants: Memorandum to the Cabinet by the Chancellor of the Exchequer', 7 October 1949.

104. 469 H.C. Deb., 5s., cols. 209-11 (1 November 1949).

105. PRO/T215/183.

106. PRO/T215/183.

107. PRO/T215/183, Bridges to Chancellor of the Exchequer, 3 July 1950.

108. PRO/T215/188.

109. PRO/T215/110 and PRO/T215/188.

110. PRO/T215/189.

111. PRO/T215/189, Winnifrith to Bridges, 23 November 1951.

112. PRO/T215/189, Bridges' minute, 28 November 1951.

113. PRO/T215/189, Bridges to Financial Secretary, 5 December 1951.

114. See *Political Activities of Civil Servants*, [Cmd. 8783], (HMSO, London, 1953), Appendix.

115. PRO/T215/190.

116. 505 H.C. Deb., 5s., cols. 1689-1704 (27 October 1952).

117. PRO/T215/190, Bridges' note, 28 January 1953.

118. *Political Activities of Civil Servants*, [Cmd. 8783].

119. PRO/T215/190.

120. 512 H.C. Deb., 5s., col *142* (12 March 1952).

121. PRO/T215/191.

122. PRO/T215/192.

123. P.J. Grigg, *Prejudice and Judgment*, (Jonathan Cape, London, 1948), p. 353.

124. PRO/T222/678, John Henry Woods to Bridges, 29 July 1954, apparently quoting views of Douglas Jay.

125. Richard A. Chapman, *The Higher Civil Service in Britain*, (Constable, London, 1970), pp. 116-17.

126. PRO/T215/96, Robson's evidence (30 November 1948).

127. *Committee on the Political Activities of Civil Servants, Report*, (Chairman: Sir Arthur Armitage), [Cmnd. 7057], (HMSO, London, 1978).

128. 958 H.C. Deb., 5s., col. *232* (15 November 1978).

129. 973 H.C. Deb., 5s., col. 403 (7 November 1979).

130. Geoffrey K. Fry, 'The British Career Civil Service Under Challenge', *Political Studies*, Vol XXXIV, 1986, pp. 533-55.

131. Douglas Wass, 'Loyalty, Neutrality and Commitment in a career Civil Service', *Occasional Paper 2/1986*, (European Group of Public Administration, Brussels, 1986).

4

The Case of Sir Christopher Bullock

There are at least six reasons why discussion of the case of Sir Christopher Bullock is important. First, it is a rare case, probably unique, of a permanent secretary being summarily dismissed from his post. Because it was an occasion of such rarity and involved the investigation of a Board of Inquiry whose report was published, there are often references to the case, though until now the full details have not been available because the papers were not released in the Public Record Office until 1987. Secondly, many facets of the case have a surprising relevance to current discussions about reforms in the civil service - especially reforms which might permit, or even encourage, civil servants to have known commitments to particular policies. Thirdly, the full details of the case provide unusual insights into various aspects of the workings and values of the civil service in the 1930s and 1940s. Some of the procedures and values today may be somewhat different, but the constraints on open government only enable the curtain of secrecy to be drawn aside long after personal sensitivities can no longer be upset. Fourthly, the case involved leading officials and the civil service generally in potential political embarrassment because of its elements of injustice. Moreover, it had the potential to cause considerable damage to morale in the civil service. Fifthly, it was a case to which Bridges devoted an enormous amount of time and energy, revealing facets of his personal leadership style, and involving him in an initiative which seriously displeased leading members of the Government. Finally, it was a case essentially involved with the ways in which civil servants should or should not behave in matters going beyond circumstances envisaged in the general rules and guidelines for conduct in the civil service.

Sir Christopher Bullock and the events of 1936

Christopher Llewellyn Bullock was born on 10 November 1891 at Whiston, Northamptonshire. His father, the Revd Llewellyn Christopher Watson Bullock, was a master at Liverpool College and later at Rugby School. His mother, Cecil Augusta Margaret Isabella, was the daugther of E.R. Spearman and granddaughter of the fifth Earl of Orkney. Bullock was educated at Rugby, where he was Captain of the Running Eight. From Rugby he gained a classical scholarship to Trinity College, Cambridge, where he had a remarkable career. He won the Abbott and Porson University Scholarships in Classics, the members' Latin Essay prize, the Browne medals for Latin Ode (twice) and Greek Epigram, the Charles Oldham Shakespeare scholarship, and the Whewell scholarship in international law (re-elected 1921). He was placed in the first division of the first class of the classical tripos in 1913 and was offered a fellowship at Trinity.[1]

After taking first place in the open competition for the Home and Indian Civil Services in 1914, he chose India; but with the outbreak of war he volunteered for service with the Rifle Brigade. He served as an infantry officer in the trenches, was seriously wounded at Ypres in 1915 and mentioned in dispatches. Later, he was seconded to the Royal Flying Corps, gaining his wings first as an observer and later as a pilot. When he became unfit for flying in 1917 he was appointed to the air staff and, in 1919, became principal private secretary to Churchill, who was then Secretary of State for Air. From 1923 to 1930 he served successive Secretaries of State in the same capacity. During this period the permanent independent Royal Air Force was established and in its creation Bullock was Lord Trenchard's right-hand man on the civilian side. This was a difficult time because there were forces in Whitehall hostile to the young Royal Air Force, particularly in the other Service departments and in the Treasury. Indeed, the survival of the Royal Air Force as a separate service was at times in doubt. Bullock was appointed OBE in 1919, CBE in 1926, CB in 1929 and KCB in 1932. According to a statement made by Bullock in a letter to the Prime Minister in 1947, Fisher (and others), before the Geddes incident, spoke of Bullock as a likely candidate in due course of time for the Headship of the Civil Service.[2]

In 1930, when he was only 38 years of age, and in the grade of assistant secretary, Lord Thomson, the Secretary of State for Air, recommended him to succeed Sir Walter Nicholson as Permanent

Secretary to the Air Ministry. This was a quite exceptional appointment for two reasons. The first was Bullock's youth. However, there were precedents for appointing officials in their 30s to permanent secretaryships: Sir John Anderson was 37 years of age when he became Chairman of the Board of Inland Revenue in 1919 and was only 40 when he became Permanent Under Secretary of State at the Home Office in 1922; and Fisher was only 40 years of age when he was appointed in 1919 as Permanent Secretary to the Treasury. Secondly, and more importantly, such a promotion within a department meant he would pass over several officials senior to him, with whom he was already working in the Air Ministry. However, Bullock's outstanding ability and general knowledge of the work of the department was unquestioned. Before making his recommendation, Thomson ascertained the views of the department by consulting Nicholson, Trenchard, Sir John Salmond, then Chief of the Air Staff, and Sir John Higgins, then Member for Supply and Research of the Air Council. All were unanimous in thinking Bullock to be the best person for the post. Fisher also agreed. On 12 June 1930, the Prime Minister, Mr J. Ramsay Macdonald wrote: 'I agree to Bullock.'[3]

Not only was Bullock widely recognised for his outstanding ability and capacity for hard work, he was also a man with a strong personality; he had plenty of drive and determination. In the 1930s he worked under considerable pressure on the expansion of the Royal Air Force (his normal working day was eleven to thirteen hours and there were occasions when he was working for eighteen hours out of twenty-four) and his personal impact on the RAF and the Air Ministry was very significant during this period. He also made a great impact in other areas: by initiating the Air Training Corps, by negotiating the 'Bullock-Bhore' agreement with India to ensure the passage of Imperial Airways' aircraft across India, and by his part in creating the Empire Air Mail scheme - to mention just a few examples. This was the period, during the rise of Nazism in Germany, when the expansion of the RAF became a matter of great importance. Bullock was personally committed to this policy and strove to awaken public and Parliament to the need to strengthen the RAF. Indeed, so involved was he with this policy that he personally drafted nearly all the important air staff papers submitted to the Committee of Imperial Defence and the Cabinet. However, this ability and energy, combined with his at times combative personality - especially when focused on matters that Bullock recognised to be of outstanding importance - did not always make for easy personal relationships, nor did it always endear him to his colleagues. A significant illustration of this occurred in 1934.

In February 1934 there were discussions in the Air Ministry about the arrangements in the ministry for controlling civil aviation. In the course of the discussion Bullock produced a draft for an Office Memorandum clarifying the existing arrangements. This draft was endorsed by the two previous permanent secretaries, Nicholson and Sir Arthur Robinson, and approved by the Marquess of Londonderry, then Secretary of State for Air, but for extraneous reasons the memorandum was never circulated. The memorandum confirmed that the Director of Civil Aviation reported to ministers through the permanent secretary, and not directly. Subsequently, following criticism from the Parliamentary Air Committee, Londonderry pointed out on 23 November that although what was in the memorandum might correspond with what had become the practice, it differed from the formal position under what he called the Air Ministry 'constitution',[4] but he said that he was not saying which was the better policy. By 26 November, however, he had made up his mind after 'considering this very important matter during the whole of this weekend'.[5]

Londonderry sent Bullock a letter on 26 November and a formal minute effectively repudiating the arrangements in the draft Office Memorandum, and laying down that in future the Director (General) of Civil Aviation would be responsible directly to him. In the February draft it had been stated that the Director of Civil Aviation 'will submit all major issues through the Secretary, *who is responsible for tendering final advice to Ministers on questions of higher policy*'.[6] Bullock was upset at the loss of responsibility as a result of the change in policy and, when he made enquiries, he found that the policy had been reversed on the advice of Fisher (apparently over the weekend before 26 November) whose involvement had been kept secret from Bullock. Bullock's reaction was clear:

That intervention behind my back was, in my opinion, a singular breach of the personal relations and good faith which should prevail between Civil Service colleagues; whilst of its entire constitutional impropriety there can be no manner of doubt. Nothing would have been simpler than for Sir Warren Fisher to have informed the Secretary of State that he could not constitutionally intervene and that, if it was desired to call

145

him into consultation informally he must, of course, acquaint me with the fact. Sir Warren did not take this obvious course and I only learnt of his intervention quite fortuitously after the event when I asked the Secretary of State the reasons for his surprising *volte face*.[7]

Bullock consulted three other senior heads of departments, to make sure that he was not overreacting. All three felt that there could be no doubt as to the constitutional impropriety of Fisher's action and that Bullock owed it to the civil service to take the matter further. Bullock tried to do this in the manner he believed to be constitutionally correct but found himself, as he later wrote, 'side-tracked and blocked by various manoeuvres'. He replied to Londonderry the same day (26 November) indicating his intention to resign, but asking permission first to seek a meeting with the Prime Minister. Baldwin, then Lord President of the Council, urged him not to resign[8] and eventually he received a communication in writing from the Prime Minister who said that he regretted that he could not intervene because the matter concerned 'a decision of the Secretary of State with regard to the administration of his Department and the regulations which control it'.[9] He was, of course, extremely busy, but it seems he was very concerned about the precedent which such an interview would establish.[10]

Before Mr J. Ramsay Macdonald, the Prime Minister, wrote to Bullock, Baldwin had asked Fisher to see him (Baldwin) about Bullock's position. Baldwin also talked to Londonderry the same morning. Immediately after seeing Baldwin on 8 December 1934 Fisher wrote to Londonderry confirming what had been agreed:

(i) Your decision, as explained in your Minute about the constitutional position of the Director - or Director-General - of Civil Aviation, will stand in its entirety.
(ii) Bullock will in writing fully acknowledge this.
(iii) Bullock will apologise for his unwarrantable activities over the past few days against his own Minister.
(iv) Bullock will promise that in future he will in this, and all other, regards act with loyalty to his Ministers.
(v) Bullock will understand that any deviation from loyalty in the future on his part will be met by summary dismissal...
  The effect of this course of action is to give Bullock the opportunity of learning a much needed lesson; and I think that is fair, though whether or not he is capable of learning the

lesson, and consequently his fortune in the Service, are matters which the future alone can show.

Londonderry replied on 10 December: '...Your suggestions are admirable.'[11] However, the file does not indicate whether, and if so how, these points of agreement between the two men were conveyed to Bullock. Perhaps they never were. Perhaps Londonderry thought it unnecessary to take any action because the new arrangements were prepared and submitted by Bullock in an Office Memorandum (OM R68/34) of 17 December. Perhaps Fisher simply did not want Bullock warned (compare this with Fisher's later failure to warn Bullock of the unwisdom of his talks with Geddes) - indeed, this is a distinct possibility because Fisher disliked Bullock so intensely that Londonderry in 1938 wrote that Bullock was the victim of Fisher's 'inveterate hatred'.[12]

This incident in 1934 provides an insight into Bullock's personality and his relations with Fisher and illustrates the official atmosphere in which he was working. It is necessary to have such an introduction before outlining the events leading up to his dismissal from the civil service in 1936 following the report of a Board of Inquiry. This inquiry, appointed by the Prime Minister, found that Bullock's conduct was completely at variance with the tenor and spirit of the Treasury Circular of 13 March 1928[13] (the circular which had been issued following the inquiry chaired by Fisher into what became known as the Francs case).[14]The Treasury Circular had, in fact, become a sort of civil service code of conduct. The Board of Inquiry which investigated Bullock's conduct used words from the Treasury Circular when it concluded: 'We do not say that he consciously used his official position to further his interests...(but) We think that the whole course of these proceedings shows on the part of Sir Christopher a lack of that instinct and perception from which is derived the sure guide by which the conduct of a Civil Servant should be regulated'.[15] On the day the report was published the Prime Minister also published a minute in which he announced that he had directed Bullock be dismissed from the Service. However, he added that, grave as Bullock's offence was from a Service point of view, he was glad to observe that no question of corruption was involved.[16] Bullock recognised that he had been injudicious, though he did not consider any action he had taken to be improper, and he found much that was wrong in the proceedings and report of the inquiry. He never recovered from its findings and the severe punishment of dismissal from the civil service. Some years later he wrote: 'Had I been grossly idle or inefficient, had I indeed been suspected of corruption or some other criminal offence, there was no severer penalty which the Government had it in their power to inflict'.[17]

The story is apparently simple, but it provides rare insights into the practice of public administration in British government in the 1930s. The essence of Bullock's 'offence' was that on three occasions in the course of two years he sounded Sir Eric Geddes, then Chairman of Imperial Airways, as to whether it would be acceptable to Geddes if Bullock were to become a Government Director of Imperial Airways at some future date (when he left the civil service before the normal retirement age, as he intended to do), and possibly succeed him as Chairman, or alternatively serve under him as Deputy Chairman. Two other factors were also involved in the inquiry. One was the relationship at the time between the Air Ministry and Imperial Airways; the other was the sounding out of Geddes to see whether he would be interested in a further honour for himself.

First, an explanation of the relationship between the Air Ministry and Imperial Airways. Imperial Airways had been created by the Government in 1924. As a semi-public corporation[18] it received a substantial subsidy and the Air Ministry had a direct shareholding in it and the right to appoint two directors to its Board.[19] In the field of diplomacy the Government negotiated on the Company's behalf with foreign countries and with the Dominions, India, Egypt and the Colonies. This meant that the relations between the Air Ministry and the Company were entirely different from relations between a department and any ordinary firm with which the Government had regular contractual relationships. Although in 1938 the Cadman Committee into Civil Aviation drew attention to Imperial Airways' role as 'a chosen instrument of the policy of the Government'[20] it also found that the Company had failed to co-operate fully with the Air Ministry and had 'been intolerant of suggestion and unyielding in negotiation'.[21] One of the Government directors in the 1930s was Nicholson, Bullock's friend and predecessor as Permanent Secretary at the Air Ministry; the other Government director was Sir John Salmond who, from 1930 to 1933, had been Chief of the Air Staff before his appointment as a director. The first Chairman of the Company, Sir Eric Geddes, was still Chairman in 1936; the Managing Director was Mr Woods-Humphery. The relationship between the top managements in the Air Ministry and the Company were very close. Bullock reckoned that during his period of office he met and discussed matters with Geddes or Woods-Humphery on something like a hundred and fifty occasions and spent well over two hundred hours in their company. When they had business to discuss, as apparently they often did, Woods-Humphery invited Bullock to lunch at the Carlton Hotel or Bullock invited Woods-Humphery to lunch at the Oxford and Cambridge Club.[22]

The way Nicholson was appointed to his directorship provides another example (supplementing those already given in Chapter 2) of the way appointments of this sort were made. At the inquiry Nicholson was asked whether he held office at pleasure or for a definite period. He replied:

> It is rather vague. In my particular case...what happened was that, if I may say so, years ago, I told Lord Thomson who was then my chief that I wanted to leave and I thought it sound to leave the Air Ministry and, of course, if I had just left like that, at the age of 55 or so, my pension would just have gone and I told Thomson I was ready to do that if it worked out, but I did not pretend I should not be quite pleased to retain my pension rights, and it was suggested - I certainly had it at the back of my mind, but I do not know that I specifically suggested it to Lord Thomson - it was suggested that I might become a Government Director because there was an understanding that the posts were held for about six years, that sort of thing. Sir Vyell Vyvyan had held the post for about six years and Sir Herbert Hambling had held it for about seven or eight years, I think. Anyhow, the long and short of it was that I was appointed to succeed Herbert Hambling, and I had a talk with Sir Warren Fisher about the conditions and he said he thought it quite correct that it should be scheduled as approved service and so there was some exchange of letters or minutes, I think, which implied that, without any pledge of course, in the natural way I should be relieved about my sixtieth birthday when I had become eligible for a pension...[23]

From mid-1934 the Air Ministry was negotiating with Imperial Airways arrangements for an Empire Air Mail Service involving a 15-year contract starting in 1937. The Air Ministry and the Post Office had decided that the cost should not exceed £1.5m p.a. but the Company was holding out for £1.8m p.a. and negotiations reached a deadlock. The deadlock was broken when Bullock intervened with an ingenious formula to provide a sliding scale of payments starting at £1.65m and declining over the period of the contract so that the average cost would be £1.5m but including a proviso that, when the first reduction became due, if the Company found the service could not be provided for that sum it should not take place. Bullock drove a very hard bargain, as the Secretary of State and others were well aware. Indeed, he pressed Geddes to accept terms materially lower than Geddes claimed were fair and Bullock later admitted that he 'refused absolutely, after prolonged discussion to entertain many of his (perfectly proper and legitimate) proposals.'[24]

Bullock had personal doubts whether the money was sufficient, but he knew from the Cabinet Sub-Committee that there was no prospect of a larger amount being made available in the atmosphere prevailing in regard to civil aviation. Furthermore, Bullock himself was committed to the pioneering idea of the Empire Mail link-up and the great merit of his formula was that it safeguarded, so far as possible, the interests of both the Exchequer and Imperial Airways. To reach agreement, he brought pressure to bear on the Company through the two Government Directors and on one occasion told Geddes that, if he would not accept, Bullock would have no option but to report to the Cabinet Sub-Committee that was dealing with the matter that negotiations had broken down. When Geddes made representations to Londonderry about the unduly hard bargain Bullock was driving, Bullock briefed the latter to resist the representations. It is quite evident that the negotiations were not easy and there is no evidence that the two men were doing other than their best for the interests they represented.

There is also no doubt that Geddes, the man Bullock had to deal with, was past his prime; indeed, in 1936 he was far from well and he died the next year. By 1936 it seems he was, according to Bullock, an overbearing and forgetful old man. Geddes rose to prominence in the First World War when, as Deputy-Director of Munitions, he won the complete confidence of Lloyd George. In 1916, when he was 41 years of age, he became director-general of transportation on the staff of the Commander-in-Chief of the British Army in France; later he was Inspector-General of Transportation for all theatres of war with the honorary rank of Major-General. In 1917 he was appointed Controller of the Navy and an additional member of the Board of Admiralty with the temporary and honorary rank of Vice-Admiral. At a by-election in 1917 he was elected Unionist MP for Cambridge and the same month became First Lord of the Admiralty and sworn of the Privy Council. He was Knighted in 1916, appointed KCB in 1917, GBE in 1917, and GCB in 1919. In 1921, when he was Chairman of the House of Commons Committee on National Expenditure, he was responsible for the 'Geddes Axe', which made devastating cuts in public expenditure; but on the break-up of the coalition in 1922 Geddes left the House of Commons.[25] He turned to industry and transport and it was then that, among other positions, he became the first Chairman of Imperial Airways - a position which paid little (about £2,000 p.a.) but which he regarded as a public service to salve his feelings of selfishness because his other activities were so purely commercial.

Geddes and Bullock got on quite well despite their personality and age differences. Geddes told the inquiry that he liked Bullock and 'found his mind agile and acute' and that he had a great ability in handling things.[26] Nevertheless, the negotiations were difficult for personality reasons as well as because of the issues involved. Geddes was apt to emphasise in discussions that he was an ex-Cabinet Minister and a serving Privy Councillor who held the Chairmanship of Imperial Airways out of public spirit and not as a business appointment. Bullock later recalled:

He stressed these points year in year out and, as an ex-Cabinet Minister and serving Privy Councillor, he asked Ministers to let him see confidential Government documents of a type which never would be shewn to an ordinary contractor; and I was specifically instructed to shew him such documents. It was my practice... to prepare a specially edited version of these documents whenever their communication to him might otherwise cause embarrassment. He continuously asked me to lunch or dine, and harped on his confidential relations with Cabinet Ministers past and present. Indeed, he was dangerously indiscreet in what he told me of some of his former colleagues...[27]

An important factor in this case was Bullock's personal commitment: he had a genuine interest in and enthusiasm for civil aviation. In particular he was confident that he could make a positive contribution in Imperial Airways at some future date when he left the civil service. Furthermore, Bullock made no secret about this interest. In 1936, both his previous minister, Londonderry, and his minister at the time, Lord Swinton, knew about his interest in civil aviation and, in particular, his hope to join Imperial Airways. So did Fisher at the Treasury and Nicholson (who, it will be remembered, had been his predecessor as permanent secretary at the Air Ministry and in 1936 was one of the Government directors of Imperial Airways). Mr Geoffrey Lloyd, who was a political aide in the Secretary of State's private office at the Air Ministry when Bullock was principal private secretary, also knew of Bullock's interest and thought it would be a good thing for Bullock if he ever left the public service and also, in view of his 'vigour and industry' a good thing for the company. Others who knew included Mr Loel Guinness, a private pilot who at all material times was Parliamentary Private Secretary to either the Under-Secretary of State for Air or the Secretary of State for Air, and thought it would be good for Imperial Airways if Bullock joined the company. So well known was this interest of Bullock's that *The Tatler* referred to it, though apparently inaccurately, as 'The perennial report about Sir Christopher Bullock leaving the Air Ministry to take up a post in Imperial Airways Ltd...'[28]

It is also clear that in the climate of the time and because of the nature of the relationship between the Air Ministry and Imperial Airways, the people who knew of Bullock's interest did not seem to think there was anything wrong in it. For example, Fisher, whom Bullock had personally told that he had aspirations someday to be appointed to a Government directorship, agreed at the inquiry that there would be nothing improper or objectionable in Bullock having ambitions to become a Government director of Imperial Airways (for which, he said, the fee was only about £500 p.a. - at a time when Bullock's salary as a permanent secretary was £3,000).[29]

Nor, indeed, did Bullock feel it was wrong. He put his position on this clearly in his minute (38 pages in length) to Swinton on 28 June 1936:

> It sometimes seems to be imagined that private and public interests must inevitably and always conflict. Often they do - but sometimes they coincide. Frankly I have felt in the past that I might one day be able to contribute something of real value to Imperial Airways and by so doing serve the interests of the State just as much as fulfil my own ambitions. That is why, despite my mind moving in different directions more recently, I have still thought that, even though my main

activities (if and when I left the public service) were to lie elsewhere, I could usefully be - and should like to be - a Government Director.[30]

Geddes, however, was very worried at the prospect of having Bullock on his Board. He consulted his colleagues and they told Geddes that if Bullock came on the Board they would resign. They recognised that for all Bullock's great ability 'he would not be a soothing influence on the Board'. Geddes told Londonderry about this and Londonderry replied: 'You have no need to worry: I shall never put him in as a Government Director'.[31]

The second factor that played an important part in the inquiry was the possibility of an additional honour for Geddes. Bullock recognised that Geddes was inordinately vain[32] but they had what amounted to a good working relationship and he thought it would be a nice gesture if Geddes were to receive an honour for his work for civil aviation. He raised the matter with Londonderry in 1934. Londonderry told the inquiry that he had great confidence in Bullock and by implication he also had confidence in his recommendations for honours. He then explained how he reacted: '...if you think that a person is a proper person to have an honour you say "Well, what does he want?"...an honour was suggested for Sir Eric Geddes and I am quite sure I made the answer which I have had to make on many occasions before, "What does he want?"[33] Geddes' reaction was also plainly revealed at the inquiry: a question was asked of him which included a reference to people wanting to cover their chests with decorations. Geddes replied: 'I am not a bit ashamed, I like them'.

Bullock telephoned Geddes and, because he thought he could find out the answer to Londonderry's question before he (Bullock) went on holiday, he asked for an urgent appointment. For this purpose Bullock called on 14 May 1934. Geddes made a note of the discussion:

> Said he had come at the S of S's instructions and asked me if he could recommend me for a Peerage in recognition of my work in Civil Air Transport. I said I thanked the S of S but I wanted no hereditary titles, that I did not believe in them at the present time, and could have had one a long time ago if I had wanted. Then he said, what about a baronetcy: I replied also hereditary.
>
> I said, was the Thistle out of the question, and he said yes.

> Then he said, would I like GCMG, and I said yes, if for 'Work linking up Empire by Air'.
>
> He then said he thought and hoped he could get that through the Honours Committee.
>
> ...I was a little flattered at the suggestion of a Peerage....[34]

In oral evidence Geddes accepted that he, rather than Bullock, raised the possibility of a GCMG, but the doubt about exactly how it was raised does not seem important. To Bullock, the procedure of sounding people out for honours was a routine business and he found it difficult to grasp how such a fantastic pother could have developed 'over a mere GCMG', a lower honour than Geddes already had.[35] What is much more important is that Geddes thought that his name would appear, just two or three weeks later, in the Birthday Honours for 1934 and was disappointed (he admitted 'I was woefully ignorant').[36] He later raised the matter with Bullock who was surprised that anyone with Geddes' experience could have imagined that such matters could be arranged in such a short time, and explained that it was to be recommended for the New Year's Honours List. Discussions about the Empire Air Mail link-up then began in earnest and Geddes began to worry about the possible connection between accepting a contract in hard-fought circumstances and being awarded an honour. Indeed, as he told the inquiry, '...I am a silly sort of person, I worried about it, I worried a lot'.

Bullock's attitude at the time was an interesting contrast to Geddes'. He wanted to see Geddes as soon as possible because it was administratively convenient for him to settle what honour Geddes might want before he went on holiday. It was urgent in the sense that Bullock 'thought it urgent to keep the old boy happy'. Bullock later explained that the offer of an honour was certainly not envisaged as a bribe by him, but he also added in his quite extraordinarily open manner: 'If it were suggested that it was to be a bribe for signing the agreement, I am afraid I should not even think that was very wicked. It was in the Government's interests and everybody's interests that the agreement should be signed'.[37]

Geddes decided on reflection that, although he had done many things for the Government since leaving the Admiralty, in view of the contract negotiations, an honour at that time would not be appropriate and told Bullock so. Meanwhile Fisher took a similar view and when the proposal came forward from Londonderry Fisher intervened and explained to the Prime Minister how unsuitable it would be when there were negotiations in progress. Later, when Geddes called on him, Fisher expressed surprise that Geddes knew he was being put forward for a GCMG, then he showed Geddes in strict confidence ('as between old friends') the letter that Bullock had written for Londonderry to sign recommending Geddes for the GCMG and also the subsequent correspondence between himself (Fisher) and Bullock. Londonderry's letter mentioned that 'Geddes could have had a Peerage years ago...' and ended by saying ' it seems to me that there is really nothing appropriate left but the GCMG'.

These matters, the contract negotiations, Bullock's untimely inquiries about his possible acceptability as a director of Imperial Airways at some future date, and the question of an additional honour for Geddes, came to a head in June 1936 when Geddes went to see Fisher, as the Head of the Civil Service, to seek his advice 'as a friendly and wise adviser'.[38] Later, Geddes saw Swinton twice about the situation in which he found himself, and on 22 June he confirmed in writing some of what he said. Meanwhile the papers on the matter were sent to the Chancellor of the Exchequer, Mr Neville Chamberlain, who read them on 21 June.

On 23 June Swinton called Bullock to see him and handed him a long account of the facts that had been drawn to his attention. His conclusions referred to the conflict of public and private interests with special reference to Bullock's personal interests in Imperial Airways while negotiating the Air Mail link-up contract. He ended by asking Bullock to reply in writing 'whether and to what extent you admit or deny the truth of the facts set out in this memorandum, and whether you desire to offer any explanations in connection with them'. Bullock read the letter in Swinton's presence and said at once that some casual conversations, of which he kept no record, but other people apparently had, had been twisted. Swinton said he was not prepared to discuss the matter:

> I told him that I had no option but to suspend him until such time as his answer had been considered; but that I wished to do this in whatever manner was least disadvantageous to himself. He said that he had in fact been far from well, and asked that he might be treated as being on sick leave, with which I agreed.[39]

Swinton then submitted both his document and Bullock's 38 page reply to the Prime Minister on 29 June 1936.

Although the Board of Inquiry was formally set up by the Prime Minister, Swinton was in close touch with Fisher on the matter and there is little doubt that Fisher played a significant role in deciding the nature of the inquiry and the membership of the Board. The terms of reference were, as Swinton outlined them to Bullock: 'to inquire into, and report upon, the discussions referred to in those minutes, namely the discussions alleged to have taken place at various times, commencing in May 1934, at your insistence between yourself and representatives of Imperial Airways concerning the possibility of your own future association with the Board of that Company'. The Board consisted of Sir G. Evelyn P. Murray (Chairman of the Board of Customs and Excise), Sir Richard Hopkins (Second Permanent Secretary to the Treasury) and Mr (later Sir) L. Granville Ram (Second Parliamentary Counsel).

The most important finding of the inquiry was that Bullock had 'interlaced public negotiations entrusted to him with the advancement of his personal or private interests'. The Board also recorded their 'opinion that he at no time appreciated the gravity or fully realised the true nature or possible consequences of what he was doing and we consider that his failure to do so goes far to explain, though it cannot excuse, what has occurred'.

The report was signed on Monday 25 July 1936 and Fisher immediately sent it to the Prime Minister who presumably consulted Fisher about appropriate action on it. On the same day that the report was published the Prime Minister published his minute embodying his decision on it. As a result of the Prime Minister's decision Fisher wrote a three sentence letter to Bullock on 28 July. The third sentence read: 'The Prime Minister accepts the findings of the Board, and as a consequence has directed that you be dismissed from the Service'.[40]

When the sentence became known Fisher was contacted by many people about it. One of these (perhaps Swinton or Sir Findlater Stewart - the signature is not clear) wrote on 28 July:

> I had hoped it would have been possible to allow CB to resign.
>
> I doubt if even now CB will realise where his fault lay, and the fact that he does not goes a long way to explain why he acted as he did; but his punishment is an appalling one...

To Sir Findlater Stewart, then Permanent Under Secretary of State for India, whom Fisher saw for two hours to discuss the case, Fisher replied on 1 August 1936:

It is a mere insult to our Service to excuse any official - let alone the Permanent Head of a great Department of State - by saying that he has not been corrupt or grossly negligent in the performance of the official duties entrusted to him. Just because Bullock's offence does not come within the purview of the Criminal Law, it is quite unjustifiable to say that his offence, of its own kind, is any less serious. In the judgment of his peers, Bullock has been guilty of a complete and inexcusable violation of the standard laid down for Civil Servants by the Treasury Circular of the 13th March 1928; and even if his own instinctive perception is insufficient to guide him, he had this code publicly brought to his notice (as to that of all members of the Service) in a printed document. The tenor and spirit of that code can be conveniently summed up in the two brief extracts - 'the Service exacts from itself a higher standard' and 'the public expects from Civil Servants a standard of integrity and conduct not only inflexible but fastidious'. Bullock's conduct is a gross betrayal of that standard and of the Service. Officials far subordinate in rank to Bullock have been dismissed, and will again be dismissed, for infringements of that code far less than Bullock's has been adjudged to be. The position of the Head of a great Department carries with it the responsibility of giving and maintaining the highest example, and therefore the degree of culpability when he betrays that trust is infinitely greater. So far from influential people endeavouring to secure preferential treatment for Officers to whom so great a trust is committed, it is axiomatic that such Officers can only receive the severest penalty in the power of the State.

I am not going to repeat to you my remarks about the greatness of the public interest at stake, whether it be the view of our Service as a national institution held and to be held by other Services of the Crown, by our own public, by foreign countries, or the great Dominions. But I am going to make one personal observation. His Majesty's Government are the constitutional authority for all purposes in this country, and the decision in all matters rightly remains with them. What, however, the Government are not entitled to expect or demand from the Official who is in a very special degree the trustee for the standards and honour of his Service, is that he should be a party to an unforgivable breach of his trust and utter indifference to his personal honour. To treat Bullock's offence as meriting anything short of dismissal is a betrayal of our Service and all it should stand for.[41]

Bridges' personal initiative

Bullock's dismissal was a major event that stimulated wide interest in the country as well as special concern within the British civil service. Whilst it is not unknown for civil servants to be dismissed for serious misconduct, this case was different. It was a case where a civil servant had risen to the most senior grade in his department as a result of outstanding commitment, drive and determination, qualities that were recognised to be of special value at that particular time. His dismissal resulted from an incident when the exercise of these personal qualities, combined with a degree of insensitivity, led to embarrassment. Bullock himself never accepted that he had acted improperly, though he did agree that he had been injudicious. Following his dismissal he received over a thousand letters of sympathy and support. Even his Secretary of State and the Prime Minister in 1936 wrote letters after the war admitting that their decision had been wrong. After a short period when he was stunned by what had happened, Bullock campaigned vigorously for many years to have his reputation restored. There is no evidence that Bridges was personally involved in the case in the years before he became Permanent Secretary to the Treasury, though he would probably have had informal discussions with colleagues within the Treasury, and perhaps also with other colleagues, in the late 1930s. However, when he became Head of the Civil Service he was the main official contact for Bullock and Bridges became concerned that if Bullock led a public campaign (which he said he was prepared to do) it might result in political embarrassment. In any case, Bridges could hardly ignore the support that Bullock marshalled within the civil service. Bridges therefore took an initiative which resulted in himself being placed in an embarrassing position where his conduct was criticised by both the Lord Chancellor (Lord Jowitt) and the Lord President of the Council (Mr Herbert Morrison).

After his dismissal, Bullock felt understandably aggrieved for a number of reasons. The most important of these was first, the composition of the Board of Inquiry. Bullock thought it ought to have included Fisher, as Head of the Civil Service, and should have excluded Ram, who was of junior rank to Bullock in the civil service grading system. The Chairman of the inquiry, Sir Evelyn Murray, was not, in Bullock's opinion, of sufficient distinction for this task, 'having been transferred from the Post Office to the Board of Customs and Excise in circumstances which had not enhanced his reputation'. In addition, because of their previous official contacts over the Empire Air Mail scheme (when, apparently, they were engaged in some hard bargaining) Bullock said he could 'hardly imagine a less suitable choice to preside over the Board of Inquiry'.[42] Bullock was not to have known, however, that Fisher might have been regarded as biased because of his earlier involvement with Bullock (especially in the incident mentioned above, in 1934). Furthermore, Fisher had consulted the Treasury Solicitor and the Parliamentary Counsel about the case and Ram was therefore chosen to serve on the Board of Inquiry, despite his more junior rank than Bullock, because of the necessity of getting a legal member without previous knowledge of the case.[43] Secondly, Bullock drew attention to the evidence by Nicholson and others that he had been particularly open in telling them about his talks with Geddes and his ambitions to be associated, at some future date, with Imperial Airways. Nicholson agreed at the inquiry that in his opinion the propriety of such conversations with Geddes could not be called in question. However, this, and other evidence in Bullock's favour, was not referred to in the report of the inquiry. Furthermore, the report contained misinformation on another aspect of Bullock's openness about his discussions and was selective, to Bullock's detriment, in some of the quotations from documents used in the report. Thirdly, the behaviour of Fisher in not warning Bullock about the dangers of his actions seemed quite extraordinary. Indeed, Bullock felt that the 'only explanation which emerged during the course of the Enquiry for Sir Warren's strange silence during all these months was that Sir Eric had pledged him to secrecy, and Sir Eric said he had done so in his evidence'. He added: 'To me it seems a breach of official propriety, if not also of personal good faith, thus to enter into a compact of secrecy with an outsider on a service matter against a colleague - whether or not that outsider be a personal friend'. Bullock found it remarkable that the report made no mention whatever of the discussions between Geddes and Fisher, which apparently resulted in Bullock being denied the sort of

cautionary advice that might have been expected from the Head of
the Civil Service to Bullock as a colleague of permanent secretary
status in the civil service. There is no doubt that Bullock felt Fisher
was responsible for his outstanding and still promising civil service
career coming to such a disastrous end. Although he said that he did
not accuse Fisher of '*conscious* prejudice' he nevertheless wrote:

> It was Sir Warren Fisher who first suggested to Sir Eric
> Geddes that my talks with the latter might be related to the
> 'Francs' case of 1928...it was Sir Warren Fisher who kept
> silence for nine months on what passed between him and Sir
> Eric, when a word of warning would have saved the whole
> situation; it was Sir Warren Fisher who was responsible for
> some at least of the more offensive matter in the original
> indictment, which I was able completely to demolish; it was
> Sir Warren Fisher who (theoretically at all events) was
> responsible for advising the Prime Minister to set up the
> Board of Enquiry, for selecting its personnel and giving them
> their instructions, and in due course for advising the Prime
> Minister as to what action should be taken on the Board's
> Report; it was Sir Warren Fisher who... communicated the
> decision to dismiss me without a syllable of regret or one
> word of recognition of such services as I had been able to
> render to the State; and finally, I have been informed that Sir
> Warren Fisher was not content to leave at least one great
> organ of the Press to make up its own mind on my case free
> from external influence.[44]

After he had received notice from Fisher of his dismissal from the
civil service, Bullock wrote to the Prime Minister on 29 July asking
that he be permitted to resign (on grounds that he was not guilty of
corruption or neglecting the interests of the State), because the
stigma of dismissal would jeopardise his chances of obtaining other
employment and resignation would have all the severe practical
penalties that were involved in dismissal. However, it seems that at
this time Baldwin was, according to Bullock, 'suffering from
insomnia so severe that he was on the verge of a breakdown and
hardly capable of digesting papers of any complexity'.[45] On receipt
of Bullock's letter to the Prime Minister, Fisher discussed it with
Swinton, who apparently expressed the view that dismissal was too
harsh a penalty,[46] then he and Sir Horace Wilson saw the Prime
Minister and it was decided that the sentence must stand and that

Fisher would reply on behalf of the Prime Minister.[47]

Bullock received great encouragement from the hundreds of friends and well-wishers who spontaneously wrote to let him know how shocked they were at the sentence, to express their sympathy, and to tell him of their good wishes and support. Many correspondents made a special point of criticising the unsatisfactory nature of the inquiry and stressing their disapproval of Bullock's dismissal. Of the various newspaper comments, the *Birmingham Post* included some very pertinent remarks:

> ...While, then, Sir Christopher Bullock's service career has ended in a manner which, happily, is so exceptional that memory may well be taxed in vain in the search for precedents, what is really more remarkable than the act of summary dismissal is the commission, by a person holding the high office of Permanent Secretary, of an offence so grave, so flagrantly against the service code, as to render the Prime Minister's decision imperative. And yet, having said so much we must, in justice to Sir Christopher, say something more: which is that readers of the official statement who begin by commending the Prime Minister's stern guardianship of public interest and service morality will be not unlikely to end by asking themselves what, after all, did this offender's transgression amount to? And how, if at all, was any public interest adversely affected, or even imperilled, by any of the conversations now held to justify his dismissal?
>
> ...The nature of Sir Christopher's offence is clear enough, then. He made suggestions which were untimely...he displayed (in the words of the Board) 'a lack of instinct and perception'. The gravity of it all is another matter and we, for our part, should hesitate to emphasise the 'gravity' of error admittedly so free from either wrong intention or mischievous result...[48]

By the time Bullock had recovered from the shock of his dismissal, war had broken out. This meant that at the beginning of the Second World War Bullock was in the frustrating position of being denied the opportunity of playing a full and active part in the war effort. Bullock asked to see Wilson, as Wilson had succeeded Fisher as Head of the Civil Service, and they met on 6 May 1940. Bullock went into his case in great detail. Then, in the spring of 1940,

Wilson offered Bullock the Headship of the Petroleum Warfare Department, which Bullock could not at the time accept because by then he had an industrial Chairmanship and was engaged in war work (he also had other directorships) and there was no one available to replace him. Furthermore, as he explained to Wilson, it was a position at less than his previous rank and he could not accept a drop in his income because of the level of his personal and family expenditure - his two sons were then 13 and 19 years of age.

During the war, in the intervals of fire-watching, Bullock spent time preparing his case. He wrote a full account of it, which he had printed, and after the war he continued preparing other evidence for the case to be officially reopened. In these preparations he was remarkably successful, as the following examples illustrate. Twelve civil service heads of department, six serving and six retired, signed a statement to the Prime Minister urging, in the interests of the civil service, reconsideration with a view to redressing what appeared to be a serious miscarriage of justice, and Bullock's reinstatement. Bullock said he could have obtained more signatures but twelve seemed ample. Baldwin and Swinton, neither of whom met Bullock at the time of his dismissal, wrote to Attlee saying they would never have taken the decision they did, had they at the time known all the facts subsequently drawn to their attention by Bullock.[49] Sir Walter Monckton and two other King's Counsel gave, without any fee, a legal opinion in support of Bullock, in which they said that the Board of Inquiry committed such misdirections or non-direction that, had they been made by a Judge, there would have been grounds for a successful appeal and quashing the sentence. Lords Trenchard, Portal and Tedder wrote to the Secretary of State for Air praising Bullock's work for the Royal Air Force and supporting his request to have his case reopened. Bullock then sent a mass of evidence to Attlee on 19 April 1947. In his covering memorandum, of 17 typewritten foolscap pages, single spaced, with numerous annexures and enclosures, he explained that on various occasions he discovered that business appointments, which he had been offered, were withdrawn because of his case in 1936 and/or because senior officials in the Treasury said the Treasury would find Bullock's appointment embarrassing. He also outlined the sort of informal but thorough review, behind the scenes rather than in public, that he hoped the Prime Minister would set up. Bullock suggested that if Attlee approved a discussion in Parliament he would have no difficulty in arranging for a series of friendly Questions by leading members in the House of Commons, the Lords, or both. Finally, he stressed his request for an interview with the Prime Minister, which he felt he had been wrongly and unfairly denied in 1936. He sent copies of this letter and enclosures to the Chancellor of the Exchequer and to Bridges.

It was Bridges' job to deal with this request, accompanied by its vast supporting documentation. Bridges' first reactions were contained in his minute to the Prime Minister on 3 May 1947. He wrote:

> ...I have never had anything to do with this case hitherto and in 1936 I shared the impression that the decision was very severe and perhaps harsh. But in common with many other people, I had the impression that the actions Sir Christopher Bullock complained of had their origin in a strain of marked egotism and insensitiveness in his character. For all his great ability and drive, he had rather more than his fair share of blind spots which prevented him from seeing how others reacted to his conduct, particularly where his own interests were concerned. Indeed I believe that owing to his strain of insensitiveness he never realised at the time or since that the actions which he took were not merely indiscreet but did not accord with the way in which a Permanent Secretary should conduct himself.[50]

Bridges continued his minute with the suggestion that the Prime Minister should refer the matter to the Lord Chancellor, Lord Jowitt. Jowitt reviewed the case, reading the written evidence and transcript of the inquiry and also all the papers submitted to the Prime Minister by Bullock. Although he recognised that the report of the inquiry may have contained blemishes, he found that nearly all the facts were beyond the realm of controversy. On the papers presented by Bullock, the Lord Chancellor said he found it difficult to use moderate language: it was 'difficult to conceive how any honourable person could put his hand to the vulgar diatribe in which Sir Christopher Bullock has criticised the Board of Enquiry and witnesses'. Jowitt said he thought it inevitable that Bullock had to leave the civil service, but

> ...that it would have met the case if he had been allowed to resign. After all, it was not a case in which any corruption had been alleged and though he adopted undesirable means to try

to get himself appointed to the Board of Imperial Airways he did so primarily because he believed that the Board was thoroughly inefficient and he believed he could put the concern to rights. He did not do it for money. He was by nature a man who so long as he could achieve his end was not troubled by niceties as to the means by which he did so. It may well be that he did not appreciate then and does not appreciate now that what he did was wrong. ...This conduct was quite unworthy of a man in the position of Sir Christopher Bullock, but excuses can be made for a man of his temperament and enthusiasm...[51]

Jowitt's general conclusion was that while the report of the Board of Inquiry was right, Bullock should have been given the opportunity to resign because 'it was really a case in which his zeal had outrun his discretion'. However, although Jowitt said he would have made a different decision from the Prime Minister's in 1936 his advice to Attlee was that he should not 'after all these years alter the decision that was then made'. On the other hand, he thought Attlee should emphasise that in the opinion of HM Government there was no reason why Bullock should not now be accepted as a fit man to occupy any position of trust.

The Prime Minister discussed the Lord Chancellor's report at a meeting on 9 June 1947 with the Lord Chancellor, the Chancellor of the Exchequer, the President of the Board of Trade and Bridges. Bridges wrote a brief for this meeting in which he thought a public announcement should be made which upheld the decision of the Board of Inquiry but said that the original sentence was too severe and should be modified. He added: 'I think this...may be urged. My heart has some sympathy with it, but my head has doubts.' Bridges recognised, however, that an announcement to this effect would not satisfy Bullock: 'He is already looking for something like a formal retrial or rehearing of his case' and Bridges thought his proposed line of action might prove to be a compromise which looked weak and pleased no one.[52] In the event, the meeting on 9 June decided that Bridges should be asked to draft a letter for Jowitt to send to Bullock inviting him to discuss the Lord Chancellor's review of the case. However, this discussion with the Lord Chancellor, which took place in August 1947, did not satisfy Bullock for numerous reasons.[53]

Soon after the Lord Chancellor's review, Attlee wrote to Baldwin on 8 September 1947, the letter being drafted for him by

Jowitt, embodying Jowitt's findings and he agreed that, if Baldwin desired, the letter might be made public. Bullock was not satisfied with these reactions, and on 16 May 1948 he sent a further letter to the Prime Minister arguing that it should be made public that the Board of Inquiry had gone wrong on several points and asking for a fuller measure of redress than was offered by the Prime Minister's letter to Baldwin. The letter of May 1948 was accompanied by a letter from six former permanent secretaries who also took the view that the Prime Minister's letter was not adequate redress and challenged the findings of the Board of Inquiry. The Prime Minister replied on 28 June adhering to his previous decision. Statements in Bullock's letter of 16 May made it clear that, if he did not get the redress he was seeking, he would launch a public campaign through Parliament and in the press, attacking the decision of ministers. Later, Bridges blamed himself to some extent because, as he said, 'the letters which I recommended ministers to write communicating their decisions to Bullock were not couched in the sort of terms which were most likely to bring about a settlement, given that we were dealing with a man in a highly disturbed and nervous frame of mind'.[54]

Activity on the Bullock case then died down for a few months until February 1949 when Bullock wrote asking for a meeting with Bridges.[55] This was arranged for 8 March and Bullock asked Bridges to take some action about the way government departments were blocking his appointments to responsible business positions. Bullock offered Bridges a draft of a letter he could send to the Governor of the Bank of England (whom Bullock did not know, but whom Bridges knew well) that might help ease the situation. Bridges knew that Wilson, Sir William Douglas, and Cripps had written such letters at Bullock's request in the past and he therefore said he was sympathetic to the request but asked for time to think the matter over and draft his own letter. It was agreed that they would meet again when a draft had been prepared and it could be shown to Bullock before being sent to the Governor, Lord Cobbold.

Later, Bridges drafted a letter to Cobbold which he discussed with both Padmore and Cobbold; then he saw Bullock on 29 March to discuss it with him before posting it. After they had discussed the draft Bridges introduced his extraordinary initiative. Bridges turned the discussion onto what Bullock called 'his case' and asked Bullock if he would like to hear how he saw the matter. Bullock said he would. Bridges then explained that he had 'from the first thought the sentence of dismissal a very severe one which was likely to be modified as time went on' but that Bullock had made things more difficult for himself by seeking to justify up to the hilt what he had done; by attacking other people and seeking to show that they had made grievous errors or had shown malice; and he was asking for more than he would get in practice by seeking complete absolution and formal reinstatement. Bridges made the point that in seeking justice for Bullock care should be taken to avoid injustice towards those who had handled the case or been involved in it.

Bullock took this well, though later he became heated in criticising the Board of Inquiry and others. After he had expressed his strong views he became appreciative of what Bridges had said. Bullock made it clear, however, that he still wanted formal reinstatement. Bridges argued that any reinstatement could be formal only and could not be expected to lead to anything (i.e. neither a permanent secretaryship in the civil service nor a pension). The interview ended with Bullock showing that he was quite moved by Bridges mentioning the matter in such a friendly way and it was agreed they would meet again to discuss the matter further. Bridges emphasised that what he had said had been an entirely personal approach, without consultation with any other person and that he could not guarantee that even if something emerged from it it would not be turned down by ministers.

Various letters were then exchanged between Bridges and Bullock, but pressure of business, especially Parliamentary business, devaluation and the national economy measures, prevented a further meeting before 4 January 1950. Meanwhile, Bridges consulted Padmore who agreed with Bridges that if Bullock did not get reinstatement in due course he was likely to embark on the public and political campaign which he had had in mind for some time. It is clear from the papers that Bridges was trying to move towards a compromise where it could be conceded that the dismissal had been unduly harsh for an error of judgment that was not a moral lapse and that ministers would agree to expunge his dismissal from the civil service. Bridges' difficulty was that this was less than Bullock was demanding and in any case he had no authority even to offer so much. There is no doubt that Bridges was only too well aware of his delicate position. On 27 July 1949 he had a discussion about it with Hopkins. Hopkins was not very sympathetic - which is not surprising as he was a member of the 1936 Board of Inquiry. His view was that one Prime Minister (Baldwin) had been made to eat his words and he did not see why another one (Attlee) should be made to do the same. Furthermore, he had no doubt that the statement signed by the permanent secretaries had been the product of Bullock's technique of energetically negotiating drafts. Bridges, however, said he wanted to stop an endless series of appeals and persecution mania in Bullock, and he explained how he envisaged an acceptable compromise statement. Hopkins made it clear that he thought reinstatement for a man who had no intention of continuing in the civil service went beyond what was justified.

When Bridges saw Bullock on 4 January 1950 he delivered himself of a long and what he thought was a moving oration. His main point was that if the matter was to be settled it could only be by a short statement in very general terms in which both sides agreed to leave many things unsaid and which breathed an atmosphere of hatchet burying. He had prepared such a statement, but it was without authority or consultation, though he thought ministers would probably accept it. He warned that if the statement was expanded he did not know whether he could get it accepted. Bullock was very moved by this gesture, read the draft and took it away for reflection and so that, with Bridges' agreement, he could show it to one or two of his friends. Bullock agreed to let Bridges know his views on the draft within 48 hours.

After reflection Bullock wrote to Bridges on 5 January saying that he could not accept the draft as it stood but he wanted to be constructive and proposed amendments. He also asked if Bridges could have a word with the Chancellor on his behalf about the possibility of being appointed to the Board of the Anglo Iranian Oil Company. He wrote again on 9 January, but at greater length. Bridges asked for his revisions; these were sent with covering notes by Bullock on 11 January. They had agreed to meet again on 13 January, but on 12 January, after Bridges had consulted Padmore, he wrote postponing the meeting because, he said, the matter was too important to risk dealing with it without adequate time for thought. Bullock replied on 13 January with more points to strengthen his own position.

About this time Bridges became ill and this was followed by pressure of work which meant their intended meeting was again postponed. Bullock wrote again on 21 February about their meeting. Again he stressed points he wished to see included in the statement to strengthen his position. Again he referred to what could, if necessary, be extracted by a series of Parliamentary Questions.

Bridges then, on 7 March, discussed his draft statement and

Bullock's revised version with Padmore and Sir Thomas Barnes, the Treasury Solicitor. Barnes expressed reservations about both drafts: in particular he made it quite clear that any statement could not imply that the Board of Inquiry had gone off the rails because the Lord Chancellor had specifically said that it had not. Because it looked as though the two drafts were irreconcilable (and if the points proposed by Bullock were inserted Bridges thought ministers would not agree) it was proposed that Bridges should ask Bullock to nominate one of his supporters to speak for him and discuss the matter again with Bridges and someone else of Bridges' choice. These three would then try to produce an agreed draft *ad referendum*. It was also agreed that there would be no need to tell ministers about this until an agreement was reached on a formula to present to ministers.

Bullock wrote to Bridges again on 11 March 1950 asking for an early meeting, mentioning again the possibility of stimulating a series of Parliamentary Questions. They met on 15 March and, as arranged, Bridges proposed a meeting with one of Bullock's supporters and another chosen by Bridges. According to Bridges, Bullock then had a violent mood and spoke with great vehemence and bitterness. Eventually Bridges stressed his doubts once more about what he could get ministers to accept but he said he would have another shot at redrafting to meet Bullock's points. Bridges noted: 'The odds are about 3 to 1 or 4 to 1 against, but the position is not quite hopeless. It is also quite clear that if we don't settle this ultimately Sir C.B. will put someone up to ask a lot of questions in April and we shall have a lot of public fuss.'[56]

Bullock wrote again at length (7 more pages of typed foolscap, single spaced) on 21 April saying again how shabbily he had been treated and that the shifts and evasions he had encountered had been unworthy. He complained that Bridges had, in effect, muzzled him for over a year. Again he referred to the possibility of public statements and Parliamentary Questions, but this time he also referred to a new pamphlet which he had ready for the printer.[57] Meanwhile Bridges, in further consultation with Padmore and Barnes, produced another redraft of the proposed statement and in a letter of 3 May he proposed a meeting of Sir Archibald Rowlands, Sir Maurice Holmes (two of Bullock's supporters), Bullock and Bridges. When Bullock saw the redraft he thought Bridges had travelled backwards and told him so in a letter of 15 May. He again referred to his determination to fight on and bring things out into the open, even though it would mean facing the unpleasantness of a public controversy: he stressed that the full truth could be extracted by 'a dozen or so judiciously distributed Parliamentary Questions' - and he had already provided outlines of the sort of questions he had in mind, in the documents he had had printed. The meeting of Rowlands, Holmes, Bullock and Bridges on 17 May agreed a draft statement and also a draft of a minute to the Chancellor of the Exchequer. The draft was phrased in generous terms. It recognised that the 1936 sentence of dismissal was not merited and should be expunged, made no mention of the Board of Inquiry, and admitted that Bullock had not been influenced by self-advancement, but by a desire to strengthen the organisation of Imperial Airways.

These drafts then went to Barnes for his comments. Barnes did not like what was being proposed because it gave the impression that Bullock had been completely whitewashed and that both sentence and findings had been overruled. He argued: 'This is not only unfair to members of the Board who carried out an extremely unpleasant task with great propriety, but it may well undermine such confidence as the general body of Civil Servants may now have in these domestic tribunals. It seems to me, therefore, essential that the statement should make it plain that the findings of the Board are not disturbed.'[58] Bridges also consulted Hopkins, who saw Bridges again on 5 June. He also thought the draft went too far to meet Bullock and he agreed with the views expressed by Barnes. Nevertheless, he proposed some suggestions for improving the draft statement and protecting the position and conclusions of the 1936 Board of Inquiry. Meanwhile Ram (who had also served on the Board of Inquiry but had since been promoted to the Office of the Parliamentary Counsel) was also consulted and sent an important reply to Bridges, recalling the events of 1936 and arguing that, contrary to Bullock's belief, Fisher had, in fact, been at pains to ensure a fair and impartial consideration of the evidence and an unprejudiced report.[59]

Eventually, on 12 June, Bridges sent his minute to the Chancellor of the Exchequer - with copies to other ministers. The Lord Chancellor then learned for the first time of Bridges' initiative and he felt strongly that the course Bridges was proposing was fundamentally wrong. He wrote in no uncertain terms about it to the Prime Minister. He also wrote to Bridges about it on 14 June 1950, enclosing a copy of the minute he had written to the Prime Minister in which he referred to Bridges' draft as 'a mere essay in appeasement'. Bridges replied the next day saying how sorry he was that Jowitt should feel so strongly that something he proposed was fundamentally wrong. He added: 'This depresses me greatly.' The same day Bridges consulted Portal, who, with Trenchard and Tedder had written some time before to the Secretary of State for Air in support of Bullock. Portal said that 'he was not enamoured of Bullock, who was an over-confident little man full of his own self-importance (cock-sparrow). But the fact remained that he had done a good job for the Air Force, and he had also had a raw deal...'[60]

Meanwhile the Prime Minister called a meeting on 21 June of himself, the Lord Chancellor, Chancellor of the Exchequer and the Lord President; Bridges was also present. Jowitt spoke critically, along the lines of his letter of 14 June, and was supported by the Prime Minister. The Lord President (Morrison) took the view that ministers ought never to have decided that Bullock ought not to have been dismissed. Moreover, to review a case so long afterwards would, Morrison feared, cast doubt upon the disciplinary machinery in the civil service and lead to demands for new arrangements for appeals from disciplinary decisions.[61] Bridges had to defend his action and explain that he had not been trying to upset any of the decisions taken by ministers but to produce a short draft within the ambit of ministerial decisions that would bring an end to a longstanding controversy. Ministers were clear that they endorsed the findings of the 1936 Board of Inquiry and rejected Bridges' draft. However, they agreed that a new draft might be proposed by Bridges for the approval of the Lord Chancellor. Bridges asked Barnes to produce this new draft. When it was prepared, Cripps, the Chancellor of the Exchequer, agreed to it and Bridges sent it to the Prime Minister on 12 July; it was then circulated to other ministers. The Lord Chancellor said he agreed with the Lord President and added that what should have happened was that his report to the Prime Minister should have been published in 1947. Jowitt and Morrison proposed amendments to the draft and Bridges received the Prime Minister's permission to show the further revised draft to Bullock. Meanwhile Bridges saw Morrison, who agreed to the proposed redraft provided the Prime Minister saw the considered opinions he had recorded in a minute of 17 July.

Bullock wrote again to Bridges on 6 July 1950 complaining that it was 16 months since Bridges' initiative began and 7 weeks since he had agreed, not without considerable hesitation, the draft with Bridges and others. He again asked for an interview with the Prime

Minister. He enclosed copies of some papers he had had printed outlining his case and summarising developments since 1945.

Bridges wrote to Bullock on 26 July 1950 explaining that the draft they had agreed had been rejected by ministers. He enclosed a copy of the latest revised version of the draft and urged him most strongly to consider that document carefully. He continued: 'You know that I have set my heart on trying to reach a solution to these troubles. And now I must add that I am afraid I have about reached the end of my tether and that I should be wrong to hold out any hopes that I could put forward anything more favourable to your point of view than this draft.' Bullock replied at length on 28 July pointing out that the draft was, in fact, based on the Lord Chancellor's review of the case, with which it was already known that he had numerous reservations.

Bullock called on Bridges on 3 August. According to Bridges, who wrote to Barnes the same day, he was highly disturbed. When Bridges' innings came, he made three points. First, that he had not realised how firmly determined ministers were that anything which was publicly said should be limited to a statement that the matter had been referred to the Lord Chancellor who had carried out a quasi-judicial enquiry and to the report which he had made. Bridges said he had misjudged the situation in this respect. Secondly, it was clear that ministers would not shift from this point of view and it was no use trying to get them to change their minds. Thirdly, that if Bullock launched an attack on the way the Lord Chancellor had carried out his enquiry this would do no good; ministers would rally behind the Lord Chancellor.

After the 1951 General Election R.A. Butler became Chancellor of the Exchequer. On 5 November Bullock wrote to him privately asking him to reopen the case and enclosing a copy of the draft statement that Bridges, Rowlands, Holmes and Bullock had agreed on 17 May 1950. Butler was sympathetic and wrote to his private secretary, William Armstrong, that he would like to see justice done: 'Please respect the private character of this and consult Sir E. Bridges.'

About the same time Bullock also re-contacted Bridges and asked for a meeting. Bridges consulted Barnes again, for advice, because Bridges recalled that Bullock had previously made it clear that if he was to publish a document about his case he intended to include a copy of the draft statement of 17 May, which had been rejected by ministers, but which was the result of Bridges' initiative. Bridges had already been unsuccessful in persuading

Bullock not to do this because of the embarrassment it would cause him. Bridges took the view that if there was a risk (he chose his words carefully and did not call it a threat) that Bullock involved Bridges in some future publication, then Bridges could no longer be regarded as a perfectly detached, impartial adviser of ministers in this matter. Bridges was proposing to tell Bullock that if there was such a risk he would have to entrust the handling of the case to one of his colleagues. Bridges went on:

> I want your advice as to whether you think this is the right course. I will not disguise from you that I have already spent too much time on the Bullock case and I should be glad to be free of it. But I do not think that this is what really influences me. I feel that I have got a little too involved personally in the affair and that it would be better that, if negotiations start again, someone should advise Ministers who could take a more dispassionate view than perhaps I could be expected to take after my unsuccessful attempts to solve the dispute.[62]

Barnes was sorry to learn that Bullock was again on the warpath: 'He is a public nuisance.' He agreed that Bridges was being placed in an impossible position if anything he wrote or said in confidential negotiations could be published by Bullock to suit his own ends. He added: 'I distrust him very much, and cannot help feeling that it is better to keep him at arms length...'[63]

Bullock called on Bridges again on 9 July 1953 asking for help to get a job with one of the Big Five Banks - he continued to feel that he was being denied job opportunities because of unfair and unfriendly gossip. Bridges agreed to contact Sir Frederick Leith-Ross, then Deputy Chairman of the National Provincial Bank, on Bullock's behalf. (Leith-Ross had joined the Treasury in 1909 and had been Chief Economic Adviser 1932-46). The next day Bullock wrote again to Bridges expressing his gratitude. He said that as far as he was concerned a Bank directorship would finally put matters right in the City. He admitted that there was very keen competition for them, but said that had it not been for the events of 1936 he would have been a certain candidate in view of his record of achievement up to that date. In case Bridges required it, he enclosed a list of his present directorships and explained that he had experience of and continuous contacts with engineering, brewing, bookselling and printing, metals, mining and insurance. He added: 'I have reason to believe that I could bring one or two of the

Companies listed to the Bank...which is a point to which I know Bank Executives attach importance.'

Bridges discussed the matter with the Governor of the Bank of England on 17 July 1953 and the Governor agreed there would be no harm in mentioning the matter to Leith-Ross. On 18 September Bullock wrote to remind Bridges that he would speak on his behalf to Leith-Ross and also to the Chancellor of the Exchequer. Bridges wrote to Leith-Ross on 22 September and suggested they meet at lunchtime in the Athenaeum during the following week or so. In fact, however, it was more convenient for Leith-Ross to call on Bridges in the Treasury, which he did on 7 October 1953. Leith-Ross could not hold out any hopes to help Bullock but, when leaving, he suggested that he might discuss the matter with Lord Selborne and invite Bullock to lunch.

Bullock called on Bridges again on 12 November 1953 mainly, it seems, to find out whether he had interceded on his behalf with the Chancellor of the Exchequer, to see whether R.A.Butler would back Bullock's application to Selborne for a job with the National Provincial Bank. Bullock made it clear that he wanted to take the matter up with the Chancellor personally; he said he had known the Chancellor's uncle very well and was sure the Chancellor would recognise a personal obligation to back his case. Bullock then again went over the history of his case and asked Bridges what he, as Head of the Civil Service, had tried to do to remedy the wrong and compensate him for it. Bridges went over what he had tried to do and said he had not succeeded because Bullock had insisted on a longer draft statement than in Bridges' judgment ministers would be willing to accept. Bullock and his friends had not been content with the original short draft statement Bridges had produced and the statement which they insisted on submitting had been rejected by ministers. Bridges then told Bullock that he thought he had shot his bolt. In particular he said that if at anytime Bullock wanted to return to the charge and referred to what had happened when Bridges had handled the matter, then he would feel obliged to stand aside and let someone else in the Treasury handle the matter. Bridges concluded that he could not do anything more and he felt detached from the whole business. Bullock accepted this, though rather reluctantly. Bullock then said that the Treasury had thousands of directorships at its disposal, yet had never offered one to him and he thought this very odd, bearing in mind the injury which had been done to him. Bridges found this difficult to handle because the reason why Bullock had never been offered a Government directorship was that he was not a very easy person to deal with and was not the kind of person officials would want to recommend as a Government representative. Bridges therefore pointed out that there were not as many opportunities as Bullock thought and in any case the final decision on appointments did not rest with officials. Bridges said he recognised that Bullock was quite entitled to make the point and he would take note that he had made it. This only produced a statement from Bullock that he was not asking for a job but was quite capable of asking for one when he did want one. Nevertheless, he thought 'the machine' had behaved very badly to him in never offering him one.

Bullock never secured the redress he desired and died in 1972 without any official statement being issued about his treatment. This is particularly sad because the injustice he suffered was privately recognised during the war when he was invited to return to the civil service as head of a government department - which as Hankey (Secretary to the Cabinet at the time) wrote later 'would have been *de facto* reinstatement ... equivalent to complete restitution'.[64]The injustice was not, however, recognised publicly until after his death, when his memorial service at the Central Church of the Royal Air Force, St Clement Danes, was attended by representatives of the Prime Minister, the Air Force Board, and the Home Civil Service.[65] Bullock's achievements, especially in relation to the Royal Air Force, have been justly recognised in accounts of rearmament and the role of the Royal Air Force during the Second World War. For example, H. Montgomery Hyde refers to Bullock as 'the brilliant Permanent Secretary to the Air Ministry'[66] and Viscount Templewood says he was 'a remarkable young man... by his departure the Air Force lost one of its ablest defenders'.[67] His achievements were also praised in the letter of condolence sent by Sir James Dunnett, then Permanent Under Secretary of State at the Ministry of Defence, to Mr R.H.W. Bullock on the death of his father. Dunnett wrote of Bullock's career:

His years of service in the Air Ministry covered a period of great importance for the Royal Air Force; in particular, during his latter years as Permanent Under-Secretary in the Air Ministry, the foundations were laid for the vast expansion of the Royal Air Force to which the survival of the country in the last war was so largely due. It was also during your father's period of office as the senior civilian officer in the Air

Ministry that the first steps were taken towards the great expansion we have subsequently seen in British Civil Aviation.[68]

However, it is not widely appreciated today that the story of his dismissal in 1936 became, as Sir William Armstrong recognised when he was Head of the Civil Service, 'one of the strands upon which the service's code of conduct has been based'.[69]

The Bullock case in retrospect

The Bullock case would never have achieved its significance without the prior inquiry, in 1928, 'to investigate certain statements affecting civil servants',[70] which became popularly known as the 'Francs' case. During a trial in the King's Bench Division of the High Court of Justice statements had been made that three civil servants had been engaged in speculative transactions in foreign currencies with a firm of foreign bankers. The details of the case are of no concern here, but the inquiry was set up to consider whether transactions for the purpose of private profit 'were proper or becoming in the case of a Civil Servant'.[71] Fisher, as Head of the Civil Service, was appointed by the Prime Minister to conduct the inquiry, together with Sir Malcolm G. Ramsay (Controller of Establishments, HM Treasury 1919-1921, and from 1921 Comptroller and Auditor-General) and Sir Maurice L. Gwyer (Treasury Solicitor).

The inquiry found that although the civil servants neither used, nor endeavoured to use, official information for the purpose of their transactions, those 'transactions ought never to have been entered upon by any Civil Servant'.[72] By engaging in those transactions the officials had acted 'in a manner inconsistent with their obligations as Civil Servants'.[73] The report concluded:

The first duty of a Civil Servant is to give his undivided allegiance to the State at all times and on all occasions when the State has a claim upon his services...But to say that he is not to subordinate his duty to his private interests, nor to make use of his official position to further those interests, is to say no more than that the Service is entitled to demand that its servants shall not only be honest in fact, but beyond the reach of suspicion of dishonesty. The Service exacts from itself a higher standard, because it recognises that the State is entitled to demand that its servants shall not only be honest in fact, but beyond the reach of suspicion of dishonesty...A Civil Servant is not to subordinate his duty to his private interests; but neither is he to put himself in a position where his duty and his interests conflict. He is not to make use of his official position to further those interests; but neither is he so to order his private affairs as to allow the suspicion to arise that a trust has been abused or a confidence betrayed ...[74] And lastly, his position imposes upon him restrictions in matters of commerce and business from which the ordinary citizen is free.[75]

...Practical rules for the guidance of social conduct depend... as much upon the instinct and perception of the individual as upon cast-iron formulas; and the surest guide will, we hope, always be found in the nice and jealous honour of Civil Servants themselves. The public expects from them a standard of integrity and conduct that is not only inflexible but fastidious, and has not been disappointed in the past...[76]

The principles outlined in the report of the inquiry were thought to be so important that a Treasury Ciruclar was issued on 13 March 1928, reprinting them and requiring them to be incorporated in departmental rules and brought to the notice of each new recruit. It was this Circular which played an important part in the Bullock inquiry and Bullock was specifically asked questions to confirm that he was aware of the rules contained in it. Bullock stressed that he was not seeking his private interests when he made enquiries about his acceptability for a directorship with Imperial Airways - and in Bullock's defence it must be reaffirmed that everyone later agreed that that was so. However, the fact remains that only a few years before Bullock's case the 'Francs' case had been enquired into by a Board presided over by Fisher. Fisher saw a parallel between the two cases and mentioned it to Geddes. The parallel became particularly significant at the Bullock inquiry which found that Bullock had departed from the standards said to be required of civil servants. According to Barnes it was because Bullock was not a junior official, but the head of a big public department who should have set an example to others, that 'it was felt right to impose a drastic sentence... in order to impress upon others that the standards laid down were not mere pious hopes but were standards to be rigidly observed...'[77]

It is evident that Fisher, as Head of the Civil Service, played an important role in the Bullock case. Fisher was a remarkable person whose actions were at times governed by intuition rather than logical reasoning and who inspired devotion in some and hostility in others.[78] In this case it seems that Fisher was determined that Bullock should become an example by which others would learn. When an example is made in this way it has to be publicised with attention given to the standard of behaviour to which others should aspire. Bullock himself seems to have believed that Fisher even went so far as to influence *The Times* in its comment on his case. Whether or not he did is difficult to prove over fifty years later, but there is certainly a remarkable similarity between passages in the leading article in *The Times* and Fisher's other correspondence at that time. *The Times* concluded:

... There are no two ways about the dismissal of a clerk or a postman or an Inspector of Taxes who violates what is no longer an unwritten law. Would any lighter punishment be tolerable in the case of the responsible head of a Ministry? That is the real test of the sentence of dismissal, and the Government - and particularly those members of it who are most directly concerned, the Prime Minister and the Secretary of State for Air - may well be congratulated on their determination, however distasteful it must have been, to face it at once and to leave nothing for concealment or for palliation. And the Civil Service above all is to be congratulated on having taken into its own hands the inflexible maintenance of its great traditions. It will not suffer in the end for this ruthless exposure. Nor is it altogether a misfortune - at a time when there must inevitably be more and more dealings between the Departments and the contracting firms - that it should have had occasion to demonstrate in such signal fashion how high is its standard and how rigorous its code.[79]

Bullock's scale of priorities, and his belief that ends could justify means, were rather different from those proclaimed by Fisher and in *The Times*. However, his enthusiastic devotion to his work, and to what he considered to be the public interest, seems in retrospect to be unquestionable. Indeed, such devotion, and the scale of values that went with it, certainly contributed to his rapid career advancement and to his appointment as the permanent head of the Air Ministry before he was 40 years of age.

However, the differences between Bullock and other civil servants were even more clearly responsible for his downfall. His thrusting personality, lack of sensitivity, and willingness to 'cut corners' to achieve his objectives, brought disadvantages to a civil service post and in some respects were more suited to a commercial enterprise. One example of this thrusting style and insensitivity emerged during the inquiry but was not mentioned in the report. In evidence it was revealed that in September 1935, and perhaps as early as May 1934, Bullock had been promised a directorship of the North British and Mercantile Insurance Office. When Bullock was discussing with Geddes the possibility of an honour for him and Geddes disclaimed his desire for a peerage, Bullock said that this made things easier for him as he wanted the peerage for someone else. In fact it seems that on 20 March 1935 Bullock spoke to Fisher about a peerage for Sir Arthur Worley, the Deputy Chairman and Managing Director (and the leading spirit) of the North British and Mercantile Insurance Company - though it is not clear whether Bullock then disclosed to Fisher that he had been promised a directorship in that firm for a later date, after his retirement from the civil service. For some time Worley had been indicating, by various means and through a variety of well-placed individuals, his desire for a peerage. The origins of the link between Worley and Bullock may have been that the North British operated for the Air Ministry a scheme of insurance against pilots' air risks. It may well have been that some of the conversations between Bullock and Worley were similar to conversations between Bullock and Geddes (at least, Hopkins thought it possible, and it was considered by the Board of Inquiry),[80] though if there were such similar conversations, they did not result in a public inquiry. Bullock, and others with similar attitudes, may not have thought there was anything wrong in such conversations simply because to some top civil servants proposals for honours were regarded as such an ordinary matter of routine.[81] The important point to note, however, is the context within which Bullock was seeking a peerage for Worley: no matter that he was acting in what he believed to be the public interest, he had in fact been promised, by Worley, a directorship on the Board of the North British and Mercantile Insurance Company. Whilst this should not have made Worley ineligible for a peerage, it almost certainly made him ineligible to be proposed by Bullock.

The Bullock case clearly reveals that there can be disadvantages as well as advantages in having in the civil service someone with the combination of personal qualities which Bullock possessed. It reveals even more about the lack of sensitivity within the civil service to questions of personnel management. Time and time again Bullock asked for an interview with the Prime Minister, the minister responsible for the civil service, but he was never granted one by Baldwin or Attlee, nor was he seen by his own Secretary of State at the time of his dismissal. It seems the denials of access to ministers in 1936 were because Fisher said it would be incorrect for Bullock to be granted an interview, the matter being in the hands of the civil service.[82] This raises further questions about Fisher's role in the case and, especially, about his relationship with Bullock.

It should also be emphasised that Bullock was not a man who lacked deference to legitimate authority: in certain respects he acted with extraordinary restraint and propriety. The pamphlet he wrote in defence of his position was by no means intemperate, though the Lord Chancellor seemed to think it was in 1947. Bullock accepted much more advice from senior colleagues than might have been expected of someone of his disposition and he showed remarkable patience in preparing what amounted to his appeal through the normal channels. Indeed, Bullock adhered quite strictly to the formal procedures in seeking redress for his grievances but he felt he could never win against what he called 'the machine'. That he felt he could not get a full and fair review of his case within the administrative system may reveal as much about the deficiencies of the system in this respect as it does about Bullock. Other cases in recent years have suggested that opportunities for review by superiors are not always, or are not always seen to be, as impartial as the expectations of natural justice might require.[83]

Expectations of natural justice and equity were matters that were mentioned during the 1948 review of the Bullock case. For example, Lord Swinton wrote to the Prime Minister:

... What then is the right and fair course to adopt now? I suggest that it is clearly a formal reinstatement. I do not think that lapse of time is any reason for not doing the fair thing now. Rather the other way.

May I add one other consideration? I have been comparing Bullock's case with that of O'Malley in the Francs case. In the latter the impropriety or indiscretion was financial and actuated by private motive. Yet O'Malley was not dismissed but censured, and afterwards promoted to high rank in the Public Service. I do not at all dissent from the course followed in that case. But I do suggest that if the two cases are compared, precedent and justice alike call for re-instatement in Bullock's case.[84]

Bridges' role in all this is not easy to analyse. Bullock and Bridges had a peculiar relationship that is difficult to explain, though their similar educational backgrounds and army service during the First World War may have helped to establish a bond between the two men. Both had been wounded in the trenches during the war and both had in later years suffered pain from arthritis (which they also discussed when they met to discuss Bullock's case). Bridges may well have been influenced by the elements of injustice in the case, but other factors were at least as important. It is quite clear that Bridges was worried about Bullock leading a public campaign with support in Parliament and the press. He was also worried by the support given to Bullock by so many serving and retired top civil servants. A public campaign would have been embarrassing and involved politicians on both sides of the House being critical of the civil service. The issues that would have been stressed by Bullock in such a campaign, because he was so critical of 'the machine', would have been particularly embarrassing for Bridges - who was always concerned to ensure that the high reputation of the civil service was untainted. In addition, at the time when the Bullock case was at its most demanding, Bridges was far from well: his illness is known to have caused delays but it may also have influenced his attitude of mind and judgment.

Bridges' initiative and the reaction of ministers is particularly interesting. Jowitt's involvement in the case and his reaction to the initiative has already been mentioned, but he was not the only minister who took a strong line when the draft statement was presented to the Chancellor of the Exchequer in June 1950: Morrison also disapproved of Bridges' initiative. Whilst there is no evidence to suggest that the matter was not considered in isolation from other matters, it should be remembered that this period of post-war reconstruction, which saw the creation of the welfare state and the expansion of governmental activity, was a particularly difficult time for top civil servants, for ministers, and for their interrelationships. Some aspects of the general environment in Whitehall are described in the next chapter, on the Machinery of Government. Among more specific difficulties, however, was the sensitive relationship between the Lord President's Office and the Treasury. For example, there was disagreement about where the new Planning Board should be located and also difficulties because Morrison wanted Max Nicholson, the head of the Lord President's Office with the grade of under secretary, promoted to permanent secretary so that he had equal status with other top civil servants. At one stage in 1947 Bridges sent a 'Personal and Private' letter to Morrison which amounted to a remarkable warning, urging Morrison not to press his point too hard on behalf of the economic responsibilities of the Lord President's Office. Morrison replied complaining of Bridges' lack of co-operation, of his hostility to Nicholson, of the efforts to subordinate him to the Treasury, and making it clear that while he was the economic boss, he would not allow questions of economic organisation to be settled over his head. But, as Bernard Donoughue and G.W. Jones put it: 'Demotion, fragmentation, isolation and ultimately elimination, were the stages by which the Lord President's independent economic powers were whittled away and the Treasury was re-established in its primacy'.[85] While there is no evidence to suggest that Morrison or Bridges bore grudges over their clashes, it seems that Morrison may have concluded that, at times, Bridges and Treasury officials were too assertive compared with decisions of ministers. It is therefore not impossible that Morrison may have thought that Bridges' initiative on the Bullock case was another example of a ministerial decision being trimmed by officials. Just as Morrison thought Bridges was trying to clip Nicholson's wings, so he may have felt that Bridges in turn needed to have his wings clipped, and it looks as though Morrison thought the initiative over the Bullock case was a suitable occasion to make the point. With such strong feelings being held by the Lord Chancellor and the Lord President it is not surprising that ministers rejected Bridges' initiative.

A factor that seems to have been important to Bridges was the continuing potential of the Bullock case to cause embarrassment. It is the duty of a civil servant to point out to ministers the possible embarrassing reactions in Parliament and the public to any government decisions, and it is a small step from this duty into the administrative culture of Whitehall which seems to require embarrassment to be avoided, almost at all costs. The Bullock case seems to have caused particular trouble to Bridges because, had it developed into a public campaign, it could have brought discredit to the system of government in general as well as to the civil service in particular. One way of containing rumours of maladministration is to institute a public inquiry. But an issue that does not die as a result of a public inquiry, and which still continues after a quasi-judicial review of the inquiry some years later, may acquire more serious cancerous characteristics.

A further question which may have troubled Bridges was how to resolve a problem that was so multi-faceted. There may have been aspects of Bullock's personality that made him unsuited to the position of permanent secretary, but by the late 1940s it was not only Bullock's injudicious and insensitive behaviour and the alleged denial of the principles of natural justice that were foci for attention. Others factors included the rights of members of the Board of Inquiry; the possible wider implications of the case for personnel management, including appeals from internal disciplinary proceedings and questions about appointments to quasi-government positions; the ethical questions of the eligibility of retired civil servants for outside appointments; the question of honours, especially the personal responsibilities of the Head of the Civil Service in relation to them; and, in addition, the responsibilities of the Head of the Civil Service in relation to ministerial decisions. At some point in a case as complicated as this someone has to decide which ethical element has priority and how it should be dealt with. In the Bullock case there was such a maze of ethical issues that Bridges may simply have felt that he had to take it in hand personally.

Even if all these factors are given the attention they deserve, it seems surprising that Bridges should have given so much time and energy to the Bullock case, and it was most unusual for him to place himself in a situation where he could be criticised for exercising an initiative beyond what was acceptable to his political masters. At the end of the day, however, criticism even from leading members of the Government at a time when the end of their term of office was evidently drawing near may, to Bridges, have been preferable to a public campaign with all the damage to the morale and to the prestige of the civil service that might have accompanied it.

Notes

1. Lord Geoffrey-Lloyd in Lord Blake and C.S. Nicholls (Editors), *Dictionary of National Biography 1971-1980*, (Oxford University Press, Oxford, 1986).
2. PRO/T273/161, Bullock to Prime Minister, 19 April 1947.
3. PRO/T273/156
4. This apparently referred to the Air Force (Constitution) Act, 1917

(7 and 8 Geo V Ch.51), together with amendments and relevant Statutory Rules and Regulations. See also *Memorandum by the Secretary of State for Air on the Report of the Committee on Control of Private Flying and other Civil Aviation Questions; together with the Report and the Appendices thereto*, [Cmd. 4654], (HMSO, London, 1934), p. 12.

5. Information from Mr R.H.W. Bullock.

6. PRO/T273/160.

7. PRO/T273/160.

8. Information from Mr R.H.W. Bullock. Bullock appears to have been in the habit of making direct approaches to Baldwin under Londonderry's regime: see J.A. Cross, *Lord Swinton*, (Clarendon Press, Oxford, 1982), p. 51.

9. PRO/T273/160.

10. Londonderry to Bullock, 4 December 1934. Source: Mr R.H.W. Bullock.

11. PRO/T273/156.

12. Londonderry to Baldwin, 29 December 1938: Baldwin Papers 171, f.184. Quoted in H. Montgomery Hyde, *British Air Policy Between the Wars 1918-1939*, (Heinemann, London, 1976), p. 387.

13. Treasury Circular E 19377 (1928).

14. *Report of the Board of Enquiry appointed by the Prime Minister to investigate certain Statements affecting Civil Servants*, [Cmd. 3037], (HMSO, London, 1928).

15. *Report of the Board of Enquiry appointed by the Prime Minister to investigate certain discussions engaged in by the Permanent Secretary to the Air Ministry*, [Cmd. 5254], (HMSO, London, 1936), para. 35.

16. *Minute by the Prime Minister on the Report of the Board of Enquiry appointed by the Prime Minister to investigate certain discussions engaged in by the Permanent Secretary to the Air Ministry*, [Cmd. 5255], (HMSO, London, 1936).

17. PRO/T273/157 and PRO/T273/160.

18. This term was used in evidence to the inquiry by Sir Walter Nicholson and subsequently quoted by Bullock on various occasions (e.g. PRO/T273/159, Bullock to Prime Minister, 29 July 1936).

19. W.A. Robson (Editor), *Problems of Nationalised Industry*, (George Allen and Unwin, London, 1952), p. 281. See also W.A. Robson, *Nationalised Industry and Public Ownership*, (George Allen and Unwin, London, 1960), p. 33.

20. *Report of the Committee of Inquiry into Civil Aviation*, [Cmd. 5685], (HMSO, London, 1938), para.45.

21. *Ibid.*, para. 46.

22. PRO/T273/157.

23. PRO/T273/157.

24. PRO/T273/156, Bullock to Swinton, 28 June 1936.

25. George Beharrell, 'Sir Eric Campbell Geddes' in L.G. Wickham Legg (Editor), *The Dictionary of National Biography 1931-40*, (Oxford University Press, London, 1949).

26. PRO/T273/157.

27. PRO/T273/160.

28. *The Tatler*, 19 June 1935. See also PRO/T273/158.

29. PRO/T273/157.
30. PRO/T273/156.
31. PRO/T273/157.
32. PRO/T273/160.
33. PRO/T273/157.
34. PRO/T273/158.
35. 'On the Case of Sir Christopher Bullock', p. 20; in PRO/T273/160.
36. PRO/T273/157.
37. PRO/T273/161.
38. PRO/T273/156.
39. PRO/T273/156.
40. PRO/T273/159.
41. PRO/T273/159.
42. PRO/T273/161, Bullock to Prime Minister, 19 April 1947.
43. PRO/T273/162, Ram to Bridges, 9 June 1950.
44. 'On the Case of Sir Christopher Bullock', p. 43; in PRO/T273/160.
45. PRO/T273/161, Bullock to Prime Minister, 18 April 1947.
46. PRO/T273/161, Swinton to Attlee, 21 April 1947.
47. PRO/T273/159.
48. Quoted in 'On the Case of Sir Christopher Bullock', pp. 16-17; in PRO/T273/160.
49. PRO/T273/161, Baldwin to Attlee, 21 April 1947; Swinton to Attlee, 21 April 1947.
50. PRO/T273/161.
51. PRO/T273/161, Lord Chancellor to Prime Minister 20 May 1947.
52. PRO/T273/161, Bridges to Chancellor of the Exchequer, 6 June 1947.
53. Bullock's 'Notes on the Lord Chancellor's Review of the Case', June 1948, in PRO/T273/162.
54. PRO/T273/162, Draft of minute from Bridges to Chancellor of the Exchequer, 19 May 1950.
55. PRO/T273/162, Bullock to Bridges, 28 February 1949.
56. PRO/T273/162, Bridges' Note, 20 March 1950.
57. PRO/T273/162, Bullock to Bridges, 21 April 1950.
58. PRO/T273/162, Barnes to Bridges, 23 May 1950.
59. PRO/T273/162, Ram to Bridges, 9 June 1950.
60. PRO/T273/162, Bridges' Note for Record, 15 June 1950.
61. PRO/T273/162, Morrison to Bridges, 17 July 1950.
62. PRO/T273/162, Bridges to Barnes, 31 December, 1951.
63. PRO/T273/162, Barnes to Bridges, 1 January 1952.
64. Hankey to Bullock, 28 October 1947, information from Mr R.H.W. Bullock.
65. *The Times*, 16 June 1972.
66. H. Montgomery Hyde, *Baldwin: The Unexpected Prime Minister*, (Hart-Davis, MacGibbon, London, 1973), p. 441.
67. Viscount Templewood (Sir Samuel Hoare), *Empire of the Air: The Advent of the Air Age 1922-1929*, (Collins, London, 1957), p. 50.
68. L.J. Dunnett to R.H.W. Bullock, 18 May 1972.
69. *The Times*, 20 May 1972.
70. *Report of the Board of Enquiry appointed by the Prime Minister to*

investigate certain Statements affecting Civil Servants.

71. *Ibid.*, para. 2.

72. *Ibid.*, para. 18.

73. *Ibid.*, para. 18.

74. *Ibid.*, para. 56.

75. *Ibid.*, para. 57.

76. *Ibid.*, para. 59.

77. PRO/T273/161, Barnes to Bridges, 3 June 1947.

78. Sir H.P. Hamilton, 'Sir Warren Fisher and the Public Service', *Public Administration*, Vol 29, 1951, pp. 3-38.

79. *The Times*, 6 August 1936.

80. PRO/T273/158, Hopkins to Fisher, 14 July 1936.

81. 'On the Case of Sir Christopher Bullock', p. 38; in PRO/T273/160.

82. PRO/T273/162, Bullock to Bridges, 6 July 1950.

83. *Seventh Report from the Treasury and Civil Service Committee, Session 1985-86, Civil Servants and Ministers: Duties and Responsibilities, Vol I, Report, together with the Proceedings of the Committee*, H.C. 92-I, (HMSO, London, 1986), p. xxxviii. See also, for example, H.C. 92-II, pp. 39 and 293.

84. PRO/LCO2/6347, Swinton to Prime Minister (Attlee), 3 June 1948.

85. Bernard Donoughue and G.W. Jones, *Herbert Morrison: Portrait of a Politician*, (Weidenfeld and Nicolson, London, 1973), p. 406.

5

The Machinery of Government

Bridges had a serious and sustained interest in the structure and organisation of government. Although he recognised that expert advice about organisation had a contribution to make to good administrative practice, in his opinion such expert advice, often the result of observation and theory, was subordinate to knowledge acquired through practice. Whilst he recognised that 'the general administrator will usually lean heavily on ... expert advice about organisation' he added that 'when it comes to a periodic overhaul the people who can give the best advice about running registries and accounts branches are those who know something of the working of not one registry, but of twenty or thirty'. An administrator must, of course, be concerned with such matters as the demarcation of responsibility, the 'span of control' of management, co-ordination and delegation, but Bridges believed that these topics were often no more than common sense: not the sort of common sense that can be divined by abstract reason, but common sense 'based on a good deal of experience of the likely points of weakness in organisations and of the fallibility of human beings and of the best ways to combat them'. In essence, the administrator concerned with such problems needed the sort of rarified common sense acquired by practice.[1]

This approach to machinery of government problems had implications for two features of British government. First, whilst ministers had the responsibility for deciding policy, the implementation of policies, involving both their detailed elements and the organisation necessary for executing them, was the preserve of administrators. This was because most ministers had neither the time nor the expertise to devote to such matters; furthermore, they had other interests and responsibilities and held particular offices in government for only a relatively short time. Officials, however, were permanent, and officials in senior positions had long practical experience in the confidential business of serving ministers. It was, quite simply, impossible to acquire this experience elsewhere or by other means.

Secondly, this contributed to the distinctive role of higher civil servants in British government. On one occasion Bridges recalled that Professor Laski said in one of his books that 'at the top of the Department the great official is nothing so much as a statesman if he is to be successful'. Bridges thought this was putting it 'a bit too high' and seemed to impinge on the ministerial sphere.[2] He thought Laski came nearer the mark when he qualified his terms to distinguish civil service statesmen from political statesmen. The truth emerges that in the British civil service ethical questions arise not only from administering policies determined by ministers but also from advising ministers and acting in their name. On no topic is this more evident than in the machinery of government. It is a sphere to which Bridges made a distinctive contribution.

More than any other Head of the Civil Service, Bridges attempted to institutionalise the means for resolving machinery of government issues. He did this in two ways. First, by persuasion and encouragement through the medium of official committees, which were intended to distil the collective wisdom of experienced civil servants. Secondly, through the creation of common services based inside the Treasury, in the machinery of government branch and the Organisation and Methods Division. Bridges' interest in the machinery of government can be traced back to his research proposal for his All Souls Fellowship, through his service in the Treasury where he worked on various establishment and machinery of government problems and also served as secretary to royal commissions, to the time when, as Secretary to the Cabinet, he assumed what Lord Trend has called the 'vital task of harnessing the whole of the intricate machinery of government to serve the war effort'.[3] However, Bridges' most significant opportunity to affect the direction of and attitudes to machinery of government developments came after the war, when he was appointed Head of the Civil Service.

His role in these developments must not be misunderstood. As Bridges' obituary in *The Times* put it: 'He was not himself an innovator, but he was always open to new ideas; he never assumed that he knew all the answers, but listened and discussed till the moment of decision came. He preached and practised cooperation between departments ...'[4] However, even if he was not an innovator, the fact remains that to these tasks Bridges brought a shrewd appreciation of the constitutional and practical limitations to what was possible, combined with uniquely relevant practical experience.

Moreover, the opportunity which presented itself in 1945 was unprecedented. In the period after the Second World War Britain faced enormous problems. These included its balance of payments difficulties and the need to adjust to the post-war international economic and commercial arrangements. Furthermore, a Labour Government had been elected with ambitious proposals to create a welfare state, inaugurating an expanded role for the state in British society, and with the declared intention of achieving its objectives by producing a national economic plan.

As Secretary to the War Cabinet, Bridges played an important part in advising the Prime Minister on the organisation and membership of the various Cabinet committees and sub-committees.[5] Among these committees one that is of special interest to students of public administration is the Machinery of Government Committee. An authoritative history of this committee and its successors (1942-52) has already been written by J.M. Lee,[6] and Bridges' influential advice and guidance is evident throughout Lee's account. Lee emphasises Bridges' cautious approach, which was to deal individually with a number of separate problems rather than preferring a full-scale investigation along the lines adopted by the Haldane Committee after the First World War.[7] He also emphasises Bridges' constant preoccupation with judgments on tactics and timing and says Bridges 'played his cards close to his chest' and 'tried to retain the initiative whenever he could'.[8] These characteristics of Bridges' style of management are well illustrated in this chapter which has two main purposes. First, it provides an account of Bridges' contribution to machinery of government issues. This includes more information about Bridges' role than is given in Lee's wide-ranging account of the Anderson Committee and its successors. Secondly, it focuses on Bridges' views on various aspects of the machinery of government, especially the role of the Treasury in British government.

An introduction to the machinery of government committees

Before dealing with Bridges' role it is necessary to give a brief introduction to the main committees concerned with the machinery of government during the Second World War and in the immediate post-war period. This is necessary to clarify the sequence of events and to ensure that readers are not lost in the complexity of committees and working parties with similar names, related functions, and overlapping memberships. Between 1942 and 1945 the main responsibility for reviewing the machinery of government was in the hands of a committee of Cabinet ministers, known as the Machinery of Government Committee (MG), under the chairmanship of Sir John Anderson (later Lord Waverley), Lord President of the Council. The other members were Sir Stafford Cripps, Lord Privy Seal; Sir Kingsley Wood, Chancellor of the Exchequer; Lord Simon, Lord Chancellor; and Mr Herbert Morrison, Home Secretary. Constitutionally, it was an off-shoot of the Lord President's Committee, which was set up in June 1940 and which was regarded by Bridges as the most important Cabinet committee in the civil sphere during the Second World War. It had the specific duty of keeping continuous watch over home front questions and the general trend of our economic development.[9]

This ministerial committee was paralleled by a small committee of officials (MGO). It consisted of three senior civil servants who were expected to act as 'three wise men'. Their duty was to collate the views of others and provide ministers with the benefit of their own experience. These officials, chosen, according to Lee, by Anderson himself, were Sir Alan Barlow, the Treasury's Second Secretary on machinery of government and establishment matters; Sir Robert Wood, Second Secretary in the Board of Education; and Sir Percivale Liesching, Second Secretary at the Board of Trade. Both the MG and MGO committees were served by part-time joint secretaries from the Treasury and the Cabinet Office.[10] From November 1943 to March 1946 they also had the services of a full-time principal from the Treasury (Bruce Fraser), together with some supporting staff.

After the 1945 General Election the MG committee was not formally reconstituted. Instead, the Prime Minister asked those members of the Government surviving from the committee under the Coalition Government (Morrison and Cripps) to join the new Chancellor (Dalton) in completing the unfinished business. This was done by separate *ad hoc* committees. Lee comments that 'what held all these different discussions together was the interlocking membership of the committees, particularly at the official level where Bridges, Barlow and Brook played an important part'.[11] In addition, Bridges, who was then both Cabinet Secretary and Permanent Secretary to the Treasury, set up a steering committee of permanent secretaries on economic development, which began work in 1945. Its main concern was expected to be co-ordination to assist in preparing the 'National plan' which the Cabinet was thinking of producing. It worked through five working parties of officials. In addition, Bridges called a meeting of heads of departments in March 1946 to consider what advice he should give the Prime Minister on 'business efficiency' questions. This meeting led to the creation of another five working parties of officials which concentrated on headquarters accommodation, recruitment, training and posting, business efficiency, and the staffing of public boards.

From 1947 a more formal committee of permanent secretaries emerged, known as the Government Organisation Committee (GOC). It had its origins in the interim report of the working party on business efficiency which recommended that

Heads of Departments should be asked to appoint a standing 'business efficiency' committee, under Treasury chairmanship, and composed of the Heads of a few Departments and two or three other officers ... to examine and pass judgment upon proposals for changes in organisation and method which are of interest to the Service as a whole, and to recommend to Departments for action proposals which they approve.[12]

When the GOC was set up Bridges became its chairman and it met when he and the machinery of government branch of the Treasury thought there was enough business to justify a meeting: in fact, it met nineteen times between November 1947 and October 1950.

The Treasury Organisation Committee (TOC) was set up in 1948, under the chairmanship of Sir John Woods, Permanent Secretary to the Board of Trade, to set an example to other departments by putting its own house in order. It surveyed the economic organisation which had been set up since the war and in particular concentrated on the position of the Central Economic Planning Staff after they had been absorbed into the Treasury.

The MG and MGO committees

The MG committee was expected to cover broadly similar ground to that covered by the Haldane Committee which reported in 1918. It had no formal terms of reference, but this was not out of character with Bridges' general approach while Cabinet Secretary. On one occasion in 1943 he warned Brook, who was then preparing a paper for the machinery of government exercise, against thinking 'that the exact set of words used in the Terms of Reference is going to be of much practical use'. Bridges believed that questions were 'settled by good sense, not by definition'.[13] The proposal for such a committee originated from Cripps, who thought there should be 'another Haldane'. Cripps at this time was immensely popular and had strong personal ambitions; the proposal therefore had a political motivation as well as an administrative one. However, Cripps was later persuaded by Anderson to change his original proposal to an 'inside' inquiry. The matter was discussed and approved by the Cabinet on 24 August 1942. Attlee was in the chair at that meeting and two days later Bridges wrote to the Prime Minister making suggestions for the membership of the committee. He said 'Sir Kingsley Wood wants to be on the committee, partly because of the Treasury interest in Civil Service administration' and commented that the Home Secretary had 'more administrative experience than the Lord Privy Seal but there is a risk that on matters of this kind he might be influenced by the rather theoretical views of, e.g. Mr Harold Laski and Mr Kingsley Martin, Editor of "The New Statesman". Bridges argued that the committee should consist of Anderson, Cripps and Wood, though he added: 'I hope this note does not exceed my brief'.[14]

Churchill was sceptical. His reply the next day included the comment: 'I hope that these speculative inquiries will not be allowed to distract the attention of any of the Ministers concerned from the urgent war tasks with which they are charged. Such academic and philosophical speculations ought, in these times to be the province of persons of leisure'.[15] But Laski wrote to him on 1 October to try to persuade him to take action on the Cabinet decision and it seems he was finaly persuaded to act by Wood, the Chancellor of the Exchequer.

There was a general feeling among officials and among ministers that the best way to proceed was not to have a formal committee engaged in a full-scale investigation along the lines of the Haldane Committee, but instead to proceed in a more cautious and pragmatic fashion. Bridges later wrote of the great and continuing influence of the Haldane Report but with somewhat muted enthusiasm - at least, it appears muted when expressed by someone who on another occasion said he was 'very interested in and very keen on O and M'.[16] He thought that the Haldane Report's title to fame arose from the encouragement it gave to think about the fundamental problems of government.[17] Bridges' attitude to it was similar to the attitudes generally found within government at that time, especially attitudes in the Treasury. These were clearly expounded in a Treasury document written in 1949 which presented three main arguments against a Haldane-type inquiry. The first argument was that information given to an outside body must be coloured by regard for what ought to be, rather than to what actually is:

> Secondly, an outside body can seldom have the first hand experience necessary to make immediately applicable recommendations. Sometimes they endorse proposals already worked out within the Government, as the Haldane Committee did on the subject of the Ministry of Health; sometimes they offer generalisations which have a certain value, but which leave most of the difficulties to be solved in their application, like the Haldane Committee's principle for the allocation of duties between Departments; and sometimes they get an unworkable idea, like the Haldane Committee's proposal that all thinking preparatory to the settlement of policy should be concentrated in a separate Ministry. Finally, it is rare for action to be taken on the recommendations of such bodies. The Haldane Report has stayed on the shelf since it was written.[18]

Although these statements were written a few years after 1942, when the Machinery of Government Committee was set up, there is no reason to believe that the attitudes and views expressed did not exist earlier. There was certainly a general feeling both in the Treasury and among ministers that the best way to proceed was not to have a formal committee involving outsiders. Instead, as Anderson, who had been a career civil servant before his election to Parliament in 1938, put it to Cripps: 'The view is held fairly strongly in certain quarters that in these quasi-constitutional matters our system is best left to develop organically - 'broadening down from precedent to precedent' - and what we need is to clear our minds in the general direction which these constitutional changes should take...'[19]

When the committee first met, Padmore, one of its secretaries (the other secretary was E.C.S. Wade, the Cambridge constitutional lawyer then on attachment to the Cabinet Office) supplied it with copies of such general material as the Report of the Haldane Committee, extracts from Ivor Jennings' book on Cabinet Government, the Liberal Party pamphlet on the Civil Service, the PEP Broadsheet *Planning* No 173, and the Sixteenth Report from the Select Committee on National Expenditure 1941/42.

The MG committee decided to reserve the following subjects for themselves to consider: the distribution of functions between departments, the role of supervising ministers and the size of the Cabinet. The MGO committee was to examine the roles of the Treasury and Cabinet Office, the use of scientists and economists, the value of non-departmental organisations such as public boards, regional administration, and recruitment and training for the civil service. Bridges does not appear to have taken a close interest in its work during the first year, but as its tempo of work increased so did the involvement of officials; this stimulated considerable activity beyond its 'three wise men', their support staff and their secretariat. The MGO committee met more than 30 times a year when it was most active, on some occasions meeting more than once a week. When Wood died, in September 1943, and Anderson succeeded him as Chancellor of the Exchequer, Bridges appears to have made every effort to keep Anderson as chairman of the MG committee.[20]

By mid-1944 the work of the MG and MGO committees had extended considerably. One of the major effects of this work on Treasury officials at this time was to focus official minds on producing all sorts of proposals for civil service reorganisation. These included proposals on such matters as the 'one class service', the Treasury control of intake numbers, the amalgamation of the HCO and EO grades, and Treasury control of class to class promotions. Within the Treasury much of this work was the responsibility of Henry Wilson Smith and Miss Evelyn Sharp, but they tended to seek Bridges' comments on drafts of their papers on the structure of the civil service after the war.[21] Bridges was, of course, also responsible for the papers that were prepared on the functions of the Cabinet Secretariat. These were mainly the work of his colleagues (particularly Brook) and went through successive drafts before being submitted. Indeed, drafts of papers prepared for the committee were often widely circulated: for example, the draft official paper on the role of the Treasury was circulated to more than 50 serving and retired members of the civil service,[22] and Bridges felt strongly that a copy of his paper on the Cabinet Secretariat should be sent to his predecessor, Lord Hankey.[23] This procedure of consultation and the circulation of proposals was characteristic of Bridges' management style and must have had a considerable influence on the development of an official consensus on particular issues. [24]

When the MG committee was created, it was generally presumed that there would be a published report, a sort of practitioners' equivalent to Haldane, but this expectation was not fulfilled. Bridges wrote to the Chancellor of the Exchequer about this on 5 March 1945 and said it was 'increasingly difficult to find time for MG matters on the War Cabinet agenda and any attempt to achieve, within the lifetime of the Government, a document which can be published on the full authority of the Government... would almost certainly fail'.[25] Consequently, the Anderson Report itself was never published. In March 1945 Bridges submitted a minute to the Prime Minister in order to get formal approval for plans that had been prepared, and as the report was never considered by the War Cabinet Anderson submitted it to the Prime Minister after the caretaker administration was announced. The published equivalent to the Haldane Report therefore became Anderson's Romanes Lecture, 1946.[26]

The period from 1945 to 1947

In 1945 ministers decided to make the Treasury responsible for machinery of government work and Bridges initially interpreted this responsibility almost as an extension of his private office. William Armstrong, one of Bridges' two private secretaries, was asked to undertake part-time MG duties in January 1946 and given a room across the passage from Bridges and the assistance of another official. However, this was not a heavy burden. Soon after his appointment Armstrong was sent to Brussels on reparations business for a month, and while he was in charge of MG work from 1946 to 1949 he found time to do a lot of reading and even write a play.[27]

Until the end of the war Bridges was thinking of the problems of transition mainly in terms of avoiding the mistakes of the First World War rather than in terms of implementing the lessons from the Second World War.[28] He appears to have conceived the Treasury MG work as the office from which *ad hoc* inquiries could be serviced. There was no call for a fully co-ordinated programme of action. However, he did at this time ask Brook and Max Nicholson, the Lord President's private secretary, to form a steering committee which would supervise the preparation of a number of small booklets on government organisation questions, though these were intended to have only a limited circulation within the civil service. [29]

After the Labour Government had been elected, Cripps began applying pressure in Cabinet for a 'National plan'. He also began advocating the transfer of the Economic Section from the Cabinet Office to the Board of Trade. On 20 August 1945, within the new Government's first month of office Bridges, as Cabinet Secretary, was asked by ministers to prepare an outline of the machinery necessary to advise ministers on the use to be made of national economic resources.[30] Bridges therefore wrote to permanent secretaries about the need for a 'high-level working party' on economic development. A steering committee of permanent secretaries on economic development was consequently set up in November 1945, and this steering committee (of seven senior officials plus Bridges as chairman) constituted the core of the machinery of government for economic planning. Grouped under the steering committee there were five official working parties: the Manpower Working Party (run by the Ministry of Labour), the Balance of Payments Working Party (run by the Treasury, Overseas Finance Division), the Economic Survey Working Party (run by the Economic Section of the Cabinet Office), the Investment Working Party (run by the Treasury) and the Statistical Working Party (run by the Central Statistical Office). Bridges explained that the object of the steering committee and its working parties was 'to survey the available national resources and to forecast the demands which are likely to be made on those resources, with the objective of having ready by mid-November a provisional plan for the calendar year 1946'. This was to be followed up as soon afterwards as possible by a three-year plan covering the years 1946, 1947 and 1948. The idea of this was that it should be the first instalment of a five-year plan, which should be the ultimate objective.[31]

This steering committee on economic development, together with its supporting working parties of officials, was therefore created without a supervising ministerial committee, and although Bridges and others had frequent contact with the four key ministers concerned (the Chancellor of the Exchequer, President of the Board of Trade, Minister of Labour and the Lord President), the group of ministers was not formally recognised as a Cabinet committee until April 1946.[32] As far as Bridges was concerned, this steering committee had its origins in the Employment White Paper of 1944 and the practical experience gained in the war of allocating resources in a period of stringency. He explained the position as he saw it to heads of departments in these words: 'The reason for starting action now is that the machinery required for carrying out employment policy will be of great use in the immediate post-war years in ensuring that we do not try to do too much with the available resources, and in directing those resources into the right channels'.[33] The official committee on economic development was firmly within the control of the Treasury: its chairman was Permanent Secretary to the Treasury, it had two Treasury second secretaries on it (Sir Bernard Gilbert and Sir Wilfrid Eady), a Treasury secretary, and its original memorandum said it could call on the assistance of the Economic Section of the Cabinet Office and the Central Statistical Office.

As a result of this economic planning exercise it is apparent that Bridges played an important part in developing an administrative machine for the co-ordination of economic policy. The steering committee received papers by economic staff with comments on various aspects of economic planning, in preparation for a possible White Paper on Economic Development. Bridges was chairman, but he seems to have made only modest contributions to the discussions. However, he was well informed as a result of the discussions in the steering committee and as a result of receiving the recommendations and conclusions of its working parties, and it was Bridges who personally became its main link with ministers. The official steering committee on central planning for economic development was therefore a rather curious body which appears now to have become an important line of communication between professional civil servants and ministers.[34]

Furthermore, the existence of this economic planning structure was not made public. Mr Francis Williams (later Lord Francis-Williams), then Adviser on Public Relations to the Prime Minister, had suggested giving it publicity because he thought it would do the Government good if its existence were known, but when the suggestion was referred to Bridges it was accompanied by a minute from Gilbert advising against it:

Public reference to the Committee as a Committee would only lead to enquiries whether they had reported and whether their Report was to be published and so on, and this would lead to questions whether there was a comprehensive plan, and if so, what it was. But I imagine that Ministers will want a plan primarily for their own guidance, and that what is announced will be simply the action to be taken on the constituent parts.[35]

A second committee of permanent secretaries was the Civil Service Manpower Committee: it had six members, including Bridges who was chairman. This was set up partly in response to parliamentary concern about the size of the civil service. In this regard Bridges advocated that his colleagues take a firm line with ministers: 'if we are to do with fewer people, we can do fewer things'.[36] The committee was also set up partly in response to demands in Parliament for greater sensitivity to 'business efficiency' (which also led to the Select Committee on Estimates in 1946 deciding to inquire into organisation and methods in central government). In April 1947 the Cabinet accepted the view of the Civil Service Manpower Committee that no substantial reduction in staffs could be expected while the civil service had to carry out its present tasks. But it was recorded that the Prime Minister recognised that it was impossible to carry out such government policies as socialisation, bulk purchase and economic controls without employing large numbers of civil servants: 'While all practical economies should be sought, Ministers should be prepared to defend a substantial increase in the size of the Civil Service'.[37]

On Saturday 2 March 1946 Bridges held a meeting with a group of fourteen other permanent secretaries to discuss various 'business efficiency' aspects of the civil service. Mr Geoffrey Cooper MP had recently written to the Prime Minister calling for a Select Committee to consider the organisation of the civil service and the Prime Minister had asked for advice on the matter. At the meeting Bridges introduced the topic and said one of the key questions to be considered was whether they felt that an inquiry would serve any useful purpose. The general feeling at the meeting was that although there were problems of organisation and training to be faced, any necessary reform should be undertaken by the civil service itself rather than imposed from outside as a result of an inquiry. Bridges himself suggested that various topics might best be tackled by separate working parties. He explained that his personal view was to favour *ad hoc* adjustments, on a practical basis, rather than raising wide issues by instituting a formal full-dress inquiry. After the meeting he wrote, on 8 March, to all permanent secretaries, whether or not they had attended the meeting, asking for lists of questions they thought should be examined by working parties.

On 19 March 1946 Bridges wrote to the Chancellor of the Exchequer with comments on Cooper's letter, for the Chancellor to reply to the Prime Minister. He mentioned that he had consulted the permanent secretaries of some departments mainly concerned and he strongly discouraged the appointment of an outside committee. Such a committee would put more work on higher civil servants and would be unlikely to report very quickly. Cooper's letter had implied that the civil service had not made use of scientific methods of business organisation, but this was not true because the Organisation and Methods branch of the Treasury increasingly used them (and it was at the service of all departments). However, he pointed out that 'many of the problems of Government organisation are inherently different from those of business. You cannot solve the problems of the Civil Service simply by applying business technique'. He hoped that the proposed committee would not be appointed, but he asked for authority to arrange for a small group of civil servants, 'who, after all, can tell better than any outsider where the shoe pinches without any long process of collecting evidence', to take a quick look at certain aspects of civil service organisation. He added: 'I feel certain that the right course in the first instance is to call for a report from a picked group of officials who are in the best position to diagnose any existing weaknesses'.[38]

On 22 March Bridges circulated a summary of the replies he received from his colleagues and this constituted the agenda for another meeting, on Saturday 30 March. In his pre-meeting notes Bridges grouped the suggestions he had received into five working parties. These five working parties (the decisions of the meeting on 30 March followed closely the lines of Bridges' pre-meeting notes) were as follows: accommodation (Chairman: Bridges, plus six other members); recruitment (Chairman: Bridges, plus five other members); training (Chairman: Sir Alexander Maxwell, plus eight other members); organisation and departmental efficiency (Chairman: Barlow, plus seven other members); and quasi-constitutional questions (Chairman: Barlow, plus five other members). Each working party had, in addition, its own secretary.[39]

Later, in November 1946, the Prime Minister and Chancellor of the Exchequer approved Bridges' proposals for appointing a ministerial committee under the Lord President and an official steering committee of permanent secretaries under his own chairmanship.[40] This proposal (which eventually resulted in the GOC) did not originate from Bridges personally, as he explained to the Select Committee on Estimates in 1947. As already mentioned, it was one of the proposals from the working party on business efficiency.

Some details of the business efficiency working party provide an insight into what was involved in this large scale and complex review into five aspects of the machinery of government. The working party took as its terms of reference the study of the numerous comments and suggestions received in response to Bridges' letter of 8 March so far as they touched upon the efficient operation of departments and had not been specifically assigned to the other working parties. To assist them in their work they invited the views 'of some of the individuals who had come from prominent positions in industry and commerce to work in the Service during the war'.[41] In fact, all the evidence received (both orally and in writing) seems to have been solicited from outsiders, all of whom were ex-civil servants.[42] The working party met on twelve occasions before issuing its interim report on October 1946.

Its first investigation concerned ancillary services (e.g. communications working conditions, and the use of secretaries), but it adopted such a narrowly practical approach that it neither defined 'business efficiency' nor explained what it thought was meant by the term. Nevertheless, in its report, marked 'Confidential', it made various recommendations for improving the speed of work with the minimum manpower, and for taking advantage of modern equipment. Some of these recommendations, as illustrated by the following examples, now appear as disappointingly low level from such a high-powered group of officials who had the advice of eight distinguished industrialists: 'Vacuum cleaners should be provided on an increased scale for the cleaning staff as supplies permit. The installation of electric plugs should be carried out as circumstances allow.' 'It is essential that the messenger services should be so organised that the discharge of their prime duties - carrying papers, and ushering visitors - is not hampered by subsidiary jobs like tea-making.' 'The wider use of the photo-copying process for reproducing printed and type-written documents should make a substantial contribution to the solution of present difficulties caused by the shortage of typists.'[43]

The final report of the business efficiency working party considered the efficiency of the organisation of departments and the efficiency of the individual. Again, the working party consulted leading business men who had served in government departments. They also consulted, informally, with heads of departments and other colleagues in the civil service. Again, the working party's report gave no definition of efficiency, though it concluded that 'for securing greater efficiency in the Civil Service, outside the ancillary services, there are few recommendations which can be put forward as of general application throughout the Service'. The following examples are representative of the recommendations in the final report: 'Ministers might be asked on appropriate occasions whether, in the interest of greater speed and efficiency, they would defend in the House, some inequality of treatment of parallel cases, for example, in case work arising from economic controls.' 'Selected Principals might undertake preparatory work on special problems on behalf of the Permanent Secretary.' 'A study of staff management in the Civil Service would be worth while.' Like the interim report, the final report was marked 'Confidential', though extracts from it for 'Official Use Only' were printed by HMSO in January 1948 with a Foreword by Bridges.[44] He wrote: 'I hope that everybody who reads it will find, as I have done, much that is stimulating, and much of that practical wisdom without which none of us can do our jobs to the utmost of our capacity.'[45]

When it was set up, the GOC had overlapping membership with both the economic development committee and the civil service manpower committee (which was primarily concerned with the imposition of manpower ceilings). Furthermore, all three committees were chaired by Bridges. When he announced the creation of the GOC to the Estimates Committee on 18 June 1947,[46] Bridges also gave details of the positive support intended to be provided by reorganisation within the Treasury. It is difficult to work out now which pressures were most significant in contributing to setting up the GOC. The most important seem to have come from the political sphere of government, but it is quite possible that Bridges' well-reasoned explanation to the Estimates Committee included an element of *post hoc* rationalisation. In addition to his announcement about the GOC he explained that it had been decided to put the small section on machinery of government already existing in the Treasury into the O and M Division under the direction of J.R. (later Sir John) Simpson.[47] This came somewhat as a surprise to the staff concerned, but it gave the MG branch a new rationale and enhanced status within the Treasury.[48]

The Government Organisation Committee

The GOC, though it was composed of officials only, in practice acquired the sort of oversight functions previously performed by the MG committee. It marked the period of increased emphasis on manpower economy and included within its ambit a major exercise of Treasury reorganisation. The real emphasis behind these developments was provided by the national fuel crisis and the crisis arising from the attempt to make sterling currency fully convertible. Although Bridges instituted a campaign to make departments more aware of the need to adhere to manpower ceilings and to intensify the work of staff inspectors, he did not give a lead in inaugurating GOC agenda items. These mainly arose from suggestions within the Treasury or from departments. After a year's experience of MG work, Armstrong complained that his separation from the Cabinet Office was a handicap to his work and as a result the GOC was converted into an official Cabinet committee. This meant that from October 1948 the committee was served by a joint secretariat from the Treasury and the Cabinet Office. At that time the committee had eleven members, including Bridges, but the papers were being circulated widely on a circulation list which included all permanent heads of departments. Brook's note of 21 October 1948 indicated the intention to change the membership of the committee from time to time, so as to give other permanent secretaries an opportunity to serve on the committee.[49]

The story of the expanding work of the GOC is an interesting one. The Estimates Committee, to whom in 1947 Bridges explained the appointment of what he then regarded as the Business Efficiency Committee (i.e. the committee he said had been set up in accordance with the recommendations in the interim report from the business efficiency working party), assumed that the Business Efficiency Committee was intended to handle not only O and M but also MG questions. The Estimates Committee recommended that urgent attention should be given to improving the machinery of government as a whole and that this should be undertaken by a review 'at the highest level'.[50] But Bridges noted that while the committee clearly favoured the appointment of 'a specially constituted body of a few highly placed and experienced persons',[51] they would apparently be satisfied if the functions were undertaken by this committee. He therefore proposed that the Business Efficiency Committee should be known as the Government Organisation Committee and should handle both O and M and MG questions. In a draft memorandum by the Treasury, commenting on the recommendations of the Estimates Committee, no reference was made to the recommendation that the committee to review the machinery of government should be 'strengthened where necessary by experts on administration from outside the Civil Service'. Instead, it focused on other aspects of the recommendations and replied:

> ... the small committee consisting chiefly of Permanent Secretaries, mentioned above, has been appropriately expanded and its terms of reference now include Machinery of Government questions. This Committee, which has been renamed the Government Organisation Committee, will meet frequently under the Chairmanship of the Permanent Secretary to the Treasury, and will be responsible, under the supervision of Ministers, for laying down the programme of investigations to be undertaken, for directing such investigations and for seeing that any necessary changes are carried into effect.[52]

Bridges therefore did not envisage the GOC in quite the same way as the Estimates Committee and he made no provision for the participation of outsiders in the committee. Indeed, he saw it having a less assertive role. In the paper he wrote about it on 25 October 1947 the procedure he suggested was that the committee should receive proposals, approve reports submitted to it, recommend the priority to be given to particular items, and invite departments to take action on proposals when approved.[53]

An important point to note about this is that the committee could not interfere in the organisation within departments. As Bridges put it in another paper he wrote on 25 October: 'It is a sound rule that those responsible for policy are also primarily responsible for the machinery to give effect to it. Each Department is therefore primarily responsible for defining its own functions, for considering possible extensions and contractions, and for determining its relations with other Departments.'[54]

He therefore saw the Treasury developing to meet some of these needs: to provide departments with advice, to make information available of general interest to departments (e.g. in the form of booklets in the 'Notes on Government Organisation' series), and to initiate studies which were beyond the responsibility of any other department. He then provided a provisional agenda which consisted of a list of topics which had come to the notice of the Treasury in recent months.

The 'Notes on Government Organisation' series was intended to provide officials with information about subjects of general interest within the civil service. The first two booklets were issued in May and June 1946 and they covered Government Information Services and Regional Organisation. Bridges presented a memorandum on this series for consideration by the GOC in March 1948. Other titles among the next ten already in preparation included: The Preparation of Bills, Central Defence Organisation, Whitley Machinery and Cabinet Committee Organisation. Bridges solicited comments and advice and, among the replies, he received a most helpful and constructive letter from Sir Harold Emmerson with detailed suggestions relating to the titles proposed for the next series (i.e. beyond the first ten booklets) together with a number of new proposals. For example, one of Emmerson's suggestions was for a booklet on The Administrative Class and the Art of Public Administration. He wrote:

> Newcomers to the Civil Service and the public at large seem to find difficulty in grasping what the Administrative Class does and the Class itself tends to be reticent. Dale's book was never wholly applicable and is out of date. Oliver Franks' lectures have brought a new but very sketchy picture. The booklet would show how the Administrative Class acts as a co-ordinating agency between Departments (a device which does not exist in business or in most foreign Civil Services). It would also show how officers are trained to do almost any Administrative work at short notice and give flexibility to the Service...[55]

Some of these booklets were very successful. In July 1949 the GOC received a report which said that in the previous fifteen months booklets had been issued on The Preparation of Bills; Private Bill and Provisional Order Legislation; Scottish Administration; Parliamentary Supply Procedure; and Staff Relations in the Civil Service. The last of these booklets had such a good reception, particularly from the National Staff Side, that it was decided to reprint it and put it on general sale to the public.[56]

In July 1948, at the 4th meeting of the GOC, it was agreed that

Bridges should write to all permanent secretaries who were not members of the committee and solicit their suggestions for future inquiries to be undertaken on behalf of the GOC by the MG branch of the Treasury. Although thirteen of the replies offered no positive suggestions, the responses again helped Bridges by ensuring that he was kept in touch with colleagues' opinions about the exercise, and this enabled him to make modest innovations. The MG branch of the Treasury increasingly controlled the direction of the work of the committee. This was particularly evident when Bridges was ill in December 1949 and January 1950: the work of the committee was not seriously affected at all. While he was unwell, the MG branch took full responsibility for its work, and when Bridges recovered he resumed chairing the GOC's special steering committee.

In 1949 Bridges received a particularly interesting suggestion from the Institute (later the Royal Institute) of Public Administration. It wanted to sponsor a series of books on the functions and organisation of selected government departments. This fitted in with the way Bridges' mind was already working. On 3 June 1949, after a meeting he had with the Treasury's Advisory Panel of businessmen on Organisation and Methods, which suggested increased publicity for the O and M work being done in the government service, Bridges wrote: 'There is at present a serious dearth of published information in permanent form about the working of the Government machine and steps ought to be taken to remedy this deficiency.' He was wondering whether some of the booklets on government organisation might be made available to the public and also whether there might be a new series of books on the lines of the 'Whitehall Series'.[57] It was on 2 September, and quite independently of the GOC's discussions, that the Director of the Institute of Public Administration asked for the Treasury's general approval and support for the commercial publication of a series of books on the functions and organisation of government departments. This was referred to the GOC, and in November the GOC agreed in principle to the proposal, on the understanding that it would be developed in close cooperation with the Treasury and other departments concerned. The Institute proposed six departments to begin the series and it was agreed that the departments should be 'warned ... to expect an approach from Mr Nottage, the Director of the Institute, seeking their cooperation and in particular their help in the selection of a suitable author'. Nottage, however, found progress difficult and a year later told Bridges that he had not succeeded in getting the authorship firmly settled for any of the volumes. Bridges commented:

> Perhaps this is not really surprising. The collection and assimilation of material for a book on a modern Government Department is an immense task for one person even when he has complete freedom of access to the records of the Department and can discuss his problems freely with the staff. There would be few if any people who would be prepared to undertake such a labour single-handed on such terms as the Institute could offer.
>
> In discussing the problem with Mr Nottage we have come to the conclusion that the only feasible way to get the books written is for the Departments themselves to collect and partially at least assimilate the material. It is, moreover, doubtful whether, even with extensive help of this kind, an outside author would be able to produce a fair and accurate picture of the Department's activities; and there might be difficulties if the Department tried to adjust his presentation of the story. We are, therefore, now inclined to the view that the books should for all practical purposes be written by the Departments themselves...
>
> We have come to the conclusion in the Treasury that if a satisfactory, consistent, and unembarrassing series of books is ever to be produced they must be written in this way.[58]

There was a further full discussion about this project at the GOC meeting in April 1951. In his note of 7 December 1950 Bridges had invited his colleagues to comment on the Institute's proposal. Before the April meeting he therefore circulated extracts from their replies. Sir John Woods (Board of Trade) said it would be impossible to contemplate diverting the energies of a good man for a departmental compilation. Sir William Douglas (Ministry of Health) thought the times were unpropitious and was not enthusiastic about either the nature of the proposed series or the suggested authorship. Sir John Maud (Ministry of Education) and Sir Alexander Little (Post Office) thought their departments were adequately covered by existing or forthcoming publications. Sir Harold Emmerson (Ministry of Works) said no one in his department could take on the preparation of a book at present. Sir Donald Fergusson (Ministry of Fuel and Power) did not agree with the proposal and thought it was not the time to undertake the work, when departments were so heavily pressed and government organisation was far from settled. Sir John Lang (Admiralty) did not dissent in principle, but said the Admiralty could not undertake the production of a book for some time. Sir Thomas Lloyd (Colonial Office) simply said he preferred his department to be left out. Sir Eric Bamford (Inland Revenue) thought there was little public demand for a book. Others were slightly less unenthusiastic, several offered the suggestion that retired civil servants would be more suitable as potential authors because they would have the time to devote to the task. Bridges added his own comments:

> My own view on this is clear. While an occasional book may be written about the Civil Service which would appeal to the general reader - we hope that Mr Wyn Griffiths' book on the British Civil Service in Collins' Britain in Pictures series will have this attraction - we must recognise that the average man will not buy or even borrow from the library a serious book on a Government Department.
>
> Nor do I think it is our function to produce a series of what, without offence, might be called rather highbrow studies of the analytical kind which would often be highly critical of Government Departments. It may be a good thing that such books should be produced, but the job is not for us.
>
> I therefore ... think that our aim should be to produce a series of books mainly historical and descriptive...
>
> It would, in any case, be undesirable to attempt to launch the whole series at the present time and my suggestion, therefore, is that we make a start with the scheme on a rather narrow front, and that other Departments should be brought within the scheme later on.[59]

During discussion Bridges reiterated the arguments in favour of having the books published by the Institute. He said that any department which found it difficult to take part in the scheme need not feel called upon to do so. He also said: 'It must be recognised that in circles outside Government there was a great demand for full and objective studies of Government Departments, and the publication of such studies would do something to meet the criticism that the Government was secretive about its methods of conducting business.'[60]

Meanwhile the various projects approved by the GOC were all making progress and by mid-1949 the GOC was receiving reports on the numerous projects undertaken by the MG and O and M staff in the Treasury. Some examples from a long list of projects will illustrate this: Co-ordinating Committee on Controls; Production Authorities; Relationship between Government Departments and Nationalised Undertakings; Housing; Ancient Monuments; Policy Control and Executive Work; Responsibility for Civil Building in the Service Departments; Relations between Government Departments and Local Authorities; Government Local Offices; National Insurance and National Registration Systems; Births and Deaths Registration; Medical Staffs in Government Departments; Administration of Overseas Territories; Payroll Procedure; Control of Forms; Messenger Services. Clearly, this was a rather odd assortment of projects. However, it is indicative of the time and energy which were being devoted to the work not only in the Treasury but also in the departments. Some of these projects were at the stage where MG staff were making preliminary surveys, others were being undertaken by O and M staff in particular departments: most had their own steering committees or inter-departmental study groups with the status of sub-committees of the GOC.

A good example of how this worked in practice is provided by the GOC Sub-Committee on Organisation and Methods, which reported on 9 July 1953. It was set up in June 1952 to review the development of Organisation and Methods work and its organisation in the Treasury and other departments, and to make recommendations. The Chairman was Sir David Milne, of the Scottish Office, and its six other members included two outsiders, one of whom was the chairman and the other a member of the O and M Advisory Panel. The sub-committee held thirteen meetings and received evidence from twenty-five departments. It also heard oral evidence from twenty-two witnesses, including a deputy secretary, nine principal establishment officers and eight officers in charge of O and M branches.

It traced the development of O and M work back to the Treasury Investigating Officers appointed as a result of one of the recommendations of the Bradbury Committee on the Organisation and Staffing of Government Offices.[61] It also drew attention to the significance of successive commissions and committees which had made relevant recommendations, culminating in the report from the Select Committee on National Expenditure (Session 1941-42) which recommended strengthening O and M work. Since then the Treasury had issued a memorandum on the status and functions of departmental O and M branches, how they should be accommodated in departments, and how they should relate to the Treasury O and M Division. In addition, the work of O and M was reviewed by the Select Committee on Estimates (Fifth Report, Session 1946-47). It found that there were seventeen departments with O and M branches of their own, in addition to the Treasury branch. Their total staff numbered well over 300 officials. These O and M branches had been involved in planning new work as well as reviewing existing structures and organisation. Since 1943 over 1,000 officers had attended O and M training courses, including 100 from Commonwealth and Colonial countries and 60 from local authorities. In addition, the report surveyed the work being done by O and M branches and made numerous assessments of progress and proposals for future projects and for the organisation of O and M work.[62]

A quite different subject considered by the GOC in July 1949 was the review of the machinery of government that had been undertaken in the United States. In 1949 the Treasury had received copies of the Report of the Hoover Commission on the Organisation of the Executive Branch of Government in the United States. This coincided with a request from the Chancellor of the Exchequer for a memorandum describing the central machinery of government, including the Cabinet and its committees, and dealing in particular with the changes and developments that had taken place in recent years. The opportunity was therefore taken to compare the British machinery with that proposed by the Hoover Commission, in order to see whether anything could be learnt from the suggestions made by the Commission. A long paper was prepared in the Treasury for this purpose. When the GOC discussed the paper it reached the general conclusion that there would be no advantage in having a public commission of inquiry, but the committee thought there was a need for a general review of a number of major questions including such issues as the number of government departments and the allocation of functions between them. It was later decided to start this inquiry by looking at the field of economic affairs, trade and industry and a steering committee was set up consisting of permanent secretaries from some of the departments concerned, together with one or two officials from other departments.[63]

J.M. Lee has drawn attention to Bridges' continuing belief in the kind of internal reform which he had been able to effect in the conditions of total mobilisation for war. Perhaps, however, this does not give sufficient credit for Bridges' change in management style from war to peace. The GOC exercise certainly illustrates a relatively low-key approach from Bridges personally, dependent on encouragement, advice and solicitation, though it was enormously time-consuming both in terms of its committee work and the associated formal and informal discussion. This is well illustrated in the report of the sub-committee on Organisation and Methods, which reported to the last meeting of the GOC, in July 1953. Furthermore, the GOC exercise was an almost exclusively internal review, though with the benefit of an Advisory Panel on Organisation and Methods, which encompassed the organisation as well as the structure of the machinery of government.

In 1950 Bridges made an attempt to reconstruct the GOC by persuading three 'founder members' to retire and bringing in replacements. When he spoke to the working party in November, to represent the steering committee's point of view, he stressed that 'the government was irrevocably committed to the review of the whole of its organisation from within'.[64] He made a further attempt to revive the work of the GOC by resurrecting the steering committee in March 1952. As he put it to Brook, then head of the three-man steering committee: 'if those of us who have lived all our working lives in Whitehall and have studied Whitehall organisation give up as hopeless all attempt to reform it from inside, then what hope is there of any reform in our time?'[65] After the 1950 General Election the GOC declined in significance and when Churchill became Prime Minister again in 1951 he made changes to reassert the Prime Minister's authority. It seems that by this time the GOC had become a meeting of officials with little interest in problems which did not affect their departments, and took a narrowly departmental line on those which did.[66] Also, some permanent secretaries became concerned when they heard that discussions had taken place relating to their areas of interest without themselves being involved. For example, in December 1949 there was a GOC discussion on the distribution of departmental functions and the possibility of merging the Ministry of Civil Aviation and the Ministry of Transport, but Sir Arnold Overton, the permanent secretary to the Ministry of Civil Aviation was not present, and made it clear in a letter to Bridges on 16 December 1949 that he was very put out about it.[67]

The Treasury Organisation Committee

Bridges noted early in 1948 that one of the criticisms made of O and

M work was that too much effort was directed into enquiries into particular aspects of a department's activities and not enough into reviews of the functions of the department as a whole. This, he observed, was one of the criticisms made by the Select Committee on Estimates in 1947, though Bridges added that he thought the criticism was made somewhat ineffectually. Although a broad review was being made of the Ministry of Supply, Bridges found it difficult to get departments to do this, so he thought the Treasury should set a good example by taking stock of its own organisation.[68]

On 18 May 1948 he wrote to the Chancellor of the Exchequer proposing such a review by a committee with the assistance of the Treasury's O and M Division. He continued:

> The members of the committee should not be restricted to the Treasury and should include two people from outside the Department. One of them should be chairman. For this post I would prefer a senior officer who has served in the Treasury and is therefore acquainted with our problems. I would like to try to persuade Sir John Woods to become chairman (or, failing him, Sir William Douglas). The second outside member I have in mind is Mr D.C.V. Perrott, Deputy Secretary, Ministry of Food, who has had wide experience of organisation in other Departments and belongs to a Department which has extensive business with the Treasury; he will bring to the problem a 'fresh' mind, since he has never served in the Department. The Treasury representatives on the committee should be Sir Herbert Brittain, Mr Padmore, and the Director of Organisation and Methods, Mr Simpson.
>
> I have considered whether we should add a complete 'outsider' but do not recommend it. I think that the hub of the Government machine can best be examined critically by those who, though not necessasrily employed in it, have some acquaintance with the working of the machine as a whole. I do not find it easy, moreover, to think of an 'outsider' who is suitably qualified...[69]

The draft of the interim report of the TOC, dealing with Overseas Finance and the Central Economic Planning Staff, was produced on 17 December 1948 and the final version of the report was sent to Bridges on 22 February 1949. One reason why Bridges had asked the committee to look at this aspect of the functions and organisation of the Treasury first, was because of the possibility of overlap between the Overseas Finance Division, Mr Rowan's Division (formerly known as the staff of the Minister of Economic Affairs) and the Central Economic Planning Staff. The committee took evidence from a number of officials in the Treasury.[70] After they had produced their report Bridges gathered views from various senior staff about the recommendations (these included views from T.L. (later Sir Leslie) Rowan, G.M. Wilson, Padmore and Wilson Smith)[71] and when the final version of the report was signed by Woods on 17 February 1949 he felt confident about making recommendations to the Chancellor of the Exchequer, which he did on 29 March.[72] It was then that Bridges proposed the new co-ordinating committee which he called the Standing Working Group of the Official Committee on Economic Development, which would have reporting to it the London Committee, Programmes Committee, Overseas Negotiations Committee, and Exports Committee. However, Bridges did not recommend the Chancellor to take action at that time on other recommendations in the Woods report, which would have involved changes in parts of the Treasury organisation.

The distinctive feature of the TOC is that it was a personal initiative of Bridges, and it is not surprising that when Woods was ill Bridges acted as chairman. The first report from this committee dealt with overseas finance, but the Chancellor of the Exchequer decided (apparently on Bridges' advice) to defer for the time being action on the recommendations for structural changes, the most important of which would have required a merger between the organisation then under Rowan and the Overseas Finance Division. Bridges kept up his pressure on the TOC by his continuous interest and queries, and the report on Establishments Business, dated 20 December 1949, was printed over his own name because he was then acting for Woods.[73] The purpose of the establishments review was, as Bridges put it to the Chancellor of the Exchequer on 27 June 1949, 'to make the work of the Treasury Establishment Division more effective, particularly in control of staff numbers'.[74] It recommended new arrangements for the control of civil service establishments, more delegation to departments, and the institution of staff inspectors; these recommendations were accepted by the Chancellor of the Exchequer and promulgated to departments in 1949. The next report was on the Treasury control of Supply, and Bridges personally gave evidence to the TOC on this.

It is quite clear that Bridges had given a lot of thought to the question of Treasury control. Some of his ideas were purely administrative or technical - for example he thought more periodic overhauls were needed to see what was happening to schemes sanctioned some years previously. But some of his ideas went beyond techniques. For example, he felt that one reason for the ineffectiveness of Treasury control of supply was the desire of the majority in Parliament to spend money, and their disbelief in Treasury control. The only way to deal with this was to produce estimates of global expenditure and to bring home to ministers that if they insisted on sanctioning further increases the result would be that the total would go up and up and the bill just would not be met. In his opinion this was very necessary because there was no room for raising taxation further and the total volume of government expenditure was, at that time, a vital factor in the whole economic life of the country. On these matters Bridges believed it was essential to institute new techniques to deal with this situation. The techniques would include: forecasts of supply expenditure and periodic reviews of the supply expenditure of the Department as a whole, planning to produce import programmes and investment programmes, and a new budget technique to estimate what the budget had got to achieve from the monetary point of view.[75] His evidence to the TOC was, without doubt, very important evidence. Both its content and style provide valuable insight into the way Bridges went about his work and some of his personal attitudes. The following extensive quotation provides such an insight:

> Recent years have seen an enormous increase in Government business and Government expenditure. Government business is also much more complex than it used to be.
>
> As the result, the time has passed when Government expenditure can be dealt with effectively by detailed control from the centre. The main fields of Government activity are much too big for detailed control to be exercised effectively from a single central position.
>
> It is, therefore, necessary to make sure that Treasury control of expenditure has been adjusted to meet modern conditions. This, in effect, means that Treasury control must be so organised and exercised as to be directed to the main issues and to the bigger questions, and that minor questions are, as far as possible, left to be settled by those who are in closer touch with the activities in question than the Treasury.
>
> This is a general doctrine and it is broadly expressed and

212

needs qualifying in particular instances. But in general I believe it is true that the Treasury does its job best when it concerns itself with the broader issues and keeps off matters of detail.

There are exceptional cases where the Treasury has to exercise more detailed control. But we should only admit these exceptions where we are satisfied there is good cause. We should not be content to exercise detailed control merely because it is a survival from the past.

I would like to make it clear that in talking in this way of the Treasury avoiding detailed control where it is not necessary, I am not merely thinking of saving staff. It is not merely a question that the work of the Treasury will not be properly organised so long as a lot of time is taken up in dealing with minor questions. It is also a question of the effect on those who exercise control and on those upon whom Treasury control is exercised. The point of view of a man who spends his time dealing with a lot of minor questions ad hoc is not conducive to the sort of forward looking outlook and concern with general tendencies and policies which one wants to cultivate. The same is perhaps even more true of the attitude of those in Departments other than the Treasury. If they find that the Treasury is too much concerned with asking what seem to them petty and irritating questions, they will not take kindly to the Treasury interest in the wider aspects of their affairs. Furthermore, I think that a lot of the irritating delays which are attributed to the Treasury will be found to relate mainly to fairly trivial matters and that a great deal of irritation would be avoided if fewer of these minor questions were asked.

As you will see, my general point of view therefore leads me to favour wider delegated powers. One of the notes circulated to the Committee outlined the main objects of control as:

1) regularity of expenditure
2) administrative control, i.e. to avoid extravagance
3) policy control, to scrutinise policy proposals in terms of money.

I regard (1) as in essence probably the least important from the point of view of actual control of expenditure. This is a field, however, in which the Treasury have certain traditional and constitutional functions which cannot be abrogated.

Nevertheless I think that it ought to be firmly impressed on the Treasury staff that (1) regularity is only one aspect and by no means the most important aspect of Treasury control.

On (2), administrative control, to avoid extravagance, it is much more difficult to generalise, but insofar as one can generalise I think my view is that we should try to get a good deal nearer to the position which we are trying to establish in such matters, namely that we put much more trust in the Departments but combine this trust with a measure of general guidance and help combined with test checks. But I admit that I am, in this matter, speaking without having enquired into the matter myself in any detail and I am not sure how far this doctrine can be pushed on supply expenditure.

You will realise from what I have said that the side of the work which I wish to see emphasised and encouraged is (3) namely policy control.

I turn now to the particular proposal for increased delegation. First, there is the question of write-offs for losses, fraud and so forth. I am in favour of a much wider delegation on this front, and I would think that such control as we exercise could largely be done:

a) by means of scrutiny of schedules sent to us in bulk post facto, and

b) by a certain amount of analytical and comparative work based on these schedules, namely to see whether the degree of fraud and losses in particular departments is unreasonably large, given the nature of their work.

On delegated authorities generally I am in favour of going a good deal further than has already been done. But I recognise that different degrees of delegation are appropriate in different types of work and I think this needs to be investigated. But I hope the investigation can be carried out against the sort of background which I am seeking to outline to you today and with the aim to see Treasury work on the policy side intensified. I imagine that there is scope for much more work to be done in following up policies and new schemes once they have been approved, and would have thought that there should be something in the nature of a continuous process of enquiry and consultation about broad issues of policy which affect expenditure. And I think it is important that this sort of work means a certain change in the relationship between the Treasury and Departments. It is not a question of the Department putting a proposal for sanction or refusal, but the Treasury getting inside the mind of the Departments concerned and influencing their forward policies and encouraging them to review policies and schemes already approved in the light of growing experience and so forth.

With this side of the picture I associate the scheme, with which the Committee are aware, for periodic forecasts of expenditure. There is a risk that unless this work is treated as something of real importance it might become stereotyped and degenerate into a paperasserie. I regard the punctual rendering of these reports and detailed work on them by Divisions as one of the most important functions of the Treasury in the future. I do not believe we shall ever succeed in bringing Ministers to a sense of real responsibility about finance until we are in a position to relate any demands for substantial increased expenditure to an up to date statement of the country's financial position, making it clear almost at a moment's notice that some bright new scheme which is brought up by Ministers means there will be an increase of expenditure next year of X millions instead of Y millions and that in terms of income tax this means so much. But we cannot do this unless the forecasts are kept thoroughly up to date.

Furthermore, the forecasts will be unrealistic unless the Treasury Divisions are encouraged to keep in the closest touch with Departments on these forecasts as to where the policies are leading or are likely to lead in terms of money, and to influence betimes in the early stages where policy is beginning to be formulated.

In saying all this I have perhaps drawn a somewhat exaggerated picture of the possibilities of a changed outlook on supply work, but if I have exaggerated a little it is because I want to make my point of view clear. And perhaps I might finish these general observations by saying just a few words on the extent to which the Treasury work has changed, and new techniques have been and are being in process of being evolved since the war. Indeed, if it is not impertinent, I would like to suggest to the Committee that it would be helpful if somewhere in their report theycould put in a paragraph or two summarising the extent to which Treasury work now depends upon methods of work or techniques which were either unknown or hardly developed before the war.

If I may mention the leading ones: on the O.F. side you have the periodic balance of payments forecasts and the more or less continuous work which is done to keep watch on the balance of payments, particularly on the dollar side, and to see to what extent happenings day by day and week by week are in step with that forecast.

Secondly, and closely allied with the balance of payments forecast, is the series of import programmes. Thirdly, there are investment programmes. Fourthly, there is the work on the national income from the point of view of enabling those who frame the Budget to know how the economy of the country is faring generally, an exercise which is of the utmost importance in framing the Budget. Fifthly, in another field there is the new establishment technique of staff forecasts, staff ceilings and staff inspectors, with added emphasis on O and M and periodic reviews. Sixthly, there is this business of forecasts of supply expenditure.[76]

Without wishing to diminish the importance of Bridges' personal work for the TOC, it should be remembered that at this time the Treasury staff employed on this work were by no means lightweight. It included five officials with the civil service status of permanent secretary (including the Chief Planning Officer) and seven officials with the status of deputy secretary (i.e. Treasury third secretaries). It is obvious that Bridges kept fairly closely in touch with them all. In addition, he read all the TOC minutes as they were produced for circulation. This enabled him to be continuously informed about what was being said - and it is important to add that although the whole exercise was dominated by 'insiders', the evidence presented was by no means inhibited or uncritical of the arrangements then in operation. Another important feature was that when Bridges himself produced papers for discussion they were often first drafted by others, amended by Bridges, then circulated and further amended until a finally agreed and polished version was ready for the purpose intended (such as circulation to ministers). This procedure may have been very time-consuming, but, again, it was a very good means by which Bridges kept in touch with what was going on and with what people were thinking. It also resulted in his views percolating throughout the Treasury and the civil service. Furthermore, since the advice was so thoroughly worked over and generally the product of many not uncritical minds, it is hardly surprising that the final versions of papers appear so well polished, politically sensitive and well balanced.

Similarly with the minutes. When Bridges chaired the committee in Woods' absence he always saw the minutes in draft. Sometimes he wanted extensive revisions ('Sorry to be so fussy. EEB'). Sometimes he was very encouraging to E.W. Maude, the secretary ('Approved (very good minutes). EEB 27.v.49').[77] The point to remember from all this is that great care was taken to get the minutes just as Bridges wanted them, even if the care required more resources to produce more drafts; and Bridges was fully informed of all that was going on as a consequence.

An example of even more meticulous preparation of evidence for a committee was the effort applied to Bridges' evidence to the Committee on Higher Civil Service Remuneration (the Chorley Committee). Bridges gave evidence to this committee in 1948, but in preparation he found out what questions were expected to be put to him, had the answers drafted by Winnifrith, Padmore, Crombie and others; then discussed the draft answers with them; after which he called a meeting of 12 Heads of Departments to discuss his proposed evidence.[78] In these circumstances it is not surprising that the actual evidence appears so well informed and authoritative, and it is not surprising that in comparison the evidence of other witnesses, especially 'outsiders', appears to be in a different class. The points to notice here are, on the one hand, the care taken to prepare evidence and the resources involved, and on the other hand, the superiority of the results compared with other evidence. When, however, the investigation was less formal and the issues less politically sensitive (as with Bridges' evidence quoted above, to the TOC) it is possible to gain the clearest insights into Bridges' own thoughts and attitudes.

Bridges on the machinery of government

The period from 1942 to 1952 was characterised by numerous committees, sub-committees, working parties and interdepartmental groups, all considering related but often overlapping aspects of the machinery of government. Large numbers of officials were involved in the numerous machinery of government investigations and the fashionable management technique during this period was organisation and methods. Bridges was heavily involved in this work. He played an important part in deciding what should be investigated and who should do the investigating. It was, moreover, a subject in which he had a considerable personal interest and the memorial to that interest is his publications on the subject, especially his book *The Treasury*,[79] which was his own contribution to the New Whitehall series of books published by the Royal Institute of Public Administration. He maintained this interest to the end of his life. For example, when Sir William Armstrong was appointed Head of the Civil Service in 1968 Bridges wrote to congratulate him and added: 'I am also very glad to think that these moves will enable you to diminish some at least of the nonsense which has resulted from the overlap between the Treasury and the DEA. This is all to the good...'[80]

There are a number of reasons why this study of Bridges' relationship to the machinery of government is important. First, his own contributions to the work. Many of the ideas that were implemented, and also many of the proposals for investigations, originated from others. Bridges did not personally present a series of brilliantly original ideas that significantly influenced the direction of government. However, it was often Bridges who influenced the choice of which projects should be studied and how the studies should take place. This, of course, is not inconsistent with the position classically expected of a top official in British government. Such officials are not recruited for their academic originality but for their qualities of judgment and abilities to work within a particular environment. Nevertheless, it seems somewhat critical to say now that he was not an innovator. It would be more correct to say that his innovative qualities were of a managerial kind. As he put it in one of his lectures: 'The administrator has to settle, not merely whether the scheme of organisation is technically sound and economical, but how it will work given the personalities of the chief members of his staff.'[81] Not only did he mastermind the administrative structure of central government during the Second World War, he used the experience he had gained to mastermind a quite different exercise in the period after the war was over. There is no doubt that he played a major role in this and that it was the distinctive and original role of a leading civil servant.

Secondly, in practice, Bridges used his experience to develop for himself a position as Head of the Civil Service different from any of his predecessors. He was personally at the centre of the whole organisation of central government and on all the key committees (many of which he chaired). Consequently he knew exactly what was going on in many individual departments as well as from an interdepartmental point of view. One of the reasons why he was in this uniquely powerful position was that he was permanent. He had played a key role at the centre of government for a long time, he had made an enormous contribution to the organisation of the government during the war, and he had the confidence of the leaders of both the main political parties. He also had the wisdom to successfully adjust his style to changing circumstances. Many of the ideas that were implemented may have originated from elsewhere but it required innovative qualities to put them into practice. This meant that in the post-war period the machinery of government studies and committees butressed and strengthened the position of the Treasury as the key department in central government. Furthermore, Bridges knew well almost all the top permanent officials. Many of them had been appointed as a result of his recommendations and he had a natural talent for gaining their confidence and distilling their collective wisdom.

Thirdly, he did not lack the resources to do the job. He was indeed hard worked, and his capacity for hard work was an important element in his success, but these reports and judgments that in their final versions read with such clarity and polish were often the result of many hands and minds producing many drafts. For Bridges' GOC work, A.E.C. Parnis, then a principal, meticulously prepared his agenda papers, with analysis of the issues and advice. This meant that for each meeting Bridges was provided with very detailed briefs.[82] Even when government staffing and other resources were being squeezed, resources were ensured for this key work.

Fourthly, developments in the machinery of government were considered and implemented in conditions of considerable confidentiality. Whenever possible outsiders were excluded. Indeed, Bridges' idea of an inspection of a department by people outside it was to institute a group of three civil servants to make a study, where only one of them came from the department concerned. On more than one occasion he said that departments could learn something from the experience of others,[83] but in practice he could not see outsiders without civil service experience having a useful role to play. Statements were made that now appear extraordinarily arrogant about the competence of those within the administrative system, though the statements were often made by officials with little or no outside experience themselves or even awareness of what was going on outside the relatively restricted circles in which they operated. Partly this is because of the conservative and secretive nature of bureaucracies. But partly also it is because of the requirements of the British constitution which maintains the fiction that decisions are made by ministers and it would be contrary to the spirit and customs of the constitution to recognise the part played by officials. This will be considered further in Chapter 7. The fact remains, however, that, as Bridges himself put it, there are certain fields of activity where ministers or Parliament have not seen their way to lay down any clear policy.[84]

This is an area where the ethical conduct of civil servants becomes particularly important. Not only do senior officials have to advise ministers - indeed, they often have to advise ministers to issue instructions to themselves - they also have to fill out the details of policies or develop policies where none already exist and where ministers have not given instructions. This is especially important in relation to the machinery of government because it is a subject which rarely has much political appeal: the electorate is unlikely to become spontaneously enthusiastic about it and there is not usually much kudos for ministers who make major contributions to it. It may seem surprising that in matters of this nature Bridges should have taken such a leading role: for example, in proposing to Churchill which ministers should be on a Cabinet committee. On the other hand, Bridges was clearly a trusted confidential adviser to Churchill and if that was the way they worked together and Churchill was prepared to accept the responsibility for decisions taken in his name it is difficult to maintain that the arrangement was wrong.

The machinery of government is a key element in government. Without good organisation and structure for their execution, government policies, however attractive they may appear to politicians or the electorate, may be unachievable or undermined. However, the constitutional constraints and the administrative culture within which officials work influences what actually happens. There are at least three reasons for this. First, this is because of the position of officials in relation to ministerial responsibility: in terms of strict formal propriety it is ministers who are responsible for policies, who give instructions, and who are accountable for what is done in their name. This accounts, to some extent, for the emphasis on official secrecy in this area. Secondly, in terms of day to day politics, ministers' intentions may be jeopardised if details of proposals and planning for government organisation become generally known before announcements can be made by politicians at what they judge to be the opportune time. This also contributes to the emphasis on confidentiality associated with machinery of government issues. There is also a third reason, associated more specifically with the administrative culture which protects Whitehall against the participation of 'outsiders'. For perfectly understandable reasons this exclusion is sometimes because of civil servants' lack of knowlege about who might be available to help and what expertise might be available. Sometimes the reason may simply be a consequence of tradition. When 'outsiders' have to be considered, the procedure seems to have evolved to consider first the participation of those 'outsiders' who were once 'insiders'. For example, when Robson was being proposed for membership of the Masterman Committee, one of the qualities Winnifrith felt it important to mention in Robson's favour was that he had been a temporary civil servant. Then, when Robson had to decline the invitation, Chester became the second choice and again one of the reasons was that he had been a temporary civil servant.[85] It is not surprising that 'outsiders' who have never been 'inside' regard this as a rather arrogant attitude, aptly expressed in the views attributed to Jay (apparently Douglas): 'that the gentleman in Whitehall knows best; and that the gentleman who dares to question Whitehall is no gentleman...' [86]

Finally, this chapter provides some insights into education and training both in the civil service, and in British society, on the subject of the British system of government. The New Whitehall series of books would probably have never been published had it not been for the recommendations of 'outsiders' on the O and M Advisory Panel making a suggestion which coincided with the initiative from the Institute of Public Administration under its recently appointed new Director, Raymond Nottage. There is no doubt, though, that the nature of the series, and the descriptive, uncritical, and certainly unembarrassing approach of the books was considerably influenced by the response of officials, especially those who were members of the GOC. The relationship of the Treasury and of Bridges in particular with the Institute, together with other aspects of education and training will be considered further in the next chapter.

Notes

1. Sir Edward Bridges, 'Administration: What is it? And how can it be learnt?', in A. Dunsire (Ed.), *The Making of an Administrator*, (Manchester University Press, Manchester, 1956), pp. 5-6.

2. Lord Bridges, 'The Relationship between Ministers and the Permanent Departmental Head', *The W. Clifford Clark Memorial Lectures, 1964*, (Institute of Public Administration of Canada, Toronto, 1964), pp. 9-10.

3. Lord Trend on Bridges in E.T. Williams and C.S. Nicholls (Editors), *Dictionary of National Biography 1961-1970*, (Oxford University Press, Oxford, 1981).

4. *The Times*, 29 August 1969.

5. PRO/CAB21/1998, Bridges' Notes for discussion, 16 December 1942.

6. J.M. Lee, *Reviewing the Machinery of Government 1942-1952: An essay on the Anderson Committee and its Successors*, (Birkbeck College, London 1977). See also Richard A. Chapman and J.R. Greenaway, *The Dynamics of Administrative Reform*, (Croom Helm, London, 1980), Ch.4.

7. *Report of the Machinery of Government Committee*, [Cd. 9230], (HMSO, London, 1919), Ch.3.

8. J.M. Lee, *Reviewing the Machinery of Government*, pp. 140, 141 and 144.

9. PRO/T199/65, 'Functions of the Cabinet Secretariat: Historical Note', para.47.

10. Authorised by the Prime Minister's minute to Bridges (C33/2), 19 October 1942, in PRO/Prem4/63/2.

11. J.M. Lee, *Reviewing the Machinery of Government*, p. 30.

12. PRO/CAB134/505, Organisation of the Civil Service: Working Party No. 4: Business Efficiency in Departments: Interim Report, October 1946, para.9.

13. PRO/CAB21/1998, Bridges to Brook, 18 February 1943.

14. PRO/Prem4/63/2, Bridges to Prime Minister, 26 August 1942.

15. PRO/Prem4/63/2, Prime Minister to Bridges, 27 August 1942.

16. *Fifth Report from the Select Committee on Estimates, together with the Minutes of Evidence taken before Sub-Committee D and an Appendix, Session 1946-47*, H.C. 143, (HMSO, London, 1947), Q. 1616.

17. Lord Bridges, 'Haldane and the Machinery of Government', *Public Administration*, Vol 35, 1957, pp. 254-65.

18. PRO/CAB134/308, HM Treasury, 'The Central Machinery of Government: American Studies and British Practice', 31 May 1949.

19. PRO/T222/71:OM290/01.

20. PRO/Prem4/63/2, Bridges to Prime Minister, 25 September 1943.

21. PRO/T162/870/E45491/07/019.

22. J.M. Lee, *Reviewing the Machinery of Government*, p. 61.

23. PRO/T222/9, Bridges to Barlow, 14 June 1944, and Barlow to Fraser, 22 June 1944.

24. See also Richard A. Chapman, *Decision Making*, (Routledge and Kegan Paul, London, 1968), pp. 102-4 and 109-10.

25. PRO/T222/71:OM290/01.

26. Sir John Anderson, 'The Machinery of Government', *Public Administration, Vol 24, 1946, pp. 75-85*.

27. J.M. Lee, *Reviewing the Machinery of Government*, pp. 36-7.

28. PRO/T273/9, Bridges to Heads of Departments, 26 February 1946.

29. PRO/T222/79:OM370/1/01 and PRO/T222/79:OM383/6/01.

30. PRO/T161/1294/S53261/1-5, PRO/T161/1295/S53261/6-7 and PRO/T273/298.
31. PRO/T161/1295/S53261/7 and PRO/T273/298.
32. J.M. Lee, *Reviewing the Machinery of Government*, p. 41.
33. PRO/T161/1295/S53261/7.
34. PRO/T161/1294/S53261/2.
35. PRO/T273/298, Gilbert to Bridges, 18 October 1945.
36. J.M. Lee, *Reviewing the Machinery of Government*, pp. 41-2.
37. PRO/CAB21/2074 and PRO/CAB134/904.
38. PRO/T273/9.
39. PRO/T162/881/E52057.
40. J.M. Lee, *Reviewing the Machinery of Government*, p. 44.
41. PRO/CAB134/505, 'Organisation of the Civil Service: Working Party No. 4: Business Efficiency in Departments: Interim Report', para. 2.
42. PRO/T162/944/E51953/025.
43. PRO/T162/881/E51953/026.
44. PRO/CAB134/505, 'Organisation of the Civil Service: Working Party No. 4: Business Efficiency in Departments: Final Report'.
45. PRO/T162/969/E51953.
46. *Fifth Report from the Select Committee on Estimates, 1946-47.* H.C. 143, (HMSO, London 1947), Q. 1624.
47. *Fifth Report from the Select Committee on Estimates,* 1946-47, Q. 1608.
48. J.M. Lee, *Reviewing the Machinery of Government*, pp. 30-1.
49. PRO/CAB134/307.
50. *Fifth Report from the Select Committee on Estimates, 1946-47,* para. 58.
51. *Ibid.*, para. 49.
52. PRO/CAB134/307, 'Fifth Report from the Select Committee on Estimates (Session 1946-1947), Draft Memorandum by the Treasury'.
53. PRO/CAB134/307.
54. PRO/CAB134/307.
55. PRO/CAB134/307, Emmerson to Bridges, 20 April 1948.
56. PRO/CAB134/308.
57. PRO/CAB134/308.
58. PRO/CAB134/309, Note by Bridges, 7 December 1950.
59. PRO/CAB134/310.
60. PRO/CAB134/310, Minutes of Meeting, 24 July 1951.
61. *Final Report of the Committee appointed to inquire into the Organisation and Staffing of Government Offices*, [Cmd. 62], (HMSO, London, 1919).
62. PRO/CAB134/903.
63. PRO/CAB134/908.
64. CR10/233 Part I, quoted by J.M. Lee, *Reviewing the Machinery of Government* pp. 111-12.
65. CR/233 Part I, minute 28 March 1952, quoted by J.M. Lee, *Reviewing the Machinery of Government*, p. 113.
66. J.M. Lee, *Reviewing the Machinery of Government*, p. 52.
67. PRO/T273/167.
68. PRO/T222/504.

69. PRO/T273/163.
70. PRO/T273/309.
71. PRO/T273/201.
72. PRO/T273/309.
73. PRO/T199/122.
74. PRO/T273/201.
75. PRO/T273/201.
76. PRO/T273/202.
77. PRO/T222/509.
78. PRO/T162/968/E51933/02.
79. Lord Bridges, *The Treasury*, (George Allen and Unwin, London, 1964).
80. Goodmans Furze Papers, Box 9, Bridges to Armstrong, 9 January 1968.
81. Sir Edward Bridges, 'Administration: What is it? And how can it be learnt?', p. 4.
82. PRO/T273/164.
83. For example, PRO/T222/678.
84. Lord Bridges, 'The Treasury as the most political of departments', The Pollak Lecture, delivered at the Graduate School of Public Administration, Harvard University, 1961, pp. 9-10.
85. PRO/T215/91.
86. PRO/T222/678, minute by Woods, 29 July 1954.

6

Publicity and the Profession

In practice all aspects of the executive work of British central government are largely shrouded in mystery. There are various reasons for this, one of the most important being the position of civil servants themselves in the system of government: they have been regarded by some authorities as officials in the fourth service of the Crown. To them the civil service is comparable to the three armed services.[1] Moreover, official attitudes of mind and modes of work retain some of the residual characteristics of confidentiality associated with personal service to the monarch. In recent times, of course, the focus of loyalty has been transferred from the King or Queen to the government of the day. Thus, whilst the reasons for maintaining confidentiality in the executive work of government are to be found in the complex traditions of administrative culture and the practical requirements of the Official Secrets Acts, the most powerful and continuing justification originates from the constitutional convention of ministerial responsibility.

It is not difficult to see how the culture and customs encouraging this confidentiality have developed from the fundamentals of the constitution. There is plenty of evidence to show how it has been maintained with the approval of the government of the day, though rarely with the approval of the opposition or even the government's own backbenchers. As Attlee put it to Bridges on one occasion: 'It is not the custom to reveal to the world the domestic arrangements for the despatch of Government business. To do so would invite undesirable criticism.'[2] The basic fact is that in the British system of government it is ministers, not officials, to whom Parliament gives power and it is ministers who are answerable in Parliament for the actions of their officials. These essential features of the constitution, and some of the consequences in terms of the relationships between officials and ministers, will be considered further in the next chapter. The purpose of this chapter is to focus on those experiences of civil service publicity and the profession of government that emerge from a selection of the numerous Treasury files concerned on the one hand with various aspects of publicity and on the other hand with the peculiar problems associated with the founding, development and financial problems of the Royal Institute of Public Administration.[3] These are topics to which Bridges gave a great deal of time and energy. They also involved matters which appear to have stimulated in him complex feelings involving enthusiasm for historical writing and sympathetic interest in civil service training (especially training in techniques and skills), but caution and frustration toward publications about government that were other than purely historical.

Publicity

Bridges was naturally interested in books and in writing. Perhaps this is not surprising in the son of a poet laureate who, during his childhood, met so many literary figures when they visited his father's home. Later in life one of his modes of relaxation was sorting his father's papers and preparing them so that they could be made available to scholars. It should also be remembered that his great interest in libraries and books became more publicly known in his work for the British Council and as Chancellor of the University of Reading. In addition, Bridges himself made a mark as an author, by virtue of the Book of Box Hill, his writings on the civil service and government organisation, and also, during the First World War, some early attempts at essay writing and fiction.[4]

It is therefore not surprising that when Bridges became Secretary to the Cabinet he took a special interest in the Historical Section of the Cabinet Secretariat, which came within his field of responsibility. The Historical Section owed its origin to a memorandum written by Lord Esher in 1906 urging the importance of forming a Historical Section of the Committee of Imperial Defence. After consideration by a sub-committee, the Committee of Imperial Defence in 1907 accepted the principle that the work of preparing histories of naval and military operations should be concentrated and placed under the Committee of Imperial Defence. This marked the beginning of the Historical Section of the Committee of Imperial Defence working under its Sub-Committee for the Control of Official Histories. In the years from 1907 to 1913 the Historical Section completed the official history of the war in South Africa (previously undertaken by the War Office) and compiled an official history of the Russo-Japanese war.[5]

Neither of these works was a financial success, and in 1913 the Historical Section's supervising Sub-Committee of the Committee of Imperial Defence, then under Esher's chairmanship, made further important recommendations. These were that the Historical Section should not normally attempt the compilation of histories of wars in which Britain had not been a belligerent but instead should translate or abridge the official histories of the belligerents themselves. Consequently the Historical Section was reduced to a very small unit, with a staff of only one officer and one clerk under the control of the Secretary of the Committee of Imperial Defence.

When war broke out in 1914 an early start was made on writing the histories of the war and from 1915 onwards considerable staff were recruited for the purpose. The staff later declined in number as the volumes were published, but the task for which they were responsible was enormous. For example, by 1944, 47 volumes had been published on the 1914-18 war; 4 more volumes had been completed and were awaiting publication; work was proceeding on another 4 volumes; and it seemed possible that 4 more volumes would eventually be compiled. By this time the staff still engaged on the history of the First World War consisted of the Head of the Branch, two narrators and an assistant.

Bridges, on appointment to the Cabinet Secretaryship, took an active part in the first meeting he attended of the Sub-Committee for the Control of the Official Histories. The most important item on the agenda was the annual report by Brigadier General Sir James Edmonds, which gave somewhat shocking information about the conditions of work. During the thaw in January 1939 icicles fell on the glass roof of the courtyard under which the records were housed, smashing part of it; one clerk barely escaped injury. The Military Branch was housed in a range of fifth floor attics, hot in summer and cold in winter, whilst the records themselves were in the basement to which the lift service was frequently interrupted. The building where the Branch was accommodated was on the Victoria Embankment in the City of London, with much noise from heavy traffic in front, the *Daily Mail* printing presses on one side, the *Evening News* presses at the rear, and the Metropolitan Railway, which shook the building, underneath. Bridges was impressed by this report and commented on the need to move the records to a place of safety as part of the general policy of decentralisation.[6]

From this time Bridges took a keen personal interest in the work in progress. The official histories of the First World War concentrated on the military operations and covered the civil side of the war effort only to a very limited extent. In 1941, however, a start was made on the narratives of military history of the Second World War, and by 1944 the staff employed consisted of the Head of the Branch and five narrators. More important - because it marked a change from the policy for the histories of the First World War - Bridges wrote to all ministries in 1939 asking them to collect material and keep a war diary of principal events and decisions affecting their share in the war effort. This was the first official paper towards work for a series of books on the civil side of the war effort.[7] In 1940 it was felt that an inspection should be made to ensure that this work was being carried out in the departments along the right lines. The Committee for the Control of Official Histories (as the supervising committee was then called), first invited Sir James Rae, who had served in the Treasury for many years before his retirement, to carry out the inspection, though it was later persuaded that only historians could really perform this function.[8] R.A. Butler, then President of the Board of Education, was Chairman of the Cabinet Committee, and he personally stressed the importance of the civilian aspect of the war effort, proposing Professor W.K. (later Sir Keith) Hancock as supervisor of the civil histories. This proposal, and a proposal for an Advisory Committee from the universities, were both approved and Hancock assumed his duties on 10 October 1941.[9] Bridges agreed with Butler and the rest of the committee that the civil volumes were a very important part of the history of the war and the committee accepted his recommendation that there should be a press notice about them. The press notice, which was eventually issued on 23 June 1942, explained that

> The whole population is concerned as never before and have a more direct part in it than perhaps in any previous war. A great volume of experiment and change is crowded into the war years; and, unless the main developments of policy are recorded, together with the measures adopted to give effect to them, there is a danger that full benefit will not be derived from the experience of the war effort as a whole...[10]

It was left to Bridges personally to propose the names for the

Advisory Committee and to prepare a plan for producing the official histories. Later, Bridges drew up precise rules to regulate access to documents; he also settled financial aspects of the work in consultation with the Treasury.[11]

Bridges consistently supported Hancock,[12] doing his best to get more help for him when it was needed,[13] and even after the end of the war, when he was no longer Secretary to the Cabinet, he maintained this personal interest in both the Military Series of volumes (concerned with the war strategy and operations), and the Civil Series of volumes (concerned with the civil war effort and the economic and social problems caused by the war).[14] At first, the intention was to print the histories for official use only, but in 1944 authority was given for them to be published in the usual way by HMSO.[15] The first volume in the Civil Series, written by Hancock and Mrs (now Professor) Margaret Gowing, was *British War Economy*, published in June 1949. It was intended that there would be between 20 and 25 volumes in the Civil Series.

Throughout the period when these histories were being prepared, there were also efforts to maintain the constitutional conventions of confidentiality. For example, a document to narrators (who were only later called historians) which Bridges may have drafted, and which he certainly amended in manuscript, said:

> A Narrator may well be disposed to take the view that only if he gets free access to all the material on record can he do his job properly. At the same time, a Department can hardly be expected to give free access to Departmental files to a Narrator until they have got to know him personally and have come to have full confidence in him and trust in his discretion and to the use he will make of the material.

It seems that on this document Sir Horace Wilson wrote in the margin (the signature is not entirely clear): 'Surely he can't do the job unless he does have access! If he is not to be trusted, get someone who is.'[16] In a memorandum of 27 February 1942 Henry Wilson Smith expressed similar sentiments:

> I would favour most strongly the suggestion that, in addition to ordinary departmental files and papers, Cabinet Papers and relevant Cabinet Minutes should be shown, where necessary, to the narrators, subject always to adequate security arrangements...To expect anyone to write a major part of an

official history of the war from the sort of files that repose in central registries seems to me quite ludicrous.[17]

Another aspect of confidentiality concerned reference by name to individual civil servants. For example, on 25 November 1945 Hancock issued an instruction to historians (presumably originating from Bridges or at least influenced by him) in which he said that reference to individual civil servants should be avoided as far as possible. He continued:

> We all remain bound in our historical writing by the constitutional convention of ministerial responsibility. Nor must we allow ourselves to give good or bad marks to officials who are debarred from explaining or defending their action... our concern is with the problems, the differing attitudes and policies put forward for tackling them, the methods followed and the results achieved. The biographical method is *taboo* for us...[18]

Nevertheless, from time to time there were queries concerning this anonymity. Bridges had discussions about it with Professor R.S. Sayers on 19 July 1951 and later wrote, with reference to his meeting with Sayers:

> An important point which has not, I think, emerged in the record of the meeting is that it is obviously impossible to treat Keynes and Keynes' contributions in this field as those of some anonymous person. Quite clearly a clear and not anonymous light must be allowed to shine on Keynes, and to some extent this light must be allowed to shine on some of those in his immediate circle. Anyhow, I think that Phillips, who was virtually the Financial Ambassador in Washington, may have to be mentioned by name. But I have and do reserve judgment as to the treatment of Horace Wilson and Hopkins, although Hopkins, of course, had a special position from the point of view of his very close and happy relationship with Keynes...[19]

A third aspect of the conventions of confidentiality was Bridges' desire to eliminate from the histories anything that was remotely sensitive. Whilst he was continuously encouraging about the official histories, and this encouragement was greatly appreciated by Hancock ('I was much encouraged by what you said about the battle to keep the series alive': 31 January 1952),[20] Bridges also took extraordinary care to ensure that anything in the draft manuscripts that could conceivably have been the slightest bit sensitive was officially approved and, if possible, desensitised. One safeguard was to read many of the drafts himself (for example, he was especially helpful in reading drafts written by Professor J.R.M. Butler, the general editor of the Military Series, though draft chapters sent by Butler to Bridges on 30 January 1953 were returned by Bridges a year later with apologies for not having had the time to read them). Sometimes Bridges sent authors several pages of detailed and very helpful comments and suggestions.[21] In 1955, for example, his comments on Chapter 10 of *Grand Strategy* Vol VI, especially his comments on Appendix IV, were so valuable that they were later included for publication in the volume.[22] Another safeguard was to ensure that the drafts were read by numerous officials and ex-officials who had been concerned with the particular subjects. For example, the circulation list for the drafts on the Civil Defence volume contained the names of 15 permanent secretaries; 10 permanent secretaries were on the circulation list to read the drafts of the Food History volume; and when the volume on Financial Policy 1939/45 was produced, the records show that copies numbered 33, 37 and 38 were sent to Mr H.C.B. Mynors at the Bank of England. Multiple copies of drafts were roneoed so that the demands of these large circulation lists could be met and the typing and secretarial resources involved in this exercise must have been considerable. In these circumstances it is not surprising that indiscretions were rare: few books prepared elsewhere have the benefit of so many friendly assessors reading the drafts and making constructive suggestions for improvement.

This help and encouragement from Bridges was gratefully received and much appreciated by the authors. Bridges himself enjoyed the work, especially as it was so compatible with his interests in history. Indeed, he was also sympathetic to the proposal made in 1945 (originating, apparently from the Society of Civil Servants) for a book that would be more popular in approach, and give an account of the civil departments in wartime. As he put it in a memorandum to Wilson Smith: '... a pennyworth of experience is better than a bob's worth of theory. Let us get from the Ministry of Information four or five of their popular booklets about the fighting services; and let us consider whether the civil service achievements in this war are capable of being treated on the same lines.'[23] It was subsequently agreed, at a meeting in the Treasury on 25 March 1946, that planning for this book should proceed, under the guidance and control of Bridges, assisted by Mr D.N. (later Sir Norman) Chester, who had left his temporary position in the Cabinet Secretariat in 1945 and had become an Official Fellow of Nuffield College, Oxford. However, it was also agreed that 'the book must not be written in such a way as to appear to be a "puff" for the Civil Service: the credit to which the Civil Service was entitled should appear out of the objective accounts given in the book'.[24] The book was to consist of a number of essays by different authors and the manuscripts were to be delivered by the end of 1946. Some of the essays were indeed written in time and Bridges wrote a draft of his introduction,[25] but there were delays caused by pressure of work elsewhere and eventually the project was abandoned in 1948 because, by then, it seemed that the intended contributors were not all likely to be able to deliver. Furthermore, at least one who had, Professor Lionel (later Lord) Robbins, had asked to withdraw his contribution as publication was uncertain, so that he could revise it to send to *Economica*.[26] The trouble seems to have been that although practitioners might have much valuable practical experience to offer, it was more difficult to get them to deliver manuscripts than it was for authors with other backgrounds. Furthermore, well-informed writings on the civil service (like the New Whitehall series of volumes) may have been factually accurate, but they avoided all criticism and evaluation and did not acquire a reputation for being stimulating to read.

This proposal for a book on the civil service in war was entirely consistent with other positive attitudes towards publicising the civil service at that time. For example, a study group was set up in 1945 under the chairmanship of E.L. Turnbull, then Director of Establishments, Home Office, to consider civil service publicity. Like the procedure for certain Cabinet committees at this time, no specific terms of reference were given, though the purpose of the study group was quite clear: it was to consider the relations between the civil service and the public, and to make suggestions for their improvement. Apart from the chairman, the study group included four other senior officials with experience of government information and public relations. It reported in 1946 and its recommendations were at the time approved in principle by Bridges who wrote a memorandum, circulated with copies of the report, commending it to departments.[27] The study group came to some very clear conclusions as indicated by the following quotations:

We conclude that the reputation of the Service is low enough to affect detrimentally, or to risk affecting, the cooperation of the public, internal morale, and the prospects of satisfactory recruitment...

...positive measures for making the Civil Service better known and understood (include): Publicity, through books, works of reference, lectures, press, radio (and possibly the screen) on Civil Service matters - recruitment, the organisation of the Service, its functions, history, relation to Parliament and ministers, how it works etc...

Even where there is no 'propaganda' object in view we consider that information about the activities of the Civil Service in any way likely to be of general interest, should be given to the press as a matter of routine...

The general education of the public in knowledge and understanding of the Civil Service should be promoted through all available avenues...

Some two years later E.C. Lester noted that the Turnbull Report, although commended by Bridges and generally approved by a meeting of establishment officers, had not been implemented by the Treasury. In fact, the Treasury had continued with its traditional rules and attitudes, which were enforced by officials at all levels. This is illustrated by the following examples. First, there is a selection of miscellaneous proposals for co-operation with authors writing about the civil service. Secondly, special emphasis is given to the particular example of how Bridges and the Treasury dealt with Dr (later Professor) W.A. Robson over the Fabian Report on 'The Reform of the Higher Civil Service'. Thirdly, there is a brief account of Bridges' attitudes to the proposed publication of *Economic Trends* and the *Quarterly Bulletin*.

Numerous examples could be quoted of proposals by authors and requests from them for official assistance during the period of nearly twenty years when Bridges held his two most important positions in the civil service. Many writers were discouraged by their initial contacts with officials, but some writers, for one reason or another, managed to secure considerable official co-operation and assistance. For example, in 1938 A.J. Brown was writing a chapter on commissions which report to the Treasury for the book on *Advisory Bodies*, edited by R.V. Vernon and N. Mansergh.[28] The file shows that the Treasury went to considerable trouble to help Brown, who was a Fellow of All Souls College, Oxford.[29] In view of some of the experiences of other authors it seems not unreasonable to wonder whether he would have received as much help had he not been at All Souls College and had Mansergh not been so well regarded in the Treasury.

A second example concerns Sir James Grigg, who had served in the Treasury and as Permanent Under Secretary of State for War before becoming Secretary of State for War 1942-45. In 1949 he had been asked to write a book on the central machinery of government for a series called 'Home Study Books' and had enquired whether the Government would be prepared to allow him access to the relevant material and give him such other help as might be required, if he accepted the offer.[30] The view of the GOC, with whom the matter had been raised by Bridges, was that there would be some advantage in agreeing to give Grigg such help as was possible in preparation for his book, but only on the understanding that the relevant chapters were submitted in proof for scrutiny and that the book contained no acknowledgment that official assistance had been afforded.[31]

A third example occurred in 1932 when S.J. de Lotbinière, Director of Talks at the BBC, was arranging a series of twenty talks on careers and asked the civil service to provide a speaker for a talk on the civil service and sought help from the Treasury. The Treasury response was unambiguous:

> ... we are not too happy about the proposal because this does not seem a very good time for advertising the Civil Service as a career. In the first place we are having the greatest difficulty in maintaining a trickle of open recruits in the interests of the service against many and varied kinds of misrepresentation and we do not want to make the position more acute than it is. Secondly, everybody knows all about the civil service as a career; and thirdly, we get far too many candidates to fill all our vacancies.[32]

A similar attitude was expressed by W.R. Codling, in a letter to Sir James Rae in 1938: 'I dislike the modern craze for publicity, and personally avoid it as much as possible. I am doubtful about the advisability of broadcast talks 'rather superficial in treatment put in an entertaining form' to make the work of Government Departments better known to the public...'[33]

The fourth example in this selection of miscellaneous illustrations of the Treasury's attitude to publicity concerns Harry

B. Price who, in 1955, wrote a book on Economic Cooperation Administration aspects of the Marshall Plan which referred by name to a number of British civil servants.[34] After a great deal of consultation and deliberation in the Treasury it was eventually agreed that, contrary to all normal practice, he should be permitted to refer to civil servants by name. This was mainly because he was writing a comparative study and British non-co-operation would have looked bad when officials from other countries had already co-operated. Various civil servants read the draft manuscript and they all had a rather low opinion of it. It was Bridges' responsibility to give the final decision. As he said in a letter to Sir Ivone Kirkpatrick on 9 November 1954: 'Broadly our view is that we dislike this business a good deal. But given the differences between the American and the British ways of looking at things: and given that the quotations themselves seem to us to be entirely innocuous, we are disposed to give consent...'[35]

A fifth example occurred when, in 1947, Winifred Davies, of the art department of *Scope*, a magazine for industry (concerned with marketing and merchandising but also with business efficiency and management problems) wrote to E.C. Lester in the Treasury asking for three photographs, one of which was to be of Sir Edward Bridges, to be published in connection with an article on planning in the civil service. When the letter was referred to Bridges by Lester, Bridges replied with a series of questions about *Scope*, ending with: 'Shall we have a chance of vetting the horrid thing?'. Later he wrote: 'I would be glad to see the article when it arrives. I must admit that my present feeling is that this is not the moment at which I should welcome publicity of a personal character about those who are engaged in planning in the civil service...' When provided with further information Bridges wrote again to Lester: 'My line is to suppress personal chat as much as possible. No flood lighting for individuals.' Eventually Bridges read the article and asked Lester to return it for him, adding:

> When returning it ...perhaps you would be good enough to say that some of your colleagues in the Treasury doubt whether the planning organisation is really susceptible of being explained in diagrammatic form on the lines of the diagram attached to the article. We do not, of course, raise objection to the inclusion of the diagram, but we fear that it is impossible to avoid any diagram on these lines being liable to give rise to some misconception as an oversimplification.[36]

A sixth illustration concerns the activities of the GOC sub-committee on regional organisation which was active in 1950: its joint secretaries were A.R. Bunker and B.C. Lumsden. It was a particularly active sub-committee, chaired by Sir John Maud (later Lord Redcliffe-Maud), focussing on problems which were likely to become politically sensitive during the forthcoming election. Not surprisingly, it attracted a certain amount of academic attention, including interest from Mr (later Professor) Henry Maddick, of the University of Birmingham, and Professor J.E. Hodgetts. Bunker wrote a note to his colleagues about these two scholars. On Maddick he wrote: 'More by luck than good judgment we have got rid of Mr Maddick - I hope - until 16th March (1950, not 1951 I fear). Can you kindly let me have a brief saying how much you are going to let me tell him when I see him?' On Hodgetts he wrote: 'A new star has appeared on the horizon - a Professor (Canadian) Hodgetts - whom Mr Padmore has been good enough to wish off upon me (I have already made verbal protest to Mr Padmore but all he would say - with a grin - was that we had better get on with it)...'[37]

The last of these relatively minor illustrations of official attitudes of mind is quite different and concerned Sir Ernest Gowers who wrote *Plain Words*.[38] He was, in fact, asked by Bridges to write this book because the Treasury's Education and Training Division wanted someone to write such a book on the use of English, with reference to the special problems confronting the civil servant. Difficulties arose because Gowers and others thought his book would sell well and he was interested in receiving royalties rather than a once-for-all fee (which was the usual practice with Stationery Office publications). The advantage of receiving royalties was that Gowers would have the income spread over a number of tax years; whereas had he been paid a fee, most of the money would have gone straight back to the government in sur-tax. When the matter came to Padmore's attention he noted: 'If it should prove essential to persuade Sir Ernest Gowers to sell his book to the Stationery Office for a fee, I think it is likely that Sir Edward Bridges will be willing to try to do so; and it is no doubt probable that Sir Ernest Gowers, being a good citizen will do as he is asked.' In the event a compromise was reached whereby Gowers was paid a fee for a number of copies with an arrangement for subsequent fees on reprinting specified quantities of the book. The first fee related to printing 40,000 copies and was equivalent to a royalty of about 12.5%. However, the book turned out to be a best seller so that by December 1949 over 200,000 copies had been sold.

Gowers wished to continue to earn from his book, and personally retain copyright of it, but this caused embarrassment in the Treasury and the Stationery Office, where it was felt that he should be paid less than before, when further printings were required. The main Treasury attitude was that Gowers should not be making money, certainly not to this extent, for work he had been asked to do in the public interest. Gowers felt the money was not taxpayers' money but money from the book-buying public and the government had already made so much profit that all the initial production expenses had been paid long ago. Had the book been published by an ordinary publisher he could reasonably have expected more royalties, not less, when it was reprinted. Eventually Gowers continued to be paid, but not until after a lot of tiresome negotiations.[39] The essential details of the negotiations seem to have revolved around matters of principle. For example, it was felt that officials should not be paid when writing during office hours, but in fact Gowers, who was born in 1880, wrote the book after he had retired from full-time employment. Also, the Treasury were unhappy that the situation did not fit their normal rules for official publications. However, the matter was made more complicated because the Stationery Office was involved as the publisher (because it had a priority supply of paper, not easily available in postwar years to commercial publishers). In addition, the Stationery Office had no normal arrangements for paying royalties rather than fees. Reading the Treasury files now, many years after the events, the Treasury attitude appears exceedingly mean towards Gowers, and short-sighted about the reflected benefits on the civil service. The sensitivity was, of course, heightened because Gowers was behaving out of character for an individual in his position. Gowers, having created an asset by his own effort in his own time did not see why he should sacrifice it to the public interest simply because the suggestion that he should write the book came from the Treasury and the Treasury was expecting him to give up his interest in the work. Bridges continued his active involvement in the matter, issuing clear instructions to Padmore who was dealing with Gowers: 'Wrestle with him, and explain that we are giving him a very substantial share of the profits: and that the sort of figures he has suggested really are not practical politics.'[40]

This example and the preceeding ones illustrate some of the official attitudes in the Treasury on questions of publicity and publications. The civil service had developed a rather arrogant attitude towards requests for information, co-operating rarely and at its own discretion. The discretion, however, was applied according to criteria which always involved judgments of the applicants, made by officials who had little knowledge of these matters beyond their official duties. For example, they seemed to know little of the academic world outside Oxford and Cambridge, especially Oxford, and dealt rather contemptuously with requests from individuals in such other institutions of higher education as happened to exist. They knew even less about the world of publishing or about specialist groups in society interested in the civil service and how government worked. Publicity seems to have been tolerated as long as it was purely factual, included no accompanying comment and avoided naming officials. But, in general, relations with citizens interested in Whitehall and its workings were seen as both time-consuming and irritatingly unwelcome by busy officials. They seem to have felt they had more important things to do than satisfy what appeared to them to be at best the idle curiosity of individuals and groups, and more often the troublesome interference of busybodies intent on causing embarrassment.

These sentiments are well illustrated by an interesting brief discussion at the GOC in 1949. Sir Godfrey Ince, of the Ministry of Labour, who had recently visited Washington, said that he had been impressed with the practice there of United States government departments throwing open their offices to public inspection. He had noticed that the attitude in the United States was that as the public maintained through taxation the departments, and the buildings which housed them, citizens felt they had a right to interest themselves in the way their money was being spent. He suggested to the GOC that the same attitude should be accepted in the United Kingdom and that, where appropriate, departments should be allowed at their discretion to admit the public. In discussion it was pointed out how inappropriate this would be. Members of the public, if allowed to walk around a department, might obtain a totally misleading impression of the way in which civil servants conducted themselves and misrepresentation might reach the press. Nevertheless, in a positive spirit of sympathy towards Ince's suggestion, it was thought that the dangers might be averted if the public were admitted on conducted tours with explanatory talks on how the department was organised. This opportunity, it was suggested, would be of particular value to schools and universities.[41]

Bridges, and some of his Treasury colleagues, had a rather clear-headed attitude towards what they thought schools and universities needed, especially when those needs were consistent with official ideas about training. Training at this time was fashionable, both inside the civil service and in business and industry. Indeed, one interesting development originating from about this time was the 'Handbook for the New Civil Servant'. F.C. Newton was writing this for new entrants into the civil service and Bridges took a close personal interest in it. He had views about what should be included, and asked Humphreys-Davies to encourage Newton to have a word with him. Later he wrote to Newton in an extremely encouraging manner saying that he would like to lend a hand if Newton got stuck at any time. When the draft of the Handbook was typed Bridges went out of his way to send five pages of comments to Padmore and Humphreys-Davies, congratulating Newton and offering criticisms aimed to achieve greater perfection.[42] The Handbook, however, was to be for official use only. It was a form of internal publicity for training, and it made hardly any advances towards the positive suggestions being made by individuals and groups outside the civil service.

One of the most significant sources of these positive suggestions was the Fabian Report, 'The Reform of the Higher Civil Service'. The Treasury response to this pamphlet reveals with such extraordinary clarity civil service attitudes and modes of working in this area that, as already mentioned, it should be considered on its own, distinct from the various illustrations already given of day-to-day attitudes towards publicity in various contexts. The report was the work of a small group chaired by Bosworth Monck, a former civil servant, whose writings on the civil service[43] were not highly regarded in the Treasury. As Padmore put it to Mrs Johnstone in 1947: 'If we had intended producing a book on the subject under official auspices, we should not have chosen Mr Monck to write it.'[44]

The group that produced the report was, in effect, a sub-committee of the Fabian Political and Local Government Research Committee, with Robson as chairman. Robson, who had been a temporary civil servant during the war, sent a copy of the report to Bridges with a note written from the London School of Economics in which he said: 'I should very much like to know your views on the proposals contained in the report, and whether you consider they are moving in the right direction. I wonder whether you would care to discuss the matter. I would gladly offer you tea in our

Common Room here or lunch either here or at Lincoln's Inn.'[45]

Bridges, it seems, was immediately apprehensive. As soon as he received the letter, on 27 November 1947, he wrote to Padmore: 'I met this man last summer when I went to lecture at Ashridge. He is fairly influential in left wing circles and it might be useful for me to go and talk to him - provided that you can tell me what I ought to say, and can trust me to say it! What do you think?' Padmore was also apprehensive and sent the note on to Winnifrith who replied to Padmore on 3 December: 'I feel that Sir E. Bridges will not be able to express final views on many of the more important proposals, which require Ministerial decisions, and altogether I think he will find it a fairly difficult interview to handle.'

Bridges therefore sent Robson an extremely tactful, carefully worded letter on 5 December. He thanked him for his letter of 25 November. He said how much he would like the opportunity of having an informal talk about the Fabian Report, though, to make the position unambiguously clear, he added: 'You would, of course, only expect me to give my own views, and that informally.' The last two sentences of his letter were masterly: 'At the moment I am rather badly tied up, and I should like a little more leisure to think about some of the points in the Report before we meet. May I therefore look forward to suggesting a time just a little later on?'

In fact, this provided Treasury officials with time to make adequate preparations for Bridges' informal talk. Winnifrith, for example, immediately wrote to six of the senior staff in the Treasury asking for their comments on the Fabian Report. All replied at some length with very helpful analyses of points in the report to which they had applied their special knowledge. On 30 December Winnifrith sent Padmore (to pass on to Bridges) a summary of the comments he had gathered. This summary amounted to 27 foolscap pages, some in single spacing. It found that there was nothing startling in the report and much of it represented the lines of thought on which the Treasury had been working for some time. Its recommendations, according to Treasury officials, fell into three groups: (i) ideas which had already been adopted (e.g. recommendations on training), (ii) ideas which the Treasury thought sound but which had not yet been put up to ministers (e.g. concerning widows' pensions and premature retirement), and (iii) ideas which, although having much to commend them, went beyond anything the Treasury thought practicable at that time (e.g. the recommendation on centralised promotion).

Bridges then sought permission from W. Glenvil Hall, Financial Secretary to the Treasury, before arranging the meeting with Robson. He provided the Financial Secretary with details of his brief for meeting Robson and argued that 'the fact that the Fabian Society have done their best to produce a practical and level-headed document is, I think, a good reason why I should be reasonably forthcoming to them.'[46] Then, with the Financial Secretary's agreement, and feeling adequately briefed by his Treasury colleagues, he arranged his informal meeting with Robson, not by accepting Robson's invitation but by inviting Robson to call at the Treasury. Robson was an exceedingly shrewd and experienced scholar, at the time he was one of the most eminent academic authorities on public administration in the country, but it is unlikely even he could have guessed at the extensive preparations before he called on Bridges on 9 February 1948.

Robson, like Bridges, had a natural formal courtesy rarely seen nowadays, and contacts between the two men were maintained intermittently from this time. When Robson suggested it would be a good thing if they established a certain measure of informal contact on administrative questions which were being studied and pressed forward in the civil service, Bridges gave a sympathetic reply. After the meeting he noted:

I said I would welcome a measure of cooperation in this matter and I hoped that if he wanted to he would always come to see me and to consult me informally. Though I did not put it to him quite in this way, I am sure it is worthwhile by means of these informal contacts to establish a degree of understanding with people of Professor Robson's position whose critical and constructive work is much more likely to be helpful to us if we take a little trouble to tell him what we are doing and to keep in touch with him.[47]

When Bridges retired Robson wrote a typically courteous letter of best wishes. With reference to Bridges' period of office as Head of the Civil Service he added: 'I immensely appreciated your willingness to cooperate with those of us who tread the academic path: and I hope that this will continue now that you are no longer burdened with official responsibility.'[48]

The last example of official publicity is chosen because it neatly encapsulates official attitudes that can be found, though rarely in such pure form, in numerous Treasury files of the late 1940s and early 1950s. It dates from 1953 and relates to two proposals. One was to publish and put on sale *Economic Trends*. The other was to make the *Quarterly Bulletin* available to the research staffs of the three main political parties. The *Quarterly Bulletin* was prepared for the National Joint Advisory Council but in fact it was at this time already being sent to hundreds of people outside Whitehall. In essence it was, as Bridges himself put it in a memorandum to Armstrong on 5 February 1952, an 'explanatory commentary on the published facts which it embodies'. It was 'drafted with care' showing 'nothing that could have been embarrassing to either of the two Governments of the Day' (i.e. since 1945).

Bridges was firmly against both proposals. He thought the proposal to make the *Quarterly Bulletin* more widely available, but in a modified form, was quite unacceptable. He put his views very clearly to Armstrong in a minute of 11 February 1953:

It would be a quarterly version with a false beard, and would be given, by an under-the-counter arrangement, to the research staffs of the three political parties to be used for briefing their leaders but not shown to them.

This sort of under-the-counter arrangement makes me pretty miserable. It is not, with respect, a suitable thing for a public department to do. And...it will give rise to trouble.[49]

R.A. Butler disagreed with Bridges and added: 'I have been Chairman of a Research Department. There is really not much mystery. They should have all we can reasonably provide.'

The problem concerning *Economic Trends* was slightly different. *Economic Trends* was technically a Cabinet paper, begun in 1947 to supply ministers, for the purpose of their platform speeches, with an appraisal of the current economic situation. By 1951 it had a circulation of 883 copies, but Bridges was far from sympathetic to the proposal to extend its circulation. He put his views clearly to the Chancellor of the Exchequer in a minute of 16 January 1953:

The argument is, of course, that if this document is published, it will help the nation as a whole to a better understanding of our economic position.

I suppose this argument should prevail, especially as there is nothing secret about the figures. But I sometimes wonder whether by this sort of process we are not making everything a little easy for would-be critics of the Government by serving up everything in such an extremely convenient form.[50]

These views about making the *Quarterly Bulletin* and *Economic Trends* more widely available reveal official attitudes towards what would now be generally termed the debate on open government.[51] Bridges was in fact being briefed on these matters by S.C. Leslie, who had been recruited to the civil service at a highly controversial salary in excess of salaries paid to permanent secretaries. At this time he was Chief of the Economic Information Unit. But when Bridges drafted his minutes on these two publications it seems he greatly exaggerated some of the points made by Leslie (by referring to false beards and under-the-counter arrangements). Whereas Leslie was in favour of making information generally available to those who asked for it - especially if they were prepared to pay, so that receipts from public sales would reduce the net cost of preparing the information for official use - Bridges used the information provided in Leslie's briefs to produce arguments opposite to those advance by Leslie.

It was almost as if Treasury officials regarded their work and the information they possessed as not public but private to them. Of course they were hard pressed and did not wish to increase their workload unnecessarily, but their attitudes toward publicity and the public, demonstrated in these files, is quite different from the attitudes Ince observed during his visit to Washington. This became evident in various ways and was especially advantageous to enquirers with the right connections. Scholars from Oxford in particular were given more co-operation than others and the reasons for this are not difficult to understand. Many of the Oxford dons in the post-war period had been temporary civil servants during the war. This gave them contacts but, more important, they had insights so that they were already fairly well informed. Another advantage Oxford enjoyed at this time was the private conferences on the central planning of economic development. The 23rd of these conferences, at Nuffield College in 1947, on the external economic relations of the United Kingdom, enabled 60 participants from the Treasury and other planning posts in the civil service to talk freely, but in private, with invited participants from the academic world.[52] Such opportunities provided valuable indirect advantages. Informal contacts build trust. Furthermore, they enable scholars to know what questions to ask: in contrast, questions from individuals without such advantages may appear naive and ill-informed so that co-operation is more justifiably denied. It is not difficult to see how self-perpetuating the advantages of established academic institutions can be in the United Kingdom.

The Royal Institute of Public Administration

The Royal Institute of Public Administration (it became Royal in 1954) is a professional institution which might reasonably be expected to enjoy many of these advantages and to act as an intermediary, providing the focus for scholarship in public administration expected of a learned society, together with services and academic stimulation for practitioners. Although it has many achievements to its credit, it has never made the impact or achieved the status to which some of its early members aspired. There are various reasons for this. For example, the nature of the British system of government, which is neither based on a written constitution nor steeped in the intricacies of law characteristic of many European countries, means that in Britain there is no distinctive professional qualification required of practising public administrators. Another reason, associated with this lack of a professional qualification, is that ministers and officials have been unwilling to allocate public money for what appears to have been sometimes regarded by them as no more than a special sort of club for government employees. The distinctive attitudes of central government towards the Institute became apparent from the time of its foundation in 1922 and although the relationship became closer as the Institute matured, some of the early attitudes are still evident today.

The Institute owes its existence primarily to the major staff associations in the public services; in particular, to the Society of Civil Servants. The Society arranged two notable series of lectures in 1920 and 1921, and these enabled those interested in founding the Institute to come together and determine its objectives. It was soon agreed that the Institute was to have two purposes. The first was the development of the civil service and other public services (both national and local) as a recognised profession. The second was to promote the study of public administration.[53]

The Institute had an unfortunate beginning as far as interest from the Treasury was concerned. The 1920 series of lectures sponsored by the Society of Civil Servants was on the theme: 'The Civil Servant and his Profession', and the impressive list of speakers

244

included Lord Haldane. This early contact was important in attracting Haldane's interest and support. According to Sir Frederick Maurice,[54] who wrote a life of Haldane, it is significant that this was soon after Haldane realised there was little prospect of official consideration being given to the Report from the Machinery of Government Committee which he had chaired. Haldane therefore determined to organise voluntary support for his campaign for the application of scientific measures to administration and the Institute of Public Administration, of which be became the first President in 1922, became a suitable project through which he could channel his enthusiasm. In these circumstances, and bearing in mind the comments from the Treasury about the Haldane Report (see chapter five of this book), it is, perhaps, hardly surprising that the Institute was not immediately favoured by the Treasury.

Its views about the Haldane Report were, however, only one example of attitudes in the Treasury at that time. When the Institute of Public Administration was being founded Mr E.F. Wise, who later became the first Chairman of its Council, wrote on behalf of the Society of Civil Servants to Sir Russell Scott, then Controller of Establishments, HM Treasury, seeking support from the Treasury. Scott's reply was not encouraging:

> I have been thinking a good deal about your scheme for the organisation of a Professional Institute for the Civil Service...
>
> Frankly, I do not like your scheme. It seems to me that it has no application to the vast majority of the people in the Civil Service. For the most part Civil Servants have no concern with administration. And so far as the administrators of the Civil Service are concerned, I should, myself, have thought that in so far as your scheme was intended to provide for instruction in the theory and practice of administration, it was not much good attempting to apply it to the administrators of the Civil Service at this stage. They are, poor creatures, badly overworked already. I do not doubt that many of them might profit from the opportunities of learning better ways of doing things that your Scheme is intended to provide but it really is not much good attempting this until they have some time to spare.
>
> So far as your Scheme provides for the inculcation of professional etiquette I am afraid I can find little justification for it. The analogy with lawyers and medical men seems to

me to be ill-founded. These people are dealing with clients and no doubt certain canons of etiquette are necessary in their case by way of restriction of the freedom of the individual in their common interest. The Civil Servant, on the other hand, is an employee. He does what he is told, he cannot devise his own professional etiquette. He may of course object to what his employer tells him to do, but in that case he rquires a Trade Union to protest rather than an Institute to define.

Apart from all this, my main feeling is that I do not like your scheme because it seems to be a glorification of the bureaucracy. We are unpopular enough already, God knows, but I tremble to think how we should be regarded if we consciously assumed the airs of superior persons. After all, we have our Whitley, and I should have thought, myself, that if there was any real desire on the part of the staff to improve the Civil Service and not merely to increase the remuneration of its constituents (and if I put this hypothetically it does not mean that I have any doubt on the subject) there is abundant opportunity on the Staff Side of our Whitley Councils to do all that is necessary in this direction.[55]

Wise next wrote to Sir Warren Fisher on 15 March 1922. He enclosed a copy of the Institute's draft constitution, asked Fisher for his help in starting the Institute, and also asked for an opportunity to call on Fisher to talk about it. Fisher replied on 7 April saying: 'I have...had a talk with Russell Scott, and find that he has been in communication with you on the subject. He has shown me the letter he wrote to you on 21st February, and I share the views he then expressed.'[56]

Despite this unfortunate response from the Treasury, the Institute soon became established on a firm basis. By June 1923 it had over 1,000 members, and by 1930 it had 2,120 members. H.G. Corner, an idealist with a genuine passion for social service,[57] became its first honorary secretary and he wrote asking Fisher to become Vice-President. Fisher accepted the invitation on 28 June 1923. Later, in October of the same year, Corner asked Fisher to write a short message of 200-300 words to develop a little the President's message and stimulate recruitment. Fisher felt able to do this but not to the extent requested. His message extended to two sentences. It read: 'The importance of sound principles of administration and their application in the sphere of Government, both central and local, is great, and any endeavour to co-ordinate the common experience and the constructive thought of the Public Services should have value. I share the President's hope that the Institute may succeed in furthering enlightened interest in the subject.' This was hardly a rousing message of encouragement, but it was consistent with Fisher's attitude to the Institute. His lack of enthusiasm is illustrated by the fact that after Fisher had been Vice-President for two years Corner wrote asking him if he would be good enough to become a member 'in order to put the matter on a formal footing'.[58] Fisher, as a Vice-President of the Institute, was regularly invited to functions; generally he had other engagements and arranged for messages to be sent saying he would not attend. Each year as long as Fisher was Head of the Civil Service the invitation was extended for him to serve as Vice-President. When Sir Horace Wilson succeeded Fisher as Head of the Civil Service he also succeeded him as a Vice-President of the Institute.

When Bridges followed Sir Richard Hopkins as Head of the Civil Service he took a more personal interest than his predecessors in the activities of the Institute. Like his predecessors, he was invited to become a Vice-President and Bridges replied that he would be much honoured. He added that he read with great interest the papers issued to members and said he would be ready and anxious to help the Institute in its activities as far as he could. During the years when Bridges was most involved in Institute activities he attended lectures and other functions and on special occasions went to some trouble to reply personally, especially if he was unable to attend.[59] When asked, soon after becoming Vice-President, to write a short message congratulating the Institute when it celebrated its Silver Jubilee, he personally wrote an encouraging message, of the required length, which was delivered within a fortnight of the request being sent. The message was typical of Bridges' approach to public administration, as the first three sentences illustrate:

The lessons taught by practical experience have always stood high in the ways of thought and methods of work traditional in this country. Many changes, which elsewhere would have meant a break in continuity have, with us, been brought about by adapting what already existed, to meet fresh needs or novel purposes.
Nowhere is this more evident than in Public Administration...[60]

Despite Bridges' interest in the work of the Institute he could not always agree to its requests - at least not in the ways the Institute may have hoped. A good example of this occurred in 1950 when the Institute asked for Bridges' help in its membership drive. Mr P.R. (later Sir Patrick) Laird, writing on behalf of the Institute, thought it would be a good idea if Bridges wrote to Heads of Departments appealing to them to join and encouraging members of their staff to do likewise. Bridges was at first quite prepared to do this, but Padmore had reservations and suggested an alternative approach which was calculated to give publicity to the Institute but not to actually recommend civil servants to join. Padmore, it seems, was very concerned about the embarrassment that might be caused if Heads of Departments decided not to follow such a recommendation from the Head of the Civil Service. In the end, Padmore's approach was adopted.[61]

Bridges' deepest involvement with the Institute was in the late 1940s when the Institute was receiving its first financial assistance from the government, and in the 1960s when the Institute was attempting to raise funds towards the cost of taking a lease on premises in Carlton House Terrace.

In the late 1940s the Institute was in financial difficulties. At that time training in management was fashionable, politicians and commentators on national affairs were stressing the need for greater efficiency and the Institute felt it had a special role to play in improving the standards of public administration. The Treasury, however, maintained its characteristic scepticism towards the Institute. Indeed, the Treasury had never had much time for the development of management studies and management techniques. For example, when Newton was serving as secretary to the Assheton Committee on the Training of Civil Servants, Mr K.S. Jeffries, who was then apparently engaged on O and M work in the Treasury, surveyed the literature for him and commented that it 'is marred by a pseudo scientific attitude which produces such peculiar high-falutin' language that one often finds difficulty in suppressing the thought - "humbug!"'. Newton then passed the papers to Wilson Smith with the comment: 'It is high sounding but unimpressive'. Wilson Smith noted 'Read with a good deal of horror! Please keep by you for the moment in case a little light relief to our labours is ever required'.[62] At about this time Sir Alan Barlow, apparently reflecting views generally held in the Treasury, referred to the futility of the Institute of Public Administration.[63]

It is against the background of other significant post-war

developments in management and management education that the relationship of Bridges and the Treasury with the Institute of Public Administration should be considered. These originated from the interest and pressures exerted from politicians and interested parties outside the civil service. One result was the creation of the Administrative Staff College at Henley-on-Thames soon after the end of the war.[64] However, even when the Staff College had been created there was no real interest in it within the civil service. Its first course was in 1948 and it was only after enormous trouble that the civil service found one official it could spare for the course (she was Miss J.M. Franks, an established principal in the Ministry of Supply who was 'very nearly assistant secretary quality'). A typical response to the Treasury request for names for the second course was the reply from Sir Percivale Liesching of the Ministry of Food. He wrote that he could not nominate anyone and added: 'Frankly, I feel that I simply cannot spare any of my good people in the near future, and I should like to see the Staff College developed further before I submit any names'.[65] In the Treasury, J.A.C. Robertson, with a sense of relief that one person had eventually been found for the first course, wrote to Padmore: 'it is better to send one good Principal ... without overstraining the administrative machine, than to attempt to put the screw on Departments'. The Principal of the College, Noel F. Hall, was disappointed by the response from the civil service, especially as it was hoped that the courses at Henley would contain a balance of participants from various backgrounds, and he let the Treasury know of his disappointment. Padmore's response was predictable: 'If this thing cannot be run successfully without substantial Civil Service participation, its sponsors had no business to go setting it up without knowing whether we wanted it or were ready for it'.[66]

The main support from the public service towards the setting up of the Administrative Staff College came, as already mentioned, from ministers, not officials. The idea had been mooted at the time of the National Expenditure Committee's report in 1942 on the Organisation and Control of the Civil Service. Cripps had been keen on the idea and Attlee was sufficiently sympathetic that he visited the College when it was opened. Bridges' concern in 1948 was to ensure that any civil servants who attended the courses at Henley were good ambassadors for the civil service and he asked Padmore to 'try by informal means to check up whether our nominees are proving up to standard'.[67] Later, Bridges was told that Sir Geoffrey Heyworth had asked Sir John Woods (Board of Trade) to become a Governor of the College. Woods asked Bridges for advice and Bridges wrote to Padmore: 'I cannot see any objection to this, but have you any comments?' Padmore replied: 'I have tried to think of reasons why not. I have failed.' Bridges therefore wrote to Woods: 'There can be no possible objection to your being appointed to be a Governor of the Administrative Staff College. In fact it is a wholly admirable idea.'[68] The overall attitude within the Treasury towards the Administrative Staff College was therefore to doubt its value and be cautious about all forms of participation.[69]

A similar attitude prevailed towards the British Institute of Management (BIM). The difference was that the Staff College had been set up as a response to initiatives from industry; in contrast, the idea for creating the BIM originated from the Board of Trade. The suggestion was formally proposed at a meeting on 9 February 1944, sponsored by the Board of Trade. In 1946 Cripps, then President of the Board of Trade, announced his full agreement with the recommendations presented to him by a committee which he had set up, presided over by Sir Clive Baillieu, President of the Federation of British Industries. When the BIM was set up the Treasury, at its request, was represented on its Council by one of its officials, J.I.C. Crombie. It was also agreed that the Treasury would make a grant of £150,000 to cover its first five years.[70] This grant was subsequently increased to £250,000 for a six year period. It also, apparently, received financial support for acquiring premises.[71]

It is in the context of the general attitudes illustrated by these developments that consideration should be given to the post-war problems facing the Institute of Public Administration. The Institute had never had any subsidy or grant from government but had continued entirely on the income from members' subscriptions. In 1948, when the Institute was running into financial difficulties, it first applied for a grant from the Nuffield Foundation, though without success because the Foundation's policy prevented it from contributing to the general costs of an applicant. Next, the Institute prepared detailed papers for the Treasury, asking for £1,500 for three years at least, plus £5,000 a year for five years for research and allied activities. The detailed accompanying papers covered the history and objects of the Institute, an explanation of the effects of the war, information about activities since 1945, details of the financial position, research, Commonwealth and International relations, and an outline of the Institute's record of co-operation with the universities. Before the submission was sent to the

Chancellor of the Exchequer, there were informal contacts between Sir John Anderson, as President, and Bridges, as Vice-President of the Institute. Bridges discussed the matter with Padmore and Mr J.R. (later Sir John) Simpson. Other Treasury officials were also involved. Mr P.D. (later Sir Dennis) Proctor provided comments for Padmore and Humphreys-Davies contacted E.M.T. Firth, at the Ministry of Health, to ascertain the interests of local authorities in the Institute. Humphreys-Davies also wrote to S. Beer of the Board of Trade because of the danger of overlapping between the BIM and the Intitute. Bridges was clearly in a difficult position. Not only was he Vice-President of the Institute (and had shown more interest in it than any previous Head of the Civil Service), he was also somewhat embarrassed that the Institute was not proving as successful as he thought it might have been, especially in increasing the number of its members.

Bridges saw many sides to the problems of the Institute and felt that, as an interested party, he had to explain them all to the Chancellor of the Exchequer. He recognised that the main argument in favour of state help was that just as the Institute of Bankers and Chartered Insurance Institute were supported by banks and insurance companies, so the state should support the Institute of Public Administration. However, he preferred the Institute to be wholly independent of government. Whilst there were many banks and insurance companies, there was only one central government and if the Institute depended on it for a subsidy it ran the danger of losing its independence and could be regarded as a sort of offshoot of government. He used similar arguments, incidentally, in support of the independence of the University Grants Committee - which he strongly defended.[72] Furthermore, Bridges recognised that one of the great advantages of the Institute was that it was a meeting place for people in all the public services. When it came to research, for example, the Institute catered for a wide field and could propose ideas of mutual benefit. The primary beneficiaries were the institutions of government and in this respect it was unreasonable for the financial responsibility to remain exclusively with the individual members of the Institute. However this, in turn, meant that if the Institute was to receive institutional help, the assistance ought to come from local government and the nationalised industries as well as from central government.[73]

Bridges therefore proposed a firm response from the Treasury. This involved not an annual subvention to meet the running costs of the Institute, but 'a once-for-all grant to enable the IPA to get on its legs, on the understanding that the grant would not be repeated'. His second proposal was for a research grant, though of less than the Institute had asked for, to see whether other public authorities would accept a similar responsibility and give grants for research. Cripps, then Chancellor of the Exchequer, was more sympathetic than Bridges to the Institute's request, and indicated that he was prepared to consider the possibility of various departments of government (not just the Treasury) each subscribing to the Institute. He therefore agreed to offer £6,000 a year for three years towards the general purposes of the Institute.

Bridges was very worried by this decision, especially as he thought it might be regarded as a precedent. He wrote a minute warning about the implications, mentioning the interests of such bodies as the Council of British Archeology, and adding: 'In my experience one has to be ruthless in the small things if one is to achieve anything substantial in the way of reductions of expenditure over the whole field of Government expenditure'.[74] The letter that Cripps signed conveying the good news to the Institute bore all the marks of being drafted under Bridges' instructions. It emphasised the need for steady growth in membership which 'should enable ... independence to be achieved in three years', adding: 'I am anxious (as you will be) at the earliest possible time to see the Exchequer playing no more prominent a role in this matter than would be involved in the taking by Government Departments of their due place as corporate members of the Institute', and 'I do not think that I ought to accept a commitment on behalf of the Government for a longer period than three years, except in the form of a commitment to examine the position afresh with the Institute towards the end of that time.' He continued by saying that a further special research payment would depend on the value of the research done and on the success of the Institute in winning the active support of other bodies.[75]

Bridges' apprehensions were to a large extent justified. For example, a Question was soon asked in the House of Commons referring to the grant to the Institute and asking whether similar grants might be made to comparable organisations which recruited their members from and took an interest in the public services such as the Institute of Personnel Management, the Institute of Works Managers, the Office Management Association, the Industrial Welfare Society and others.[76] However, one of the benefits of this grant to the Institute of Public Administration was that the Institute was motivated to consider sponsoring a series of books on the functions and organisation of government departments (which resulted in the publication of 'The New Whitehall Series', as explained in Chapter 5 of this book).

Bridges continued to be worried about the Institute. In October 1949 he asked Padmore to arrange for someone to keep a friendly eye on what the IPA was doing. Mr R.C. Griffiths was assigned to this task and on 23 November reported his impression that Mr Nottage, the Director of the Institute, 'was an extremely sensible administrator' and 'the IPA was both in a sound financial position and in very good hands'. Griffiths continued to report back, through Padmore, but Bridges continued to be worried. For example, in response to Griffiths' report of 22 August 1950 Bridges wrote:

> But in the long run it is members which count, and I am still somewhat perturbed by the fact that, although we began to talk about a campaign for increased members over a year ago, the membership and income from membership has in fact remained stable for about eighteen months. We must, therefore, I think, continue to keep a pretty close watch on this side of things. We should find difficulty in justifying our position if at the end of the period for which grant had been promised the Institute has not increased its membership and income substantially.

By this time the British Institute of Management was developing nicely. A Treasury minute of 4 January 1951, commenting on the First, Second, Third and Fourth Reports from the Select Committee on Public Accounts (session 1950) reported that the grant to the BIM at that time was £240,000 and to this the Government found it necessary to give an additional special grant of £20,000 towards the cost of the BIM moving to more permanent premises.[77] However, soon after this the O and M Division in the Treasury was making strong comments about the money being given to the BIM. For example, on 9 July 1952 Simpson wrote:

> It now appears that all this money has gone down the drain. The Institute has acquired fine offices and built up a large staff, it has such things as a library, a club and an imposing Council but has achieved little or nothing in establishing itself as an instrument for improving the standard of management in industry generally.[78]

Meanwhile, Bridges, as a Vice-President of the Institute of Public Administration, was receiving its Council papers and minutes. On 14 February 1951 he wrote to Padmore: 'The finances of the IPA do not seem to be getting on awfully well. Last year notwithstanding the £6,000 grant they lost £70, although it is true they had non-recurring expenditure'.[79] On 16 July he wrote: 'I have been thoroughly dyspeptic for some time about the progress in building up membership and I cannot say that the latest figures make me any less unhappy ... for the life of me I don't for the moment see any particular evidence to suggest that the Institute will do any better in the next two years than they have in the last three years.' Consequently, Bridges was becoming increasingly anxious that the Treasury would be asked for more support. He wrote to Winnifrith on 19 July: 'I take a dyspeptic view of the way these people manage their affairs. And although it is early days to consider this matter before an approach has been made to us, there will be no harm in getting our thoughts in order.'[80]

This anxiety, so regularly expressed by Bridges, was probably a major factor in moving towards the arrangement introduced in the early 1950s for corporate memberships of the Institute. The grants for the general purposes of the Institute, begun when Cripps was Chancellor, soon became an annual subscription paid by the Treasury on behalf of all government departments. At the time this seemed a sensible solution and, with similar corporate membership fees from other public authorities, it meant that the continuance of the Institute was assured. It is difficult now to say where the main encouragement came for this idea. Bridges and his Treasury colleagues played an important though somewhat ambiguous part. On the one hand they recognised that central government had to make a financial contribution if the Institute was to continue, but on the other hand they did not necessarily approve of all types of Institute activities. They were sympathetic to O and M and the provision of certain sorts of training courses, but they thought that administration could not be taught; it required commonsense but it was essentially something one simply did. Cripps, however, was sympathetic to anything which held out the prospect of improved management efficiency, especially in government. Treasury officials in one respect had the last word. For example, Griffiths wrote in a minute to Padmore on 21 February 1951 that he and his colleagues intended to examine the Institute's proposals for corporate membership with 'stony-hearted realism'.[81] The outcome was reflected in Bridges' memorandum of 29 January

1952:

> I have consulted a number of my Permanent Secretary
> colleagues who, in general, agree that there is a case for
> giving some overall financial assistance to the IPA as a body
> engaged in fostering the study and practice of public
> administration. They feel, as I do, that the size of the
> contribution should be a lot less that the £5,000 p.a. for which
> the IPA have asked; and a figure of £1,500 would accord with
> my view as well as theirs.[82]

Nevertheless, corporate membership arrangements in these
circumstances, for an Institute that was not responsible for a
professional qualification, probably killed all hope of significantly
increasing individual memberships because senior officers of
public authorities which were paying corporate fees came to feel
that personal membership was superfluous. Therefore, from this
time the Institute became financially dependent to a large extent on
corporate membership fees. Perhaps, too, it is fair to say that this
arrangement, and the attitudes in the Treasury revealed by it, had a
more significant effect on the nature of the Institute than could
have been predicted at the time. This is well illustrated by the
events in the 1960s, when Bridges was President of the RIPA.

When Bridges became President of the Institute in 1958 he
thought it was a great honour, 'almost overwhelmingly when it is
to succeed the late Lord Waverley'. He said he was very proud to
accept the office and committed himself to do his best to further its
work.[83] Indeed, writing at the end of his period of office, he
referred to his profound belief in the value of the work of the
RIPA.[84] He served the Institute well over the years, giving lectures,
chairing meetings and writing messages of encouragement when
appropriate occasions required them. His lack of success in helping
the Institute to raise funds in the late 1960s must therefore have
been a profound disappointment, especially as he had previous
experience of fund raising both for Eton College (when the appeal
for reconstruction and renovation raised £490,000 in the 1950s)[85]
and the Oxford Historic Buildings Fund.

At the end of the 1950s the Institute had acquired a 14-year lease
on accommodation at 24 Park Crescent, London W.1, and it moved
to its new premises in September 1961. It was not long, however,
before the Institute was again seeking new accommodation and
entered into detailed discussions with the Crown Estate

Commissioners concerning 3 and 4 Carlton House Terrace. Unfortunately, these premises required a great deal of renovation and the cost was to be met by the incoming tenant. For this purpose the Institute had to find £50,000 of the £100,000 needed to reach an agreement with the Commissioners.[86] This was because the Treasury said that if the Institute raised £50,000 the government was prepared to provide the other £50,000 at the rate of £10,000 a year for five years.[87] A particularly frustrating aspect of these efforts was that while the Institute was endeavouring to raise £50,000 the government announced a further grant of £100,000 to the BIM.[88]

Nottage briefed Bridges who wrote to various trusts in attempting to raise the money. He lobbied Lord Bullock, a Trustee of the Wolfson Foundation, to gain his interest in the Institute's application for funds. He also wrote to Lord Murray of Newhaven, Director of the Leverhulme Trust, Mr McGeorge Bundy, President of the Ford Foundation, the Joseph Rowntree Memorial Trust, and the Clerks of the Drapers Company and the Goldsmiths Company. Most of these requests were politely but firmly rejected, but Bridges kept trying. He wrote a special personal letter to Lord (Ifor) Evans of Hungershall because Evans was a consultant to the Wates Foundation. Bridges was convinced, as a result of his other fund-raising experience, that if he could persuade the Foundation to give a lead by granting, say £5,000-£10,000 then other grant awarding bodies would be sympathetic and the money would soon be raised. In the event it was therefore an enormous disappointment that after Bridges' personal appeal to Evans the Wates Foundation offered only £500.[89] Although Bridges managed to secure a grant of £5,000 from the Pilgrim Trust (of which he was chairman) the funds raised were quite insufficient for the target set by the Treasury, and by November 1968 Bridges conceded defeat by writing to the Civil Service Department: 'It seems, alas, that our Carlton House Terrace ambitions have been thwarted. The Air Centre, which is better breeched than the RIPA, came on the scene during the summer and have made a firm offer which we cannot hope to better.'[90]

Taking this and all the other examples of Bridges' connections with the Institute into account, it seems clear that he had a very ambiguous attitude towards the Institute. There is plenty of evidence to show that he approved of it in principle and had a high opinion of much of the work that the Institute was doing. He also appreciated the efforts being made by Nottage and his colleagues at the Institute. However, he also had various reservations which, because of his character, he was probably incapable of hiding. The expression of these reservations was unlikely to have helped the interests of the Institute. For example, on one occasion he wrote to the Chancellor of the Exchequer: 'Sometimes I have read articles in the journal which I should hate to think came from a body subsidised by the Government.'[91] The apparent contradictions are, however, largely understood in the context of his attitude towards public administration as a profession. Bridges' attitude had the characteristics of a previous period (rather like his sense of humour which has been variously described as 'wispish', 'Edwardian', 'like that of a school prefect' and, in terms of modern expectations, 'non-existent').[92] His approach was that of the generalist - the type of official much criticised by the Fulton Committee and by other commentators in the 1960s. To Bridges, administration, like rowing, was an activity where improvement followed practice. His attitude was clearly and succinctly expressed when, as chairman at the first of the 1949 series of lectures sponsored by the Institute he said: 'I hope that more of the younger Civil Servants will join the Institute and take part in its activities. By doing so, I am confident that they will not only find added zest in their work but also be doing something which is of permanent value in the public interest.'[93] Like other Treasury officials, Bridges may have disapproved of grants going in the proportions they did to the BIM, and regarded the BIM experience as a good reason for *not* asking the state to subsidise their own professional organisation. In general, one might say that his views about the Institute, though genuinely felt and honestly expressed, were not the sort of views best suited for use in fund raising appeals.

These attitudes of both encouragement and discouragement towards the Institute have been apparent for most of the Institute's life. Some activities have been readily appreciated and encouraged by officials but others have not. Two examples illustrate this. In 1955 Bridges and others were obviously delighted when, in launching a course for Methods Officers, the Institute sought assistance from Treasury O and M officials.[94] However, in 1971, when the Institute was again reviewing ways to stimulate more individual members, it was suggested that central government could help at modest cost or inconvenience by enabling its staff to have subscriptions deducted from their pay on a monthly basis (like union subscriptions and other authorised deductions). It was a great disappointment when even this modest proposal was rejected on the grounds of expense because the Civil Service Department said the numbers involved would not justify the procedure being adopted.[95] Similarly in the 1940s and 1950s when Simpson and other Treasury officials went out of their way to be supportive and encouraging, their support was sometimes stunted by relatively minor incidents. For example, Robson, as chairman of the Institute's Research Committee, made great efforts to secure Treasury co-operation but when, at a committee meeting, he expressed the enthusiasm he had for local government and regretted that its functions were being taken away, then everything else he had to say was largely discounted, even by a friendly and sympathetic Treasury representative like Simpson.[96]

Another strand in this attitude is reflected in Treasury comments in relation to the report of the Clapham Committee on the Provision for Social and Economic Research.[97] In a minute to Padmore in 1948 Proctor said he had 'sounded a good many people inside and outside the Service on their views' and he had come to the conclusion that 'the field of the social sciences is one which the State ought to keep out of, at all events while social science studies are still in their present subjective and highly political stage of development'.[98] This attitude was consistent with attitudes observed by Keynes in 1945. According to Professor James E. Meade, Keynes said the Treasury officials at that time 'were utterly incapable and incompetent to deal with technical economic matters ... Economics was not yet taken as a serious subject.'[99]

In the post-war years there was almost a sense of pride among some Treasury officials that they were distant from these matters. When Nottage was trying to persuade the Treasury to be more supportive in 1960 he was not slow in sending information about the Institute's activities. Bridges counselled him to be more persuasive on the grounds that 'the Treasury do not really understand what the Institute is doing at the moment and I think they may have got to be brought round rather gradually'.[100] Of course, some of the attitudes of Treasury officials may have been simply the result of a professional concern to limit public expenditure. It was evidently a suspicion in Sir Russell Scott's mind in 1922 that the creation of a professional institute was likely to lead to demands for increased remuneration, and that apparently constituted one reason for his non-cooperation.

Publicity and the profession

Many of the attitudes of Treasury officials towards the Institute, as with attitudes to government publicity and all aspects of open government, have their origins in the ways officials have seen their own position in the British system of government. How they have felt they ought to behave has been determined as much by this constitutional dimension as it has by any other element, and this is further illustrated by the discussion in the next chapter on the position of civil servants in the British system of government and their attitudes to the constitution.

However, one lesson that emerges very clearly from these insights into publicity and the profession is the extraordinary ignorance about the workings of British government by otherwise well-informed citizens outside the relatively small circle encompassed by the system of government. This is evident over and over again from numerous files that could be quoted. Bridges was fully aware of this and went some way to resolve it. The recommendations of the Turnbull Committee may not have been fully implemented even in the Treasury, but he supported the Committee's recommendations and made his own contributions to speaking and writing about the system of government in general and the civil service in particular. Let there be no doubt about his attitude: Bridges clearly enjoyed giving these talks and spending time writing. As he put it to Lt Gen Sir Frank Simpson after giving a talk at the Imperial Defence College: 'I really like coming to the IDC and it is one of the things I believe in and care about.'[101]

Nevertheless, for the purposes of the present discussion, Bridges' enjoyment was not as important as the content of his talks. They were all, apparently, elementary, though they were elegantly written in his own very clear style of English. For example, the main feature of Bridges' lecture on the Machinery of Government which he regularly gave at the IDC was its simplicity of approach: it was purely descriptive but the content was at such a basic level that it might today be regarded as inadequate by British Government students reading for GCE examinations. There is no reason to believe that Bridges misjudged the level required: indeed, he was always profusely thanked after his visits and he was always invited back to speak to subsequent courses. Instead, Bridges' approach may be interpreted as evidence of the ignorance of the Brigadiers, Air Commodores and Captains to whom he spoke. As Simpson put it to Bridges in what appears to be a very genuine letter of thanks in 1953: 'Most students here nowadays know very little of the Machinery of Government and it is a great thing for them when they are told about it from someone of the experience and authority of yourself.'[102] The interesting point to emphasise is that this ignorance was so clearly apparent to people working inside the system of government; and it was widespread, even in unexpected places. In 1948, for example, when Bridges was recording details of a talk with Sir Guildhaume Myrddin-Evans he noted: 'we touched on the point that a good many of the present Ministers do not really understand what an impartial Civil Service is or how to use it'.[103] The reason for this ignorance is inseparable from certain of the fundamental features of the British system of government, as Bridges himself was only too well aware. This is well illustrated by a passage in one of his Broadcast talks in 1952:

> You must not expect me to tell you what advice Permanent Secretaries give to Ministers, or, even, to discuss in detail how the relationship works. For the essence of the relationship between Ministers and Civil Servants is that it is a confidential one; a relationship in which each can speak to the other with perfect frankness and confidence, and with the knowledge that what he says is for the ear of the other, and will go no further.[104]

Indeed, there is a case for arguing that Bridges genuinely believed that official secrecy was necessary for good government. In a letter to Lord Gladwyn in 1967 about the House of Lords debate on the Public Records Bill, which was intended to reduce the number of years before which documents could be released in the Public Record Office, Bridges wrote:

> I entirely agree with your point that the 30-year period, if universally applied, will discourage bright young men from writing things on files which they ought to write on files. I made the point in debate and added that the result of having too short a period is that important material will never get on to files at all.[105]

The important point therefore is that attitudes to publicising the workings of government are an integral part of the administrative culture of the British civil service: they are, in a sense, part of the profession of government. Furthermore, there are constitutional reasons for them - as explained in part in this chapter and further in the next chapter. The dangers inherent in making government more open are often most evident at the administrative levels in the civil service, where 'administration' is used in the peculiarly civil service sense (as it was by Scott in his discouraging letter when the Institute of Public Administration was being created), and where officials are most sensitised to the possibilities of political embarrassment. This sense reserves the use of 'administration' for the policy-making levels in the civil service, it applies to the sort of work primarily associated with the 'administrative class' before the Fulton recommendations began a reform of the civil service terminology. In the context of the British civil service it would be myopic to pretend that there is no distinctive administrative profession with well defined ethical standards and a code of conduct. That its main features are not embodied in a single document or even a collection of documents does not make its standards and rules invalid or unworkable. Indeed, such characteristics ensure that the British civil service is uniquely well suited to the standards and requirements of the British constitution.

Notes

1. Richard A. Chapman and J.R. Greenaway, *The Dynamics of Administrative Reform*, (Croom Helm, London, 1980), Ch. 2.
2. PRO/T273/74, Attlee to Bridges, 10 November 1946.
3. PRO/T1/12181/30535/18.
4. Some of these still exist as possessions in the Bridges family. I am grateful to Mrs Shirley Corke, Bridges' daughter, for letting me read two of them.
5. PRO/T166/65.
6. PRO/CAB16/53.
7. PRO/CAB98/13.
8. PRO/CAB98/8.
9. PRO/CAB98/13.
10. PRO/CAB98/14.
11. PRO/CAB98/14.
12. PRO/T273/72.
13. PRO/CAB98/16.
14. PRO/CAB134/104 and PRO/CAB21/779.
15. PRO/T166/65.
16. PRO/T273/72.
17. PRO/T273/72.
18. PRO/T273/72.

19. PRO/T273/72.
20. PRO/T273/72.
21. PRO/T273/233.
22. PRO/T273/72.
23. PRO/T215/118.
24. PRO/T215/118.
25. PRO/T215/120.
26. PRO/T215/119.
27. PRO/T162/965/50877.
28. R.V. Vernon and N. Mansergh (Eds.), *Advisory Bodies: A Study of their uses in relation to Central Government 1919-1939*, (George Allen and Unwin, London, 1940).
29. PRO/T162/526/E38178.
30. P.J. Grigg, *Prejudice and Judgment*, (Jonathan Cape, London, 1948).
31. PRO/CAB134/308, Minutes of meeting on 27 July 1949.
32. PRO/T162/977/E28481, Fraser to Wolfe, 15 December 1932.
33. PRO/T162/977/E28481, Codling to Rae, 13 April 1938.
34. Harry Baynard Price, *The Marshall Plan and its Meaning*, (Cornell University Press, Ithaca, 1955).
35. PRO/T199/256.
36. PRO/T162/965/E50877/3.
37. PRO/T222/261, Bunker to Lumsden, 14 February 1950.
38. Sir Ernest Gowers, *Plain Words: A Guide to the Use of English*, (HMSO, London, 1948). See also Sir Ernest Gowers, *ABC of Plain Words*, (HMSO, London, 1951), and Sir Ernest Gowers, *The Complete Plain Words*, (HMSO, London, 1954).
39. PRO/T199/452. Similar attitudes by the Treasury prevailed in other cases. For example, on the publication of books by J. Wheeler Bennett and R. Dean see PRO/T162/836/E9913/018.
40. PRO/T199/452, Bridges to Padmore, 8 June 1948.
41. PRO/CAB134/308.
42. PRO/T199/190.
43. Bosworth Monck, *How the Civil Service Works*, (Phoenix House, London, 1952).
44. PRO/T162/933/E45806/3.
45. PRO/T162/933/E45806/3, Robson to Bridges, 25 November 1947.
46. PRO/T162/969/E51965, Bridges to Financial Secretary, 19 January 1948.
47. PRO/T162/969/E51965, Bridges' Note, 9 February 1948.
48. Goodmans Furze Papers, Box 9, Robson to Bridges 27 October 1956.
49. PRO/T273/367.
50. PRO/T273/367.
51. Richard A. Chapman and Michael Hunt (Editors), *Open Government: A study of the prospects of open government within the limitations of the British political system*, (Croom Helm, London, 1987).
52. PRO/T161/1296/S5321/10.
53. PRO/T1/12181/30535/18. See also Raymond Nottage and Frieda

Stack, 'The Royal Institute of Public Administration 1922-1939', *Public Administration*, Vol 50, 1972, pp. 281-302.

54. Sir Frederick Maurice, *Haldane (Vol II) 1915-28*, (Faber, London, 1939), pp. 119-20.

55. PRO/T273/18.

56. PRO/T273/18.

57. A.J. Waldegrave, 'Miss G. Kemball: An Appreciation', *Public Administration*, Vol 24, 1956, p. 189.

58. PRO/T273/18, Corner to Fisher, 10 June 1925.

59. PRO/T273/19.

60. PRO/T273/18.

61. PRO/T273/19.

62. PRO/T162/752/E47687/08.

63. PRO/T162/806/E47867/06.

64. Richard A. Chapman and J.R. Greenaway, *The Dynamics of Administrative Reform*, Ch. 3.

65. PRO/T216/1.

66. PRO/T216/1.

67. PRO/T216/1, Bridges to Padmore, 7 June 1948.

68. PRO/T216/1, Bridges to Woods, 26 July 1948.

69. PRO/T249/64.

70. PRO/T222/157.

71. *The Times*, 2 February 1968. See also Goodmans Furze Papers, Box 9, Nottage to Bridges, 28 May 1968.

72. *First, Second and Third Reports from the Committee on Public Accounts, together with the Proceedings of the Committee, Minutes of Evidence, Appendices and Index, Session 1948-49*, H.C. 104-I, 186-I, 233-I, (HMSO, London, 1949), Q. 269 and 274.

73. PRO/T273/18 and PRO/T199/475, Bridges to Chancellor of the Exchequer, 24 November 1948.

74. PRO/T273/18, Bridges to Trend, 10 December 1948.

75. PRO/T273/18, Cripps to Anderson, 11 December 1948.

76. 463 H.C. Deb., 5s., cols. 1854-5 (5 April 1949).

77. PRO/T199/475.

78. PRO/T222/159.

79. PRO/T199/475.

80. PRO/T199/475.

81. PRO/T273/19.

82. PRO/T273/19, Bridges to the Chancellor of the Exchequer, 29 January 1952.

83. RIPA archives: Bridges to Williams, 1958.

84. RIPA archives: Bridges to Nottage, 12 May 1969.

85. Goodmans Furze Papers, Box 9.

86. Raymond Nottage, 'The Royal Institute of Public Administration, 1939-72', *Public Administration*, Vol 50, 1972, pp. 419-43.

87. Goodmans Furze Papers, Box 10, and RIPA archives: Helsby to Bridges, 3 May 1967.

88. *The Times*, 2 February 1968.

89. Goodmans Furze Papers, Box 10.

90. RIPA archives: Bridges to Collier, 19 November 1968.

91. PRO/T273/18, Bridges to Chancellor of the Exchequer, 24 November 1948.

92. Interviews with ex-colleagues of Bridges.

93. Goodmans Furze Papers, Box 9.

94. PRO/T222/694, Bridges to Milner Barry, 28 January 1955.

95. Royal Institute of Public Administration, 'Review of Activities Committee Report 1970' (Chairman A.L. Adu), para 26. This report was printed for the use of the Institute and its members, but not published.

96. PRO/T222/694.

97. *Committee on Social and Economic Research, Report* (Chairman: Sir John Clapham), [Cmd. 6868], (HMSO, London, 1946).

98. PRO/T199/475, Proctor to Padmore, 25 October 1948.

99. The Diary of Professor James Meade, British Library of Political and Economic Science. Entry for 7 January 1945.

100. RIPA archives: Bridges to Nottage, 31 October 1960.

101. PRO/T273/187, Bridges to Simpson, 1 February 1952.

102. PRO/T273/187, Simpson to Bridges, 27 January 1953.

103. PRO/T249/30.

104. PRO/T273/222, 'A Day in the Life of the Permanent Secretary to the Treasury', BBC (GOS) Broadcast talk, 1952.

105. Goodmans Furze Papers, Box 5. See also 282 H.L. Deb., 5s., cols. 1666-9 (11 May 1967).

7

The Civil Servant and the Constitution

Constitutionally, British civil servants are accountable to ministers and ministers are accountable in Parliament for the actions and conduct of their officials. However, there may in practice be many differences between what actually happens and the formal requirements of the constitution. Indeed, the gap between actuality and the formal presentation of it in terms of constitutional proprieties varies according to two factors: first, the circumstances at particular times in relation to particular cases; and secondly, the degree of confidentiality that is maintained concerning the role of civil servants. As in many other spheres of life in Britain, much depends on trust - both in terms of all participants working according to the rules and conventions and also in terms of mutual confidence in their integrity, between ministers and officials who work together.

What in fact happens is that behind the 'dignified' facade of ministers and Parliament, officials, who are permanent, often assume the roles of non-partisan politicians. Sometimes, unknown to ministers in advance, they engage in negotiations or make important decisions which ministers subsequently have to defend; sometimes ministers themselves are involved in the decision-making processes, occasionally by formally issuing instructions to officials which the officials themselves have advised ministers to issue; often officials have to assess a sensitive situation and make a judgment and take other necessary action to resolve a disagreement. In these and other circumstances it is hardly surprising that officials are referred to as 'statesmen in disguise',[1] 'politicial administrators',[2] 'cloistered politicians',[3] or a 'permanent government'.[4]

It is not difficult to understand how they have become permanent politicians. Whereas the average time spent by a minister in a particular post is about eighteen months or two years, officials generally serve in one department over long periods of time. Such officials, recruited for relevant abilities, then acquire considerable experience through their own administrative practice. Furthermore, they have access to all departmental records, including details of precedents, whereas ministers are denied access to the papers of previous governments; they have networks of contacts including formal and informal relationships not only in Whitehall and Westminster but beyond; and they have the experience of working together as a team so that over periods of time they develop what Bridges referred to as a 'departmental view'.[5]

Whilst these generalisations may be so widely accepted that they appear as truisms about the civil service, Bridges may be seen as the prime example of all that they say or imply. One reason for this was that he served in the Treasury for most of his career and had exceptional opportunities to acquire constitutional and practical experience. It should also be remembered that no other civil servant had the distinction of serving as secretary to three royal commissions. A second reason was that he was secretary to the Official Side of the National Whitley Council (and, later, Chairman of the National Whitley Council) and thus, for nearly forty years, he was consequently associated with many of the major constitutional issues which were raised in connection with Whitleyism. A third reason was his academic interest in constitutional matters. The research project for his fellowship at All Souls College was on such a topic and he received great satisfaction from working on historical and constitutional issues. A further reason was the trust and esteem in which he was held by so many people: especially by leading politicians and senior officials but also by major figures in many other spheres of activity. He had a personality which inspired confidence and because he lived simply it was quite evident that he sought no material advantages for himself. In these circumstances it is not surprising that Bridges became an eminent authority on Britain's peculiar constitution. Although the extent and significance of his influence in government will never be fully known, there were numerous occasions when he played a crucial part, often by establishing the rules for procedure or through contributing to joint decisions. Some of these are illustrated by the following examples.

Constitutional and political advice

From the days when Bridges was a relatively junior official in the Treasury he was involved in advising ministers on matters of constitutional importance. His advice was usually, but not always, accepted. Churchill, in particular (but also Attlee and other leading politicians) greatly valued Bridges' advice on these matters.

An early occasion when Bridges' advice was not accepted was in connection with the Trade Disputes and Trade Unions Act 1927, when Churchill was Chancellor of the Exchequer. Some of the union leaders had set up the Civil Service Civil Rights Defence Committee to represent the interests of civil servants because the Staff Side of the National Whitley Council was precluded from making representations on the Government's proposed legislation. In February 1927 they wrote to the Chancellor asking him to receive a deputation from the Committee. Bridges, who was then a principal, took a strong line when drafting the initial advice for the Chancellor. He argued that while in theory the Civil Service Civil Rights Defence Committee was a committee of civil service unions, it was in fact in the closest possible contact with the Trades Union Congress and the Labour Party and was therefore just such an example of the intimate connection between civil service unions and political parties as it was desired to avoid. His view was that 'we should, if possible, be extremely chary of recognising the Committee', and he added: 'I would suggest that the reply to the letter of the 7th might be that the Chancellor is not in a position to see a deputation from the Civil Rights Defence Committee without being first informed as to the Constitution, objects of the committee (and its relations to other bodies?)...'[6] Despite Bridges' analysis Sir Russell Scott offered different advice to the Chancellor, ending his minute: 'I think it would be expedient to receive the deputation'. Churchill later noted: 'I will'.

In a later minute on the same subject Bridges attempted to clarify the situation by commenting on the meaning of 'political' as it appeared in Section 5 of the 1927 Act. It will be recalled from Chapter 3 that this Act prevented established civil servants from belonging to associations which were associated with political parties. Bridges' minute is revealing for the insight it provides into his attitude to political activity. Bridges' conception of politics was somewhat inflexible and by no means sophisticated. In this context, and in others in which he used the term, it seems that by politics he meant simply party political activities. He regarded political activity as a lower arena of operations than the one in which he and his colleagues worked, and from that perspective he did his best to give a clear interpretation of the implications of the Act. He wrote:

> ... I quite agree that if an organisation is an off-shoot, or a would-be-hanger-on, of a political party that organisation must be regarded as a political organisation...
> ... my feeling is that a political organisation is an organisation which exists mainly or wholly to promote political ends...
> As to what a 'political end' is, a definition is obviously out of the question. For one thing the question of what is a political end varies from year to year... But clearly one has in mind not abstract political ends, but something political in the practical everyday sense.
> Nor, I think, is it possible to attempt to settle whether an organisation is a political organisation by whether it seeks to exercise influence in the political sphere. I think one must recognise that the most non-partisan organisations may from time to time have cause to descend into the political arena, in order to defend some point in their general scheme of objects, which they regard as threatened by proposed legislation or what not... I do not, therefore, think that there is any means of obtaining a definition of 'political organisation' by consideration of whether it indulges at any time in political activities. I come back to the idea that in determining whether an organisation is or is not political one has simply got to look at its ends or objects and see whether they are mainly or wholly political...[7]

In this, as in other matters, Bridges had a clear idea of what was right and what was wrong, and this clarity was particularly useful in dealing with the unions. Nearly twenty years later, when he became Head of the Civil Service, this earlier experience of the 1927 Act was very valuable. Thus, in November 1945 he noted that the Act did not forbid strikes by civil servants, except in so far as they might be sympathetic strikes designed to coerce the Government. He then added:

> ...quite apart from any statutory provision, the Government as employer has the power to take disciplinary action against any Civil Servant who commits the disciplinary offence of striking. In certain circumstances, that is if the offence were

considered sufficiently serious, there can be no doubt that the disciplinary penalty would be dismissal without question of reinstatement. For example, a strike of Prison Officers, which would make the maintenance of law and order impossible, might necessitate action of this sort. This sanction, rather than a statutory provision declaring particular types of strike illegal, seems to be the most appropriate way of dealing with the matter.[8]

Bridges' service as principal and assistant secretary in the Treasury was followed by his experience in the Cabinet Office during the war. Here, too, he acquired useful experience of many aspects of government and managing the civil service. Indeed, in this post he regarded himself as responsible for advising the Prime Minister on War Cabinet Committee organisation: that is, on details concerning the various Cabinet committees and their sub-committees.[9] Three examples, all in connection with Churchill as Prime Minister, illustrate this well. The first example dates from 1942 in relation to the duties of the Minister of Production. Bridges was asked to prepare a draft definition of the duties for the post and in doing this he had to propose which government functions should be transferred from other ministries. The arrangements he proposed were to be promulgated in a White Paper on the Office of the Minister of Production.[10] Bridges had a difficult time with this problem because he had to reconcile Churchill's instructions with the view of Beaverbrook, who was then Minister of War Production, and other ministers. Beaverbrook wanted an increase in his powers and a redistribution of functions between departments, but other ministers, especially Oliver Lyttleton, then Minister of State, were determined to maintain the functions they already had. Beaverbrook felt his position did not enable him to make the contrtibution he wished and ill-health gave him the excuse to ask to be relieved of his duties. Churchill, however, found that he then had to answer Parliamentary Questions on a matter which involved tension between his ministers. About midnight on 11/12 March 1942 Bridges was summoned to 10 Downing Street, where the Prime Minister complained that the briefing that had been prepared for him was not in a form which he could use as an oral statement in the House of Commons (on 12 March).[11] Instead it was in a form more suitable for a White Paper, but he did not want another White Paper which would inevitably be contrasted with the arrangements in the White Paper on the subject which were withdrawn before publication the previous month. Eden was then consulted by telephone, and agreed with the Prime Minister. The amount of work created by such controversies within government was enormous, and much of it was left to be dealt with by Bridges personally - at hours that may have been normal working hours for Churchill but were not necessarily for others.[12]

The second example occurred in 1944. In February of that year Churchill had the intention of separating the Offices of Prime Minister and First Lord of the Treasury and he asked Bridges to prepare a paper for him on the subject, with the 'specific instructions' that it was to be done without reference to any other person. Bridges did some research and wrote his paper on 16 February. In it he drew attention to the links between the two offices, showing that until 1937 the office of Prime Minister had no statutory significance, but pointing out that the last time the offices had been separated was in 1895-1902 when Lord Salisbury was Prime Minister and A.J. Balfour was First Lord. Bridges outlined the consequences if the offices were to be separated. These would include legislation to pay a salary to the Prime Minister who was not the First Lord, authority to pay a salary to a First Lord who was not Prime Minister, and reconsideration of the duties of the two offices. Bridges, however, was very unhappy about this exercise. Later, he gave copies of his paper to Sir John Stainton, then Second Parliamentary Counsel to the Treasury, and Sir Richard Hopkins, then Head of the Civil Service. Hopkins deplored the separation envisaged and asked Bridges to point out to the Prime Minister how much this separation would be deplored by the Treasury and also how disadvantageous it would be when a strong Treasury was needed again after the war. Bridges felt so uncomfortable at having expressed an opinion on a legal question without consulting the lawyers, that he found an opportunity to get a confirmatory opinion from Sir Granville Ram, the Parliamentary Counsel, without in any way indicating that such a separation of office might be in immediate contemplation.

The matter came to a head when, on 4 April 1944, the Prime Minister spent about 40 minutes before dinner discussing ministerial arrangements with the Foreign Secretary, the Chief Whip and Bridges. It was at Bridges' suggestion that the Prime Minister agreed to call for reinforcements in the form of the Attorney General and the battle resumed at 10.30 p.m. when the Attorney was also present. Bridges later recorded that after a long encounter the Prime Minister was disposed to accept the view that the changes he had in mind could be brought about without separating the offices of the Prime Minister and the First Lord of the Treasury, and he asked the Attorney General to send him a note setting out the grounds, both parliamentary and constitutional, on which objections would be raised by separating the two Offices by issuing a Defence Regulation. After the meeting Bridges sent a note to T.L. (later Sir Leslie) Rowan, then the Prime Minister's Private Secretary, to let him know that 'the matter discussed with the Prime Minister on Tuesday is off for the time being at any rate'.[13]

The third example was after Churchill resigned on 23 May 1945 and was asked to form a new administration. Bridges advised the Prime Minister on the size of his new Cabinet. There had been eight ministers in the War Cabinet. Bridges thought this number might have to be increased but he outlined arguments in favour of increasing the number to (say) about 12 rather than to 18 or 20. He wrote:

1. An increase to 18 or 20 might, to United States eyes, look like a return to the peace-time form of government and seem to betoken a relaxation of the war effort against Japan.

2. Would public opinion in this country be favourable to the restoration of a big Cabinet at this juncture?

3. It is always easier to enlarge than to reduce the Cabinet. Why not therefore retain as much freedom as possible to deal with the position after the General Election?

4. Before the war there were 26 Departments of State, and a Cabinet of 23 meant that only a very few Ministers were excluded from the Cabinet viz:-

   Postmaster General
   Paymaster General
   Minister of Pensions

Today there are 41 Ministers, including the four Ministers Resident overseas. No doubt this number can be reduced, by abolition and doubling up, to somewhere about 34. But it is very much harder to draw a satisfactory line which will include 20 and exclude 14 Ministers than it is to include (say) 12 and exclude about 20.

5. This is particularly the case because today there are so many Ministries which deal with particular subjects - Food, Agriculture, Fuel, Transport, Civil Aviation etc. The inclusion in the Cabinet of Ministers representing some, but not others, of these interests would raise difficulties.

Attached as a cockshy is a suggestion as to who might be in a Cabinet of, say 12...[14]

These examples from Bridges' inter-war service in the Treasury and his time as Secretary to the Cabinet built up his stature as a constitutional authority in two ways. First, the incidents themselves provided valuable experience because they involved questions that were central to the working of the system of government. Although only three examples have been quoted here, it should be remembered that more examples could easily be quoted and, in addition, Bridges was responsible for preparing numerous authoritative documents of constitutional significance: some of these were necessary because they were about unwritten elements of the constitution. Thus, he began his 1944 authoritative statement of the position and functions of the Cabinet Secretariat by saying that 'The functions of the Cabinet Secretariat have never been defined in any legal instrument, or other formal document...'[15] Secondly, Bridges' unique experience as Secretary to the War Cabinet meant that he came to know, closely, senior politicians of both the major political parties. His well-prepared, authoritative guidance became widely accepted.

This experience was called upon subsequently and its effects could well have been (at least) as significant when he was Head of the Civil Service as it was when he was Secretary to the Cabinet. Again, space permits only four illustrations from the latter, post-war period. The first example concerns the Masterman Committee on the Political Activities of Civil Servants. Herbert Morrison, then Lord President of the Council, had been asked to give oral evidence some time in the autumn of 1948 and sought Bridges' advice on whether it would be proper and desirable for him to do so. He was inclined to accede to the request, provided it was understood that he would be giving his personal views only, and that the evidence would not be published, but as there had been some recent controversy over the Minister of Health giving evidence before the Royal Commission on the Press, he particularly wanted to know Bridges' views. Bridges, it will be remembered (see Chapter 3) was taking a close interest in this inquiry, in which he was determined to ensure the presentation of clear evidence from senior officials. He therefore put his views to Morrison with tact as a well as firmness:

I ... told him that, although his experience would, I was sure,

272

be very valuable to the Committee, I saw great difficulty in his giving evidence before the Committee. My reason for taking this view is explained in the note which I have written to the Prime Minister about Ministers giving evidence before Royal Commissions etc. After all, by appointing this Committee Ministers have in fact declared that they want advice from an impartial body on the issues of policy concerned. And it is not really consistent with this action for an individual Minister to give evidence. Nor do I see how it will be possible for the Lord President to give evidence on the understanding that at least the broad purport of his evidence would not be disclosed. This I think would put the Committee in an impossible position.

There is, of course, the further point that all Ministers may not - and indeed probably do not - think alike on this subject, and that if the Lord President gives evidence other Ministers may wish to do so. I suppose the question might also arise whether leading members of the Opposition should not be invited to give evidence.

The Lord President threw out the suggestion that the best plan might be that he should have a private talk with Mr Masterman on some occasion. At first sight this seems a much more feasible suggestion. But on reflection I feel bound to say that I do not think it is wise. The fact that such a meeting had taken place could not, if it was to serve any useful purpose, be concealed from the Committee as a whole, and would, therefore, certainly become known. And, if known, would it not be assumed that the Lord President has sought to influence the Committee by devious means?

I can see no real alternative to the view that the Government, having selected an impartial Committee to advise them on this very difficult issue, Ministers should leave the Committee to frame the best recommendations they can.[16]

There is no reason to believe that this advice to Morrison was other than perfectly correct and proper, but it provides a distinct contrast to Bridges' advice to his civil service colleagues. It will be remembered that his advice to Morrison was given about four months after Bridges had written to his twelve permanent secretary colleagues telling them what evidence he intended to give, warning them that they might be called to give evidence, and saying that he wanted to exchange views with those who were likely to give evidence.[17]

The second example indicates the routine, day-to-day fashion in which some of Bridges' guidance was given on matters of constitutional propriety. The following extract, from the Minutes of the Second Meeting of the Chorley Committee on Civil Service Remuneration speaks for itself:

> Mr Gibson referred to annual leave allowances: he thought forty-eight days too much, and damaging to the Service in the eyes of the public. The Chairman pointed out that it was one of the few points on which the Civil Service provision was very much more generous than those prevailing in business. Sir Edward agreed, and said it would be quite proper for the Committee to make a recommendation on this point if they thought fit.[18]

At various later meetings Bridges also influenced aspects of the recommendations of the Chorley Committee. For example, when the Committee was considering its draft report, Bridges gave further evidence and suggested that a certain paragraph might be reworded so as to avoid the suggestion that posts should be created purely in order to provide for promotion: the suggestion should rather be that the cadres in each class should be looked at as a whole to ensure that they provided a sufficiently attractive career. He also told the Committee that he was strongly opposed to their proposal that permanent secretaries should be paid at varying rates on the range £4,000 to £5,000. He outlined his reasons, and added, furthermore, that he had, in confidence, consulted a few of his colleagues among permanent secretaries and they unanimously endorsed his view. Finally, he gave his views on the controversial issue of pay for top specialists compared with permanent secretaries:

> It should be clearly understood that the function of the Permanent Secretary was that of general manager. Provided that that was recognised, Sir Edward thought it did not matter if occasionally a technical officer recruited ad hoc for a particular job was paid more than the Permanent Secretary, but it should be exceptional. The Permanent Secretary was the conductor of the orchestra; the brilliant technical man, the solo performer.[19]

The third example concerns Bridges' influence in relation to writings and interpretations of the working of the British system of government. From time to time questions originating from the colonies and foreign countries were referred to Bridges so that he could indicate authoritatively how government worked in Britain and this experience could be used as a guide for practice elsewhere. One occasion of this sort arose in 1950 when the Governor of Kenya, Sir Philip Mitchell, asked the Colonial Office for guidance on the relationship between ministers and permanent secretaries. The Colonial Office produced a draft which was referred to Bridges by Sir Thomas Lloyd, and as the draft was not very good Bridges asked some Treasury colleagues (Padmore, P.S. Milner-Barry and R.C. Griffiths) to redraft it. The new version was then discussed and agreed by all the Treasury officials, including Bridges.[20] Since there is no formal legal basis to such aspects of British government the statements produced with such care by Bridges and under his direction had the potential for wide and important effects in the Commonwealth as well as in the United Kingdom.

Similar procedures related to other aspects of government, including the monarchy. For example, in 1946 Owen Morshead was drafting the entry on King George V for publication in the *Dictionary of National Biography*.[21] Morshead referred the draft to Sir Alan Lascelles, then Private Secretary to King George VI, for comment. Lascelles had doubts about a reference to the month of February 1914 in the context of the Irish Home Rule crisis 1913/14. The passage as drafted read: 'On the 5th the King saw Asquith at Windsor and told him bluntly that when the bill was presented for assent he should feel it his duty to do what in his own judgment was best for his people generally; and this broad hint took the Prime Minister considerably aback'. Bridges consulted Ram and also checked on the constitutional position in the works of both Anson and Maitland. After reflection, Bridges told Lascelles that he did not think the passage ought to be suppressed because it was of historical significance (i.e. that the King had seriously contemplated using the formula 'Le Roi s'avisera') and also the attitude of the King added to the prestige of the monarchy. However, Bridges thought the incident ought not to be revealed in a way which highlighted it as a dramatic episode unless the whole story of the King's efforts was set out in due sequence and detail.[22]

The fourth example is probably the most significant of all illustrations of Bridges' influence in a matter of lasting constitutional significance. During the crucially important House of Commons debate on the Crichel Down case the Home Secretary contributed what has since been regarded as the definitive statement on ministerial responsibility. The statement had such an impact that it has since been widely used as the basis for discussions on the subject in academic monographs and textbooks.[23] Although Sir David Maxwell Fyfe has always been given the credit for the statement (and, indeed, constitutionally this credit is due since he personally made it in the House of Commons), in fact it drew heavily - in parts word for word - from a memorandum on 'Ministerial Responsibility' prepared by Bridges at the request of the Prime Minister.[24] In fact, therefore, the definitive encapsulation of the constitutional convention that later became so authoritative was prepared by Bridges and approved and used but not created by the Home Secretary himself.

Bridges trod a cautious path between on the one hand giving constitutional advice and on the other hand giving political advice. Sometimes he managed to resolve difficulties by the simple expedient of turning a potentially sensitive request for advice into an opportunity to offer practical comments on specific recommendations. For example, in 1948 the Cabinet received a paper from its Committee on the reform of the House of Lords. The Chancellor of the Exchequer asked Bridges for his comments on it and on 3 January 1948 Bridges, turning what could have been a partisan matter into a practical one, began by safeguarding his position. He replied: 'This paper is political, and I would not have commented on it unless invited to do so.'[25]

After Bridges' retirement he continued his interest in constitutional matters. Indeed, in 1967, when the Hansard Society for Parliamentary Government sent a questionnaire to peers to solicit their opinions, Bridges produced his response in the form of a statement instead of a series of answers to the questions. This statement included his analysis of the duties of the House of Lords and his proposal that the sittings of the House might be divided into groups: (a) the House in full session and (b) a large Standing Committee of the House. The Permanent Standing Committee (as he called it) would consist of all Life peers; all persons raised to the peerage as Hereditary peers; and a number of Hereditary peers not of the first generation, who would be elected by the whole body of Hereditary peers. This proposal for reform would have two main advantages: it would not involve any direct conflict with the Writ of Summons, since all peers could come to meetings of the House in Full Session; but it would make the election of a certain number of Hereditary Peers to the Permanent Standing Committee a reality. He recognised that the acceptability of the scheme would depend on the balance of power resting in the cross-benchers and their numbers might need to be increased. However, he thought there was no point in proposing more details unless there was a likelihood that such a reform might be acceptable.[26]

On all matters where Bridges gave advice to Prime Ministers on questions about the machinery of government or, indeed, to anybody where constitutional propriety was involved, Bridges maintained his position of strict neutrality and impartiality. He was never partisan; indeed, it may be wondered whether he was capable of being partisan. Furthermore, he was always the disciple of Warren Fisher, especially in matters of controversy involving the various elements in government. One of these matters was the relationship between ministers and civil servants. This was put clearly by Fisher to the Prime Minister in 1938, in words that on later occasions seem to have become models for Bridges' own responses. Fisher wrote: 'The relationship between Ministers and Crown Servants is conditioned by the recognition that the position of the latter is in the wings and that the footlights are the monopoly of the politician who is constitutionally the sole responsible authority. From the point of view of public responsibility the Crown Servants are anonymous and power is vested solely in governments'.[27] Remarkably similar wording and sentiments appeared in a leading article in *The Times* within a few days of Fisher's minute. *The Times* said:

> The essential point is that Civil Servants should be allowed to remain anonymous in the discharge of whatever duties may be assigned to them. They cannot answer public criticism themselves. They are the servants of their political chiefs, to whatever party the latter may belong. They have a well-balanced reputation in this country for complete impartiality, which they for their part are bound to maintain by scrupulous avoidance even of the suspicion of intrigue or partisanship. Any failure on their part to maintain it would rightly meet with discredit and might well meet with dismissal. But it would assuredly be tarnished if it were to become the common practice of those outside the Service to identify them personally with Government decisions of which they are the instruments and not the authors.[28]

Nevertheless, Bridges, as Head of the Civil Service, was never slow when it came to ensuring that the civil service was defended. Some examples of this have already been given in earlier chapters. He was very strict with officials whose conduct was unworthy and he made sure that whenever doubt was cast on the integrity of the service, someone was well briefed to present an appropriate defence. This was particularly evident in his own well-engineered defence of the civil service through the Civil Service Manpower Committee, at the time when the committee was still a Cabinet committee. The ministerial committee was in fact wound up in 1948, though Bridges continued to convene the official committee which had been created to work alongside it.

An interesting feature of the Cabinet Committee on Civil Service Manpower was the way Bridges and his colleagues were effectively in control of it. The committee had J. Chuter Ede as Chairman. The rest of the committee consisted of three politicians together with Bridges and four other officials. The membership changed from meeting to meeting as far as the three politicians and four officials were concerned, but the committee met ten times in 1947 and on eight of those occasions the officials outnumbered the politicians. The main finding in the draft report approved on 2 April 1947 was that the numbers of non-industrial civil servants were barely adequate to discharge efficiently the tasks placed upon them by the policy of the Government. The committee said that the corollary of this was that the position in regard to civil service numbers should be defended in the face of outside criticism. The last paragraph of its report was the most important. It said:

> In conclusion, we would emphasise that in defending the position in Parliament as an essential part of the Government's declared programme, every opportunity should be taken to underline the vital part which the Civil Service plays in the national economy. No organisation has any right to expect to be defended unless its own house is seen to be in order. No doubt there are improvements still to be made in the organisation and work of the Civil Service, but we are convinced that those in authority are determined to pursue these vigorously and open-mindedly. This being so we regard it as inconsistent with the political beliefs of His Majesty's Government, to treat those who operate the machine of Government, provided that their numbers are kept at the minimum necessary for the efficient discharge of the

Government's work, as parasites on the community. Any tendency in this direction might have a highly adverse effect on morale, and this in itself decreases efficiency and increases numbers. It seems to us essential that the Service should be publicly defended by Ministers, in order that it may be encouraged by its own employees to take a proper pride in their work. The new entrants on whom the building up of a more efficient Service largely depends will disappoint us if the heart is taken out of them by an unanswered campaign of unjust criticism.[29]

This influence of officials on the Cabinet committee had the desired effect and Attlee made a vigorous defence of the civil service in the House of Commons soon after. At one point he said: 'I regret the fashion, now current in some quarters of speaking slightingly of the Civil Service as though its members were less useful members of the community than other people.'[30]

Bridges did not only defend the constitutional position of the civil service by such circuitous means. As Head of the Civil Service he was determined to safeguard it in every possible way. One was to ensure that all public presentations by the civil service were of the highest possible standard. Another was to ensure that its own rules and conventions were as good as they might be, and to develop new guidelines whenever they might help achieve this end.

A good example of Bridges' ensuring a high standard of public presentations in this context occurred in relation to the Royal Commission on Scottish Affairs. The terms of reference of the Royal Commission were 'to review with reference to the financial, economic, administrative and other considerations involved, the arrangements for exercising the functions of Her Majesty's Government in relation to Scotland, and to report'. Bridges presented a memorandum which Treasury officials prepared for him and in acknowledging it Lord Balfour wrote on 23 February 1953 that it would be an advantage if Bridges were to give oral evidence in public.

As soon as Bridges was fully aware of how the commission was working he wrote personal letters to the permanent secretaries of thirteen government departments. He let them know that they were likely to receive an invitation to give oral evidence and that the invitation would be to do so in Edinburgh. Bridges added: 'I hope you won't mind me saying that I think that wherever possible it is very important that Permanent Secretaries should give this evidence themselves (even though it may involve a visit to Edinburgh). In this matter I am practising what I preach, and have agreed to give evidence on behalf of the Treasury in Edinburgh'. He went on to ask them what arrangements they were making and to stress that a bad impression would be given if representatives of most departments were not permanent secretaries.[31] As with other occasions when Bridges gave evidence, an enormous effort was applied to preparing it for him. Many officials were involved and much factual evidence was accumulated. Great care was also taken to get advance warning of the line the oral questions might take.[32] Bridges used a similar approach when preparing evidence for the Chorley Committee on Higher Civil Service Remuneration. On that occasion a first draft was discussed with his closest advisers; then Bridges sent it to twelve heads of departments and asked them to meet in his room to discuss his proposed evidence.[33] The important point to stress is that on this and on similar occasions considerable energy and resources were applied to preparing answers to questions and presenting the facts in the best possible light. In spite of the economies in the public services, Bridges only had to ask for some research to be done on a particular topic and a full report was presented to him, often in a matter of days or a few weeks, following sometimes extensive research and wide consultations.[34] In the case of the Chorley Committee, Bridges was particularly active in calling meetings with staff associations, then reporting back to the Chancellor of the Exchequer and advising him. On occasions like these Bridges, whilst always non-partisan, seems nevertheless to have been acting in a very political manner with politicians, with his colleagues and with the staff associations.[35]

There were other occasions, too, when he gave advice that could have been construed as political. This happened, for example, when Bridges was advising ministers in his capacity as Permanent Secretary to the Treasury. One occasion when this occurred was when he commented on defence expenditure in 1950. Four sentences show the type of advice Bridges felt he had to give on such occasions:

Ministers will probably find themselves in a dilemma. The political situation will, I imagine, demand a pretty definite statement, setting out in hard terms without any surrounding vagueness exactly what H.M. Government mean to do to increase our defence preparedness. And comparison is inevitable with what President Truman has announced...

I believe that there is no prospect that we should be able to get away with less defence expenditure than £800 millions next year, and I would have thought that it was probably worth while to make an announcement to this effect now in order to avoid the risk of trouble here and the accusation that we are dragging our feet.[36]

Nevertheless, Bridges was on some occasions very sophisticated about policy and politics. This was so, for example, in his Pollak Lecture on 'The Treasury as the most political of departments'. In that lecture he drew attention to the fact that 'policy' and 'political' both spring from the same root, and cover much common ground. He then differentiated between them in the civil service context. He explained that 'In the British Civil Service, when we speak of "political influence" we mean rather the extent to which the Cabinet, or Ministers in their submission to the Cabinet, are influenced by their views of what the House of Commons or the general public will tolerate on any particular issue.' However, on the same occasion he gave a superb illustration and justification for the title of his lecture. He said:

Let us imagine some sudden emergency which involves changing one of the policies pursued by one of the spending departments. Let us picture the Permanent Secretary having a talk with his Chief financial adviser and some of his staff about the sort of lines on which they think a solution might be found. After a while the Permanent Secretary may ask 'Have you been to the Treasury yet?'. 'No' might be the answer, 'we didn't think we had anything sufficiently definite to take to them'. 'Well,' the Permanent Secretary replies 'I think you had better talk to them pretty soon'. And he may add as his reason, either 'You never know they *may* have some point which might be helpful', or (if he is a diplomat by nature) 'the Treasury will be easier to bring along with us if they are brought into the discussion early'. In his own mind he may think that he would be behaving in a rather caddish way if he allowed discussions in his Department to go any further without bringing in the Treasury.

It is this degree of exceptional early involvement of the Treasury with formulation of policies which is my excuse for the title of this talk, for since nearly all policies involve some expenditure, the Treasury gets an opportunity to know about the principles and has some hand in the shaping of nearly all departmental policies.[37]

Bridges was also very good at developing internal rules and conventions for good management practice in a political context. For example, he produced a most useful document of notes for the guidance of secretaries of royal commissions (based on his unique experience of serving as secretary to three of them). The document was of a basic factual type covering the advantages and disadvantages of using questionnaires and convening commission conferences; guidance on matters of office routine; hints on reporting verbatim evidence; the importance of the members of the commission meeting at informal lunches; and managing the demands on the chairman.[38]

Another important area in which Bridges had to develop rules for operation concerned his responsibilities as Accounting Officer to the Treasury when matters of party political interest were referred to him for decision. A good example was when, in June 1945, Churchill went on a political tour using the special train which accommodated his office staff, so that he could continue his duties as Prime Minister while on tour. Questions arose about what should be paid for from public funds and what paid for by the Prime Minister personally. When it reached Bridges, he made a note of his decision, for the record:

> I said that I thought the use of the train could be justified on the grounds that it was the Prime Minister's movable office which had to accompany him during the war. But I thought that unless payment was made for the travelling done in the train by the Prime Minister and Mrs Churchill and any persons who accompanied him in his political capacity, the Prime Minister would be open to attack on the grounds that facilities provided at public expense were used for political purposes. While I thought the dividing line which I suggested was a sound one I recognised that the point was very largely one of political judgment...[39]

The action Bridges took to ensure that the civil service learned appropriate lessons from the Crichel Down case (and in particular the report by Sir Andrew Clark) was another example, typical of the way he operated, in the management context. First, he asked Sir John Woods to chair an internal committee to consider whether certain officials named in the inquiry should be transferred to other work. Later, the report of the Woods committee was published.[40] Then, on 21 July 1954, he discussed with a small group of close advisers (Sir Norman Brook, Sir Bernard Gilbert and Sir Thomas Padmore) what steps might be taken on various other facets of the case. These details were noted in minutes taken by D.J. (now Sir Derek) Mitchell. Bridges then listed some of these suggestions in a letter to a selection of permanent secretaries. Later, he invited a group of twelve permanent secretaries and other senior officials to meet for a discussion of the whole matter in his room at 10.30 on 30 July 1954.[41]

This procedure resulted in a trawl of ideas from which a line of action could be selected. For example, some interesting views were expressed on the possibility of promulgating a code of conduct. Typical of comments on this were the reactions of Sir John Rowlatt, then Parliamentary Counsel:

> On civil service discipline, I myself would be for avoiding anything like a formal published code of procedure if you possibly can. I am sure the letter kills, and that what you want is 'natural justice'. After all, civil servants ought to be intelligent enough to administer natural justice and to recognise and appreciate it where they see it.
>
> I would agree in general with what you say about the tone of semi-official letters. The 'old boy' atmosphere is all wrong. But I doubt the practicability of abolishing Christian names, if only because, as far as I can make out, people at the Universities today never dream of using surnames to one another, and it may be that in a few years' time addressing a man in a letter by his surname would be about as unnatural as ending up as his obedient servant.[42]

Sir Percivale Liesching, of the Commonwealth Relations Office, in his reply to Bridges, said: '... the opportunities for guidance, precept and example at a small post are very great. We do not have anything in the nature of a written code of conduct, but I am pretty confident that by other less obvious means we succeed in instilling the right traditions.' [43]

The idea of stimulating if not a code of practice, then certainly a booklet on the outlook and traditions of the civil service had been considered from time to time since about mid-1948 when the suggestion was put to Bridges and he raised it at a meeting of the

GOC. The original idea was that a book of this nature, adopting a historical approach, would help not only new civil servants but also the public to understand what to expect of the civil service and the qualities of political impartiality it possessed. Bridges was concerned to make it clear to ministers - and anyone else who might be interested - what could be expected of higher civil servants. He felt that all too many ministers seemed to expect high officials to be replicas, or pale replicas, of ministers; and so far as civil servants exhibited different characteristics from ministers they seemed to think civil servants were not what they ought to be. Bridges thought Gowers might be a good person to write a book along these lines but Gowers was at the time preoccupied with the *ABC of Plain Words* and his other duties including preparing the report of the Committee on the Preservation of Historic Houses and chairing a New Town Corporation and the governing body of the National Hospital for Nervous Diseases.[44] In the end this particular idea was never developed because Gowers could not take it on and it seems that Bridges and his circle of close advisers could think of no other suitable authors. Indeed, as has already been mentioned, they had great difficulty suggesting names for any jobs of this sort. Another example was the difficulty they had in proposing people for the category of specialists in the 'theory of public administration' to serve on the 1953 (Priestley) Royal Commission on the Civil Service, and in fact the only name for that category on the list was Noel Hall, then Principal of the Administrative Staff College.[45]

There were a number of reasons why civil servants found some of these tasks so difficult. The circles within which they moved tended, then as now, to be diminishing circles. The wide contacts many officials may have had at university or soon after contracted as pressures of work increased and also with increased seniority. They also contracted because so much time was spent in commuter travel between home and work. Nevertheless, a pattern emerges from these experiences of Bridges and his colleagues which provides insights into the role of civil servants and the civil service in the constitution. Bridges on numerous occasions found himself being asked by ministers for advice that was not only constitutional but also political - simply because in the British system of government it is often impossible to make a clear division between the two. Indeed, there is a sense in which the civil service is the guardian of the constitution because it alone has access to all the precedents and has a degree of permanence and operational knowledge which is not available elsewhere. One facet of this important role of the civil service is revealed in what Bridges has referred to as the departmental view.

The departmental point of view

One of the most important, if not undoubtedly the most important of Bridges' writings was his 1950 Rede Lecture, 'Portrait of a Profession: The Civil Service Tradition'.[46] In it he set out to describe 'the inhabitants of Whitehall in terms of the training and tradition, the outlook of mind and aspirations which play so big a part in determining men's actions'. He began by distinguishing three main causes which brought about a 'service' in the place of a series of departmental staffs. These were the introduction of a common system of recruitment, the transferability of staff between departments and the growing interdependence of departments as a result of economic factors which affect the whole range of government. He then explained that as the civil service organisation got into its stride, 'there has been built up in every department a store of knowledge and experience in the subjects handled, something which eventually takes shape as a practical philosophy, or may merit the title of a departmental point of view'.

Bridges explained that this departmental point of view, or departmental philosophy, was the result of nothing more startling than the slow accretion and accumulation of experience over the years. 'And in making and reshaping it, things have been learnt which could only be fully grasped by practical experience; as, for example, that certain problems can only be treated by certain administrative methods, and that if certain limits or marks are overstepped, a public outcry can be confidently expected'. He continued:

> These departmental philosophies are of the essence of a Civil Servant's work...Every Civil Servant going to a different job, unless it be an entirely new one, finds himself entrusted with this kind of inheritance. He knows that it is his business to contribute something of his own to this store of experience, and that he should play his part in moulding it and improving it to meet changing conditions. Equally he knows that it is something that he will ignore at his peril.

In another lecture, his Romanes Lecture, which he delivered in

1958 on 'The State and the Arts' Bridges elaborated on the departmental view in this way:

> Those who have done battle in or against Whitehall will know that, at some stage in the fray, you are apt to encounter what may be described as say the 'Home Office point of view' or the 'Foreign Office attitude'. You are unlikely to find out exactly who holds it, still less to be told how it can be changed. At its best, such a view is a synthesis of many opinions welded together into a unity with some political experience: and at its best, if continuously reshaped to meet changing views and conditions, such a collective point of view can play a useful part in enabling the staff of an office to act with reasonable consistency. At its worst, if allowed to ossify, it becomes a deadly menace. And I have heard a cheerful cynic describe a departmental point of view as something that no single individual believes in, but by which all feel bound.[47]

Clearly, as Bridges himself recognised, the departmental view has an important bearing on the relationship between administration and policy. Indeed, he regarded it more highly than this. He said that 'it is a cardinal feature of British administration that no attempt should be made to formulate a new policy in any matter without the fullest consultation with those who have practical experience in that field, and with those who will be called upon to carry it out'.[48] Although ministerial responsibility to Parliament and the public covers every action of the department and ministers are more interested in policy than in detailed administration 'this does not mean that their advisers have no part to play in framing policy'. In fact, Bridges explained, 'it is the duty of a Civil Servant to give his Minister the fullest benefit of the storehouse of departmental experience, and to let the waves of the practical philosophy wash against ideas put forward by his Ministerial master'. Consequently, it is not surprising that 'at the middle levels of an organisation... it can fairly be said that policy and administration merge and are only distinguished with difficulty'.[49]

Bridges queried whether departmental philosophies could harden into a rigid point of view and perhaps conflict with the needs of government policy; but he decided that there were safeguards to prevent this. One safeguard was that staffs changed their jobs every three years or so within departments, and in addition there were staff changes between departments. This was not only an aspect of training, it was also an aspect of the tradition of the civil service. As Bridges put it: 'when a man has done five jobs in fifteen years and has done them all with a measure of success, he is afraid of nothing and welcomes change. He has learnt the art of spotting what points are crucial for forming a judgment on a disputed question even when he has the most cursory knowledge of the subject as a whole'.[50] Another safeguard was the need for departments to work closely together. He noted that they now have to co-operate more, and have become more or less interdependent - with elaborate systems of interdepartmental committees having interlocking memberships.

This in turn, Bridges argued, made the civil servant the least political of all animals, since the departmental experience of which he is the exponent is part of the stock of things which are common to all political parties. It is something which stands apart from the creed of any political party and thus makes a civil servant 'avert himself, almost instinctively, from party politics'.[51]

The insights Bridges provided into this phenomenon are amply illustrated from details of administrative practice described in the earlier chapters of this book. The departmental view emerges from the experience, precedents and the accumulation of knowledge in a department's subject matter. It is reinforced to some extent by training but more often by socialisation and the 'training' procedure that is often popularly known as 'sitting with Nellie' (i.e. learning a job by doing it alongside someone more experienced in the work). The civil service may lack some of the physical manifestations of a corporate life found in a College, as Bridges somewhat regretfully recognised; but it certainly does not lack the collegiate approach to decision making. This approach ensures that anyone involved in the consequences of a decision, as well as those responsible for making a particular decision, is brought into the decision-making process. It involves consulting and informing a wide network of people within the administrative system, not necessarily so that they can offer relevant advice important in the decision-making process, but often, simply, so that an agreed policy or line of action is not subsequently upset.[52] In this context - the procedure of formulating a departmental view - much depends on who the top decision-makers decide are the key people to consult and inform. This process is well illustrated in earlier chapters, where Bridges' key role becomes apparent. It was his regular practice to involve many people in collegiate decision-making; wide consultation is the key element in the development of such processes.

In its most developed state a 'departmental view' may therefore become a 'departmental policy'. This is easy to appreciate because a department is likely to have its conception of how best to achieve certain goals. Often, it is easy to evaluate this process in operation, especially when a department identifies with the interests of clients because there is a close working relationship between officials and clients or their representatives. It is then that the safeguards to which Bridges drew attention become so important. If the safeguards are removed or diminished - for example, by making staff postings less frequent or by changing the balance between formal training and socialisation - then there may be serious consequences in terms of the relationships of ministers and officials which affects the balance between the partisan elements of policies and the elements drawn from the departmental view.

A number of leading politicians have drawn attention to the consequences of the departmental view and the inconveniences and dangers they have experienced as a result of events in their own experience, and these are well illustrated in the following three examples.

The first example is taken from Richard Crossman's *The Diaries of a Cabinet Minister*. Crossman gives the impression of permanent department officials virtually running the lives of their ministers and soon after he assumed office in 1964 he noted:

> At first I felt like someone in a padded cell, but I must now modify this. In fact I feel like somebody floating on the most comfortable support. The whole Department is there to support the Minister. Into his in-tray come hour by hour notes with suggestions as to what he should do. Everything is done to sustain him in the line which officials think he should take. But if one is very careful and conscious one is aware that this supporting soft framework of recommendations is the result of a great deal of secret discussion between the civil servants below. There is a constant debate as to how the Minister should be advised or, shall we say, directed and pushed and cajoled into the line required by the Ministry. There is a tremendous *esprit de corps* in the Ministry and the whole hierarchy is determined to preserve its own policy. Each Ministry has its own departmental policy, and this policy goes on while Ministers come and go. And in this world, though the civil servants have a respect for the Minister, they have a

much stronger loyalty to the Ministry. Were the Minister to challenge and direct the Ministry policy there would be no formal tension at first, only quiet resistence - but a great deal of it. I am therefore always on the look-out to see how far my own ideas are getting across, how far they are merely tolerated by the Ministry, and how far Ministry policies are being imposed on my own mind.[53]

The second example is from Tony Benn who, a few years ago, called for more analysis and public discussion of the working relationship and the balance of real power between ministers and officials. He argued that the power, role, influence and authority of the senior levels of the civil service in Britain have grown to such an extent as to create the embryo of a corporate state. The problem arose not from the political partiality of civil servants but from the fact that the civil service 'sees itself as being above the party battle, with a political position of its own to defend against all comers'. Much of what Benn said about the use of power by civil servants can be applied to the process of putting into practice the departmental view. Benn argued that civil servants have power in various ways and he gave numerous examples, illustrating each category: by setting the framework within which ministers make decisions, by the control of information, by the mobilization of Whitehall, by the mobilization of external pressure, by the use of expertise, by the use of patronage, and by the use of national security. For example, Benn noted that the briefing document prepared for incoming ministers after an election is used in this way. From his perspective he concluded that 'It may be dressed up to look like a range of options for implementing his manifesto, but beneath that presentational language it reveals the departmental view.'[54] One of the most significant examples to which Benn referred was the widely quoted remarks of William Armstrong who, referring to his service in the Treasury, said:

Obviously I had a great deal of influence. The biggest and most pervasive influence is in setting the framework within which questions of policy are raised. We, while I was at the Treasury, had a framework of the economy basically neo-Keynesian. We set the questions which we asked Ministers to decide arising out of that framework and it would have been enormously difficult for any Minister to change the framework, so to that extent we had great power... We were very ready to explain it to anybody who was interested, but most ministers were not interested, were just prepared to take the questions as we offered them, which came out of that framework without going back into the preconceptions of them.[55]

The third example is from Shirley Williams. She found that when she was a minister in the Home Office advice tended to take a monolithic form:

People contribute to the brief as it goes up towards the Minister, but dissenting opinions are gradually knocked out so that in the last two or three stages from Assistant Secretary, Under Secretary to Deputy Secretary - or if it is an extremely important policy, from Under Secretary, Deputy Secretary to Permanent Secretary - all dissenting views disappear from the files and what you are left with finally is the official view.[56]

It is not suggested that there is anything sinister about what Bridges called the departmental view. Indeed, the departmental view is a necessary and inevitable aspect of British government. The main point being made is that Bridges first expounded what it was, how it came to be, and drew attention to necessary safeguards to ensure that its significance was appreciated in the balance of power network within the British constitution. This study of Bridges as Head of the Civil Service and of his writings on public administration shows more clearly than from any other source how it works and its significance in the British system of government. More than this - the evidence in this book is unique in the insights it gives into how the phenomenon works in practice.

It is clear that, in the ways described in this chapter, civil servants play a uniquely important role in the constitution. They offer advice on constitutional practice, they interpret the constitutional conventions and sometimes write them down for the guidance of others, they produce detailed rules and administrative procedures that may affect and influence the way government works on a day-to-day basis, and by the development and maintenance of departmental policies they ensure continuity in government and have a vital role to play in the balance between policy and administration. The clear demarcation between policy formation and execution is now to be seen only in the most elementary textbooks and superficial statements of individuals who have little conception of political reality. However, it is in these circumstances that the role of civil servants becomes so crucial. How they should behave when they are carrying out instructions of ministers, when they are acting on behalf of ministers, and when they are making policy proposals and advising ministers is not written down in the British system of government. Indeed, no comprehensive statement along these lines can be produced without fundamental changes in the constitution. It is in this context that lessons may be drawn and further consideration should be given to ethics in the British civil service.

Notes

1. The phrase originates from Sir James Stephen, giving his opinion on the plan proposed by Sir Stafford Northcote and Sir Charles Trevelyan, for a better organisation of the civil service: *Papers on the Reorganisation of the Civil Service*, P.P. (1854-5), xx, 71-80. See also G. Kitson Clark, '"Statesmen in Disguise": Reflections on the History of the Neutrality of the Civil Service', *The Historical Journal*, Vol. 2. 1959, pp. 19-39, and O. MacDonagh, *Early Victorian Government*, (Weidenfeld and Nicolson, London, 1977), Ch. 11.

2. Hugh Heclo and Aaron Wildavsky, *The Private Government of Public Money: Community and Policy inside British Politics*, (Macmillan, London, 1974).

3. Richard Rose, *The Political Status of higher civil servants in Britain*, (SPP 92), (CSPP, University of Strathclyde, 1981), p. 38.

4. Geoffrey K. Fry, *The Changing Civil Service*, (Allen and Unwin, London, 1985), p. 21.

5. Sir Edward Bridges, *Portrait of a Profession: The Civil Service Tradition*, (Cambridge University Press, Cambridge, 1950).

6. PRO/T162/832/E8641/1, Bridges to Upcott, 16 February 1927.

7. PRO/T162/832/E8641/2.

8. PRO/T162/832/E8641/3.

9. PRO/CAB21/1998, Machinery of Government, Functions of the Cabinet Offices: Notes for Discussion, 16 December 1942.

10. *Office of the Minister of Production*, [Cmd. 6337], (HMSO, London, 1942).

11. 378 H.C. Deb., 5s., cols. 1205-9 (12 March 1942).

12. PRO/CAB127/259.

13. PRO/T199/87.

14. PRO/CAB127/274.

15. PRO/T199/65.

16. PRO/T215/101, Bridges to Stephens, 9 August 1948.

17. PRO/T215/103.

18. PRO/T162/968/E51933/02, Minutes of Evidence to the Second Meeting of the Committee on Civil Service Remuneration, held on 24

March 1948.

19. PRO/T162/968/E51933/02, Minutes of the Ninth meeting of the Committee on Civil Service Remuneration, held on 4 August 1948.

20. PRO/T215/61.

21. L.G. Wickham Legg, *The Dictionary of National Biography, 1931-1940*, (Oxford University Press, London, 1949).

22. PRO/T273/237, Bridges to Lascelles, 3 June 1946.

23. For example, see D.N. Chester, 'The Crichel Down Case', *Public Administration*, Vol 32, 1954, pp. 389-401 (reprinted in Richard A. Chapman and A. Dunsire, *Style in Administration: Readings in British Public Administration*, (Allen and Unwin, London, 1971); see also Geoffrey Marshall, *Constitutional Conventions: The Rules and Forms of Political Accountability*, (Clarendon Press, Oxford, 1984).

24. PRO/T273/209, 'Ministerial Responsibility', 8 July 1954. See also Sir Ronald Harris, *Memory-soft the air*, (The Pentland Press, Edinburgh, 1987). Cf. 530 H.C. Deb., 5s., cols. 1284-94 (20 July 1954).

25. PRO/T273/69.

26. Goodmans Furze Papers, Box 5.

27. PRO/T162/788/E37837, Fisher to Prime Minister, 11 November 1938.

28. *The Times*, 18 November 1938.

29. PRO/CAB134/122.

30. 439 H.C. Deb., 5s., col. 198 (24 June 1947).

31. PRO/T222/578.

32. PRO/T222/579.

33. PRO/T162/968/E51933/02.

34. PRO/T222/185.

35. PRO/T215/82.

36. PRO/T273/288, Bridges to Chancellor of the Exchequer, 22 July 1950.

37. Lord Bridges, 'The Treasury as the most political of Departments', the Pollak Lecture, delivered at the Graduate School of Public Administration, Harvard University, December 1961.

38. PRO/T162/525/E37512.

39. PRO/T273/213, Bridges' Note for Record, 22 June 1945.

40. *Report of a Committee appointed by the Prime Minister to consider whether Civil Servants should be transferred to other Duties*, [Cmd. 9220], (HMSO, London, 1954).

41. PRO/T222/678.

42. PRO/T222/678.

43. PRO/T222/678.

44. PRO/T249/30.

45. PRO/T215/203.

46. Sir Edward Bridges, *Portrait of a Profession: The Civil Service Tradition*.

47. Lord Bridges, *The State and the Arts*, (Oxford University Press, London, 1958), pp 8-9.

48. Sir Edward Bridges, *Portrait of a Profession: The Civil Service Tradition*, p. 19.

49. *Ibid.*, p. 19.

50. *Ibid.*, p. 23.

51. *Ibid.*, p. 28.

52. Richard A. Chapman, *Decision Making*, (Routledge and Kegan Paul, London, 1968), Ch. 6.

53. Richard Crossman, *The Diaries of a Cabinet Minister, Volume One, Minister of Housing 1964-66*, (Hamish Hamilton and Jonathan Cape, London, 1975), p. 31.

54. Tony Benn, 'Manifestos and Mandarins', in *Policy and Practice, The Experience of Government*, (Royal Institute of Public Administration, London, 1980), pp. 57-78.

55. *The Times*, 15 November 1976.

56. Shirley Williams, 'The Decision Makers' in *Policy and Practice*, pp. 79-102.

8

Ethics in the British Civil Service

Ethics in the British civil service is about the application of moral standards in the course of official work. The practical dimension of the topic is that area of official conduct and actions where civil servants are not simply carrying out specific instructions or orders from higher authority but are making value judgments that have implications for their professional standing. Of course, the judgments of civil servants do not all have an ethical element, but the number which do is a matter of increasing concern and debate for political parties and interest groups, for staff associations, and for individual civil servants. Indeed, recent cases involving ministers and civil servants have led the Treasury and Civil Service Committee of the House of Commons to examine the matter in some detail and to rationalise what seems to have become a relationship of practical uncertainty by defining and distinguishing between 'actions' and 'conduct'. It defined 'actions' as those activities of civil servants which are carried out on the instructions of or are consistent with the policies of the minister concerned. In contrast, it defined 'conduct' as activities which fall outside that definition and may amount to 'misconduct'.[1]

Even this attempt at definition may not be as helpful as first appears. It suffers from being influenced by recent cases, especially the Westland Affair,[2] which have focused attention on a particular aspect of the constitution of the United Kingdom and led to attempts to demand more precision and rigidity than is, perhaps, consistent with its uniquely flexible character. A less precise but more workable approach may be more appropriate. In this present discussion ethics in the British civil service therefore refers to moral standards in official work within the context of a specific political environment. The study of Bridges as Head of the Civil

Service has thrown considerable light on a number of facets of ethics in the British civil service. Bridges was not only a splendid upholder of the traditions of the civil service in this respect; he also contributed to the standards expected of civil servants and was an exemplar of them.

Political and administrative perspectives

Public administration is different from business management primarily because of the constraints imposed from the political environment within which the management processes are conducted. British civil servants are, in the words of the classic definition in the Report of the Tomlin Royal Commission on the Civil Service (for which Bridges served as secretary) 'servants of the Crown... employed in a civil capacity'.[3] This may at the most elementary level of study be unambiguous, but beyond the most elementary level difficulties arise from the largely unwritten nature of the British constitution. Formally, and in a 'dignified' sense (adopting Bagehot's terminology), the Crown means the Queen. But for all practical purposes the Crown is the Government - not a particular Government with a constitutionally limited period of office, but the executive branch of the state which is ultimately controlled by the Cabinet.

This aspect of the British constitution makes the United Kingdom unique. There are only two major countries of the modern world with so-called unwritten constitutions: the United Kingdom and the Kingdom of Saudi Arabia. But Britain is the only country in which the unwritten elements of its constitution have so much day to day relevance for the conduct of its officials. Unlike most other countries the United Kingdom has no Civil Service Act. There is therefore no fundamental legal document to which officials can refer which contains a statement of their organisation and their responsibilities. Particular government departments may similarly lack such basic documents. Indeed, departments can be created or abolished virtually overnight by Order in Council.[4] Acts of Parliament are not necessary.

One of the practical implications of this constitutional peculiarity is that there can, quite legitimately, be a variety of opinions about what is constitutionally correct in particular circumstances. This applies in the administrative sphere of government as well as the political sphere. For all day to day purposes loyalty and duty to the Crown has meant loyalty and duty to the Queen's ministers who act in her name and are accountable to the Queen's Parliament. If civil servants were unhappy with this line of authority they could resign - but, in fact, research shows that people to whom this line of authority was unacceptable were unlikely to be attracted to careers in the civil service.[5] However, recent events, especially the Ponting case where a civil servant leaked information because he believed his minister was lying to Parliament, have focused attention on an area of growing sensitivity for individual civil servants. In the past, ministerial accountability to Parliament was of a higher order of generality than now. The reforms of the parliamentary committee system within the last ten years have meant that representative committees, having authority from Parliament, can probe into minute details of administration across a very broad spectrum. These committees have gone way beyond the detailed examinations that have been conducted for many years by the Public Accounts Committee. One of the effects is to greatly increase the opportunities for public knowledge of anomalies between details of administration and ministerial statements. To minimise the difficulties for civil servants various statements of guidance have been issued - including the 1977 Croham Directive on the Disclosure of Official Information,[6] the 1980 Memorandum of Guidance for Government Officials appearing before Parliamentary Select Committees,[7] and the 1985 statement by Sir Robert Armstrong on the Duties and Responsibilities of Civil Servants in relation to Ministers.[8] However, even with the guidance provided by these documents, senior administrators have been unable to avoid difficult situations arising from their relations with ministers.

This, however, is only a new facet of what has always been recognised as the political dimension of the work of administrators in the British civil service. Indeed, the generalists in the civil service who were so strongly criticised in the 1960s and 1970s for being amateurs were often denied the recognition they deserved as specialists with particular expertise and skills in dealing with the political environment. Constitutionally, the position is quite clear: a civil servant's duty is to his minister; he carries out ministerial instructions and ministers are answerable in public, i.e. in Parliament, for the management decisions that are made in their name. Furthermore, all decisions made by civil servants, other than those that could be construed as misconduct, are constitutionally expected to be defended by ministers on behalf of officials who cannot answer publicly for themselves. This constitutional position is clear for all practical purposes and has been well documented in authoritative statements and in textbooks on the subject.[9] However, within the last fifteen years difficulties have arisen as a result of ministers failing to act in accordance with accepted constitutional practice. Not only have ministers not accepted full responsibilitiy for decisions made in their name, with Parliament colluding in this constitutional transgression,[10] but in the Ponting case the evidence suggests that ministers can intentionally mislead or misinform Parliament and its committees. The civil servant in such circumstances may then find himself in the difficult position of deciding where his duty lies - to Parliament or to his minister. He has to make a personal judgment about how he should behave in circumstances where the responsibilities of the Crown to Parliament are less clear and unambiguous than expected.

The recent public discussion of this dilemma, which has revolved around the highly publicised case of Clive Ponting and the Westland Affair, together with the published reports and evidence of the Treasury and Civil Service Committee and public lectures, books and articles by leading authorities on the subject, are not, however, the only area where there has been discussion about ethics in the British civil service. Two other, more general areas are the consequences of discretionary decision-making and the concepts of efficiency and effectiveness.

Much of the discussion about the relationships of ministers and civil servants revolves around the procedures, consequences and safeguards for individual citizens where decisions are made by civil servants in the name of the minister. Laws, regulations and orders cannot be drafted to cover every conceivable circumstance. Even where that is the intention of the drafters, provision is usually made for the totally unexpected and unpredictable circumstances that do, in fact, occur. Often the rules provide for a ministerial decision about what is reasonable in the circumstances of individual cases. There may be rules of guidance and case law to help the officials but there are nevertheless many thousands of such decisions made every day.

In the United Kingdom we do not have a codified system of administrative law with courts to which individual citizens can appeal, but instead we have numerous administrative tribunals and other procedures so that citizens may appeal against discretionary decisions which are in their opinion unacceptable. We also have procedures within the administrative system and in the political system to enable citizens to obtain redress of grievances. The courts, too, may apply tests to determine whether decisions have been properly made - i.e. by taking into account all the relevant factors and excluding irrelevant factors, by ensuring that there is no bias and that the principles of natural justice are not set aside.

These checks and safeguards have been developed over many years. The oldest, dating from before the development of the welfare state, were almost entirely in the political system - they are, in fact, specific developments of the constitutional conventions that redress of grievances should precede the grant of Supply in the House of Commons: they include opportunities for parliamentary questions and for grievances to be raised on motions for the adjournment of the House of Commons. The newest safeguards, with elaborate systems for advising citizens, hearing appeals through tribunals, and the work of Ombudsmen, have been developed only within the past twenty or twenty-five years. There is also, as one would expect in a healthy political system, a continuous demand for more safeguards and more checks. This is typified in the Report of the Whyatt Committee on *The Citizen and the Administration* which, in 1961, said that 'Ideally it is always in the interests of the individual that there should be a tribunal which can give an impartial adjudication on discretionary decisions'.[11]

In a perfect world, or perhaps even in a world dominated by lawyers with much to gain from such provisions, there may, indeed, be scope for more safeguards and appeals procedures. But in the world in which we actually live government business has to be carried on and there is a limit to the resources that can be allocated to safeguards and appeals procedures. If there were, in fact, appeals against every discretionary decision the work of government would soon come to a halt. Management decisions involving discretionary judgments in individual cases, or where conceptions of the national interest have to be weighed against private interests, are made every day by thousands of officials throughout the country. Those making such decisions are expected to apply the highest possible standards. But in circumstances where there is, in theory, no limit to the care that might be taken, a balance has to be maintained between the rights and interests of individuals and groups, and the national interest as indicated by the Crown and as interpreted by individual officials.

Another area of concern in public administration at the present time relates to the frequently-used concepts of efficiency, effectiveness and economy. Economy is a well understood term concerned with the cost elements of an activity and the relationship of inputs and outputs. The meanings of efficiency and effectiveness are not, however, so widely agreed. Sometimes efficiency and effectiveness are used as if they were synonymous, or when linked together (as they frequently are) they are used as if they simply mean economical and convenient. Sometimes, especially when the approaches of economists are in vogue, efficiency is basically used to refer to the extent to which maximum output is achieved in relation to given costs or inputs, and effectiveness is used to refer to the extent to which overall goals are achieved. Often efficiency is so loosely used that it is no more than a 'hurrah' word of exhortation towards some ill-defined goal implying a perfect but in practice unattainable quality of management.

It may be helpful to use these words more precisely and consistently in public administration. A start would be to go back to some of the classics in the literature[12] and to accept that management activity is directed towards advancing two ends: goals and objectives. Goals may be taken to refer to the higher level of authority, which may be general in nature and the responsibility of the highest levels of management; for example, providing a particular service or achieving a stated purpose. Objectives may be taken to refer to more specific and measurable activities, the responsibility of lower levels in the management hierarchy, often relating to output within a given time. If effectiveness is then reserved for the achievement of specific, measurable, desired objectives, the manager's effectiveness can be quantified according to the extent to which he achieves the objectives specified for him. Efficiency may then be reserved for the achievement of the ends set by the higher level of management, some of which may include quantifiable elements but because these ends will also include unquantifiable elements and take into account the unplanned consequences of management activity, efficient management will be mainly concerned with unquantifiable elements. This provision is necessary because the achievement of management objectives might be at the cost of inhuman working conditions or be at the expense of other standards expected in society. Consequently, when the terms are used in this way it may be possible for effective management to be inefficient or for effective action that is efficient in one society or at one time to be unacceptable and/or inefficient in another society or at a different time.

Because so much of the work of public administration has to do with these qualitative, political, or human elements in our society, the qualitative elements of the personal conduct of officials becomes important not only for individual citizens but also for the quality of life in our society. Top civil servants may be regarded as leaders because, by the examples they set and by the quality of the decisions they make, they influence those under them to make judgments according to similar criteria. In most countries, which have written constitutions, behaviour in these circumstances is codified in laws and decrees, which change from time to time and which guide the decision-making of officials who behave bureaucratically (in the sense of Max Weber's ideal type of bureaucracy). In Britain, with its so-called unwritten constitution, there may be conventions and statements of guidance from time to time, but the quality of our administrative system is seen in the overall pattern produced by many individual decisions of civil servants making individual judgments. Responsibility for initiating change or influencing quality rests in practice with many individuals - civil servants as well as politicians - who are all expected to play their part. The exercise of this responsibility primarily involves the professional skills and knowledge of officials working in a political environment. The quality of the judgments they make is a distinctive feature of their profession. Moreover, these judgments are often more significant than the judgments of politicians in two respects. One is that the judgments of politicians are often dependent on the guidance and advice of officials; in this sense politicians may be constitutionally accountable but they are rarely original. Considerable responsibility therefore rests in practice on the shoulders of officials who initiate action, create or modify policies and design the plans and specify the objectives for achieving the goals. The other is that calling on politicians to make a judgment, and to accept their constitutional responsibility whether or not an issue has partisan significance, requires a prior decision from officials that the time and circumstances require direction from politicians. Much therefore depends on elements of tactics and timing in the advice and judgment of officials. That is why to Bridges and to many other practitioners and writers on British public administration the profession has always appeared more an art with skills that are learned by practice than a science or craft with laws and techniques that can be discovered by scientific or quasi-scientific methodology.

Leadership and the role of individual civil servants

At another level some elements of ethics may be seen in the personal attitudes of individual civil servants in their day to day administrative activities as officials. In general, the British civil service embodies most of the features of a classical bureaucracy as outlined by Max Weber. For the purposes of this present discussion, however, one of Weber's characteristics deserves special attention. Max Weber said that the ideal official conducts his office in a spirit of formalistic impersonality, without hatred of passion, and hence without affection or enthusiasm. In general this is true, mainly because of the nature of the work in the British system of government and the selection procedures and criteria used to recruit its civil servants. It is also true because of post-entry socialisation, the administrative culture, and the personnel management procedures that include particular approaches to career planning.

As far as political attitudes are concerned, British civil servants are a distinctive type of citizen, generally lacking in strong allegiance to any political party. Research has suggested that administrative civil servants are likely to vote at elections much as individuals of their age group and social standing would be expected to vote in a particular election.[13] Individuals with strong political motivations in one direction or another are unlikely to be attracted to a career in the civil service. Indeed, in a survey conducted at a time when jobs were more plentiful than at present, it was discovered that a considerable majority of a particular cohort of principals said they would have gone into university teaching or some other form of public administration had they not joined the civil service.[14] It seems reasonable to conclude that individuals with a high commitment to a particular ideology choose to work for that ideology either as an occupation or by taking a job which would enable them to pursue their commitment outside working hours. The British civil service is simply not attractive to them.

Passionate commitment in civil servants for or against particular areas of policy is, in any case, soon neutralised in the administrative system. For example, a civil servant with a strong and conscientiously-held personal conviction on a particular social or moral issue, but who is selected according to the regular and known criteria to have the potential to become a successful civil servant, is unlikely to seek a position in a department where his or her opinions are likely to be an embarrassment or cause difficulties; nor is the Civil Service Commission likely to knowingly post him or her there. Strong enthusiasms of any sort are likely to become evident in the rigorous selection system at the recruitment stage, and they are likely to be borne in mind when allocating successful candidates to departments.

There have recently been suggestions that more politically committed civil servants should be recruited and that a future government with radical policies should require officials to be more highly committed to the 'success' of its policies. Political advisers already exist in many departments and they seem to be making valuable contributions to government that career civil servants welcome. This is because roles have been developed for political advisers which complement the work of permanent civil servants, and political advisers perform duties, such as speech writing, which civil servants are often not qualified to do well. But if tests of political commitment were applied to civil servants in Britain they would bring a fundamental change to the system of government and so far there seems to be no general demand for such a change. As in certain other countries, any requirement for political commitment would be likely to involve changing large numbers of senior officials after each election.

However, individual enthusiasms are not only to be found in political attitudes. The consequences of Sir Christopher Bullock's enthusiasm for aviation may be seen as a warning in this context. Another example was revealed by the Crichel Down inquiry. The report of Sir Andrew Clark's inquiry into the Crichel Down case, which was published in 1954,[15] was clearly critical of some attitudes he found in the civil service. It found that the Lands Service and the Land Commission had become 'infatuated with the idea of creating a new model farm'; it also found inaccuracies in an official report which 'arose solely from the passionate love of secrecy inherent in many senior officials'. Mr (now Sir) Melford Stevenson QC, one of the lawyers appearing at the inquiry, asserted that, while officials concerned in the case had no corrupt motive, 'they derive(d) great satisfaction from the exercise of personal power' and he declared 'There is a time when the public administrator can become, if not drunk, unfit to be in charge of his personal power'.[16] The Crichel Down case illustrates some of the defects in the professional standards of the civil servants involved, but the dangers to society were not apparently from corruption, because none was found. Instead, it seems, the dangers included the enthusiasms of civil servants for a particular policy which happened to have been developed by a previous Labour

302

Government but which was inconsistent with the philosophy of the new Conservative Government. One way that personnel management procedures help to check such ill-advised enthusiasms is the approach encouraged by Bridges involving the regular postings of officials. Much criticised though too frequent postings were by the Fulton Committee and by other critics of the civil service, they provide an effective check against influence in some areas of government activity (especially areas like the Tax Inspectorate): they moderate the perfectly understandable enthusiasms of officials; they minimise demoralisation in the civil service when policies are reversed; and they help to maintain common standards of professional conduct in the civil service as a whole.

Sometimes civil servants allow their enthusiasms to influence their actions, but this is rare - so rare, in fact, that it is akin to exceptions proving a rule. Bullock's enthusiasm for aviation has already been referred to in connection with his downfall in 1936. Less widely known (though not revealed until comparatively recently, and not connected with his downfall) is his practice in the 1930s of supplying Churchill with figures of German air strength while Churchill was not in the Government.[17] As has already been related, Bullock's civil service career was later abruptly ended, but it should not be assumed that such exceptional conduct has always resulted in personal disaster. If one account is accurate, Sir Norman Brook, then Head of the Civil Service, behaved quite exceptionally when in 1956 he communicated the Eden Government's confidential plans for the Suez adventure - of which he disapproved - to the Americans through the intelligence network.[18] Even Ponting's permanent secretary, Sir Frank Cooper, said on television in 1984 that the leaking of information by service chiefs, worried about the consequences of government defence reviews, could be justified.[19] As a rule, however, the professional discretion of civil servants and their duty to the Government of the day prevails even when it involves acute personal discomfort and difficulties for particular officials. Enthusiasms remain curbed or officials resign. Bridges, it seems, was not lacking in enthusiasm but his enthusiasm was in acceptable areas, tempered with caution, and exercised with discretion.

One of the features that has caused most anxiety among some civil servants in recent years is the consequences of government cuts and economies, but even this phenomenon is not new. Recently released files in the Public Record Office indicate that there was almost certainly a link - though not necessarily a direct consequential relationship - between the Crichel Down case and the economies in the civil service introduced by the Conservative Government elected in 1951.[20] Indeed, the files suggest that in this context Bridges may have been more sensitive to the relationship of effectiveness, efficiency and economy than was realised at the time. In the period of Conservative government since 1979 various measures have again been introduced to cut government activity and to introduce economies. Most of these measures are not relevant to the present discussion, but one of the consequences is most definitely relevant and, because it affects the quality of some government decision-making, the effects are felt by citizens and also cause anguish to conscientious officials who are genuinely concerned about the decline in the quality of their work. The point here is that it is generally thought that the essential characteristics of liberal democracy as seen in Britain include equality, fairness and justice in the treatment of citizens by government; and cuts in resources give rise to questions among citizens and their leaders, and also among civil servants seeking to maintain high professional standards, of how much 'fairness' and how much 'justice' can be afforded, and how these qualities are to be defined and applied. Bridges himself set high standards of fairness and justice, even at some personal cost, as illustrated by the time and trouble he spent with his initiative on behalf of Bullock. His regard for fairness and justice may also be seen in areas not considered in detail in this study: for example pay differentials and the equal treatment of men and women within the civil service.

Ways in which civil service leaders have traditionally sought to encourage officials to practice the highest professional standards include themselves setting high standards as well as issuing statements to staff. After the publication of the report on the Crichel Down Inquiry, Bridges took the unusual step of writing to all civil servants telling them to 'read and take to heart' the comments made by the internal committee of officials which considered the future of the civil servants implicated in the case. The committee had written: 'In present times the interests of the private citizen are affected to a great extent by the actions of Civil Servants ... (they) should constantly bear in mind that the citizen has a right to expect ... that his personal feelings, no less than his rights as an individual, will be sympathetically and fairly considered'.[21] Bridges also quoted from the report of the inquiry chaired by Sir Warren Fisher into the irregularities revealed by the Francs case which said that

304

'The public expects from Civil Servants a standard of integrity and conduct not only inflexible but fastidious'. [22] Bridges ended his circular: 'It will do no harm if each one of us goes over the ground himself, and makes sure there is nothing amiss'.

Another means to encourage members of professions to aim for higher standards of conduct is the promulgation of codes of behaviour. Various professional bodies have done this and some of these codes have been well received by the public in addition to being well regarded by their professions. Two have been produced for public administrators. The first was the result of a project in the Australian Institute of Public Administration and published in 1965. [23] However, when this and other comparable codes of good practice are studied they appear to be little more than lists of commonsense maxims, or rules and procedures that most managers already bear in mind because they are good general rules. As far as some topics are concerned, equivalent advice is given for British civil servants in the Pay and Conditions of Service Code and the Establishment Officers' Guide, but those official documents are mainly concerned with official rules for conduct and discipline, financial propriety, the scope for political activities and references to the Official Secrets Act; they say nothing about professional or ethical considerations. Indeed, the Establishment Officers' Guide says that it has never 'been thought necessary to lay down a precise code of conduct because civil servants jealously maintain their professional standards. In practice, the distinctive character of the British civil service depends on the existence and maintenance of a general code of conduct which, although to some extent intangible and unwritten, is of very real influence'. [24] Two years ago the First Division Association produced a short draft code of ethics for civil servants. It can be compared with codes produced by other professional bodies in the United Kingdom, though it does, of course, have special reference to the civil service and bears in mind questions arising from such recently controversial cases as those involving Sarah Tisdall and Clive Ponting.

Such codes of behaviour have limited but not unimportant uses. For example, they can be valuable as teaching aids and as guides to individuals who are facing ethical dilemmas. Codes of ethics could be made stronger and have a significant impact if, for example, an independent official or body were appointed, much like an Ombudsman, with power to look into individual difficulties whether or not the subject matter is covered by a security classification, to offer advice to individuals and to issue case reports to permanent secretaries and an annual report to, say, a parliamentary committee. Those who argue that such an Ombudsman is unnecessary and that officials in difficulty should consult their permanent secretary or, ultimately, the Head of the Civil Service, should bear in mind the lessons of the Bullock case and the relationship there revealed between a particular permanent secretary and the then Head of the Civil Service.

Many of the formal safeguards against the most extreme features of unethical behaviour have existed in the civil service for some considerable time. Patronage and corruption at the recruitment stage was largely eliminated in the last century with the introduction of open competitive examinations; relationships with staff associations and unions have been formalised and regularised since the introduction of the Whitley system (with which Bridges was so closely associated for many years) after the First World War; and, as has already been mentioned, many of the remaining topics of controversy were codified during the Second World War and promulgated soon afterwards in Estacode, which was the predecessor of the current Pay and Conditions of Service Code and Establishment Officers' Guide.

Nevertheless informal safeguards remain of considerable importance, and these are conveyed mostly by post-entry training and socialisation into the administrative culture. These are important for developing in individuals the values and beliefs that contribute to the set of patterns and guidelines for behaviour that are so important in the administrative culture of the civil service. It is not surprising that when Sir William Armstrong, as Head of the Civil Service, was questioned on television about his personal attitude to the considerable power he had, he explained that for him being accountable to oneself was the greatest taskmaster. He added: 'I am accountable to my own ideal of a civil servant'.[25] Bridges had similar thoughts. From his wide practical experience he found that there was 'in every Department a store of knowledge and experience in the subjects handled, something which eventually takes shape as a practical philosophy, or may merit the title of a departmental point of view ... in most cases the departmental philosophy is nothing more startling than the slow accretion and accumulation of experience over the years ...Every civil servant ... finds himself entrusted with this kind of inheritance.'[26]

The informal safeguards and processes of socialisation that have in practice evolved over many years are parallel and consistent with the nature of the British constitution. As with the constitution, customs and conventions that become out of date or irrelevant fall into disuse or are replaced with more formal, written rules. Indeed, in recent years it has sometimes been the case that defects in the political system have resulted in important effects in the civil service. Leaks of official information have occurred many times more frequently from political sources than from civil service sources, and there have been breakdowns, without subsequent corrective action, in the convention of ministerial responsibility. [27] The consequence is that now it may appear necessary, perhaps even urgent, to produce a code of behaviour for ministers before turning further attention to producing a definitive code for officials. In Bridges' day because of the peculiar personal standing he had, in addition to his official position, Bridges could virtually make personal contributions to constitutional developments. Moreover, he could call ministers in to tell them when they were behaving badly (as sometimes they were, according to instances referred to in this study). But again, if a formal code were produced to guide ministerial practice it could have fundamental implications for the system of government, especially if it resulted in less freedom for ministers to act according to their political judgment.

In relation to all these considerations it is clear that the approved high standards of professional conduct at all levels in the British civil service depends largely on the controls and influence exercised by outstanding civil servants who may be called leaders. There are numerous reasons why this is so, including the so-called un-written nature of the British constitution, the values and standards of British society, the nature of the work civil servants do, and the ways in which they are recruited, trained and promoted. Questions may then be asked about the special qualities that are to be found among the few outstanding civil servants who have made it to the top and achieved positions of recognised leadership. It is against the background of the environment in which he worked that the achievements of Bridges must be considered. This environment may to some extent have changed since Bridges was Head of the Civil Service, so it is the environment both then and now that must be considered - even though the similarities from time to time in this century may in fact be more significant than the differences.

Edward Bridges as Head of the Civil Service

At Bridges' Memorial Service on 15 October 1969 Sir John

Winnifrith gave an address during which he made many comments similar to those offered by others, already quoted in Chapter 1, who spoke or wrote in praise of Bridges. He emphasised Bridges' prodigious energy and his genuine enjoyment of work: whatever the work was, he enjoyed getting it done. In particular, however, Winnifrith commented on Bridges' personal code of professional ethics which, he said, 'was a very serious matter for him'. He went on:

> This code, in particular his conviction that truth was something that was not to be tampered with, was not a code he consciously worked out. It was just part of his nature. That was what made so entirely human and lovable what might otherwise have seemed almost too austere a character ... And he never preached it. His standards and his rules became known by example, not by precept.[28]

It cannot be denied that Bridges lived a remarkable life. He was a lucky survivor of the generation massacred in the First World War. After being wounded he benefited from being temporarily employed in the Treasury: this gave him a modest advantage in being posted to the Treasury after he had competed for an established position in the post-war reconstruction examinations. As a result of this posting he worked at the centre of the central government administrative system, where he was noticed by Fisher and others and where he had the unique opportunity of serving as secretary to three royal commissions. He was not quickly promoted, but promotion was slow in the 1920s and 1930s and during that time Bridges acquired valuable experience in various capacities in the Treasury. He learned not only how the Treasury worked but also gained experience of the work of parliamentary committees, the control of expenditure and staff, and interdepartmental relations in the period of rearmament before the Second World War. All this was important in terms of what would now be called Bridges' career profile. Then, immediately before and for the duration of the Second World War he had the remarkable opportunity to serve in one of the most difficult and demanding of all jobs: Secretary to the Cabinet. The work was exhausting, and working with Churchill in a post which was central in the design and practice of the civilian parts of the wartime administrative machinery of government, though it may have been an inspiring privilege in some respects was also stressful and gruelling.

Bridges was successful in these positions because he had the physical, intellectual and personal qualities that made him so well suited to the personalities and circumstances at that time in those offices. More than this, Bridges progressed from being Secretary to the Cabinet to become Head of the Civil Service at a time of unique challenge to the civil service, when government departments were not only concerned with the problems and tasks of reconstruction but were also concerned with developing the plans and interpreting the ambitious policies of the post-war Labour Government. Bridges had remarkable opportunities and more than adequately met the requirements of the positions in which he found himself. His friends and colleagues have amply borne testimony to his success in these respects and extracts from what they have said and written have already been quoted in this book. It therefore seems fair to ask how he appears to a student of politics who never met him and most of whose knowledge is dependent on Bridges' own writings and the inadequate resources of official files (after often erratic weeding). Comments may be grouped into three areas: Bridges' personal qualities; his relationships with others; and the eminent position in which he found himself.

In terms of qualities, the important conclusion emerges that Bridges' personal attributes were, indeed, appropriate for the positions in which he found himself. It is fair to say, as nearly everyone who knew him has said, that he was industrious, enjoyed his work and had well-developed abilities to express himself, and these qualities were crucial to his success. Moreover, his enthusiasm for his work extended to the capacity to motivate others through it. Although he became a permanent civil servant as a result of his success in the reconstruction competition after the First World War, with its in some respects less rigorous requirements for success, there seems little doubt that he would have met the more precise requirements of civil service selectors in the second half of the twentieth century. Several commentators have remarked on Bridges' lack of originality - they say, for example, that he was not an innovator. The evidence in this book confirms this assessment; for example, it seems very surprising that Bridges never gave a lead in inaugurating agenda items for the Government Organisation Committee when he was apparently so interested in the subject matters relevant to the GOC's work. However, it should also be remembered that in compensation he exercised judgment in selecting advisers whom he thought had imagination and flair and he was willing to accept their advice and adopt their ideas. It should also be remembered that the machinery of government developments which Bridges pushed ahead, and which were so important during the Second World War and while he was Head of the Civil Service, owed much to his persistence and industry. Other comments have indicated how difficult it was for others to get to know him and this, paradoxically, seems to have given him added strength in the context of the civil service so that some officials, with respect, recognised in him a sense of cunning and a political astuteness. He was 'a loner' who could take risks without authority - presumably because he had such an intimate knowledge of how government worked and could confidently assess what the risks were likely to be. Probably more than anyone else Bridges knew about the 'mysteries' of government - it was not only the promotions system to the most senior positions that was shrouded in mystery: there is a sense in which Bridges seemed to have a firm belief in the Bagehotian ideas about the dignified and the efficient elements of government. The dignified parts, stretching the term beyond Bagehot's useage, extended in Bridges' time to factual explanations even about the machinery of government, but in speaking and writing as freely as he did the shutters were even more tightly closed over the efficient elements of how decisions were actually made and how ministers and civil servants worked together. Indeed, Bridges usually only thought of the top 1% when he spoke or wrote about the civil service, and it is not surprising that in a matter like the initiative he took in relation to Bullock's case he kept knowledge of what he was doing to a very small circle of colleagues. His concern with confidentiality about the working of government is also illustrated by the restrained approval given under his leadership to the preparation of the New Whitehall series of studies of government departments. But these comments about Bridges' personal qualities seem rather commonplace observations in this context and many facets of his character will already have emerged from the earlier chapters of this book. Three other qualities seem much more worthy of comment: these are his judgment, his code of ethics and his conception of the national interest.

In terms of Bridges' judgment - which was highly regarded and commented on by his colleagues - more can, perhaps, be now learned from his comparative 'failures' than from his successes. This is partly because for one reason or another there is more evidence of them in the official files, but also partly because it is in the nature of life that more can be learned from failures than from successes. In any case, it is quite clear from the remaining evidence that much of Bridges' work, especially his most successful work, was done in discussion and relatively little was written down unless sensitivities were involved or repercussions were thought possible. Two 'failures' are well documented in earlier chapters: the story of the consequences of the Masterman Report on the political activities of civil servants and the case of Sir Christopher Bullock. Whilst it seems hardly fair to call them failures because the word seems so harsh, failures in a sense they undoubtedly were. These experiences seem to have demonstrated, at least to Bridges himself, that he would have done things differently if faced with similar problems and it seems clear that at the time they resulted in personal disappointment for him. In both cases his weakness seems to have been in his appreciation of the political perspective and in his insecure assessment of elements beyond his own experience. What they also reveal, however, is personal strengths in that Bridges had nothing personal to gain, he conscientiously upheld the traditions of the civil service, and he was by no means inexperienced or unwilling when it came to what C.P. Snow referred to as the 'closed' politics of Whitehall. [29] Indeed, contrary to the behaviour of officals in other contexts, especially in other countries, these events reveal an almost monastic disregard for his personal interests. Admittedly, Bridges was not living at the poverty line, but it should not be forgotten that he was not paid well for the responsibilities he carried: on the contrary, he was paid less than certain other officials, who had been specially recruited for their highly demanded qualities, who worked under him (such as S.C. Leslie and Sir Edwin (later Lord) Plowden).

These qualities and his career experience make it all the more interesting that Bridges achieved the eminence he did and especially the close relationship with Churchill. Martin Gilbert has confirmed the powerful influence Bridges had on the day to day conduct of the Second World War and how he became the link between Churchill and the main civil and military departments of state, just as Ismay was the link with the Chiefs of Staff and their various committees. Sir John Martin has contributed complementary observations on the same situation in a manner that encompasses reference to Bridges' personal qualities and standards and the consequent influence he had:

> His advice was honest and fearless and he was ready to stand
> up to Churchill if he disagreed with him. In return the Prime

Minister came to place great reliance on his judgment and turned to him to ensure the execution of his policies. Thus, though not one of the boon companions, Bridges was constantly brought into oral consultation and was often on the guest list at Chequers...

One of Bridges' contributions to the smooth working of the machine was his insistence that, as far as practicable, any meeting of Ministers that was more than a huddle should be attended by an officer of the War Cabinet Office to keep a record, especially of any conclusions reached. He himself was a master of the art of recording in clear, unambiguous terms the outcome of even the most rambling and apparently inconclusive meeting.[30]

Secondly, these examples, and also the personal cases mentioned in Chapter 2, reveal a code of expected behaviour that, if not puritanical, could on occasions be unyielding. This is by no means a criticism - but it seems important to record that it was Bridges' personal integrity that was of considerable importance in the regard others had for him and which also had great practical effects on the British civil service which was (and still is) so influenced by him. Nevertheless, Bridges emerges as a shy man, whose sense of fun was more intellectual than boisterous and in whose presence others - particularly those who did not know him well - did not always feel relaxed.

Thirdly, Bridges had a clear conception of the national interest, a conception which often guided his own decision-making but which was also acceptable to those with whom he worked. This gave him a position of authority, though it was not necessarily an authority which would have been so readily conferred in the same way, in other circumstances or at other times. It seems quite extraordinary today to find, in the post-Second World War period, other officials accepting so willingly and without question statements of what Bridges thought the national interest was, and this experience stimulates questions about the concept.

The national interest is by no means as clear a concept as it at first appears. At an elementary level in the British system of government it may be argued that the national interest is what the democratically elected government declares it to be. This is the purpose of elections and officials exist to implement government policies in accordance with the enactments of legislation by Parliament. The government, however, has other strengths as well as those arising from its election. For example, it is thought to have access to important information, relevant to particular issues, that is not available to ordinary citizens. At the other extreme the word is almost denied any meaning because it is used by all and sundry as a sort of 'hurrah' word to apply to what are often little more than political tactics to advance personal or group interests. In between these extremes there are numerous other possibilities. Clearly, the national interest, if the words are to have any acceptable meaning, must include elements of Bridges' approach where personal and group interests are subordinated to more general interests. Questions may then be raised about variations in conceptions of the national interest. For example, how much weight should be given to ruling groups or classes in society, how much knowledge of all the facts should be required before pronouncements are made, how should all the evidence be accumulated and interpreted, and what procedures should exist to ensure the balance between the public interest(s) being promoted and private interests being disturbed. It may not be acceptable to argue that the national interest on a particular issue (the death penalty for certain crimes, for example) can, in its purest sense, be expressed in a referendum. It is well known that referendums have serious disadvantages in this context and in any case they do not fit comfortably in the practice of British government. It must in practice be recognised that civil servants have an important role to play in interpreting the national interest as stated by Parliament and the Government, in filling out the details of policies (especially in areas that attract little partisan interest), in producing plans to implement policies and, of course, in designing the administrative machinery without which policies could not be implemented. In these, and other, respects it may not be acceptable to pay no regard at all to such personal factors as the age and class backgrounds of individuals who play roles in formulating and interpreting that national interest (as, for example, when the War Office and others in the Second World War objected to Vera Lynn's songs on the grounds that they were contrary to the national interest because it was believed that they would sap the will to win the war). [31]

Bridges' approach in these respects may in some ways be sharply contrasted with the different approaches now favoured in the civil service. For example, Mrs Thatcher, as Prime Minister, has recently written (January 1987) that the Government is aiming to cherish the traditional virtues of the civil service while also encouraging new ones. [32] One of the new virtues is illustrated by the performance bonus experiment, launched in 1985 to test and develop performance-related pay as part of a strategy to improve efficiency and effectiveness. [33] This seems to be a positive stimulant to thoughts of private advantage and therefore contrary to the traditions advocated and exemplified by Bridges. It appears to be in stark contrast to Bridges' view that civil servants should be influenced 'by no thoughts of private advantage or advancement' and that they should have 'no end in view but that the work may be carried out faithfully and well.'[34]

The lesson emerges as far as Bridges was concerned that his authoritative statements as Head of the Civil Service were accepted by others for a combination of reasons. Not only were they the statements of a man known to be industrious and apparently well-informed, they were also made in a manner that was transparently without any personal or private advantage. They were accepted, therefore, for reasons of Bridges' personal qualities and as much as anything else it was his personal standing with others that mattered. Take away any of these elements and Bridges' position of authority and leadership is shattered. After reviewing the events related in this book, and many more that could have been related but for limitations of length, this element of truth is brought into focus by the rather sad vignette provided by Peter Hennessy in his book *Cabinet:*

> As the (Suez) crisis deepened, Bridges was in his last weeks as Permanent Secretary to the Treasury. He, who had been so close to the innermost of inner circles since succeeding Hankey in 1938, was receiving only fragmentary details of the inner Cabinet's war-planning, despite having to advise the Chancellor on the financial implications. He was not even receiving the minutes of the Egypt Committee. He sent his private secretary down the corridor to see Sir Norman Brook to ask if they could be provided. The Cabinet Secretary was most apologetic. But the Prime Minister himself had compiled the circulation list and Sir Edward's name was not on it.[35]

Unless there are fundamental changes in the British system of government it is unlikely anyone again will assume the significant position of authority occupied by Bridges when he was Head of the Civil Service. The civil service has changed: there are new methods of selection for recruiting personnel expected to rise to the highest positions; career patterns for officials are now different from the 1920s and 1930s; the role of the Treasury and the tasks of government have changed; there are unlikely again to be developments as enormous in scale as the creation of the welfare state and the inauguration of numerous public corporations - all involving appointments in which the Head of the Civil Service had such peculiarly personal responsibilities and influence. The system of government has changed: the work of Parliament and its committees is of a different order and a different mix from earlier decades in the twentieth century; the relationships of civil servants and ministers, and of civil servants and Parliament, have been modified by new codes and guidelines; unions now play a different and more assertive role in the civil service than they did when Bridges was at the Treasury; Britain is now a member of the European Community; there may even be the possibility in the not too distant future of a written constitution involving a bill of rights and a Civil Service Act. British society has also changed with demands for more open government; new attitudes towards race and class; different emphases on education and training; and a different and possibly less respectful attitude towards civil servants in the community. However, what remains is the example of Edward Bridges as a great public servant of the twentieth century. Moreover he was - and still is - the greatest defender of the values of generalist administration and his leadership is respected even though his values, and the traditions in the civil service for which he stood, have become widely criticised. What also remains is a civil service towards which he made significant contributions of lasting value, and a continuing flow of issues and cases involving ethical questions which will have to be resolved by the judgments of numerous individuals acting both collegiately and independently. The qualities in individuals needed to resolve contemporary issues and cases may be somewhat different from those of 40 or 50 years ago, but it is unlikely that public administrators today will be as successful without the standards of integrity Bridges had or the trust and respect he inspired in others.

Notes

1. *First Report from the Treasury and Civil Service Committee, Session 1986-87, Ministers and Civil Servants, together with the*

proceedings of the Committee, H.C. 62, (HMSO, London, 1986).

2. *Fourth Report from the Defence Committee, Session 1985-86, Westland plc: The Government's Decision Making*, H.C. 519, (HMSO, London, 1986).

3. *Royal Commission on the Civil Service 1929-31, Report*, [Cmd.3909], (HMSO, London, 1931), para. 9.

4. Richard A. Chapman, 'The Rise and Fall of the CSD', *Policy and Politics,* Vol 11, 1983, pp. 41-61.

5. Richard A. Chapman, 'Profile of a Profession: the Administrative Class of the Civil Service', *The Civil Service, Vol 3(2), Surveys and Investigations: Evidence submitted to the Committee under the Chairmanship of Lord Fulton, 1966-1968*, (HMSO, London, 1968), pp.1-29.

6. Letter dated 6 July 1977 from Sir Douglas Allen, the Head of the Home Civil Service, on the Disclosure of Official Information (the Croham Directive). Reprinted in Dermot Englefield, *Whitehall and Westminster*, (Longman, London, 1985), Appendix 3.

7. Memorandum of Guidance for Government Officials appearing before Parliamentary Select Committees (May 1980). Extract reprinted in Dermot Englefield, *Whitehall and Westminster*, Appendix 2.

8. The Duties and Responsibilites of Civil Servants in relation to Ministers, by Sir Robert Armstrong, Head of the Home Civil Service (February 1985). Reprinted in Dermot Englefield, *Whitehall and Westminster*, Appendix 4.

9. For example, Sir Ivor Jennings, *Cabinet Government*, (Cambridge University Press, London, 1936); Herbert Morrison, *Government and Parliament: A Survey from the Inside*, (Cambridge University Press, London, 1954); R.M. Punnett, *British Government and Politics*, (Heinemann, London, 1968).

10. See, for example, Richard A. Chapman, 'The Vehicle and General Affair: Some Reflections for Public Administration in Britain', *Public Administration,* Vol 51, 1973, pp. 273-290.

11. Report by Justice, *The Citizen and the Administration*, (Stevens, London, 1961), para. 20.

12. For example, Chester I. Barnard, *The Functions of the Executive*, (Harvard University Press, Cambridge, Massachusetts, 1938); and F.J. Roethlisberger and William J. Dickson, *Management and the Worker*, (Harvard University Press, Cambridge, Massachusetts, 1939).

13. Richard A. Chapman, *The Higher Civil Service in Britain*, (Constable, London, 1970), Ch. 6.

14. Richard A. Chapman, 'Profile of a Profession: The Administrative Class of the Civil Service'.

15. *Public Enquiry ordered by the Minister of Agriculture into the disposal of land at Crichel Down, Report*, [Cmd. 9176] (HMSO, London, 1954).

16. R. Douglas Brown, *The Battle for Crichel Down*, (The Bodley Head, London,1955), p. 102.

17. H. Montgomery Hyde, *British Air Policy Between the Wars 1918-1939*, (Heinemann, London, 1976), p. 462.

18. Anthony Verrier, *Through the Looking Glass: British Foreign*

Policy in an Age of Illusion, (Jonathan Cape, London, 1983).

19. Richard Norton-Taylor, *The Ponting Affair,* (Cecil Woolf, London, 1985), p. 15.

20. PRO/T222/662.

21. TC/No. 2/54 (20 August 1954) in PRO/T222/661.

22. *Report of the Board of Enquiry appointed by the Prime Minister to investigate certain Statements affecting Civil Servants,* [Cmd. 3037] (HMSO, London, 1928), para. 59.

23. 'Draft of a Code of Ethics for Public Servants', *Public Administration* (Sydney), Vol 24, 1965, pp. 195-9.

24. Paragraph 4060 of the *Establishment Officers' Guide,* quoted in *FDA News,* December 1984.

25. 13 April 1969. Quoted in Richard A. Chapman, *The Higher Civil Service in Britain,* p. 141.

26. Sir Edward Bridges, *Portrait of a Profession: The Civil Service Tradition,* (Cambridge University Press, London, 1950).

27. Richard A. Chapman, 'Minister-Civil Servant Relationships' in Richard A. Chapman and Michael Hunt (Eds.) *Open Government,* (Croom Helm, London, 1987), pp. 49-66.

28. Treasury file: T118.

29. C.P. Snow, *Corridors of Power,* (Macmillan, London, 1964), Penguin Edition, 1966, p. 40. See also C.P. Snow, 'The Corridors of Power', *The Listener,* Vol 57, pp. 619-20 (18 April 1957).

30. Quoted in Martin Gilbert, *Winston S. Churchill, Volume VI, Finest Hour 1939-41,* (Heinemann, London, 1983), p. 594.

31. Peter Lewis, *A People's War,* (Thames Methuen, London, 1986).

32. Margaret Thatcher, 'Message from the Prime Minister', in Cabinet Office (Management and Personnel Office), *The Challenge of Change in the Civil Service,* (Cabinet Office, London, 1987).

33. Cabinet Office, (Management and Personnel Office), *The Challenge of Change in the Civil Service,* p. 9. See also *The Times,* 29 January 1987.

34. Sir Edward Bridges, 'Professional Standards: The Civil Servant', BBC (GOS) Broadcast talk 1952. Script in PRO/T273/222.

35. Peter Hennessy, *Cabinet,* (Blackwell, Oxford, 1986), p. 58.

Index

Attorney General 270–1
Australian Institute of Public
   Administration 305
authority 312, 314
Avery Ltd, W. and T. 105
aviation 302–3

Bagehotian 310
Baillieu, Clive 250
balance of payments 188, 216
Balance of Payments Working
   Party 195
Baldwin, Stanley 27, 146, 160,
   162, 164–5, 179
Balfour, A.J. 270
Baliol Scott, N. 66
Balogh, Thomas 35
Bamford, Eric 206
Bank of England 14, 58, 71,
   165, 173, 231
Bankruptcy Court 77
Banks, Big Five 172
Banks, Donald 98
Barker, Ernest 29
Barlow, Alan 57, 112, 189, 190,
   198, 248
Barnard, E. 61
Barnes, Thomas 167–9, 170–2,
   176
Barnes, William Gorrell 10
Barron, A.W. 80–1
BBC Overseas Service 64
Beaverbrook, Lord 269
Beer, S. 251
Beloff, Nora 100
Benn, Tony 289
Berchtesgarten 27
betting 104
Bevin, Ernest 111
bill of rights 315
Bird's nest orchid 18
Birley, Robert 21, 66
Birmingham Post 161
Births and Deaths Registration
   207
Blanesburgh Committee *see*
   Parliamentary
Blanesburgh, Lord 6, 109–10
Blatch, William 74
Bligh, T.J. 17, 99

Board of Enquiry
   on the Bullock case 142, 147,
   155–6, 159–61, 162–71,
   178–9, 181
   on the Francs case 80, 175
Board of Trade 11, 73, 164,
   189–90, 195, 205, 249
Boers Hill 2
Book of Box Hill, The 18
Bowman, James 58
Box Hill xiv, 18, 226
Boyd-Carpenter, John A. 129
Bracken, Brendan 67
Bradbury, John 26
Bradbury Committee *see*
   Organisation and Staffing of
   Government Offices
Braithwaite, W.J. 24
'Bridges Collection' of files xv
Bridges, Edward Ettingdene
   Accounting Officer to
   Treasury 282
   a constitutional authority 272
   advice offered to/sought by
   71–2, 220–21, 267, 269,
   271–2, 276, 280–1, 284
   appointments of staff 10, 31,
   52–6, 60, 66–9, 226, 314
   attitudes and beliefs 15
   biographical outline ix
   character 79; *see also* personal
   qualities
   clubs xviii, 21
   commissions and committees;
   Estimates 5; National Whitley
   Council 6, 81; Reduction of
   National Debt 6;
   Remuneration of Scientific
   and Technical Officers 5–6;
   secretary to 187, 266, 295,
   308; Tomlin Royal
   Commission 81
   compared to or contrasted
   with; Fisher 30–1, 106;
   Hankey 22–4
   defender of civil
   servants/service 35, 67, 277
   died 23, 65
   disciple of Fisher 30, 85, 106,
   277

education xviii, 3
establishment work 10, 51,
80, 110
ethics/morality xviii–xix, 15,
19, 65
evidence to; Committee on
Higher Civil Service
Remuneration 217; Fulton
Committee 39; Masterman
Committee 102, 108, 116–18;
Priestley Royal Commission
103; Scottish Affairs Royal
Commission 279 Treasury
Organisation Committee
212–16
goods works, discreetly 15
his example xiv, 1, 295
his honours/honorary degrees
19, 20
illnesses 11, 167, 180, 204
influences; on civil service
15; Quaker 2, 15; Warren
Fisher 106
initiatives 142, 211, 305, 310
interests; architecture 3;
calligraphy 22; disregard for
personal 311, 313; history 3,
12, 37, 93, 226, 231; House of
Lords 19; lectures 13;
machinery of government
186–221; music 2; natural
environment 2–3, 18; Oxford
xiv, 3, 17–20; study of public
administration xix, 23, 247
job satisfaction 63, 82
knowledge of rules 81
leadership style 15, 103, 142,
219
machinery of government
xvii, 11, 13, 32, 103, 186–221
management style 194, 208,
218
Memorial Service for 307
Ministers call on 70
minutes, revisions of 216
personal qualities; he
possessed/inspired 9–16, 21,
52, 58, 62, 65–6, 69, 77–8,
81–3, 86–7, 97, 129, 188,
219, 239, 254–5, 266, 307–9,

312, 313; he respected 16
political; activities/attitudes
xvii, 92–138; judgements 13;
astuteness 310
politician 103, 280
politics; conception of 266–7;
defined 96, 267–8
power xviii
public service xiv, 3, 19, 21
relations with; Churchill 309,
see also Churchill; Ismay
8–10, 12, 14
retirement 18, 100
secrecy xvii–xviii
Secretary to Cabinet/War
Cabinet xv–xvii, 10–11, 24,
28, 93, 187–91, 195, 226,
229, 269, 272, 308–9, 312
sense of humour 129, 256
views on education and
training 14–15
visits to; Potsdam 11;
Washington 31; Yalta 11
War Service xviii, 4, 308
writings 16–17, 83–4, 218,
226, 259, 281, 290, 309–10
Bridges, Katherine (Kitty) 11
Bridges, Robert Seymour 1–2
Bridges, Tom 2
British Airways 19
British Broadcasting
Corporation (BBC) 234
see also BBC Overseas
Service
British Council 21, 61, 99, 226
British Institute of Management
(BIM) 250–1, 253, 256–7
British Travel and Holidays
Association 73
British War Economy 229
Brittain, Herbert 210
Brook, Norman
biographical outline ix
booklets on government
organisation 195
career planning 17
Crichel Down case 282
Deputy Secretary in Cabinet
Office 29
Head of Civil Service 301

change of bowling 67–9
Charing Cross Hotel 115
Chartered Insurance Institute
251–2
Chequers 310
Chester, D. Norman 115, 221,
232
Chief Economic Adviser 172
Chief Planning Officer 216
Chiefs of Staff 309
Chiesman, W.E. 75–6
Chorley Committee *see* High
Civil Service Remuneration
christian names 283
Churchill College xiv, 19
Churchill, Mrs 282
Churchill, Winston
as Chancellor of the
Exchequer 28–30, 80, 110,
267
as Secretary of State for Air
143
Chancellor of Bristol
University 19
choosing Secretary to Cabinet,
1945 12, 29
close relationship with
Bridges 311–12
funeral 18
his papers/archives xiv, 19
Hopkins, Richard 28
influenced Bridges' career 28
information from Bullock 303
methods of work 11, 308
on Bridges 12, 102
political tour 281
Prime Minister (1951) 17–18,
209
Prime Minister during Second
World War 191–2, 220,
267–10
Prime Minister of caretaker
administration 194
valued Bridges' advice 267,
269
Churchill's Indian Summer 32
*Citizen and the Administration,
The* 298
Citizens' Advice Bureau Service
99

civil aviation
Cadman Committee 148
Director of 145–6
Office Memorandum on 145,
147
Civil Aviation, Ministry of 209,
271
Civil Defence volume 231
Civil Series of volumes 229
Civil Service Act 315
Civil Service Civil Rights
Defence Committee 110, 267
Civil Service Clerical
Association 110–11
Civil Service Commission 300
Civil Service Department 85,
137, 256–7
Civil Service Manpower
Committee 278–9
civil service regulations 107
Civil Service, Royal
Commission on
(1929–31) 6, 81, 295
(1912–14) 26
(1953–55) xiv, 37, 103, 284
Civil Service Selection Board
xiii
Clapham Committee on the
Provision of Social and
Economic Research 258
clarinet 2
Clark, Andrew 282, 302
classification 26
'cloistered politicians' 265
'closed politics' 311
club memberships xviii
Clutterbuck, Alexander 60
Cobbold, Lord 58, 165
code(s) of
behaviour/conduct/practice
106, 114, 147, 157, 175, 177,
261, 283, 305, 307–8, 310,
312, 315
Codling, W.R. 234
'cold table' 11
collegiate 287, 315
Colonial Office 58, 206, 274
Colonies, the 148, 207, 275
Columbia Broadcasting System
Network 16